Road Atlas

Uni
Canada
Mexico

*Also has downtown city map

Road data for Pennsylvania and Ohio based upon data from Navigation Technologies Corporation.

American Map Corporation
46-35 54th Road
Maspeth, New York 11378
Printed in Canada
Cover Photo: Bixby Bridge, BigSur, by Andrew McKinney, New York Stock Photo
Index Photos: PhotoDisc™

Tourism Information

WHERE TO CALL OR WRITE

UNITED STATES

Alabama
Alabama Bureau of Tourism & Travel
401 Adams Ave, P.O. Box 4927
Montgomery, AL 36103
800.252.2262, 334.242.4169
www.touralabama.org

Alaska
Alaska Div. of Tourism
P.O. Box 110801
Juneau, AK 99811-0801
907.929.2200
www.dced.state.ak.us/tourism

Arizona
Arizona Office of Tourism
2702 N. Third St., Ste. 4015
Phoenix, AZ 85004
800.842.8257, 602.230.7733
www.arizonaguide.com

Arkansas
Arkansas Dept. of Parks & Tourism
One Capitol Mall
Little Rock, AR 72201
800.628.8725, 501.682.7777
www.1800natural.com

California
California Div. of Tourism
P.O. Box 1499, Dept. TIA
Sacramento, CA 95814
800.862.2543, 916.322.2881
www.gocalif.ca.gov

Colorado
Colorado Travel & Tourism Authority
P.O. Box 3524
Englewood, CO 80155
800.265.6723
www.colorado.com

Connecticut
Connecticut Office of Tourism
505 Hudson St.
Hartford, CT 06106
800.282.6863, 860.270.8080
www.ctbound.org

Delaware
Delaware Tourism Office
99 Kings Highway
Dover, DE 19901
800.441.8846, 302.739.4271
www.visitdelaware.net

Florida
Visit Florida
P.O. Box 1100
Tallahassee, FL 32302
888.735.2872, 850.488.5607
www.flausa.com

Georgia
Georgia Dept. of Industry, Trade & Tourism
P.O. Box 1776
Atlanta, GA 30301-1776
800.847.4842, 404.656.3590
www.georgia.org

Hawaii
Hawaii Visitors & Conv. Bureau
2270 Kalakaua Ave., Ste. 801
Honolulu, HI 96815
800.464.2924, 808.923.1811
www.gohawaii.com

Idaho
Idaho Dept. of Commerce
P.O. Box 83720
Boise, ID 83720-0093
800.635.7820
www.visitid.org

Illinois
Illinois Bureau of Tourism
100 W. Randolph St., Ste. 3-400
Chicago, IL 60601
800.226.6632
www.enjoyillinois.com

Indiana
Indiana Tourism
1 N. Capitol Ave. Suite 700
Indianapolis, IN 46204
800.759.9191, 317.232.4685
www.enjoyindiana.com

Iowa
Iowa Div. of Tourism
200 E. Grand Ave.
Des Moines, IA 50309
800.345.4692, 515.242.4705
www.traveliowa.com

Kansas
Kansas Travel & Tourism Development Div.
700 S.W. Harrison, Ste. 1300
Topeka, KS 66603
800.252.6727, 785.296.2009
www.travelks.com

Kentucky
Kentucky Dept. of Travel
Capital Plaza Tower
500 Mero St., Ste. 22
Frankfort, KY 40601
800.225.8747
www.kentuckytourism.com

Louisiana
Louisiana Office of Tourism
P.O. Box 94291
Baton Rouge, LA 70804
800.334.8626, 225.342.8100
www.louisianatravel.com

Maine
Maine Publicity Bureau
P.O. Box 2300
Hallowell, ME 04347-2300
888.624.6345, 207.287.8070
www.visitmaine.com

Maryland
Maryland Office of Tourism Development
217 E. Redwood St.
Baltimore, MD 21202
800.445.4558
www.mdisfun.org

Massachusetts
Massachusetts Office of Travel & Tourism
10 Park Plaza, Suite 4510
Boston, MA 02116
800.447.6277, 617.973.8500
www.massvacation.com

Michigan
Michigan Travel Bureau
P.O. Box 30226
Lansing, MI 48909-7726
888.784.7328, 517.373.0670
www.michigan.org

Minnesota
Minnesota Office of Tourism
100 Metro Square
121 Seventh Place East
St. Paul, MN 55101
800.657.3700, 651.296.5029
www.exploreminnesota.com

Mississippi
Mississippi Development Authority/Tourism
P.O. Box 849
Jackson, MS 39205
800.927.6378, 601.359.3297
www.visitmississippi.org

Missouri
Missouri Div. of Tourism
301 W. High St., P.O. Box 1055
Jefferson City, MO 65102
800.519.2300, 573.751.4133
www.visitmo.com

Montana
Travel Montana
1424 Ninth Ave.
P.O. Box 200533
Helena, MT 59620
800.847.4868, 406.444.2654
www.visitmt.com

Nebraska
Nebraska Travel & Tourism
P.O. Box 94666
Lincoln, NE 68509-4666
800.228.4307, 402.471.3796
www.visitnebraska.org

Nevada
Nevada Commission on Tourism
401 N. Carson St.
Carson City, NV 89701
800.638.2328, 775.687.4322
www.travelnevada.com

New Hampshire
New Hampshire Office of Travel & Tourism Development
172 Pembroke Rd., P.O. Box 1856
Concord, NH 03302-1856
800.386.4664 (seasonal), 603.271.2666
www.visitnh.gov

New Jersey
New Jersey Office of Travel & Tourism
20 W. State St., P.O. Box 820
Trenton, NJ 08625-0820
609.292.2470, 800.537.7397
www.visitnj.org

New Mexico
New Mexico Dept. of Tourism
491 Old Santa Fe Trail
Santa Fe, NM 87503
800.733.6396
www.newmexico.org

New York
New York State Div. of Tourism
P.O. Box 2603
Albany, NY 12220-0603
800.225.5697, 518.474.4116
www.iloveny.com

North Carolina
North Carolina Div. of Tourism, Film & Sports Development
301 N. Wilmington St.
Raleigh, NC 27601
800.847.4862, 919.733.4171
www.visitnc.com

North Dakota
North Dakota Tourism
604 E. Boulevard Ave.
Bismarck, ND 58505-0825
800.435.5663, 701.328.2525
www.ndtourism.com

Ohio
Ohio Div. of Travel & Tourism
77 S. High St., 29th Fl.
Columbus, OH 43215
800.282.5393
www.ohiotourism.com

Oklahoma
Oklahoma Dept. of Tourism & Recreation
P.O. Box 60789
Oklahoma City, OK 73146
800.652.6552, 405.521.2406
www.travelok.com

Oregon
Oregon Tourism Commission
775 Summer St. NE
Salem, OR 97301-1282
800.547.7842, 503.986.0000
www.traveloregon.com

Pennsylvania
Pennsylvania Office of Travel, Tourism & Film Promotion
Rm. 404, Forum Building
Harrisburg, PA 17120
800.847.4872, 717.787.5453
www.experiencepa.com

Rhode Island
Rhode Island Tourism Div.
1 W. Exchange St.
Providence, RI 02903
800.556.2484
www.visitrhodeisland.com

South Carolina
South Carolina Dept. of Parks, Recreation & Tourism
P.O. Box 71
Columbia, SC 29201
888.727.6453
www.travelsc.com

South Dakota
South Dakota Dept. of Tourism
711 E. Wells Ave.
Pierre, SD 57501-3369
800.732.5682
www.travelsd.com

Tennessee
Tennessee Dept. of Tourist Development
320 Sixth Ave. N
Rachel Jackson Building
Nashville, TN 37243
800.468.6836, 615.741.2159
www.tnvacation.com

Texas
Texas Dept. of Economic Development, Tourism Div.
P.O. Box 12728
Austin, TX 78711-2728
800.888.8839, 512.462.9191
www.traveltex.com

Utah
Utah Travel Council
Council Hall/Capitol Hill
Salt Lake City, UT 84114
800.200.1160, 801.538.1030
www.utah.com

Vermont
Vermont Dept. of Tourism & Marketing
6 Baldwin St., Drawer 33
Montpelier, VT 05633-1301
800.837.6668, 802.828.3237
www.1-800-vermont.com

Virginia
Virginia Tourism Corporation
901 E. Byrd St.
Richmond, VA 23219
800.847.4882, 804.786.4484
www.virginia.org

Washington
Dept. of Community Trade & Economic Development, Washington State Tourism Div.
P.O. Box 42500
Olympia, WA 98504-2500
800.544.1800
www.experiencewashington.com

Washington, DC
WCVA Visitors Services
1212 New York Ave. NW, Ste. 600
Washington, DC 20005
800.422.8644, 202.789.7000
www.washington.org

West Virginia
West Virginia Div. of Tourism
2101 Washington St. E
Charleston, WV 25305
800.225.5982, 304.558.2286
www.callwva.com

Wisconsin
Wisconsin Dept. of Tourism
P.O. Box 7976
Madison, WI 53707-7976
800.432.8747
www.travelwisconsin.com

Wyoming
Wyoming Div. of Tourism
I-25 at College Dr.
Cheyenne, WY 82002
800.225.5996, 307.777.7777
www.wyomingtourism.org

UNITED STATES TERRITORIES

Puerto Rico
Puerto Rico Convention Bureau
255 Recinto Sur
San Juan, PR 00901
787.725.2110
www.meetpuertorico.com

Virgin Islands
U.S. Virgin Islands Dept. of Tourism
P.O. Box 6400
St. Thomas, VI 00804
800.372.8784, 340.774.8784
www.usvi.org/tourism

CANADA

Alberta
Travel Alberta
17811 116 Ave.
Edmonton, AB, Canada T5S 2J2
800.661.8888
www.travelalberta.com

British Columbia
Super, Natural British Columbia
Box 9830
Stn. Prov. Govt.
1803 Douglas St., Third Floor
Victoria, BC, Canada V8W 9W5
800.663.6000, 250.387.1642
www.hellobc.com

Manitoba
Travel Manitoba
155 Carlton St., Seventh Floor
Winnipeg, MB, Canada R3C 3H8
800.665.0040
www.travelmanitoba.com

New Brunswick
Tourism New Brunswick
P.O. Box 12345
Campbellton, NB, Canada E3N 3T6
800.561.0123
www.tourismnewbrunswick.ca

Newfoundland
Newfoundland & Labrador Tourism Marketing
P.O. Box 8730
St. John's, NF, Canada A1B 4K2
800.563.6353, 709.729.2830
www.gov.nf.ca/tourism

Nova Scotia
Tourism Nova Scotia
2695 Dutch Village Rd.
Halifax, NS, Canada B3L 4V2
800.565.0000, 902.453.8400
www.explorens.com

Ontario
Ontario Tourism
Eighth Floor, Hearst Block
Toronto, ON, Canada M7A 2E1
800.668.2746, 416.314.0944
www.ontariotravel.net

Prince Edward Island
Dept. of Economical Development & Tourism
P.O. Box 940
Charlottetown, PE, Canada C1A 7M5
800.463.4734, 902.368.7795
www.peiplay.com

Québec
Tourisme Québec
P.O. Box 979
Montréal, QC, Canada H3C 2W3
877.266.5687
www.bonjourquebec.com

Saskatchewan
Tourism Saskatchewan
1922 Park St.
Regina, SK, Canada S4P 3V7
877.237.2273
www.sasktourism.com

MEXICO

Mexico Ministry of Tourism
Mariano Escobedo, No. 726
Col. Nueva Anzures
11590 México, D.F. Mexico
800.446.3942
www.visitmexico.com

CROSSING BORDERS

CANADA

U.S. citizens entering Canada from the U.S. are required to present passports or proof of U.S. citizenship accompanied by photo identification. U.S. citizens entering from a third country must have a valid passport. Visas are not required for U.S. citizens entering from the U.S. for stays of up to 180 days. Naturalized citizens should travel with their naturalization certificates. Alien permanent residents of the U.S. must present their Alien Registration Cards. Individuals under the age of 18 and travelling alone should carry a letter from a parent or legal guardian authorizing their travel in Canada.

U.S. driver's licenses are valid in Canada, and U.S. citizens do not need to obtain an international driver's license. Proof of auto insurance, however, is required.

For additional information, consult http://travel.state.gov/tips_canada.html before you travel.

UNITED STATES (FROM CANADA)

Canadian citizens entering the U.S. are required to demonstrate proof of their citizenship, normally with a photo identification accompanied by a valid birth certificate or citizenship card. Passports or visas are not required for visits lasting less than six months; for visits exceeding six months, they are mandatory. Individuals under the age of 18 and travelling alone should carry notarized documentation, signed by both parents, authorizing their travel.

Canadian driver's licenses are valid in the U.S. for one year, and automobiles may enter free of payment or duty fees. Drivers need only provide customs officials with proof of vehicle registration, ownership, and insurance.

MEXICO

U.S. citizens entering Mexico are required to present passports or proof of U.S. citizenship accompanied by photo identification. Visas are not required for stays of up to 180 days. Naturalized citizens should travel with their naturalization certificates, and alien permanent residents must present their Alien Registration Cards. Individuals under the age of 18 travelling alone, with one parent, or with other adults must carry notarized parental authorization or valid custodial documents.

In addition, all U.S. citizens visiting for up to 180 days must procure a tourist card, obtainable from Mexican consulates, tourism offices, and border crossing points, which must be surrendered upon departure. However, tourist cards are not needed for visits shorter than 72 hours to cities along the Mexico/U.S. border.

U.S. driver's licenses are valid in Mexico.

Visitors who wish to drive beyond the Baja California Peninsula or the Border Zone (extending approximately 25 km into Mexico) must obtain a temporary import permit for their vehicles. Permits may be obtained from a Mexican Customs Office at border crossing points as long as the original and two copies of the following documents bearing the driver's name are provided: passport/proof of U.S. citizenship, tourist card, vehicle registration, driver's license, and a major international credit card for use in paying the prevailing fee. Permits are valid for 180 days, and they must be surrendered upon final departure from Mexico.

All visitors driving in Mexico should be aware that U.S. auto insurance policies are not valid and that buying short-term tourist insurance is virtually mandatory. Many U.S. insurance companies sell Mexican auto insurance. American Automobile Association (for members only) and Sanborn's Mexico Insurance (800.638.9423) are popular companies with offices at most U.S. border crossings.

Adventure Awaits

Explore a passion, not just a place, ...

Explore your world — whether across the state or across the country — in a host of exciting locations around the U.S. Adventure awaits you whether you prefer communing with whales, climbing through underground passageways, or panning for gold. Explore a passion, not just a place, as you plan your travels around the country. These unusual destinations and surprising twists on familiar places are organized by regions to help you plan anything from family vacations of a lifetime to day trips close to home.

Northwest

Watch for a Whale

Find on Page: 114 Grid: H-5

If you're planning a winter vacation in the Pacific Northwest in late November, December, or January, or a spring trip starting in mid March, you'll be visiting at the best times to see some of the more than 22,000 gray whales that make annual round trips from Mexico to Alaska. In fact, now that a group of about 200 whales summers off the Oregon coast, almost any time of year offers the potential for sightings, with the exception of early to mid November and mid February. The peak of the winter migration — when some 28 whales pass per hour — generally falls in the first week of January.

Whalewatching tours start from Westport, Washington, and at least a half-dozen ports in Oregon. If you're not up for riding the waves, you can watch from the air: A number of firms offer whale-watching tours via airplane. These are much more expensive than the boat tours, and pilots must maintain an altitude of 1,000 feet when near a whale, but the air tours nearly guarantee you'll see whales, a promise the boats can't make.

But it's not necessary to leave dry land to see these huge mammals: There are many overlooks along Highway 101 that offer the potential for sightings, albeit at a distance. Much of Washington's most accessible coastline is too flat for this, but bluffs at Kalaloch, Second Beach, Rialto Beach, and Cape Flattery are elevated enough. The Oregon coast's easily accessible headlands and an acclaimed whale-watching assistance program make it a magnet for cetacean sighters. Between Christmas and New Year's Day and again for a week in late March, several hundred volunteers trained by the marine science center in Newport are on duty at 30 overlooks from Harris Beach State Park just north of the California border to Fort Stevens State Park at the Columbia River's south jetty. Rain or shine, from 10 A.M. to 1 P.M. daily, they give tips to visitors and sometimes offer a peek through a spotting scope.

Oregon Coast Visitors Association
313 SW 2nd Street, Suite B, P.O. Box 74,
Newport, Oregon 97365;
tel: 541-574-2679 or 888-628;
www.visittheoregoncoast.com
Washington State Tourism
P.O. Box 42500, Olympia, WA 98504-2500;
tel: 800-544-1800; www.experiencewashington.com

Tour the Haunts of Haunts

Find on Page: 19 Grid: C-5

From the 1,000 suicides who have leapt from the Golden Gate Bridge since it opened in 1937 to the Winchester Mystery House, which Sarah Remington built in nearby San Jose to appease the spirits of those killed by Remington rifles, the Bay Area is rife with the kind of history that inevitably gives rise to stories of haunts. One of the most lasting tales is that of the 19th-century clipper ship Tennessee, which sank with all hands in the dense fog of the Golden Gate Strait. Many have said it sails still, including crew members of the USS Kennison, who, in 1942, watched in amazement as the ship sailed past, leaving a visible wake but no matching blip on the radar screen.

There are more stationary hauntings in a number of hotels, including the Mansions Hotel, the San Remo Hotel, the Sir Francis Drake, and the York Hotel. The latter is not only haunted by the tuxedo-clad shade of a pianist who died mid-performance here in the 1920s, but also was used as a location in Alfred Hitchcock's *Vertigo.* The San Francisco Art Institute is said to be plagued by strange lights and footsteps in empty rooms. And, of course, haunts are said to frequent several cell blocks at Alcatraz, which is now a national park site rather than an infamous prison. Visitors have reported hearing agonizing cries and rattling chains in cell blocks A, B, and especially C; others have reported cold spots and the sound of banjos in the rooms once occupied by Al Capone.

San Francisco Convention and Visitors Bureau
900 Market Street, Lower Level,
San Francisco, CA 94103;
tel: 415-283-0177; www.sfvisitor.org

Stand at Little Bighorn

Find on Page: 67 Grid: J-15

To people all over the world, a mass grave atop a rise near Hardin, Montana, is the ultimate symbol of the Wild West. Here in 1876, Lieutenant Colonel George Armstrong Custer and every one of his more than 200 men died fighting warriors from the Sioux, Cheyenne, and Arapaho tribes. The tribes were angry over federal violations of the 1868 Fort Laramie Treaty, but the battle here was not only Custer's last stand, but also that of the tribes. Within months of their greatest victory, they were forced to give up their nomadic ways of life and return to reservations.

Much of what happened here that day remains a mystery, but the stone markers scattered around Last Stand Hill show where soldiers fell. Custer's tablet naturally draws attention, but particularly poignant are the simple stones like the one that reads "U.S. Soldier, 7th Cavalry, Fell Here June 15 1876."

Visitors can listen to frequent ranger talks on such topics as "The Road to the Little Bighorn" or "Life in the 7th Cavalry" and walk the battlefield, starting about five miles southeast at the Reno-Benteen Battlefield. Guided tours also are offered. If you're lucky enough to happen through on the last weekend of June, you can see a re-enactment of the battle, held six miles west of Hardin as part of the five-day Little Bighorn Days celebration.

Travel Montana
424 9th Avenue, P.O. Box 200533,
Helena, MT 59620;
tel: 800-847-4868; www.visitmt.com

Take Sanctuary in Monterey

Find on Page: 12 Grid: M-2

Scuba fans are drawn to Monterey Bay National Marine Sanctuary, where the bay itself and the coast along the peninsula south to Carmel offers some of the best diving in the world. But you don't have to don a wetsuit to see what's under the surface: Right in town on Cannery Row is the Monterey Bay Aquarium, a state-of-the-art facility that's been redefining what an aquarium can do since it opened in 1984.

One of the main exhibits features a living three-story kelp forest inside a 335,000-gallon tank. Within, shafts of natural light strike the sinewy giant kelp fronds while leopard sharks, orange garibaldi, surf perch, and rockfish swim among them. Sea urchins, anemones, and other invertebrates fill the nooks and crannies. Nearby, seven-gilled sharks cruise between mussle- and barnacle-encrusted pilings that reproduce a Monterey wharf, complete with litter-laden "harbor" floor. The Outer Bay Gallery offers the illusion of a window on the open sea, and another gallery focuses on the denizens of the offshore trough near the coast here, a formation as deep as the Grand Canyon.

But the centerpiece is a million-gallon tank for yellowfin tuna, bonito, blue shark, and ocean sunfish. Fronted by the world's largest single-pane window, the setting is languid and serene until a tuna tucks its dorsal fins and blasts off in a bubble-trailing burst.

Monterey Bay Aquarium
886 Cannery Row, Monterey, CA 93942;
tel: 800-756-3737 or 831-648-4800;
www.mbayaq.org

Watch Waterfowl on the Wing

Find on Page: 12 Grid: A-8

When the first white trappers and explorers saw the Klamath Basin's 185,000-acre marsh they were astonished by the six million waterfowl that packed the basin as they followed their annual migratory patterns, with immense flocks of geese and ducks that darkened the sky. Only about 25 percent of the marsh remains today, but it still hosts a total of 433 species of wildlife. October through March are the best months to visit the complex, which is composed of six separates refuges that encompass an array of habitats.

The best refuges for waterfowl sightings are Lower Klamath and Tule Lake, both of which offer auto tour routes, maps, and bird checklists. Waterfowl include northern pintails and white-fronted geese; mallards; and green-winged, blue-winged, and cinnamon teals. Snow geese, Ross's geese, and Canada geese all appear at about the same time. The basin is also a good site for viewing migrating tundra swans and trumpeter swans. In addition to waterfowl, the basin offers many chances to see birds of prey, especially bald eagles, whose numbers can swell to 1,000 by late winter, and hawks of many varieties.

Large numbers of neotropical songbirds, including vireos, warblers, and thrush, pass through during the spring, each in its own season. In summer, birders can watch ducks brood their young as herons, egrets, and bitterns fish in the marshes or stalk the fields for mice and other rodents. Some white-faced ibises breed here, arriving in the spring and staying through summer. Summer is also the best time to see the basin's symbol: the beautiful white pelican.

Klamath Basin National Wildlife Refuge Complex
4009 Hill Road Tulelake, CA 96134;
tel: 530-667-2231; www.klamathnwr.org

Observe Some Observatories

Find on Page: 7 Grid: M-7 Flandrau Science Center
Page: 9 Grid: P-9, P-8 Fred Lawrence Whipple Obs., Kitt Peak National Obs.

The Arizona desert's largely clear and very dark skies have made it the site of so many observatories that it could be nicknamed The Astronomy State. The hills near Tucson have become home to a number of important observatories, including the Fred Lawrence Whipple Observatory, in Amado; and the Kitt Peak Observatory, 56 miles southwest of the city. Standing on Mount Hopkins at an elevation of 8,550 feet, the Whipple observatory was opened in 1979, making use of a groundbreaking design featuring six 1.8-meter mirrors that were mounted in an elaborate steel cage and constantly aligned by lasers. This unique design answered the need to build ever-larger, but lighter, single mirror telescopes in order to peer farther into the heavens. Tours of the observatory are offered, as are guided bus tours of the spectacular desert surrounding the site.

In operation since 1964, the 2.1-meter telescope at Kitt Peak has had many discoveries to its credit. Visitors here can view exhibits in the visitor center and take hour-long guided tours. But the real attraction is the public evenings, held for only 20 people each night, which last for three hours and include observation of the night sky through a 16-inch reflector telescope.

In Tucson itself is another major astronomical attraction, the Flandrau Science Center. Here are fascinating exhibits that include optical illusions, echo chambers, and a model of colliding asteroids. The lower level contains a mineral museum that displays dozens of meteorites, including 200-pounders. Visitors can look through the center's own telescope, a 16-inch Cassegrain in a rooftop observatory. The center also contains a 50-foot-diameter planetarium.

Fred Lawrence Whipple Observatory
P.O. Box 97, Amado, AZ 85645;
tel: 520-670-5707; cfa-www.harvard.edu/flwo
Kitt Peak National Observatory
P.O. Box 26732, Tucson, AZ 85726-6732;
tel: 520-318-8726; www.noao.edu/kpno
Flandrau Science Center
1601 East University Boulevard, Tucson, AZ 85719;
tel: 520-621-7827; www.flandrau.org

Bone Up on Dino Fossils

Find on Page: 20 Grid: G-6

Grand Junction, Colorado, offers a sight you definitely won't see anywhere else: People in a store window exposing dinosaur bones to the light of day. The Dinosaur Valley Museum, one of the three branches of the Museum of Western Colorado, opened here in a vacant department store in 1985. Its surprising but unassuming entrance belies the wealth of informative and innovative displays that occupy its compact space. Children should head straight for Kid's Quarry, where, instead of playing with plaster copies, they can play with real dino bones — big ones. The 10-foot-wide pit contains crushed walnut shells that they can brush away to reveal a dozen sauropod fossils, after which they can match the bones to a sauropod skeleton.

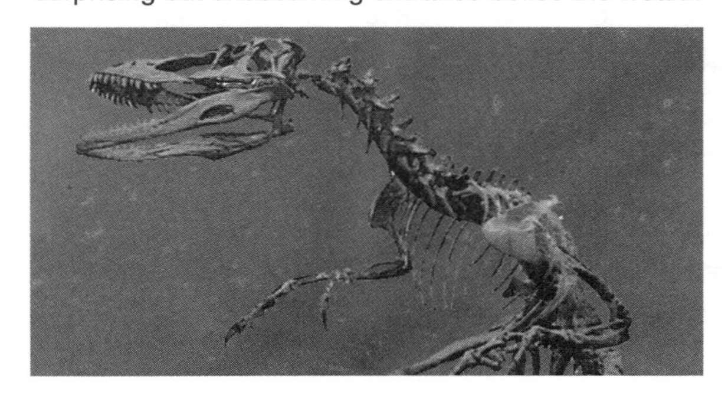

These aren't the only bones visitors can touch; a number of hands-on displays offer the chance to see and touch actual fossil bones. One of these contains a series of thigh bones from seven different dinosaurs, which range from three inches to five feet in length. Other displays let visitors view moving rubber dinosaur robots.

The museum also contains a complete mounted skeleton of Colorado's state fossil, Stegosaurus, which was uncovered in the nearby Book Cliffs; specimens from the Mygatt-Moore Quarry west of town; and discoveries made during excavations at the Dalton Wells Quarry near Moab, Utah. The latter display includes bones from eight kinds of early Cretaceous dinosaurs, including a pair of previously unknown sauropods, and a complete skeleton of recently discovered ankylosaur, Gastonia burgei.

Dinosaur Valley Museum
P.O. Box 2000, Grand Junction, CO 81501;
tel: 970-242-0971;
www.wcmuseum.org

Visit a Sky Island

Find on Page: 9 Grid: N-10

Unlike such parts of the American West as the Rockies, where wildlife sightings are restricted by winter weather, Coronado National Forest offers year-round viewing. Beginning at Tucson's city limits, the national forest spreads in 12 sections across the southeastern part of Arizona, totaling nearly two million acres. Each section protects a "sky island," an isolated mountain range that rises from the surrounding sea of low desert. Many of the birds that spend the summers on top of the sky islands can be seen in winter foraging along lowland streams. Species include yellow-eyed juncos, ruby-crowned kinglets, Bell's vireos, yellow-rumped warblers, and clay-colored and grasshopper sparrows. Raptors abound, especially red-tailed hawks and golden and bald eagles. Even in winter, temperatures may reach the low 80s, making it possible to take a comfortable hike while the rest of the area is dealing with blizzards.

Spring brings spectacular displays of desert wildflowers, as well as the breeding season for many birds and animals: Gila woodpeckers, vermillion flycatchers, painted redstarts, Gambel's quail, coyotes, and gray foxes frequently can be seen. Summer makes water holes, springs, and small creeks good sites for wildlife viewing, but autumn is a favored season in the sky islands as foliage turns and the ripening wild grapes and falling black walnuts and acorns attract skunks, bears, and many other animals. Sandhill cranes can also be seen as they arrive in mid-autumn to settle in for the winter. Winter itself begins another "vertical migration," as deer and other fauna come down from the mountaintops to the canyon bottoms.

The gems of the forest are the numerous species of hummingbird that can be seen here; southern Arizona is the wintering ground for 16 species. The best times to see them are April, when a major spike in northern migration passes through, and August into September, when there is a second increase following the summer "monsoons."

Coronado National Forest, *Federal Building, 300 West Congress, Tucson, AZ 85701;*
tel: 520-670-4552; www.fs.fed.us/r3/coronado

Walk on an Ancient Sea

Find on Page: 15 Grid: P-18

The Great Basin is a 250,000-square-mile desert covering western Utah, eastern California and Oregon, and most of Nevada. Here, between the Rockies and the Sierra Nevada, rivers flow in and evaporate, leaving behind deposits of salt, borax, and gypsum, but not much that will sustain life. Death Valley National Park, in eastern California, is the Great Basin at its most mysterious. Covering 3.3 million acres, it's the largest national park in the Lower 48. It made the record books as the hottest place on earth on July 10, 1913, when a temperature of 134 degrees Fahrenheit was recorded at the aptly named Furnace Creek.

Some of the quintessential Death Valley experiences can be had within a few miles of the Borax Museum on Route 178 near the Furnace Creek Ranch. Not far away on Route 190 is Zabriskie Point, which offers a stunning view of badlands of hardened mudhills and the distant Amargosa Mountains. Other spectacular views can be had during an afternoon's trip around Artist's Drive, which offers mineral-rich rock formations awash in yellows, purples, greens, pinks, and browns.

All of this stark beauty came about because of glacial lakes that once filled the valley during the Pleistocene Era. These evaporated, leaving behind ponds, salt flats, and briny streams. You can get a feel for this south of Artist's Drive at Badwater. Near here is the lowest point in the Western Hemisphere — 282 feet below sea level. Park your car at Badwater, walk out onto the salt pan, and imagine the ancient seas and lakes that once lapped the mountains and buttes.

Death Valley National Park
P.O. Box 579, Death Valley, CA 92328;
tel: 760-786-3200; www.nps.gov/deva
Death Valley Chamber of Commerce
P.O. Box 157, Shoshone, CA 92384;
tel: 760-852-4524; www.deathvalleychamber.org

Paddle Lake Powell

Find on Page: 109 Grid: N-6

When the Glen Canyon Dam backed up the Colorado River for 186 miles upstream, it created Lake Powell. Here, in the heart of Glen Canyon National Recreation Area, sparkling water reflects a clear turquoise sky and chiseled orange cliffs cut cleanly down to the water's edge. And there's a lot of water's edge: nearly 2,000 miles of shoreline in one of the most stunning landscapes in the Southwest. Much of the traffic on the lake is given over to motorboats, houseboats, and jet skis, but this is also spectacular scenery for sea kayaks because they can venture into tight slot canyons where their noisier cousins can't go. Nearly 100 canyons spill into the lake, many of these winding ribbons of vaulted rock containing shallow streams and pools of cold water.

If you're interested in a taste of what the one- or two-week boat trips down the Grand Canyon involve, you can take a day excursion or paddle yourself down a 13-mile-long stretch of the Colorado, from the dam to Lees Ferry. The scenery here is a sample of the rest of the trip, with tawny cliffs towering 1,400 feet above the river. Although there is much white water farther down the river, the placid water here is perfect for paddling, and the trout fishing is great, too. If you're paddling solo, you can rent a canoe in Page and arrange for a motorboat to take you back to town after your trip.

Glen Canyon National Recreation Area
Box 1507, Page, AZ 86040;
tel: 928-608-6404; www.nps.gov/glca
Grand Canyon National Park
P.O. Box 129, Grand Canyon, AZ 86023;
tel: 928-638-7888; www.nps.gov/grca

See a Star Among Observatories

Find on Page: 98 Grid: J-5

Perched on a grassy hilltop in Riverview Park only three miles north of downtown Pittsburgh, the romantic turn-of-the-century Allegheny Observatory is a symbol of an earlier era in astronomy. A research facility of the University of Pittsburgh, the observatory was completed in 1912 during an age that considered public observatories "temples of the sky" and decorated them accordingly. From the classic Greek columns that flank the portico to the three white domes that house the telescopes, the building does indeed resemble a temple. The oldest telescope here is a 13-inch refractor that was the third-largest in the world when it was dedicated in 1860; in 1895 this historic instrument was used to prove that Saturn's rings were not solid. It was moved here in 1912 and was recently restored to nearly original condition.

The impressive 1912 30-inch Thaw telescope, with its long riveted tube and its massive pier, is a reminder of the Steam Age machinery envisioned by Jules Verne and H.G. Wells. It is still used every clear night to look for very small shifts in positions of stars caused by the gravitational pull of unseen planets. The third dome contains the 31-inch Keeler reflector, which was one of the world's first medium-to-large reflecting telescopes when it was built in 1906.

The grounds are open to the public, but public access to the building is limited to prearranged tours, which are offered April through October. Visitors see a slide show before touring the building, which includes a visit to the Thaw refractor. Weather permitting, visitors can view the Moon or one of the planets through the 13-inch refractor. The tours are free, but are limited to 45 people. Call between 10 and 4 Monday through Friday to make a reservation.

Allegheny Observatory, Observatory Station
Pittsburgh, PA 15214;
tel: 412-321-4200; www.pitt.edu/~aobsvtry

See the Sea at Work

Find on Page: 55 Grid: G-19

One of the greatest places to get an idea of the power of the ocean is Cape Cod. This peninsula extending 35 miles into the Atlantic Ocean, along with the islands of Nantucket and Martha's Vineyard, was laid down by an Ice Age glacier that extended this far 20,000 years ago. As the climate warmed, the glacier retreated, leaving behind vast heaps of clay, sand, gravel, and boulders. At about this time, what is now Cape Cod Bay was a freshwater lake. Then the sea broke through, and it's been trying to erode the cape away ever since.

If you stand on the viewing platform at Chatham Light, at the cape's southeastern tip, you can get a feel for the forces at work on this slender spit of land. Across from you is North Beach, a barrier beach that once spanned the entire horizon to the east. In January of 1987, the sea breached North Beach during a violent storm. Since then, it's opened the gap to more than a mile. If you descend the staircase to the beach from the parking lot and walk north at low tide you can see wells, septic tanks, and the remains of foundations — the remnants of the summer houses that once stood here.

If you want to see some giant sand dunes, the Province Lands Visitor Center, off Route 6 near Provincetown, is the place for you. The center has an observation deck that offers a 360-degree view of sand, dune grass, and ocean. This section of the cape was not formed by glacial deposits, but by sand washed here from the southern cape. Most of the cape's dunes are only 30 or 40 feet high, but here, some dunes, like Mount Ararat, are 100 feet tall. They are constantly moving; in fact, several times a year, plows must push the dunes back from Route 6 in order to keep the road open.

Cape Cod National Seashore
99 Marconi Site Road, Wellfleet, MA 02667;
tel: 508-487-1256; www.nps.gov/caco
Cape Cod Chamber of Commerce
307 Main Street, Suite 2, Hyannis, MA 02601-4043;
tel: 508-862-0700; www.capecodchamber.org

Paddle Around a Desert Island

Find on Page: 49 Grid: T-12

Not only did the explorer Champlain's name for Maine's rocky Mount Desert Island stick, but also his pronunciation of it: To this day it's called Mount de-SERT. The largest of Maine's islands is 12 miles wide by 15 miles long and is connected to the mainland by a causeway. In the late 19th century, Rockefellers, Fords, Vanderbilts, and Pulitzers summered here in shingle and stone mansions, drawn by the gorgeous rocky scenery. Today, more than 2 million visitors each year come to Acadia National Park, which encompasses nearly half the island. Miles of elegant carriage roads wind through the park, but many visitors travel by mountain bike.

One way to avoid the crowds is to take a sea kayak tour with one of the many outfitters based along Cottage Street in Bar Harbor. If you're paddling on your own, put in at mid to low tide at the gravel and mud spit that runs from Bar Harbor to Bar Island. Then paddle southeast along the shore past downtown Bar Harbor and some of the island's grand mansions, several of which have been converted to inns. Slanting offshore brings you to the Porcupine Islands, where you may see bald eagles, harbor seals, porpoises, and the occasional whale. The superb view back toward the mainland includes 1,530-foot Cadillac Mountain, the highest point on the Atlantic coast north of Rio de Janeiro.

Whether by kayak or car, one of the sights to see is Somes Sound, the only glacier-carved fjord on the east coast. The sound runs roughly halfway through the island, with hills rising to about 1,000 feet on either side. If you're driving, use scenic Sargeant Drive, which parallels the sound.

Acadia National Park
P.O. Box 177, Bar Harbor, ME 04609;
tel: 207-288-3338; www.acadia.net/anp
Bar Harbor Chamber of Commerce
93 Cottage Street, Bar Harbor, ME 04609;
tel: 800-288-5103 or 207-288-5103;
www.barharbormaine.com

Watch the Water Fall

Find on Page: 76 Grid: C-1

Even as notorious a chatterbox as Theodore Roosevelt was moved to silence by the awe he felt upon his first sight of Niagara Falls. It's not the world's highest or widest waterfall, but it's certainly the best known. What the more than 10 million visitors a year see here is the drainage from the four upper Great Lakes, which in turn collect water from an area larger than Sweden. All that water goes over the falls in one unhindered 167-foot dive: More than 200,000 cubic feet per second pass over the falls or through its electric power generators.

From the American side, fine views of the 2,100-foot-wide Horseshoe Falls (which carries 90 percent of the flow) and the 1,075-foot-wide American Falls can be had at Niagara Reservation State Park, just off the Robert Moses Parkway. An early stop at the Schoellkopf Geological Museum, also on the parkway, is a good idea. Here displays explain the geological history of the Niagara River and the Great Lakes region. Near the museum, Prospect Point has a observation tower with a superb view of both falls. After visiting the museum and the tower, many people go for a boat ride on the Maid of the Mist, which motors very close to the base of the falls for a spectacular view from below. Much-needed rain gear is provided.

Other popular places to visit include Goat Island, the small island that divides the river into two falls, and Cave of the Winds. At the base of the Bridal Veil section of the American Falls, the cave is reached by winding walkways on which visitors clad in yellow slickers venture behind the falling veil of water. Finally, a visit to the falls doesn't have to end at twilight: The falls are illuminated at night, offering a view that in some ways is even more impressive than the daytime version.

Niagara Falls, New York, Convention and Visitors Bureau *310 4th Street, Niagara Falls, NY 14303; tel: 800-421-5223 or 716-285-2400; www.nfcvb.com*

Bring Your Binoculars

Find on Page: 97 Grid: M-20

In 1932, a young ornithologist traveled to a spot along Kittatinny Ridge in eastern Pennsylvania north of Reading and brought back photographs of hundreds of dead birds of prey that had been killed in an annual shoot. His grim pictures came to the attention of New Yorker Rosalie Edge, who with some friends purchased an option on 1,393 acres here, including the rocky outcropping from which the birds had been shot. She hired a resident ornithologist, and after many confrontations, the guns were silenced. Hawk Mountain Sanctuary represented the founding of the raptor conservation movement, which has since spread around the world.

Today, the sanctuary remains in the forefront of the movement, attracting thousands of birders every year to witness the migration of kestrels, ospreys, and bald eagles, which begins in mid-August. For their part, the birds are attracted by the updrafts rising from the ridges, which they use for more efficient travel than riding rising thermal waves or even slower wing-flapping flight. Hawk Mountain is so heavily frequented because it sits at the southern end of a long line of ridges. In effect, the mountain offers the birds their last chance to ride the updrafts out over the flatter lands of the Piedmont on their way south.

Broad-wing hawks arrive in mid-September and sharp-shinned hawks later in the month. October brings the greatest variety of raptors, and November brings waves of red-tail and red-shouldered hawks bolting south before waves of cold fronts and snow flurries. Experienced birders know that the big broad-winged hawk push will come one or two days either side of September 17 and that the peak for golden eagles is often a few days either side of November 1, depending on cold fronts. They also know that the 20,000 birds of prey that pass through the sanctuary each fall draw thousands of visitors, so the less busy weekdays are best for watching. An excellent visitor center is open year round.

Hawk Mountain Sanctuary
1700 Hawk Mountain Road, Kempton, PA 19529;
tel: 610-756-6000;
www.hawkmountain.org

Midwest

Ride Along the Ridgetops

Find on Page: 10 Grid: G-6

Although their northern neighbors the Ozarks have become a major tourist destination, the Ouachita Mountains, in west-central Arkansas and eastern Oklahoma, have many attractions of their own. Here in the Ouachita National Forest are gorgeous forested mountains, sparkling Lake Ouachita, and numerous waterfalls.

For a quick and easy visit to the top of the Ouachitas, take a drive on the Talimena Scenic Byway, a spectacular route that winds along ridgetops for 54 miles between Mena, Arkansas, and Talihina, Oklahoma. The byway runs along 2,681-foot Rich Mountain, the highest point in the range.

In places along the road, twisted and folded sandstone and shale strata demonstrate the awesome power of the tectonic forces that created the mountains. Overlooks provide excellent views of Black Fork Mountain, with its curious, boulder-strewn expanses, known as "rock glaciers." The cooler, moister north slope of Rich Mountain harbors colorful wildflowers and a wide array of trees and shrubs, including beech, black walnut, sugar maple, umbrella magnolia, pawpaw, Carolina silverbell, and Ohio buckeye. Many birds nest here, and hidden among the leaf litter live two amphibian species endemic to these mountains, the Rich Mountain and Ouachita red-backed salamanders. For a closer look, take advantage of the byway's easy access to the Ouachita National Recreation Trail, which parallels the road for several miles atop Rich Mountain. You probably won't see the black bears and bobcats that live in the mountains, but don't be surprised if you see a flock of wild turkey.

Ouachita National Forest, Forest Supervisor,
P.O. Box 1270, 100 Reserve Street,
Hot Springs, AR 71902; tel: 501-321-5202;
www.fs.fed.us/oonf/ouachita

See a Sky Show

Find on Page: 37 Grid: E-14

Much has changed since Chicago's Adler Planetarium and Astronomy Museum opened as the western hemisphere's first planetarium in 1930, but not the grand entrance, which was recently restored to its original glory. Inside, light-filled spaces beckon visitors to explore galleries filled with interactive exhibits. A gallery entitled Our Solar System invites visitors to drive a clone of the Mars Pathfinder rover across a simulated Martian landscape. Also here are a 1,000-pound nickel-iron meteorite, a Moon rock, and a meteorite that came from Mars. Next door, the Milky Way Gallery has internet terminals for access to astronomy information. Another terminal has a display of live images of the sun, which are sent down from a satellite orbiting far out in space. There's also one of the world's finest collections of historic astronomical instruments, including a handmade reflector telescope from the 17th century.

But the showstopper here is the sky show. Walking into the StarRider Theater on the lower level, a visitor who has seen an Omnimax movie will feel right at home because of the sloping floor, domed ceiling, and high-backed tilting seats. But the resemblance ends there. StarRider is not a movie, but a series of computer-generated images; a keypad at each seat allows the audience of up to 197 people to respond interactively. The show features digital images and 3-D graphics depicting planetary surfaces, exploding stars, distant galaxies, and other wonders, giving viewers an astronaut's view of the universe. There's more history outside the theater, where visitors can experience the state of the art in planetariums in the early 20th century: The Atwood Sphere, built in 1913, is just large enough for six people, who view the night sky depicted by hundreds of tiny pinpricks in its thin metal skin.

Adler Planetarium and Astronomy Museum,
1300 South Lakeshore Drive, Chicago, IL 60605; tel: 312-922-7827; www.adlerplanetarium.org

Watch the Wildlife

Find on Page: 10 Grid: C-8

Most of us think of the North Woods when we think of elk. But they exist much farther south: If you're very lucky you might see one of these magnificent animals in Arkansas, along the Buffalo River in the northeastern part of the state. The land here is still extremely wild, thanks to the Buffalo's designation in 1972 as the first national river. The Buffalo River elk were first released in 1981, more than a century and a half after they last roamed the area. They've established themselves so well that a very limited hunting season was announced in 1998. The best chance to see them is at Boxley Valley on the upper (western) river and the Steel Creek and Erbie areas farther downstream to the east.

The Buffalo winds its way through Arkansas for 150 miles to a confluence with the White River, through mountain slopes covered with oaks, hickories, sweet gums and maples that in fall seem to glow with every possible shade of yellow, orange, and red. Thanks to a corps of conservationists who fought a long and contentious battle to ward off dams along the river in the 1950s and 1960s, the undammed river flows freely today, alternately rushing in churning rapids and flowing lazily along through long pools. Most of the whitewater enthusiasts concentrate on the upper river, particularly in spring. Here, the river between the tiny hamlet of Ponca and the Highway 7 bridge north of Jasper offers kayakers thrilling rides down whitewater chutes between limestone bluffs that tower in places 500 feet over the water. Wildlife fans concentrate on the lower river, whose placid waters make for leisurely paddling. Here visitors may see ospreys and eagles taking a meal from the river. Other wildlife includes otters and mink, numerous songbirds, woodchucks, gray foxes, turkeys, raccoons, and even armadillos.

***Buffalo National River**, 402 North Walnut, Suite 136, Harrison, AR 72601; tel: 870-741-5443; www.nps.gov/buff*

Ponder the Paranormal

Find on Page: 37 Grid: C-13

Chicago doesn't offer the same length of history as such notable locales as Salem, Massachusetts. But the city's history has not only been intense and tough, but also sometimes violent. No wonder then that there are those who say that Chicago and its environs are home to a fairly high concentration of ghosts.

One of the most infamous events to take place here was the Valentine's Day Massacre of seven of "Bugs" Moran's men by the notorious Al Capone. Of course, Capone was on a beach in Florida at the time, but it was he who ordered the hit — the latest in his battles with Moran over the profits from North Side vice operations. Today, a nursing home occupies the site of Moran's garage at 2122 North Clark, where the shootings took place, but passersby have claimed to hear screams and moans through the chain-link fence that surrounds the front yard. The garage itself, which was torn down in the late 1960s, spread its own grisly reputation beyond the site: When a Canadian businessman sold its bricks as souvenirs, rumors began to circulate about the illnesses, financial ruin, or other bad luck suffered by those who had bought the bricks.

The ghost of bank robber and murderer John Dillinger is said to haunt the alley behind the Biograph Theater on Halstead Street, where he was shot by federal agents after being betrayed by his girlfriend. Witnesses allegedly have seen a ghostly figure running down the alley that would suddenly trip and fall, then disappear. Cold spots and inexplicable feelings of dread have also been reported.

Resurrection Mary, probably Chicagoland's most famous spook, is associated with Resurrection Cemetery in the suburb of Justice on the far southern edge of the city. Stories about her began in 1939, when drivers heading past the cemetery on Archer Avenue reported that a young blonde girl had tried to jump from the side of the road onto their cars' running boards. Other witnesses said they had met Mary at a dance near the cemetery and given her a ride home, only to have her leap from the car and disappear into the mists of the cemetery. Mary is also said to haunt Chet's Melody Lounge, across the street from the graveyard, where patrons have seen her numerous times. One frantic driver burst into the bar one morning saying that he'd just run over a young woman on Archer Avenue but couldn't find her body. A truck driver confirmed his story, but no body was ever found. Mary sightings have been so frequent in this part of town that many residents simply accept the ghost as real. Just in case she gets thirsty, a Bloody Mary always stands at the end of the bar at Chet's.

*Several local companies offer ghost tours. Contact the **Chicago Office of Tourism***
78 East Washington Street, Chicago, IL 60602;
tel: 800-887-2442 or 312-744-2400;
www.ci.chi.il.us/Tourism

Have Launch at the Cape

Find on Page: 27 Grid: C-19

The Soviet Union may have been first into space, but the most famous space site is still Cape Canaveral, where more than 500 launches have taken place since 1958. Now part of Kennedy Space Center, the cape is the perfect place to launch a rocket. It has the advantage of enabling launches to the east, which makes use of the Earth's rotation and allows rockets to be destroyed over open water if necessary.

One way to experience the excitement of a launch is to simply find a good spot along U.S. Highway 1 in Titusville or Highway A1A in Cape Canaveral or Cocoa Beach, like millions of others. But if you can arrange to be at the space center on launch day, you can purchase a Launch Viewing Opportunity ticket on a first-come, first-served basis. The ticket allows you to ride a bus to the viewing site about six miles from the launch pad. You'll want your binoculars, and you should also be aware that launches are subject to delays of one or more days or even weeks.

The space center itself is a place where you could spend days. At the visitor complex you can stroll among rockets like those that sent such pioneering astronauts as Alan Shepard and John Glenn into space. Inside, the center is packed with exhibits, including two IMAX films, spacesuits and spacecraft, and a full-scale walk-through mockup of the space shuttle orbiter.

In stark contrast to all of this high technology are nearby Merritt Island National Wildlife Refuge and Canaveral National Seashore, which together encompass more than 200,000 acres of coastal dunes, woodlands, marshes, and estuaries that sustain 15 endangered species, including the gentle manatee, or sea cow. Here egrets or cranes pick their dainty way unconcerned along drainage ditches beside the road, looking for their lunch while tourists watch from only a few feet away.

*Mail Code **DNPS, Kennedy Space Center,***
FL 32899; tel: 321-867-2121; www.ksc.nasa.gov
Phone 321-449-4444 for information on
***Launch tickets** or purchase online at*
www.ksctickets.com/lttandmaxac
***Merritt Island NWR**, P.O. Box 6504,*
Titusville, FL 32782; tel: 321-861-0667;
merrittisland.fws.gov
Canaveral National Seashore
308 Julia Street, Titusville, FL 32796-3521;
tel: 321-867-4077; www.nps.gov/cana

See the Sods

Find on Page: 117 Grid: D-9

If the notion of West Virginia backcountry brings to mind forested mountain ranges, a visit to Monongahela National Forest's Dolly Sods Wilderness in the north-central part of the state will have you thinking you've been dropped on another continent, or perhaps in Canada near the Arctic Circle. This 10,215-acre area is a checkerboard of sphagnum bogs, boulder flats, and windswept plains where spruce trees grow branches only on the downwind side of their trunks. Spectacular vistas from enormous rock promontories are too numerous to count. This type of scenery makes Dolly Sods a popular destination, but to get to the really good stuff you'll have to ford creeks and scramble over boulder gardens.

This crazy countryside takes its name from a family of 19th-century German settlers named Dahle, who grazed sheep on open areas they called "sods." As the 20th century began, those meadows were hemmed in by one of the East's most magnificent spruce and hemlock forests, with centuries-old trees growing to 12 feet in diameter. But once the timber barons discovered the woods, the trees' days were numbered. Their total removal dried out the deep organic soils, and burning cinders from logging equipment sparked huge fires that laid bare the rocky core of the sods.

In 1975, Congress ensured that the lumbering equipment would never again scar the sods, which left the land to berry pickers and backpackers, along with a healthy population of black bears. Thirty miles of trails score the windy, open sods. In late spring, rhododendrons and wild azaleas burst into colorful bloom, and in late June and early July, blueberries and huckleberries are ripe for the picking.

Monongahela National Forest, Headquarters
200 Sycamore Street, Elkins, WV 26241;
tel: 304-636-1800; www.fs.fed.us/r9/mnf

See a Secret Seashore

Find on Page: 31 Grid: Q-12

Just north of the Florida border in extreme southeastern Georgia is Cumberland Island National Seashore, a 17.5-mile-long barrier island that has been almost completely left alone by humans while the forces of nature were allowed free reign. There are only a handful of private residences on the island, which was protected in 1972 as a national seashore. Only 300 visitors per day are allowed onto the island, and the only way to reach it is by ferry (reservations required) from the mainland town of St. Marys River. The ferry docks at the island's southern tip, from which visitors can walk up the island's only road through live oaks hung with Spanish moss and resurrection ferns or walk two and a half miles southeast from the ferry dock to the beach at Pelican Point. Here, on the beach or in the salt marshes, they may see feral horses and pigs, raccoons, opossums, gray foxes, great blue herons, or numerous shorebirds. Offshore, pelicans coast above the water as bottle-nosed dolphins arc into the air. Nearly 9,000 acres in the northern section of the island have been set aside as a nature preserve and are criss-crossed by a network of trails. Also here is The Settlement, the site of the Cumberland Museum, where specimens of flora and fauna are collected and catalogued for research.

The restriction against bicycles (they can only be brought by private boat) and other vehicles (they're prohibited) make Cumberland Island a site for serious walkers, but the island's isolation and its severe environment are the very things that have kept it in an almost pristine state. Camping is allowed by permit and reservation, but lodgings are available on the mainland. The ferry runs only five days a week October through February.

Cumberland Island National Seashore
P.O. Box 806, St. Marys, GA 31558;
tel: 912-882-4336; www.nps.gov/cuis
***Ferry reservations**: 912-882-4335.*
St. Marys Tourism Council
P.O. Box 1291, St. Marys, GA 31558;
tel: 912-882-4000 or 866-868-2199;
www.stmaryswelcome.com

Go See the River of Grass

Find on Page: 28 Grid: T-19

In the early 20th century, Marjory Stoneman Douglas was one of those who were most influential in protecting what most people thought of as a snake-infested swamp. Her book *Everglades: River of Grass* was published in 1947, the year that President Truman dedicated Everglades National Park. The book did more to explain the misunderstood landscape than any other single action.

Although at 1.5 million acres the everglades are only one-fifth of their original size and the flow of water is controlled by canals and impoundments, these mangrove estuaries are still amazingly productive ecosystems. The dry season, November through April, is the time to visit, because lower water tables concentrate wildlife in and around ponds and the insects, although they never disappear, are less bothersome. One road, the 38-mile Main Park Road, cuts through the park from Florida City south of Homestead to Flamingo, following the water's path. Along it are hiking trails, observation towers, boardwalks, and other viewing sites. Near the Royal Palm Visitor Center are the trailheads for the Anhinga and Gumbo Limbo Trails. The former winds alongside a cattail marsh, where visitors may see namesake anhinga birds drying their wings almost within reach. The birds are known as snake birds for their habit of swimming with only their long necks and heads exposed. Gumbo Limbo Trail winds through a dense tropical hardwood hammock that is home to white-crowned pigeons, raccoons, white-tailed deer, cotton mice, green treefrogs, and gorgeous multicolored tree snails. The road winds through endangered slash pines to Flamingo, at the peninsula's end. Here, tourist boats leave for tours of Florida Bay. If the tide is out, all kinds of sea and wading birds will be prob-

ing the mudflats for dinner and elusive crocodiles may be seen curled on exposed banks.

Everglades National Park
40001 State Road 9336, Homestead, FL 33034;
tel: 305-242-7700; www.nps.gov/ever
Florida Division of Tourism,
126 West Van Buren Street, Tallahassee, FL 32399;
tel: 904-487-1462

Visit the Refusal Room

Find on Page: 111 Grid: J-9

Some say that the spirit that inhabits Carter's Grove plantation on the James River, near Williamsburg, Virginia, is motivated by regret because it has a bizarre way of making its presence known. People who've left white carnations in a wood-paneled first-floor parlor return later to find them shredded and scattered, as if in anger. Housekeepers have never managed to trap the usual suspects, such as mice. The resulting speculation about the "refusal room," as the parlor is known, lays the blame on one or both of the two ladies who rejected marriage proposals from two future presidents of the United States in the room. In the mid-18th century, Mary Cary is said to have turned down a proposal from none other than George Washington. Years later, in the same room, Rebecca Burwell reportedly rejected a proposal from Thomas Jefferson.

The sprawling Georgian plantation house was begun in 1750 by Robert Carter, one of the wealthiest men in colonial America. He died before it was completed, and the property passed to his grandson, Carter Burwell, who finished it and expanded the plantation. At one point, the property encompassed 300,000 acres and was worked by 1,000 slaves. Open for tours, the house today remains as it was when the last of the Carters to live there occupied it in the early part of the 20th century.

Although there have been no reports of hauntings by earlier residents than Mary Cary and Rebecca Burwell, it wouldn't be surprising if there were. In the 1970s, excavations in a large field between the house and the James River turned up a surprising find: evidence of an early settlement that predated Jamestown. Through international investigations that resembled attempts to solve a murder mystery more than typical historical research, it was determined that the residents of this small community had been massacred by native Americans before their settlement was burned to the ground. Today, displays show the situation and outline of the buildings. The story of the discovery can be read in the book *Martin's Hundred* by Ivor Noel Hume.

Carter's Grove
Route 60, P.O. Box 1776, Williamsburg, VA 23187;
tel: 800-447-8679;
www.williamsburg.com/plant/carter.html

The national parks of the United States

The national parks are a promise that we Americans have made to ourselves. As a people, we have resolved to protect a small portion of our precious wildlands from the ravages of "progress," to leave room for the bears and butterflies, wildflowers and ancient forests, and to preserve as a "vignette of primitive America" the crown jewels of America's natural and cultural heritage.

But the parks are more than islands of nature. They are sanctuaries of the human heart. More than just pretty places where one can snap a few pictures, they are an acknowledgment of the human need for wilderness. These are places, as Colin Fletcher wrote of the Grand Canyon, where people can move "closer to rock and sky, to light and shadow, to space and silence." Where there's room for lone hikers to lose, or find, themselves; for mountaineers to test their mettle against the elements; for scientists to study the natural world in a nearly pristine environment; and for ordinary visitors to gape at something greater than themselves and let their dreams run wild.

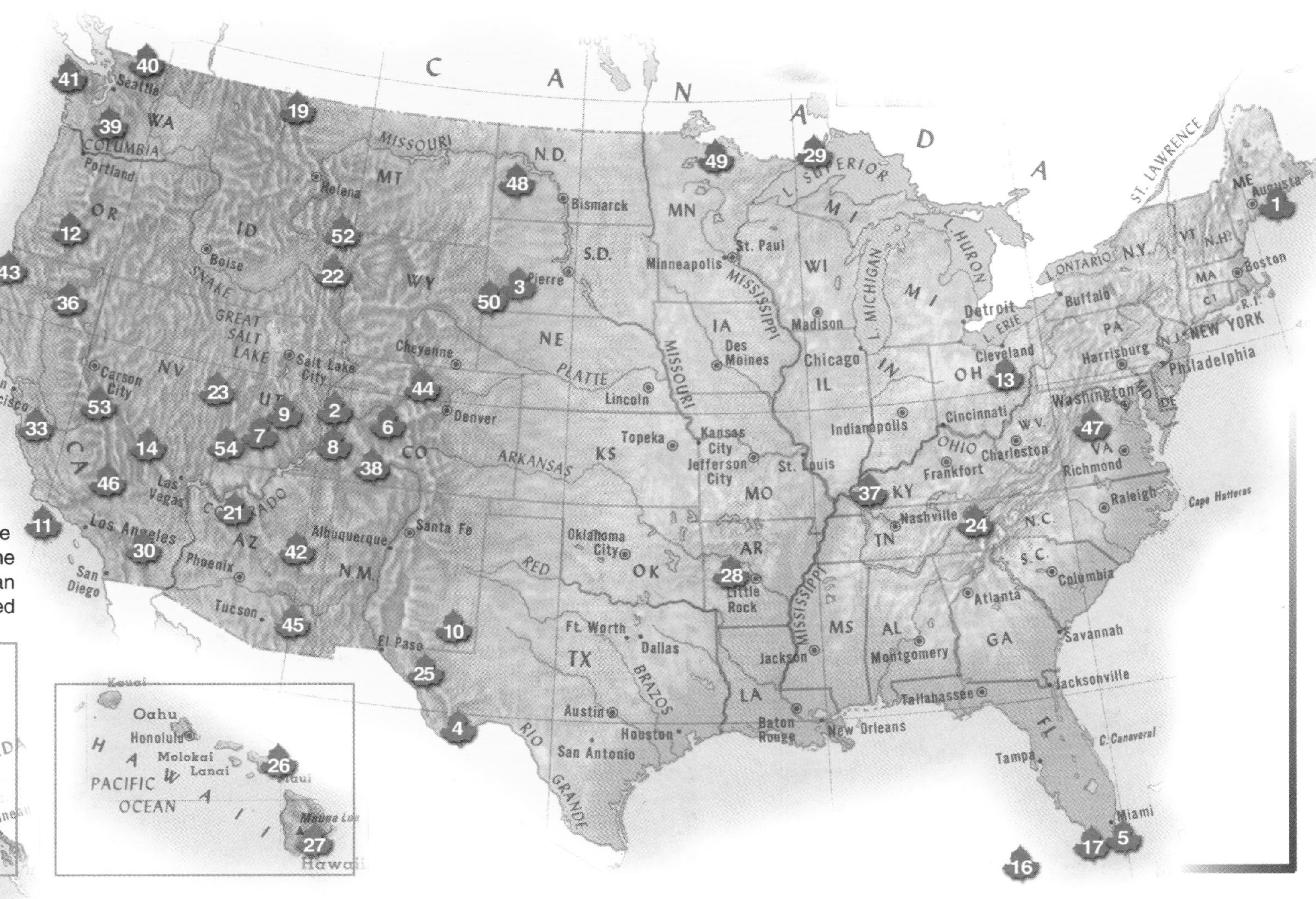

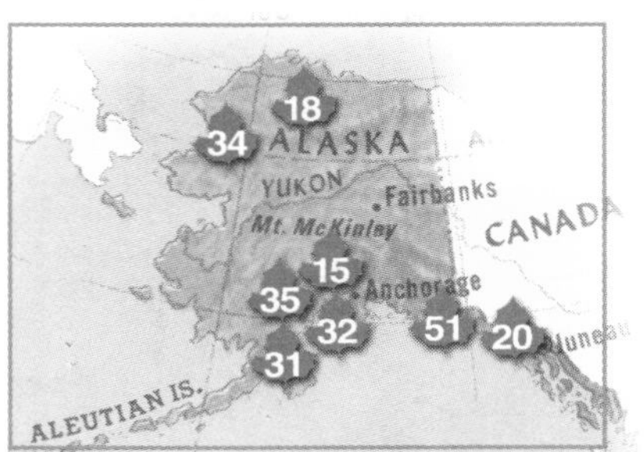

Best time to visit

The parks — particularly the popular mountain parks — tend to be crowded in summer. Traffic jams, inadequate parking, and crowded facilities are common at Grand Canyon, Yellowstone, Yosemite, Mount Rainier, and many other parks during the peak of the season. To avoid the rush, consider visiting in late spring or early fall. In the northern parks, the weather may not be quite as balmy. There may even be some snow on the ground, but it's worthwhile to see the parks without the crowds. Weekends are the busiest times, so try to visit on weekdays. Some park roads and most trails may be closed in winter, but snowshoeing, cross-country skiing and other winter activities are often permitted and give visitors a unique perspective on the parks.

In desert parks such as Death Valley, Joshua Tree, Organ Pipe Cactus, Saguaro, Carlsbad Caverns, Guadalupe Mountains, and Big Bend, fall, spring, and winter are the busy seasons. With summer temperatures in excess of 100°F (38°C), it is too hot then to do much sightseeing or hiking.

#	PARK NAME	STATE	INFORMATION ADDRESS	TELEPHONE	AREA SQ.MI.	ATLAS LOCATION	
						PAGE	GRID
1	Acadia	Main	P.O. Box 177, Bar Harbor, ME 04609.	(207) 288-3338	71	49	P - 9
2	Arches	Utah	P.O. Box 907, Moab, UT 84532.	(435) 259-8161	120	109	K - 8
3	Badlands	South Dakota	P.O. Box 6, Interior, SD 57750.	(605) 433-5361	364	101	F - 3
4	Big Bend	Texas	P.O. Box 129, Big Bend NP, TX 79834.	(915) 477-2251	1,252	105	Q - 7
5	Biscayne	Florida	9700 SW 328 St., Homestead, FL 33033.	(305) 230-7275	270	28	T - 20
6	Black Canyon of the Gunnison	Colorado	102 Elk Creek, Gunnison, CO 81230.	(970) 641-2337	43	20	H - 8
7	Bryce Canyon	Utah	P.O. Box 170001, Bryce Canyon, UT 84717.	(435) 834-5322	55	109	M - 4
8	Canyonlands	Utah	2282 S. West Resource Blvd., Moab, UT 84532	(435) 719-2313	527	109	L - 7
9	Capitol Reef	Utah	HC 70, Box 15, Torrey, UT 84775.	(435) 425-3791	378	109	L - 5
10	Carlsbad Caverns	New Mexico	3225 National Parks Hwy., Carlsbad, NM 88220.	(505) 785-2232	73	75	N - 10
11	Channel Islands	California	1901 Spinnaker Dr., Ventura, CA 93001.	(805) 658-5700	390	14	V - 12
12	Crater Lake	Oregon	P.O. Box 7, Crater Lake, OR 97604.	(541) 594-3100	286	92	K - 5
13	Cuyahoga Valley	Ohio	15610 Vaughn Rd., Brecksville, OH 44141.	(216) 524-1497	51	87	F - 15
14	Death Valley	California	P.O. Box 579, Death Valley, CA 92328.	(760) 786-3200	5,262	15	N - 17
15	Denali	Alaska	P.O. Box 9, Denali Park, AK 99755.	(907) 683-2294	9,375	6	E - 6
16	Dry Tortugas	Florida	P.O. Box 6208, Key West, FL 33041.	(305) 242-7700	101	*	
17	Everglades	Florida	40001 State Rd. 9336, Homestead, FL 33034.	(305) 242-7700	2,356	28	S - 18
18	Gates of the Arctic	Alaska	201 First Ave., Fairbanks, AK 99701 .	(907) 692-5494	13,281	6	C - 6
19	Glacier	Montana	West Glacier, MT 59936.	(406) 888-7800	1,584	66	A - 4
20	Glacier Bay	Alaska	P.O. Box 140, Gustavus, AK 99826.	(907) 697-2230	5,040	6	G - 10
21	Grand Canyon	Arizona	P.O. Box 129, Grand Canyon, AZ 86023.	(928) 638-7888	1,902	8	C - 6
22	Grand Teton	Wyoming	P.O. Drawer 170, Moose, WY 83012.	(307) 739-3300	484	120	C - 5
23	Great Basin	Nevada	100 Great Basin National Park, Baker, NV 89311.	(775) 234-7331	121	70	F - 10
24	Great Smoky Mountains	Tennessee	107 Park Headquarters Rd., Gatlinburg, TN 37738.	(865) 436-1200	814	103	E - 19
25	Guadalupe Mountains	Texas	HC 60, Box 400, Salt Flat, TX 79847.	(915) 828-3251	135	105	K - 4
26	Haleakala	Hawaii	P.O. Box 369, Makawao, HI 96768.	(808) 572-4400	47	32	E - 9
27	Hawaii Volcanoes	Hawaii	P.O.Box 52, Hawaii NP, HI 96718.	(808) 985-6000	328	32	M - 9
28	Hot Springs	Arkansas	P.O.Box 1860, Hot Springs, AR 71902.	(501) 624-2701	8	10	H - 7
29	Isle Royale	Michigan	800 East Lakeshore Dr., Houghton, MI 49931.	(906) 482-0984	893	56	B - 2
30	Joshua Tree	California	74485 National Park Dr., Twentynine Palms, CA 92277.	(760) 367-5500	1,590	15	V - 20
31	Katmai	Alaska	P.O.Box 7, King Salmon, AK 99613.	(907) 246-3305	5,741	6	G - 5
32	Kenai Fjords	Alaska	P.O.Box 1727, Seward, AK 99664.	(907) 224-3175	1,048	6	G - 6
33	Kings Canyon	California	47050 Generals Highway, Three Rivers, CA 93271.	(559) 565-3341	722	15	N - 14
34	Kobuk Valley	Alaska	P.O. Box 1029, Kotzebue, AK 99752.	(907) 442-3890	2,735	6	C - 5
35	Lake Clark	Alaska	4230 University Dr., Ste. 311, Anchorage, AK 99508.	(907) 781-2218	4,120	6	F - 6
36	Lassen Volcanic	California	P.O. Box 100, Mineral, CA 96063.	(530) 595-4444	167	12	D - 9
37	Mammoth Cave	Kentucky	P.O. Box 7, Mammoth Cave, KY 42259.	(270) 758-2251	83	44	L - 7
38	Mesa Verde	Colorado	P.O. Box 8, Mesa Verde NP, CO 81330.	(970) 529-4465	81	20	M - 6
39	Mount Rainier	Washington	Tahoma Woods, Star Route, Ashford, WA 98304.	(360) 569-2211	368	114	H - 10
40	North Cascades	Washington	810 State Route 20, Sedro Woolley, WA 98284.	(360) 856-5700	789	115	B - 11
41	Olympic	Washington	600 East Park Ave., Port Angeles, WA 98362.	(360) 565-3130	1,442	114	E - 6
42	Petrified Forest	Arizona	P.O. Box 2217, Petrified Forest NP, AZ 86028.	(928) 524-6228	146	8	F - 11
43	Redwood	California	1111 Second St., Crescent City, CA 95531.	(707) 464-6101	172	12	B - 3
44	Rocky Mountain	Colorado	1000 Highway 36, Estes Park, CO 80517.	(970) 586-1206	415	21	C - 12
45	Saguaro	Arizona	3693 Old Spanish Trail, Tucson, AZ 85730.	(520) 733-5153	143	9	N - 10
46	Sequoia	California	47050 Generals Highway, Three Rivers, CA 93271.	(559) 565-3341	629	15	P - 14
47	Shenandoah	Virginia	3655 U.S. Highway 211 East, Luray, VA 22835.	(540) 999-3500	307	113	E - 11
48	Theodore Roosevelt	North Dakota	P.O. Box 7, Medora, ND 58645.	(701) 623-4466	110	85	D - 2
49	Voyageurs	Minnesota	3131 Hwy. 53 South, International Falls, MN 56649.	(218) 286-5258	341	60	E - 9
50	Wind Cave	South Dakota	R.R. 1, Box 190, Hot Springs, SD 57747.	(605) 745-4600	44	101	F - 2
51	Wrangell-St. Elias	Alaska	P.O. Box 439, Copper Center, AK 99573.	(907) 822-5234	20,588	6	F - 8
52	Yellowstone	Wyoming	P.O. Box 168, Yellowstone NP, WY 82190.	(307) 344-7381	3,468	120	A - 4
53	Yosemite	California	P.O. Box 577, Yosemite NP, CA 95389.	(209) 372-0200	1,189	13	K - 12
54	Zion	Utah	SR 9, Springdale, UT 84767.	(435) 772-3256	229	109	N - 3

* #16 not shown on state map. Located approx. 70 miles west of Key West, in the Gulf of Mexico.

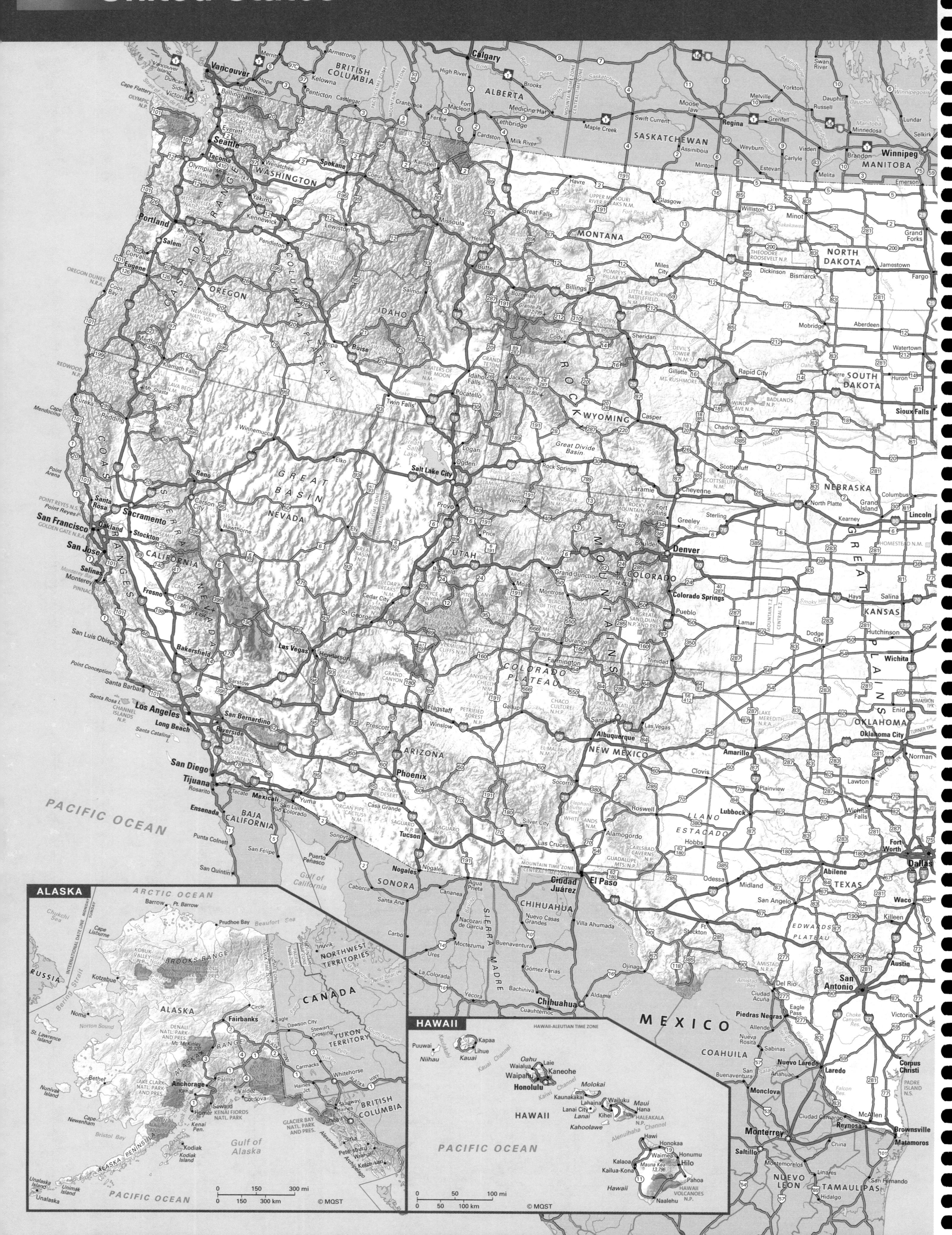
BRITISH COLUMBIA
ALBERTA
SASKATCHEWAN
MANITOBA
WASHINGTON
OREGON
IDAHO
MONTANA
NORTH DAKOTA
SOUTH DAKOTA
WYOMING
NEVADA
UTAH
COLORADO
NEBRASKA
KANSAS
CALIFORNIA
ARIZONA
NEW MEXICO
OKLAHOMA
TEXAS
BAJA CALIFORNIA
SONORA
CHIHUAHUA
COAHUILA
NUEVO LEON
TAMAULIPAS
MEXICO
PACIFIC OCEAN
Gulf of California
GREAT BASIN
COLUMBIA PLATEAU
COLORADO PLATEAU
ROCKY MOUNTAINS
GREAT PLAINS
LLANO ESTACADO
EDWARDS PLATEAU
SIERRA MADRE
COAST RANGES
SIERRA NEVADA
CASCADE RANGE
Vancouver
Calgary
Regina
Winnipeg
Seattle
Spokane
Portland
Boise
Helena
Great Falls
Billings
Bismarck
Fargo
Pierre
Rapid City
Sioux Falls
Salt Lake City
Reno
Sacramento
San Francisco
Oakland
San Jose
Fresno
Bakersfield
Los Angeles
Long Beach
San Diego
Tijuana
Las Vegas
Phoenix
Tucson
Denver
Colorado Springs
Cheyenne
Albuquerque
Santa Fe
El Paso
Ciudad Juárez
Lubbock
Amarillo
Oklahoma City
Wichita
Lincoln
Dallas
Fort Worth
Austin
San Antonio
Corpus Christi
Laredo
Nuevo Laredo
Monterrey
Chihuahua
Brownsville
Matamoros
ALASKA
ARCTIC OCEAN
Gulf of Alaska
BROOKS RANGE
ALASKA RANGE
CANADA
NORTHWEST TERRITORIES
YUKON TERRITORY
RUSSIA
Anchorage
Fairbanks
Juneau
0 150 300 mi
0 150 300 km
© MQST
HAWAII
HAWAII-ALEUTIAN TIME ZONE
Kauai
Oahu
Honolulu
Molokai
Lanai
Maui
Kahoolawe
Hawaii
Hilo
0 50 100 mi
0 50 100 km
© MQST

"In God We Trust"

One inch equals approx. 145 MI or 234 KM

MI 125 250

KM 125 250 375

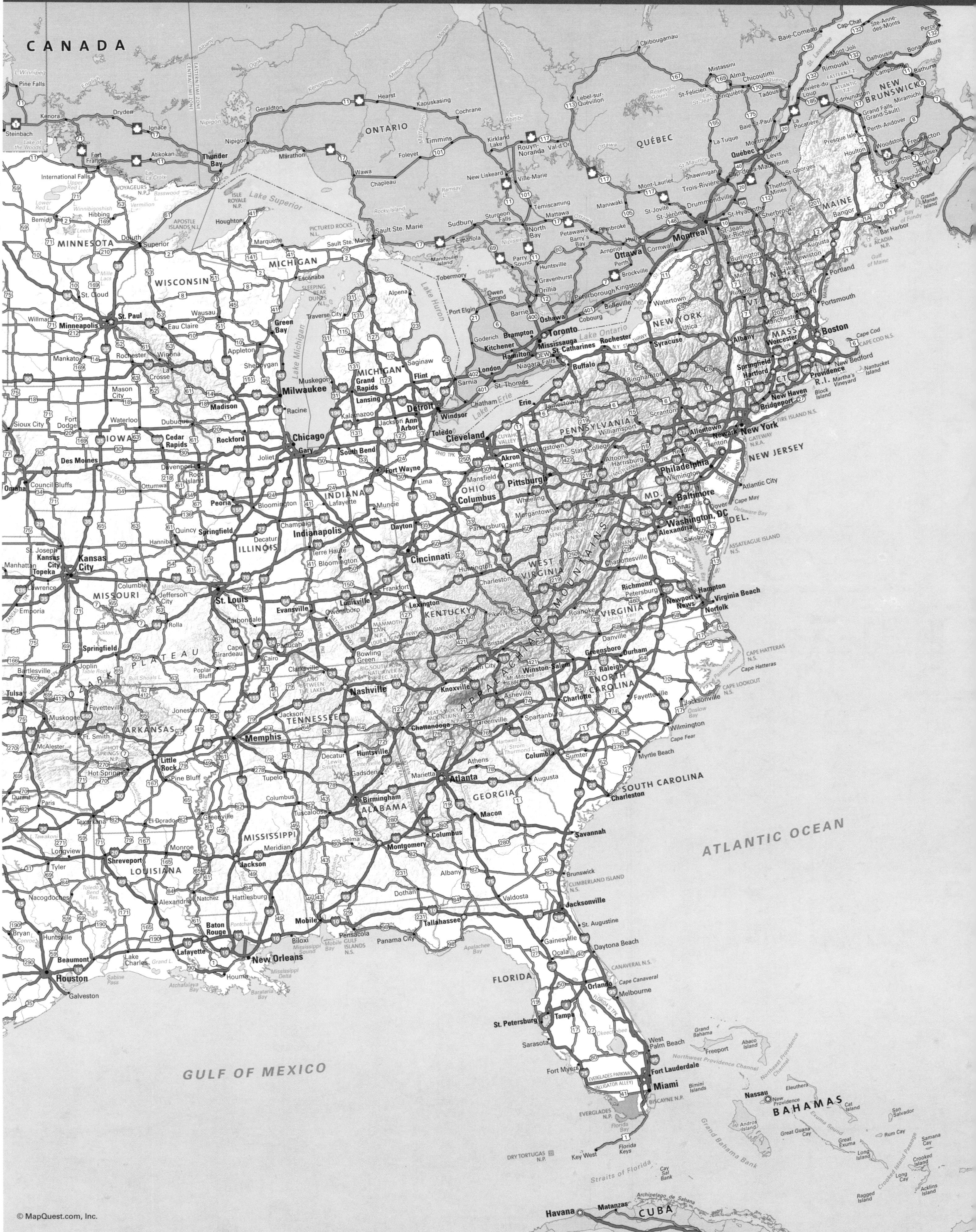
CANADA
ONTARIO
QUÉBEC
NEW BRUNSWICK
MAINE
MINNESOTA
WISCONSIN
MICHIGAN
IOWA
ILLINOIS
INDIANA
OHIO
PENNSYLVANIA
NEW YORK
VT.
N.H.
MASS.
R.I.
CT.
NEW JERSEY
DEL.
MD.
WEST VIRGINIA
VIRGINIA
KENTUCKY
MISSOURI
ARKANSAS
TENNESSEE
NORTH CAROLINA
SOUTH CAROLINA
GEORGIA
ALABAMA
MISSISSIPPI
LOUISIANA
FLORIDA
OZARK PLATEAU
APPALACHIAN MOUNTAINS
Lake Superior
Lake Michigan
Lake Huron
Lake Ontario
Lake Erie
ATLANTIC OCEAN
GULF OF MEXICO
BAHAMAS
CUBA
Minneapolis
St. Paul
Milwaukee
Chicago
Detroit
Cleveland
Toronto
Ottawa
Montreal
Québec
Buffalo
Pittsburgh
Philadelphia
New York
Boston
Baltimore
Washington, DC
Indianapolis
Columbus
Cincinnati
Louisville
St. Louis
Kansas City
Nashville
Memphis
Atlanta
Charlotte
Jacksonville
Orlando
Tampa
Miami
New Orleans
Houston
Havana

Alabama

Index page 134

	ANNISTON	AUBURN	BIRMINGHAM	CHATTANOOGA, TN	COLUMBUS, GA	DECATUR	DEMOPOLIS	DOTHAN	FLORENCE	GADSDEN	HAMILTON	HUNTSVILLE	MERIDIAN, MS	MOBILE	MONTGOMERY	OPP	SELMA	TUSCALOOSA
BIRMINGHAM	66	141		149	167	83	120	191	121	63	92	101	149	258	88	166	94	61
DOTHAN	207	125	191	311	97	273	198		310	251	282	291	246	199	103	66	147	237
HUNTSVILLE	100	241	101	109	266	25	215	291	65	74	104		245	357	187	265	194	156
MOBILE	279	227	258	403	252	340	144	199	377	317	286	357	132		173	146	194	205
MONTGOMERY	106	54	88	234	79	170	100	103	207	148	179	187	153	173		81	51	134

DRIVING DISTANCES IN MILES

SEE ALSO MILEAGE AND DRIVING TIME MAP ON PAGE 144

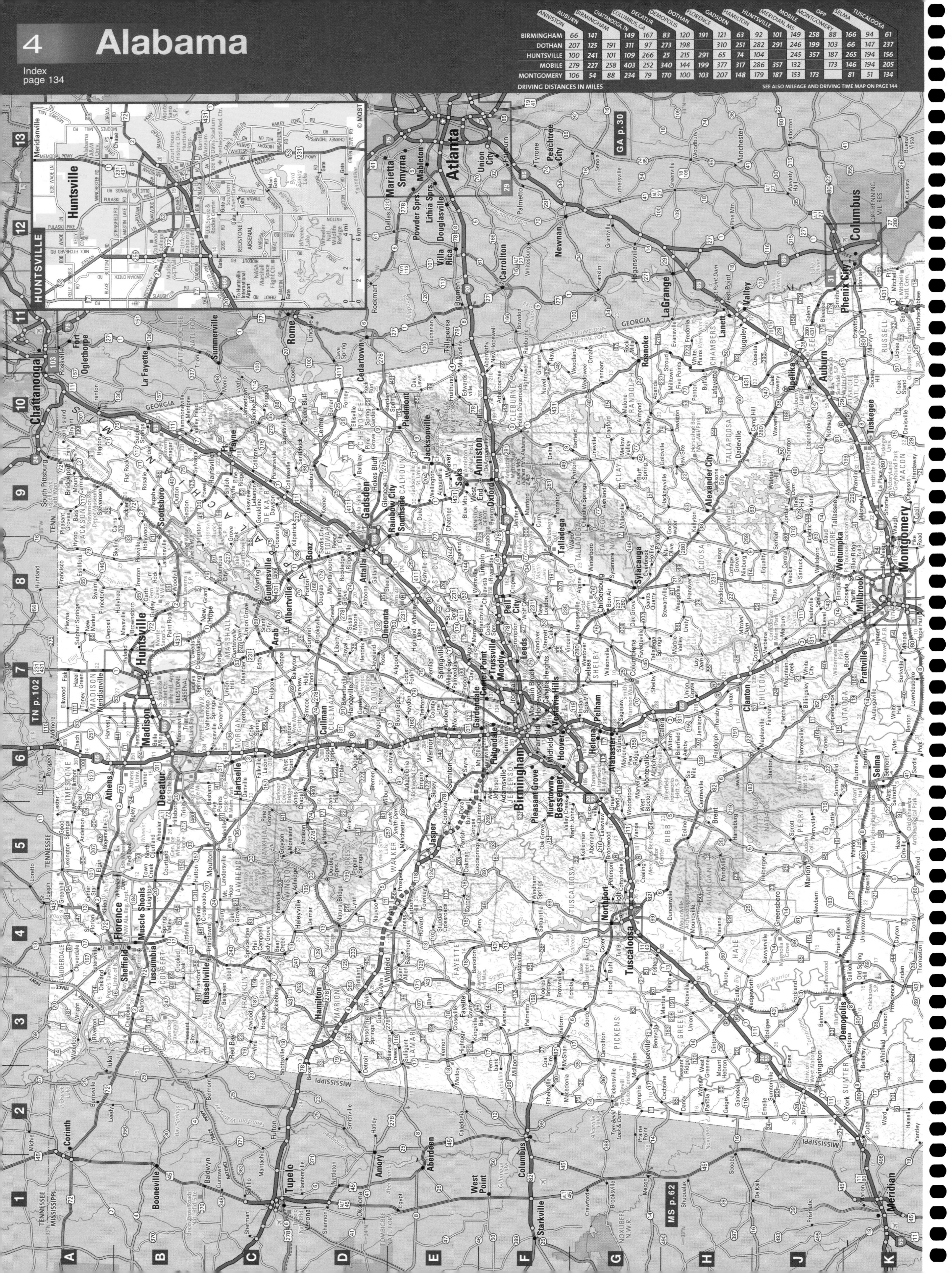

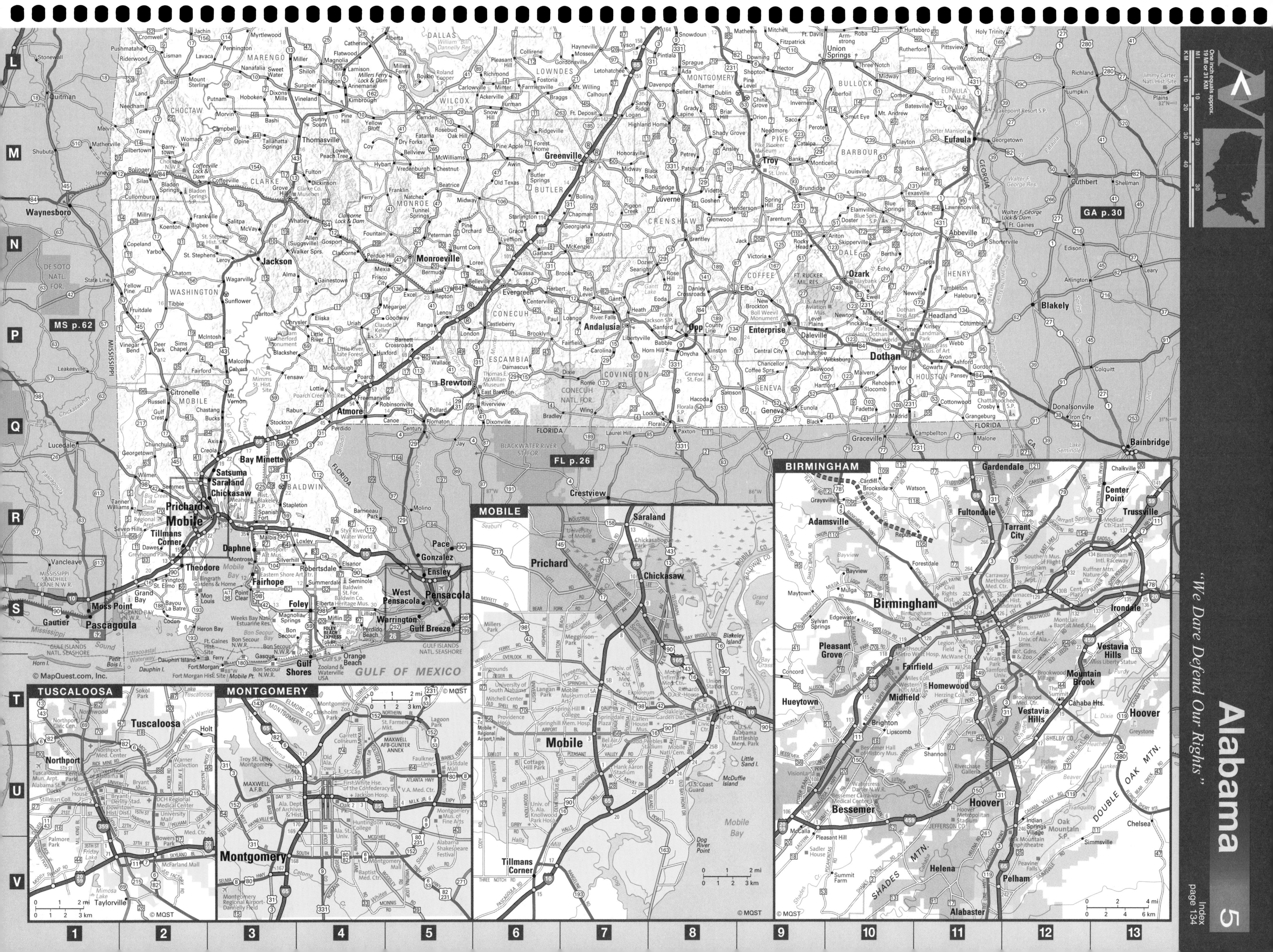
Alabama
5
"We Dare Defend Our Rights"
Index
page 134
One inch equals approx. 19 MI or 31 KM
GA p.30
FL p.26
MS p.62
BIRMINGHAM
MOBILE
MONTGOMERY
TUSCALOOSA
GULF OF MEXICO
Birmingham
Mobile
Montgomery
Tuscaloosa
Dothan
Enterprise
Greenville
Troy
Eufaula
Pensacola
Pascagoula
© MapQuest.com, Inc.

Alaska

Index page 134

"North to the Future"

	ANCHORAGE	FAIRBANKS	GLENNALLEN	HAINES	HOMER	JUNEAU	KENAI	KETCHIKAN	SEWARD	SKAGWAY	TOK	VALDEZ
ANCHORAGE		378	184	760	225	841*	161	1608*	129	807	323	301
FAIRBANKS	378		249	645	603	726*	539	1493*	507	691	207	366
HOMER	225	603	408	985		1066*	87	1833*	172	1031	547	525
SKAGWAY	807	691	623	27	1031	101*	968	954*	935		484	740
TOK	323	207	139	438	547	518*	484	1258*	451	484		256

DRIVING DISTANCES IN MILES

* DISTANCE INCLUDES FERRY TRAVEL

One inch equals approx. 143.5 MI or 233 KM

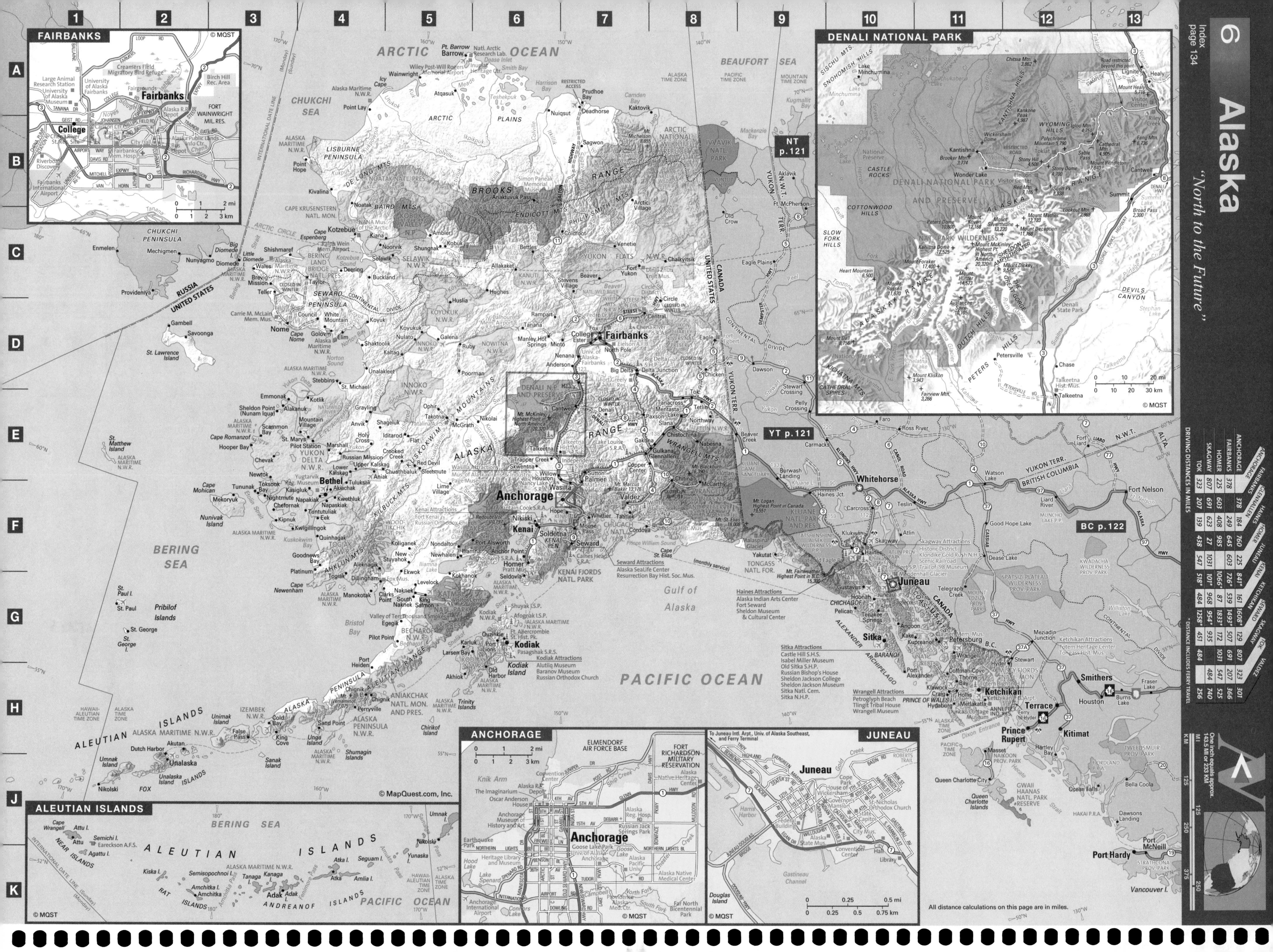

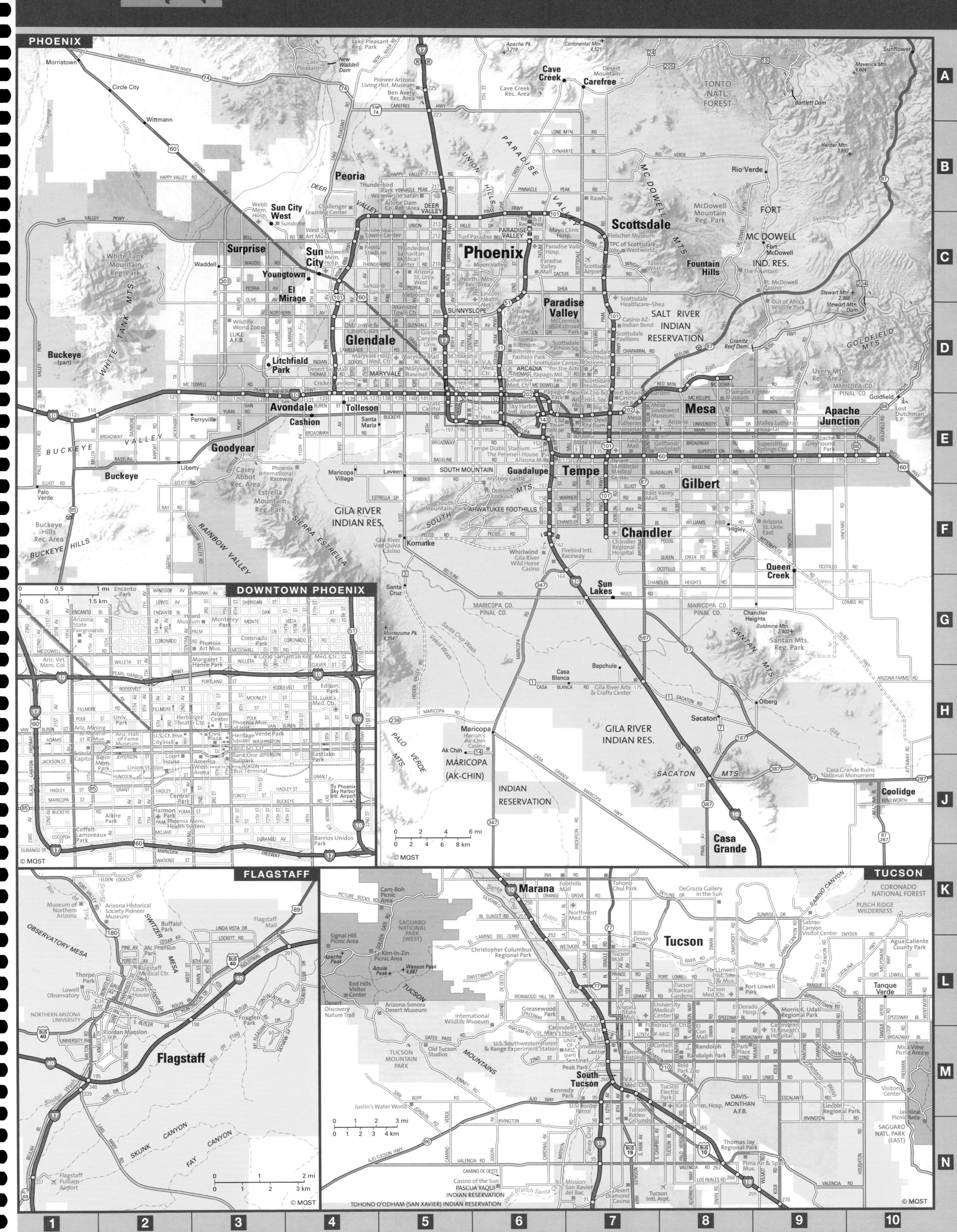

PHOENIX
Morristown
Circle City
Wittmann
Lake Pleasant Reg. Park
New Waddell Dam
Pioneer Arizona Living Hist. Museum
Ben Avery Rec. Area
Apache Pk. 3,219
Continental Mtn. 4,521
Cave Creek
Carefree
Desert Mountain
Cave Creek Rec. Area
Bartlett Res.
Bartlett Dam
Sunflower
Maverick Mtn. 4,604
TONTO NATL. FOREST
Herder Mtn. 3,693
Rio Verde
FORT MC DOWELL
Fort McDowell
IND. RES.
The Fountain
Ft. McDowell Casino
McDowell Mountain Reg. Park
MC DOWELL MTS.
Fountain Hills
Stewart Mtn. 2,988
Stewart Mtn. Dam
Saguaro Lake
GOLDFIELD MTS.
Out of Africa Wildlife Park
Usery Mtn. Rec. Area
Granite Reef Dam
SALT RIVER INDIAN RESERVATION
Scottsdale
PARADISE VALLEY
UNION HILLS
Peoria
Thunderbird Park
Waterworld Safari
Adobe Dam Co. Rec. Area
Sun City West
Sundome
Webb Mem. Hosp.
Sun City
Boswell Mem. Hosp.
Surprise
Waddell
Youngtown
El Mirage
White Tank Mountain Reg. Park
WHITE TANK MTS.
Wildlife World Zoo
LUKE A.F.B.
Litchfield Park
Buckeye (part)
Phoenix
Moon Valley
North Mtn. Rec. Area
Lincoln Health Net
Sunnyslope
Squaw Peak Rec. Area
Paradise Valley
McCormick Railroad Park
Scottsdale Healthcare-Shea
Casino AZ-Indian Bend
Scottsdale Pavilions
Glendale
Arizona Biltmore
Biltmore Fashion Park
Scottsdale Fashion Sq.
ARCADIA
Papago Mill
Maryvale
Avondale
Tolleson
Cashion
Perryville
Goodyear
BUCKEYE VALLEY
Buckeye
Liberty
Palo Verde
Buckeye Hills Rec. Area
BUCKEYE HILLS
Casey Abbot Rec. Area
Phoenix International Raceway
Estrella Mountain Reg. Park
SIERRA ESTRELLA
RAINBOW VALLEY
Santa Maria
Maricopa Village
Laveen
SOUTH MOUNTAIN
GILA RIVER INDIAN RES.
Komatke
Gila River Vee Quiva Casino
Santa Cruz
Montezuma Pk. 4,354
Papago Park
Phoenix Zoo
Desert Botanical Garden
Ariz. Hist. Soc.
Sky Harbor Intl. Airport
Old Town Tempe
Sun Devil Stadium
Arizona State Univ. Main
Tempe
Tempe Diablo Stadium
The Petersen House
Arizona Mills
Guadalupe
Mystery Castle
Dobbins Lookout
South Mountain Park
AHWATUKEE FOOTHILLS
Mesa
Mesa Southwest Museum
Fiesta Mall
Golfland/ Sunsplash
Apache Junction
Goldfield
Lost Dutchman S.P.
Superstition Springs Ctr.
Gilbert
Chandler
Chandler Regional Hospital
Firebird Intl. Raceway
Whirlwind Gila River Wild Horse Casino
Sun Lakes
Queen Creek
Higley
Chandler Heights
Goldmine Mtn. 2,403
Santan Mts. Reg. Park
SANTAN MTS.
MARICOPA CO.
PINAL CO.
Casa Blanca
Gila River Arts & Crafts Center
Bapchule
Sacaton
Olberg
Maricopa
Harrah's Ak-Chin Casino
Ak Chin
MARICOPA (AK-CHIN) INDIAN RESERVATION
PALO VERDE MTS.
SACATON MTS.
Casa Grande Ruins National Monument
Coolidge
Casa Grande
© MQST
DOWNTOWN PHOENIX
Encanto Park
Arizona State Fairgrounds
Heard Museum
Monterey Park
Coronado Park
Phoenix Art Mus.
Good Samaritan Reg. Med. Ctr.
Ariz. Vet. Mem. Col.
Margaret T. Hance Park
Edison Park
St. Luke's Med. Ctr.
Univ. Park
Herberger Theater Ctr.
Arizona Center
Phoenix Mus. of Hist.
Ariz. Mining & Mineral Museum
Hall of Fame Museum
U.S. Ct. Hse.
City Hall
Civic Plaza
Heritage Square
Verde Park
Ariz. Sci. Ctr.
Bank One Ballpark
America West Arena
Jackson Bus Terminal
Eastlake Park
Ariz. St. Capitol
Bolin Mem. Park
Court House
Union Station
Central Park
Harmon Park
Phoenix Mem. Health System
Alkire Park
Coffelt-Lamoreaux Park
Barrios Unidos Park
To Phoenix Sky Harbor Intl. Airport
FLAGSTAFF
Museum of Northern Arizona
Arizona Historical Society Pioneer Museum
Buffalo Park
Flagstaff Mall
OBSERVATORY MESA
SWITZER MESA
Mc Pherson Park
Flagstaff Med. Ctr.
Thorpe Park
Lowell Observatory
NORTHERN ARIZONA UNIVERSITY
Riordan Mansion
Foxglen Park
Flagstaff
SKUNK CANYON
FAY CANYON
Flagstaff Pulliam Airport
TUCSON
CORONADO NATIONAL FOREST
PUSCH RIDGE WILDERNESS
Marana
Foothills Mall
Tohono Chul Park
DeGrazia Gallery in the Sun
Cam-Boh Picnic Area
SAGUARO NATIONAL PARK (WEST)
Signal Hill Picnic Area
Kim-In-Zin Picnic Area
Amole Peak
Wasson Peak 4,687
Red Hills Visitor Center
TUCSON MOUNTAINS
Desert Discovery Nature Trail
Arizona-Sonora Desert Museum
Christopher Columbus Regional Park
Northwest Med. Ctr.
Rillito Downs
Tucson
Sabino Canyon Visitor Center
Agua Caliente County Park
Tucson Mall
Fort Lowell Hist. Site & Mus.
Tucson Med. Ctr.
Fort Lowell Park
Tanque Verde
Tucson Botanical Gardens
Greasewood Park
International Wildlife Museum
University Medical Center
Arizona State Mus.
UNIV. OF ARIZ.
El Dorado Hosp.
Morris K. Udall Regional Park
St. Joseph's Hospital
Mica View Picnic Area
Old Tucson Studios
TUCSON MOUNTAIN PARK
U.S. Southwestern Forest & Range Experiment Station
Sentinel Peak Park
Convention Center
Barrio Historico
Reid Park Zoo
Randolph Park
South Tucson
Kennedy Park
Tucson Electric Park
DAVIS-MONTHAN A.F.B.
Kino Comm. Hosp.
Visitors Center
Lincoln Regional Park
Javelina Picnic Area
SAGUARO NATL. PARK (EAST)
Justin's Water World
Tucson Rodeo Grounds
Thomas Jay Regional Park
Pima Air & Space Mus.
Casino of the Sun
PASCUA YAQUI INDIAN RESERVATION
Mission San Xavier del Bac
Desert Diamond Casino
Tucson Intl. Arpt.
TOHONO O'ODHAM (SAN XAVIER) INDIAN RESERVATION

Arizona

Index
page 134

	BULLHEAD CITY	CASA GRANDE	CHINLE	DOUGLAS	FLAGSTAFF	GRAND CANYON	HOLBROOK	KINGMAN	LAKE HAVASU CITY	NOGALES	PAGE	PHOENIX	PRESCOTT	SAFFORD	SHOW LOW	TUCSON	WICKENBURG	YUMA
FLAGSTAFF	180	188	216	374		89	93	148	209	318	135	137	89	271	140	255	147	320
KINGMAN	34	235	364	421	148	175	240		60	365	281	184	150	353	288	302	134	215
PHOENIX	217	50	353	237	137	226	230	184	193	181	272		96	169	178	118	51	183
TUCSON	335	68	366	120	255	345	240	302	311	65	390	118	214	128	193		169	241
YUMA	222	179	536	360	320	409	413	215	155	304	455	183	213	368	352	241	170	

DRIVING DISTANCES IN MILES

SEE ALSO MILEAGE AND DRIVING TIME MAP ON PAGE 144

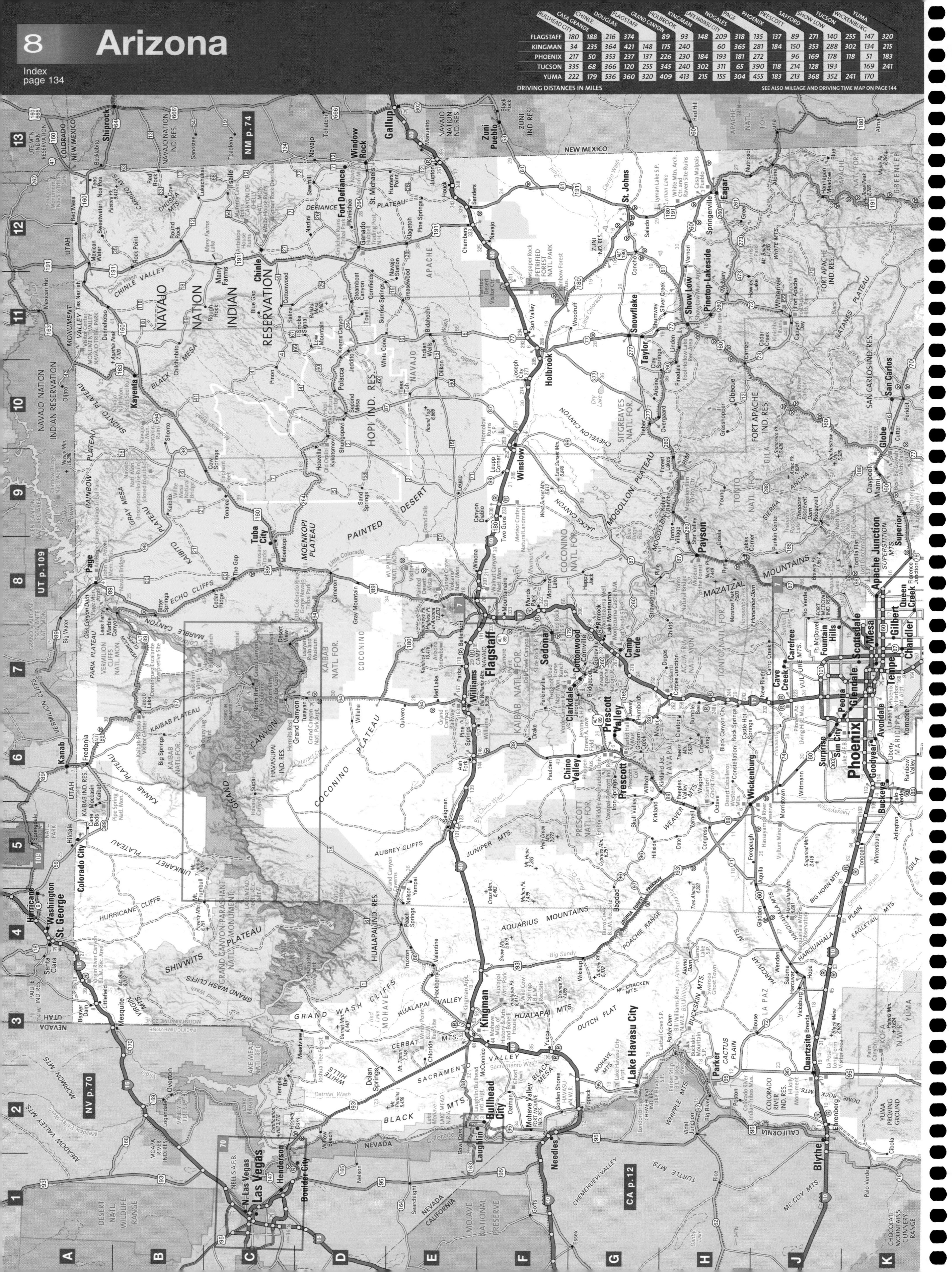

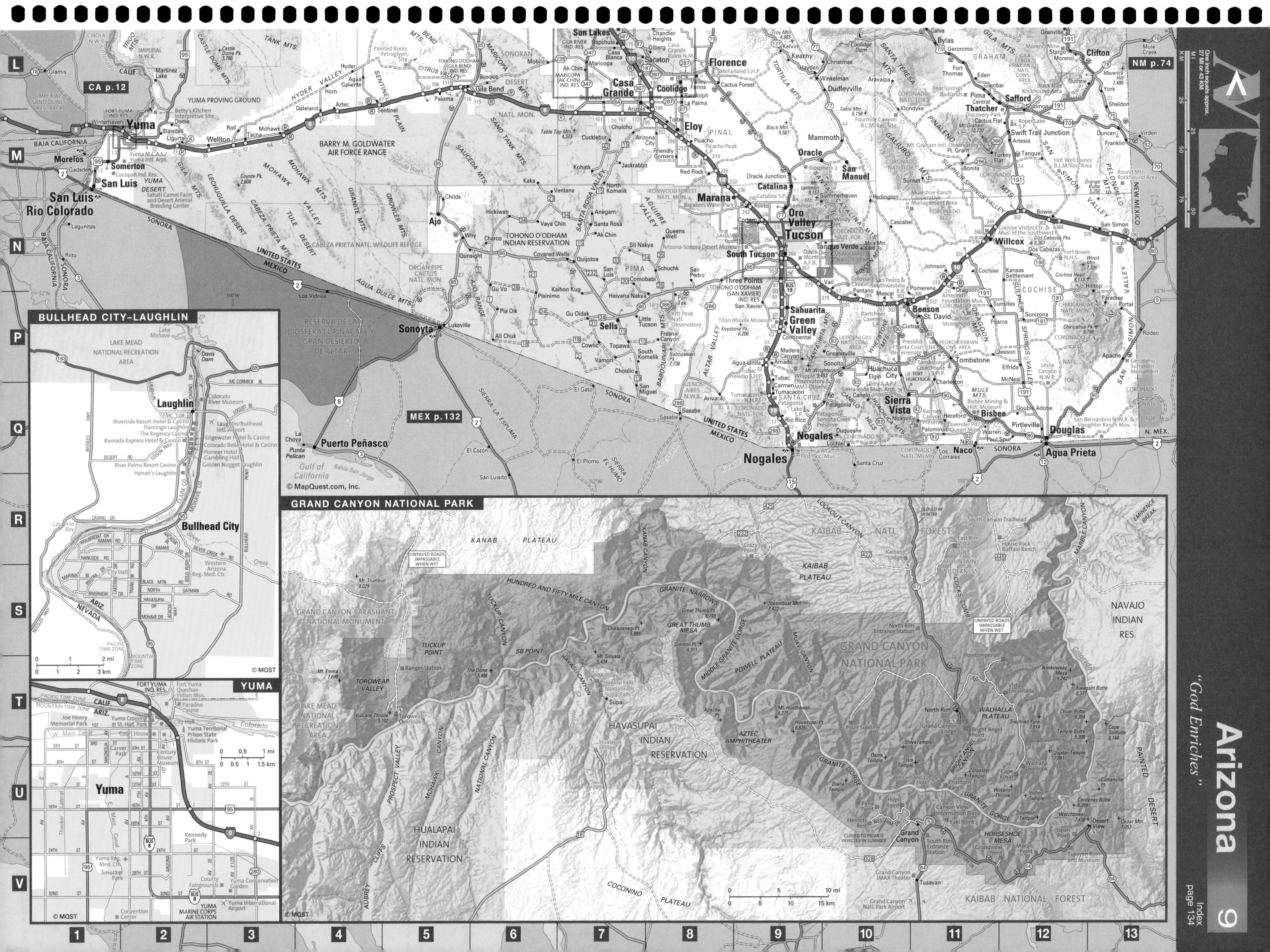
One inch equals approx. 27 MI or 43 KM
MI 25 50
KM 25 50 75
NM p. 74
CA p. 12
MEX p. 132
GRAND CANYON NATIONAL PARK
BULLHEAD CITY–LAUGHLIN
YUMA
© MapQuest.com, Inc.
© MQST
Tucson
Nogales
Sierra Vista
Douglas
Agua Prieta
Bisbee
Benson
Willcox
Safford
Florence
Casa Grande
Eloy
Marana
Oro Valley
Sells
Ajo
Gila Bend
Yuma
San Luis
San Luis Río Colorado
Sonoyta
Puerto Peñasco
Laughlin
Bullhead City
Grand Canyon
North Rim
Tusayan
UNITED STATES
MEXICO
NEW MEXICO
TOHONO O'ODHAM INDIAN RESERVATION
BARRY M. GOLDWATER AIR FORCE RANGE
HAVASUPAI INDIAN RESERVATION
HUALAPAI INDIAN RESERVATION
KAIBAB NATIONAL FOREST
NAVAJO INDIAN RES.
LAKE MEAD NATIONAL RECREATION AREA
GRAND CANYON-PARASHANT NATIONAL MONUMENT
KAIBAB PLATEAU
COCONINO PLATEAU
PAINTED DESERT
CLOSED TO PRIVATE VEHICLES IN SUMMER
UNPAVED ROADS IMPASSABLE WHEN WET

Index page 134

	BLYTHEVILLE	CAMDEN	CONWAY	DUMAS	EL DORADO	FAYETTEVILLE	FORT SMITH	HARRISON	HELENA	HOT SPRINGS	JONESBORO	LITTLE ROCK	MEMPHIS, TN	MENA	NEWPORT	PINE BLUFF	RUSSELLVILLE	TEXARKANA
FORT SMITH	353	201	134	255	232	64		141	280	126	266	165	298	81	220	210	87	180
JONESBORO	53	236	133	185	253	287	266	178	111	200		135	70	276	46	180	182	49
LITTLE ROCK	195	101	31	90	118	186	165	136	122	65	135		140	141	89	45	81	110
PINE BLUFF	213	76	76	45	93	231	210	181	106	76	180	45	157	151	134		126	128
TEXARKANA	99	210	104	129	227	259	238	193	62	174	49	110	49	250	53	128	154	

DRIVING DISTANCES IN MILES

SEE ALSO MILEAGE AND DRIVING TIME MAP ON PAGE 144

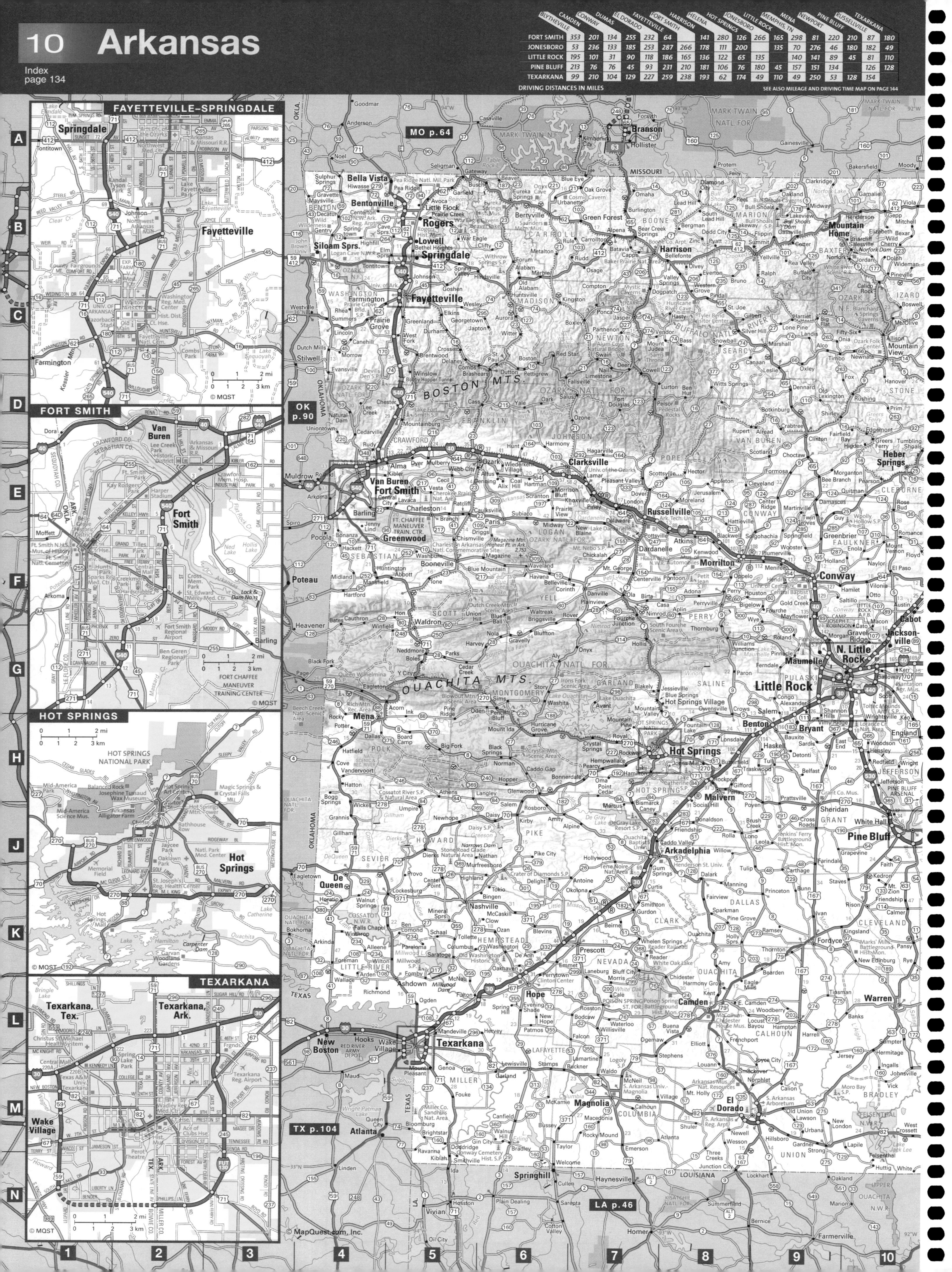

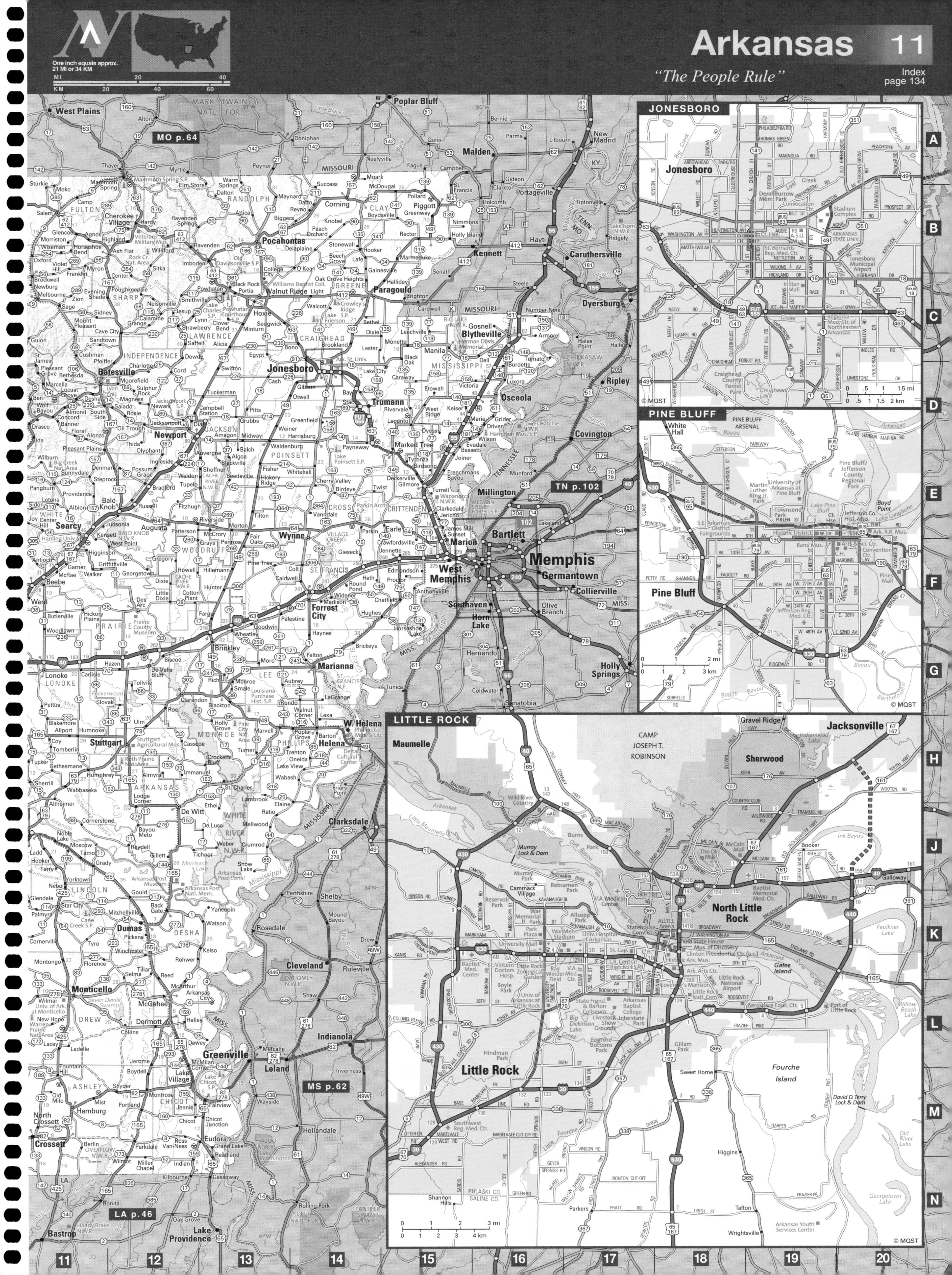
Arkansas
11
"The People Rule"
Index page 134
One inch equals approx. 21 MI or 34 KM
MO p.64
TN p.102
MS p.62
LA p.46
JONESBORO
PINE BLUFF
LITTLE ROCK
West Plains
Poplar Bluff
Malden
Kennett
Caruthersville
Dyersburg
Blytheville
Osceola
Ripley
Covington
Millington
Bartlett
Memphis
Germantown
Collierville
West Memphis
Marion
Southaven
Horn Lake
Olive Branch
Holly Springs
Jonesboro
Paragould
Pocahontas
Walnut Ridge
Piggott
Corning
Batesville
Newport
Trumann
Searcy
Bald Knob
Augusta
Wynne
Forrest City
Brinkley
Marianna
Helena
W. Helena
Clarksdale
Stuttgart
De Witt
Lonoke
Beebe
Dumas
McGehee
Dermott
Monticello
Greenville
Leland
Cleveland
Indianapolis
Lake Village
Eudora
Hamburg
Crossett
Bastrop
Lake Providence
Cherokee Village
Camp Joseph T. Robinson
Maumelle
Jacksonville
Sherwood
North Little Rock
Little Rock
Gravel Ridge
Galloway
Shannon Hills
Sweet Home
Fourche Island
Gates Island
Pine Bluff
White Hall
Pine Bluff Arsenal
© MQST
A
B
C
D
E
F
G
H
J
K
L
M
N
11
12
13
14
15
16
17
18
19
20

	BISHOP	CHICO	EUREKA	FRESNO	MERCED	MONTEREY	NAPA	OAKLAND	REDDING	SACRAMENTO	SAN FRANCISCO	SAN JOSE	SANTA ROSA	SOUTH LAKE TAHOE	STOCKTON	SUSANVILLE	UKIAH	YOSEMITE VILLAGE
EUREKA	537	186		444	385	380	235	262	133	278	263	306	208	379	336	247	148	436
REDDING	426	74	133	344	284	323	193	213		166	222	250	228	266	214	114	193	336
SACRAMENTO	260	88	278	178	118	188	58	78	166		87	115	93	100	48	183	153	170
SAN FRANCISCO	283	182	263	190	131	114	47	9	222	87		43	56	185	82	277	116	183
SOUTH LAKE TAHOE	179	165	379	267	208	286	156	176	266	100	185	213	191		142	146	251	180

DRIVING DISTANCES IN MILES

SEE ALSO MILEAGE AND DRIVING TIME MAP ON PAGE 144

One inch equals approx. 27.5 MI or 44 KM

MI 25 50

KM 25 50 75

SACRAMENTO

LAKE TAHOE

STOCKTON

FRESNO

YOSEMITE NATIONAL PARK

LASSEN VOLCANIC NATIONAL PARK

KINGS CANYON–SEQUOIA NATL. PARKS

NV p.70

© MQST

Index page 134

	BAKERSFIELD	BARSTOW	BISHOP	EL CENTRO	FRESNO	LAS VEGAS, NV	LOS ANGELES	MERCED	MONTEREY	PALM SPRINGS	SAN BERNARDINO	SAN DIEGO	SAN FRANCISCO	SAN JOSE	SAN LUIS OBISPO	SANTA BARBARA	VISALIA	YOSEMITE VILLAGE
FRESNO	111	246	219	451		399	219	59	158	324	277	342	190	153	134	258	43	90
LOS ANGELES	111	118	270	234	219	274		278	327	110	62	124	385	342	190	97	183	308
MONTEREY	229	365	315	559	158	517	327	122		432	385	450	114	74	149	242	204	201
SAN DIEGO	234	181	366	117	342	337	124	401	450	143	111		508	465	314	221	306	431
SAN FRANCISCO	287	423	283	617	190	575	385	131	114	490	443	508		43	234	327	233	183

DRIVING DISTANCES IN MILES

SEE ALSO MILEAGE AND DRIVING TIME MAP ON PAGE 144

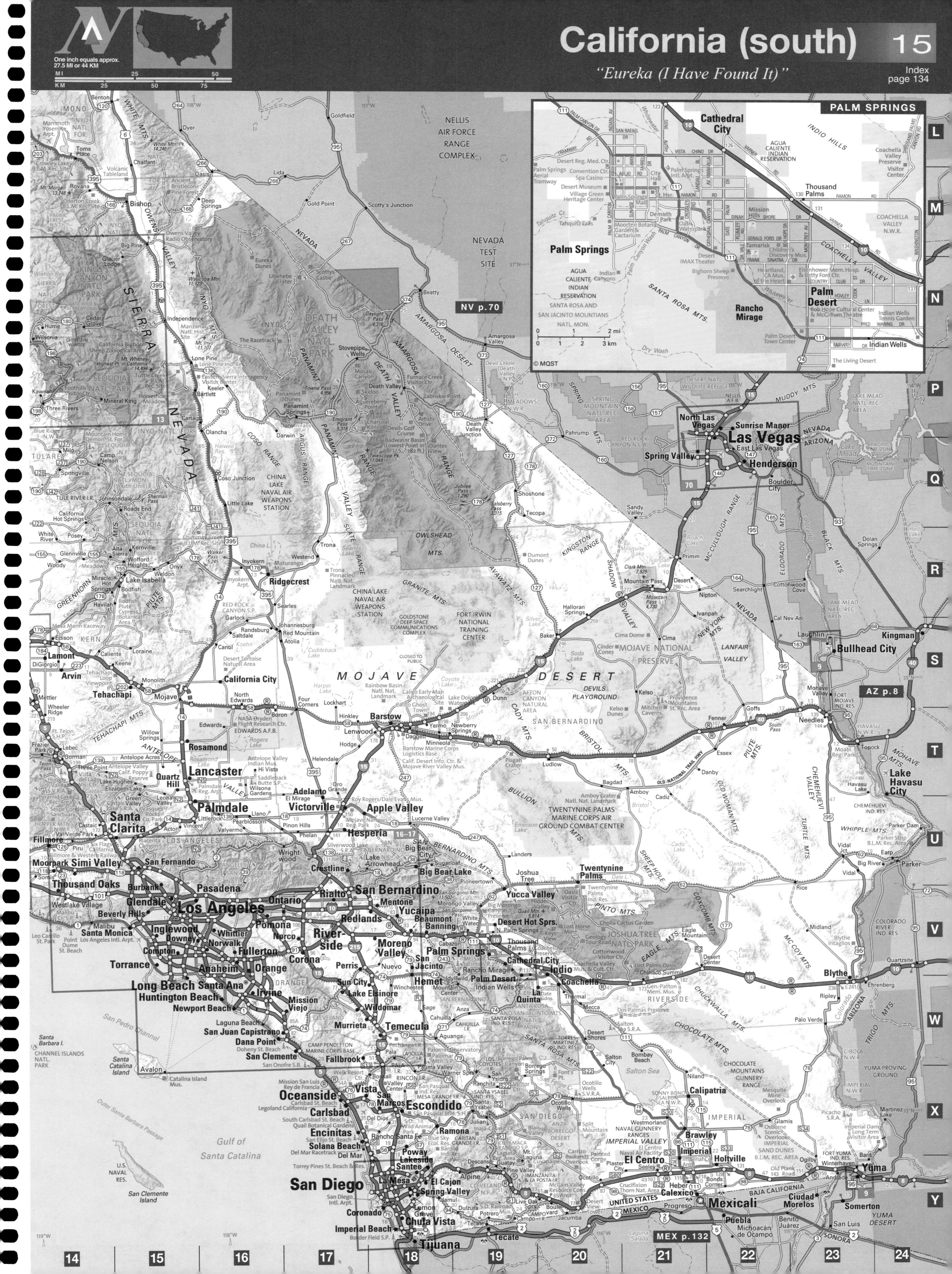

California (south)
15
"Eureka (I Have Found It)"
Index page 134
One inch equals approx. 27.5 MI or 44 KM
PALM SPRINGS
Cathedral City
AGUA CALIENTE INDIAN RESERVATION
Thousand Palms
Palm Springs
Palm Desert
Rancho Mirage
Indian Wells
SANTA ROSA MTS.
INDIO HILLS
COACHELLA VALLEY
© MQST
NELLIS AIR FORCE RANGE COMPLEX
NEVADA TEST SITE
NV p.70
DEATH VALLEY NATL. PARK
SIERRA NEVADA
KINGS CANYON NATL. PARK
SEQUOIA NATL. PARK
Las Vegas
North Las Vegas
Sunrise Manor
East Las Vegas
Spring Valley
Henderson
Boulder City
Bishop
Big Pine
Independence
Lone Pine
Ridgecrest
China Lake Naval Air Weapons Station
Baker
MOJAVE DESERT
MOJAVE NATIONAL PRESERVE
Barstow
Needles
Bullhead City
Kingman
Laughlin
AZ p.8
Lake Havasu City
Parker
Blythe
Tehachapi
Mojave
California City
Lancaster
Palmdale
Victorville
Apple Valley
Hesperia
Santa Clarita
Simi Valley
Thousand Oaks
San Fernando
Pasadena
Los Angeles
Glendale
Burbank
Santa Monica
Inglewood
Torrance
Long Beach
Anaheim
Santa Ana
Orange
Irvine
Huntington Beach
Newport Beach
Ontario
Rialto
San Bernardino
Redlands
Riverside
Moreno Valley
Corona
Yucaipa
Big Bear Lake
Yucca Valley
Twentynine Palms
Banning
Beaumont
Hemet
Temecula
Murrieta
Palm Springs
Indio
Coachella
JOSHUA TREE NATL. PARK
Mission Viejo
San Clemente
Oceanside
Vista
Carlsbad
Escondido
Encinitas
Ramona
Poway
El Cajon
San Diego
Chula Vista
Tijuana
Tecate
El Centro
Brawley
Imperial
Calexico
Mexicali
Calipatria
Yuma
Salton Sea
Gulf of Santa Catalina
Santa Catalina Island
San Clemente Island
CHANNEL ISLANDS NATL. PARK
MEX p.132

Los Angeles (CA)

Index page 134

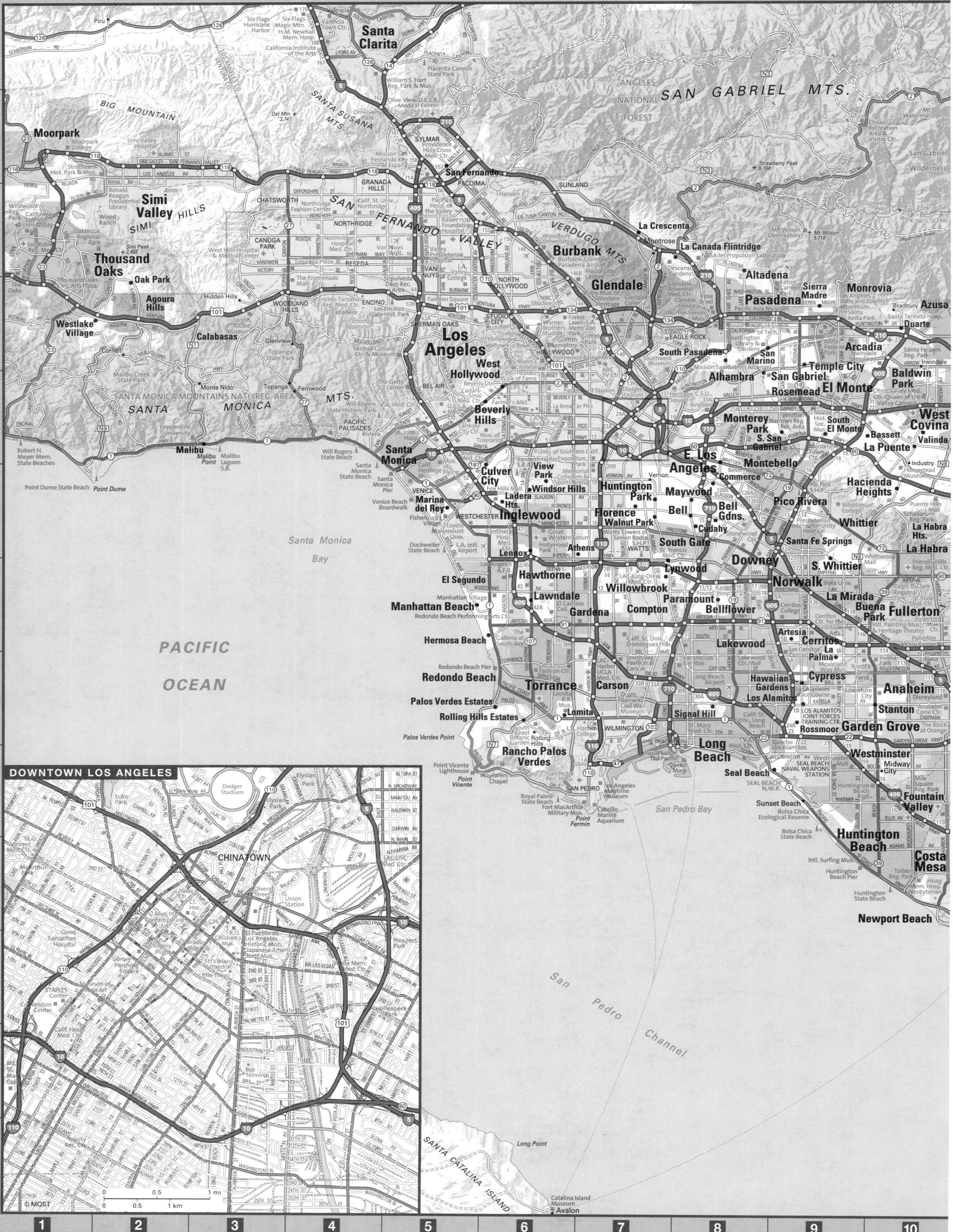

A B C D E F G H J K L M N

1 2 3 4 5 6 7 8 9 10

Santa Clarita
SAN GABRIEL MTS.
ANGELES NATIONAL FOREST
BIG MOUNTAIN
SANTA SUSANA MTS.
Moorpark
Simi Valley
SIMI HILLS
Thousand Oaks
Oak Park
Agoura Hills
Westlake Village
Calabasas
SAN FERNANDO VALLEY
VERDUGO MTS.
Sylmar
San Fernando
Pacoima
Burbank
Glendale
La Crescenta
Montrose
La Canada Flintridge
Altadena
Pasadena
Sierra Madre
Monrovia
Arcadia
Azusa
Duarte
Los Angeles
West Hollywood
Beverly Hills
SANTA MONICA MOUNTAINS NAT'L REC. AREA
SANTA MONICA MTS.
Malibu
Topanga
Fernwood
Monte Nido
Pacific Palisades
Santa Monica
Venice
Marina del Rey
Culver City
View Park
Windsor Hills
Ladera Hts.
Inglewood
Westchester
Lennox
Hawthorne
Lawndale
El Segundo
Manhattan Beach
Hermosa Beach
Redondo Beach
Torrance
Gardena
Palos Verdes Estates
Rolling Hills Estates
Rancho Palos Verdes
Lomita
Carson
San Pedro
Wilmington
Long Beach
Signal Hill
Seal Beach
Huntington Beach
Costa Mesa
Newport Beach
Fountain Valley
Westminster
Midway City
Garden Grove
Stanton
Anaheim
Cypress
Los Alamitos
Hawaiian Gardens
Rossmoor
La Palma
Cerritos
Artesia
Lakewood
Bellflower
Paramount
Compton
Willowbrook
Lynwood
South Gate
Downey
Norwalk
Santa Fe Springs
S. Whittier
Whittier
La Mirada
Buena Park
Fullerton
La Habra
La Habra Hts.
Hacienda Heights
La Puente
Valinda
West Covina
Bassett
Baldwin Park
El Monte
South El Monte
Rosemead
Temple City
San Gabriel
San Marino
South Pasadena
Alhambra
Monterey Park
Montebello
Commerce
Pico Rivera
E. Los Angeles
Bell Gdns.
Bell
Cudahy
Maywood
Huntington Park
Vernon
Walnut Park
Florence
Athens
Santa Monica Bay
PACIFIC OCEAN
San Pedro Bay
San Pedro Channel
SANTA CATALINA ISLAND
Long Point
Avalon
Point Dume
Point Vicente
Point Fermin

DOWNTOWN LOS ANGELES

Dodger Stadium
Elysian Park
Echo Park
CHINATOWN
Union Station
Olvera Street
Little Tokyo
Pershing Square
STAPLES Center
Convention Center
Hollenbeck Park
Prospect Park
Good Samaritan Hospital
Trinity Rec. Ctr.

0 0.5 1 mi
0 0.5 1 km

Index
page 134

One inch equals approx.
5.5 MI or 9 KM

MI 5 10
KM 5 10 15

TRAVEL NOTE: Beginning January 2002, California started numbering freeway exits using a mileage-based numbering system. Full implementation is expected to take three years. For more details, including a complete listing of California's exit numbers, go to *www.dot.ca.gov/hq/traffops/signtech/calnexus/index.htm.*

A B C D E F G H J K L M N

11 12 13 14 15 16 17 18 19 20

San Francisco Bay area (CA)

Index page 134

One inch equals approx. 5.5 MI or 9 KM

MI 5 10
KM 5 10 15

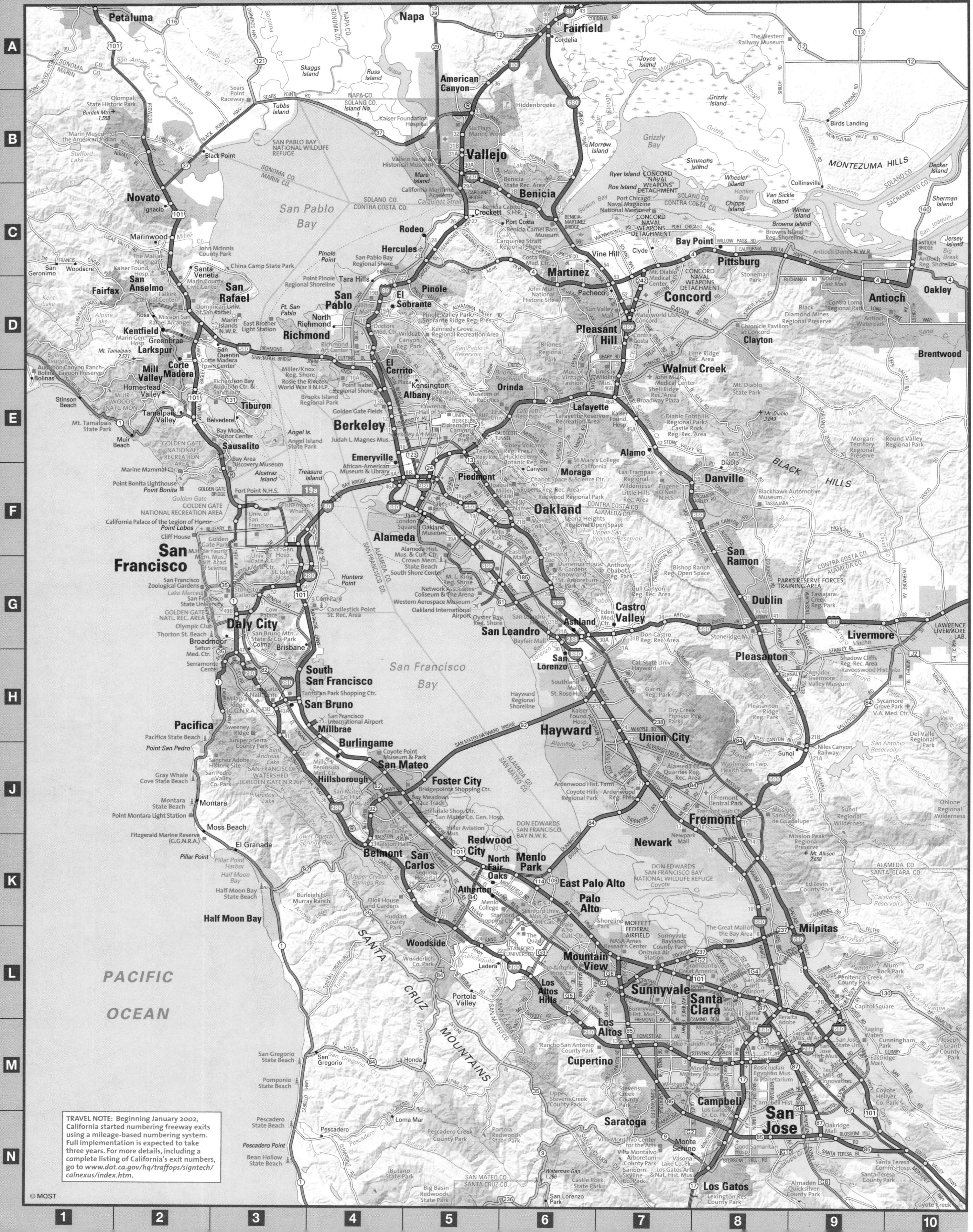

PACIFIC OCEAN

San Francisco Bay

San Pablo Bay

TRAVEL NOTE: Beginning January 2002, California started numbering freeway exits using a mileage-based numbering system. Full implementation is expected to take three years. For more details, including a complete listing of California's exit numbers, go to *www.dot.ca.gov/hq/traffops/signtech/calnexus/index.htm.*

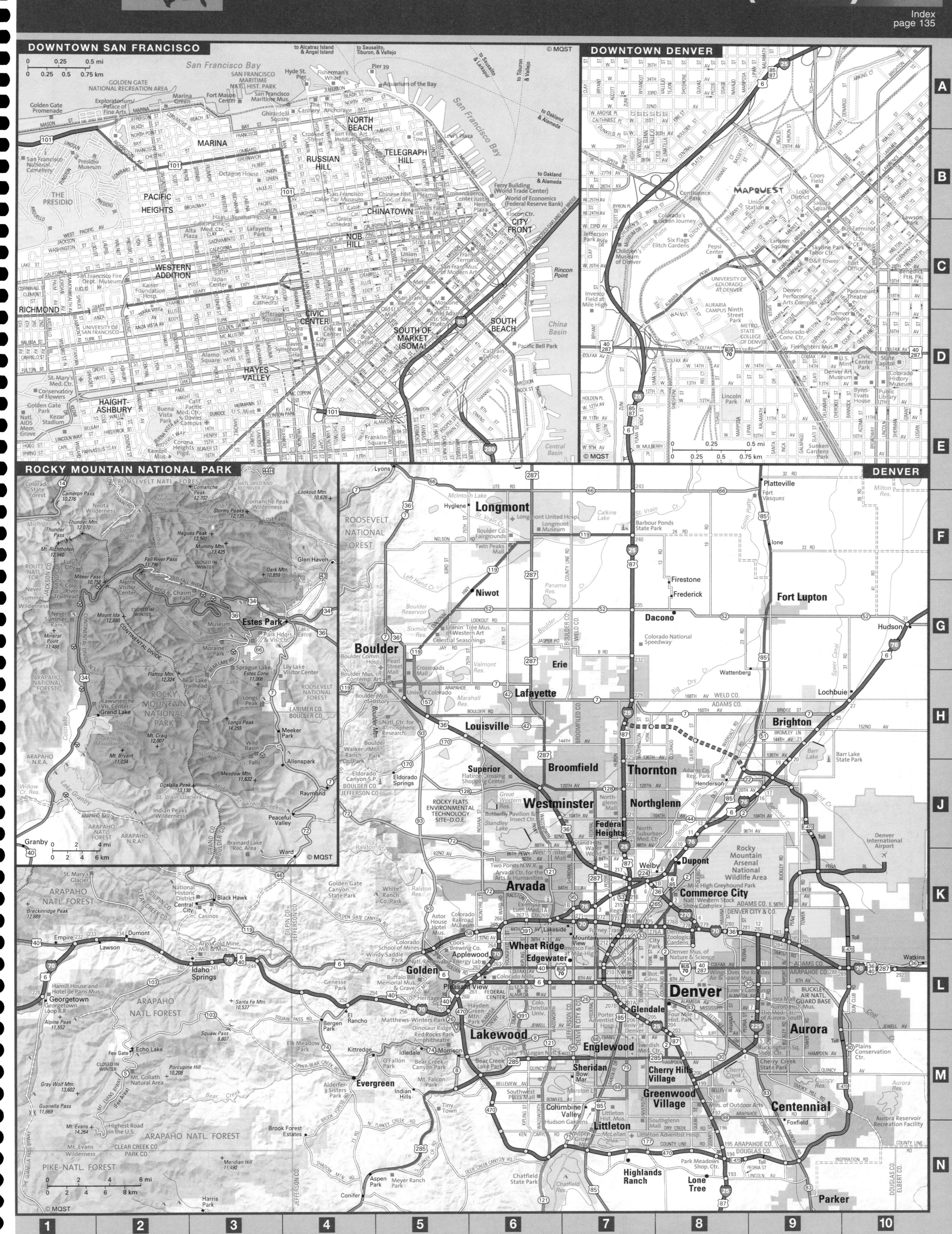
DOWNTOWN SAN FRANCISCO
San Francisco Bay
MARINA
PACIFIC HEIGHTS
RUSSIAN HILL
NORTH BEACH
TELEGRAPH HILL
CHINATOWN
NOB HILL
WESTERN ADDITION
RICHMOND
CIVIC CENTER
HAYES VALLEY
HAIGHT-ASHBURY
SOUTH OF MARKET (SOMA)
SOUTH BEACH
CITY FRONT
THE PRESIDIO
GOLDEN GATE NATIONAL RECREATION AREA
Fisherman's Wharf
Pier 39
Aquarium of the Bay
Coit Tower
Ferry Building (World Trade Center)
Rincon Point
China Basin
Pacific Bell Park
Central Basin
© MQST
DOWNTOWN DENVER
Coors Field
LoDo District
Union Station
Confluence Park
Larimer Square
Sakura Square
Six Flags Elitch Gardens
Pepsi Center
Children's Museum of Denver
Invesco Field at Mile High
UNIVERSITY OF COLORADO AT DENVER
AURARIA CAMPUS
Ninth Street Park
METRO. STATE COLLEGE OF DENVER
Denver Performing Arts Complex
Colorado Conv. Ctr.
Civic Center Park
State Capitol
Denver Art Museum
U.S. Mint
Lincoln Park
Sunken Gardens Park
MAPQUEST
© MQST
ROCKY MOUNTAIN NATIONAL PARK
ROCKY MOUNTAIN NATIONAL PARK
ROOSEVELT NATL. FOREST
Estes Park
Glen Haven
Allenspark
Meeker Park
Bear Lake
Longs Peak 14,255
Grand Lake
Granby
Lake Granby
Continental Divide
Indian Peaks Wilderness
© MQST
DENVER
Longmont
Boulder
Louisville
Lafayette
Erie
Niwot
Broomfield
Superior
Westminster
Thornton
Northglenn
Federal Heights
Arvada
Wheat Ridge
Golden
Lakewood
Edgewater
Denver
Glendale
Englewood
Sheridan
Cherry Hills Village
Greenwood Village
Littleton
Centennial
Aurora
Commerce City
Brighton
Fort Lupton
Dacono
Firestone
Frederick
Platteville
Hudson
Lochbuie
Wattenberg
Henderson
Dupont
Welby
Highlands Ranch
Lone Tree
Parker
Evergreen
Idaho Springs
Georgetown
Central City
Black Hawk
Empire
Dumont
Lawson
Kittredge
Idledale
Morrison
Indian Hills
Conifer
Aspen Park
Harris
Denver International Airport
Rocky Mountain Arsenal National Wildlife Refuge
Roosevelt National Forest
Arapaho Natl. Forest
Pike Natl. Forest
Chatfield State Park
Barr Lake State Park
© MQST

Index
page 135

	ALAMOSA	ASPEN	BOULDER	BURLINGTON	COLORADO SPRINGS	CRAIG	DENVER	DURANGO	ESTES PARK	FORT COLLINS	GLENWOOD SPRINGS	GRAND JUNCTION	GREELEY	LAMAR	MONTROSE	PUEBLO	STERLING	TRINIDAD
COLORADO SPRINGS	162	157	97	152		270	70	314	134	133	226	318	133	161	236	43	194	127
DENVER	230	164	27	168	70	203		337	64	64	158	250	64	208	277	111	130	196
DURANGO	152	244	366	461	314	321	337		402	399	226	169	399	354	107	271	465	260
GRAND JUNCTION	261	135	254	418	318	152	250	169	291	311	92		311	458	62	360	377	444
PUEBLO	119	185	139	191	43	312	111	271	175	175	268	360	175	119	229		236	84

DRIVING DISTANCES IN MILES

SEE ALSO MILEAGE AND DRIVING TIME MAP ON PAGE 144

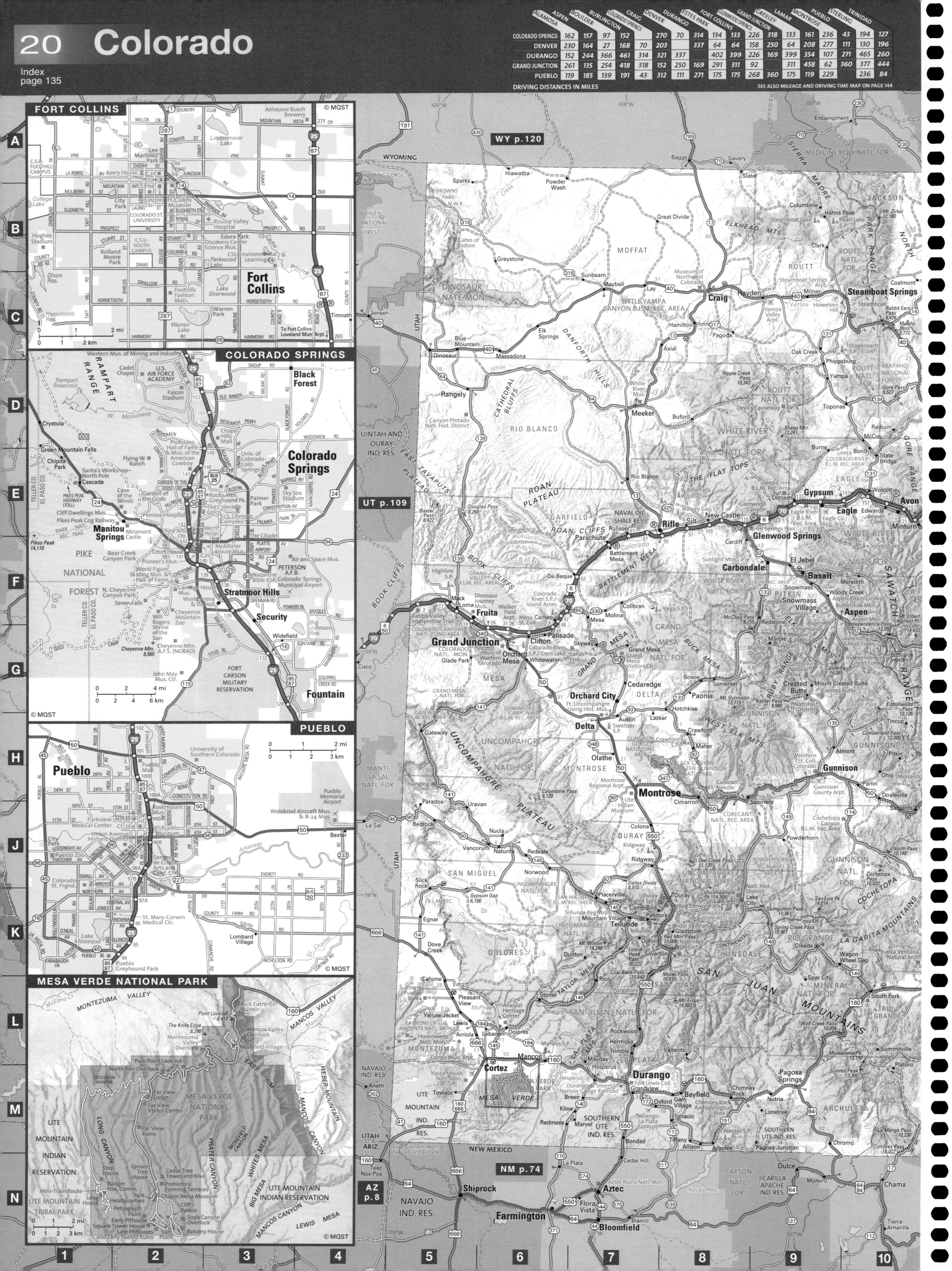

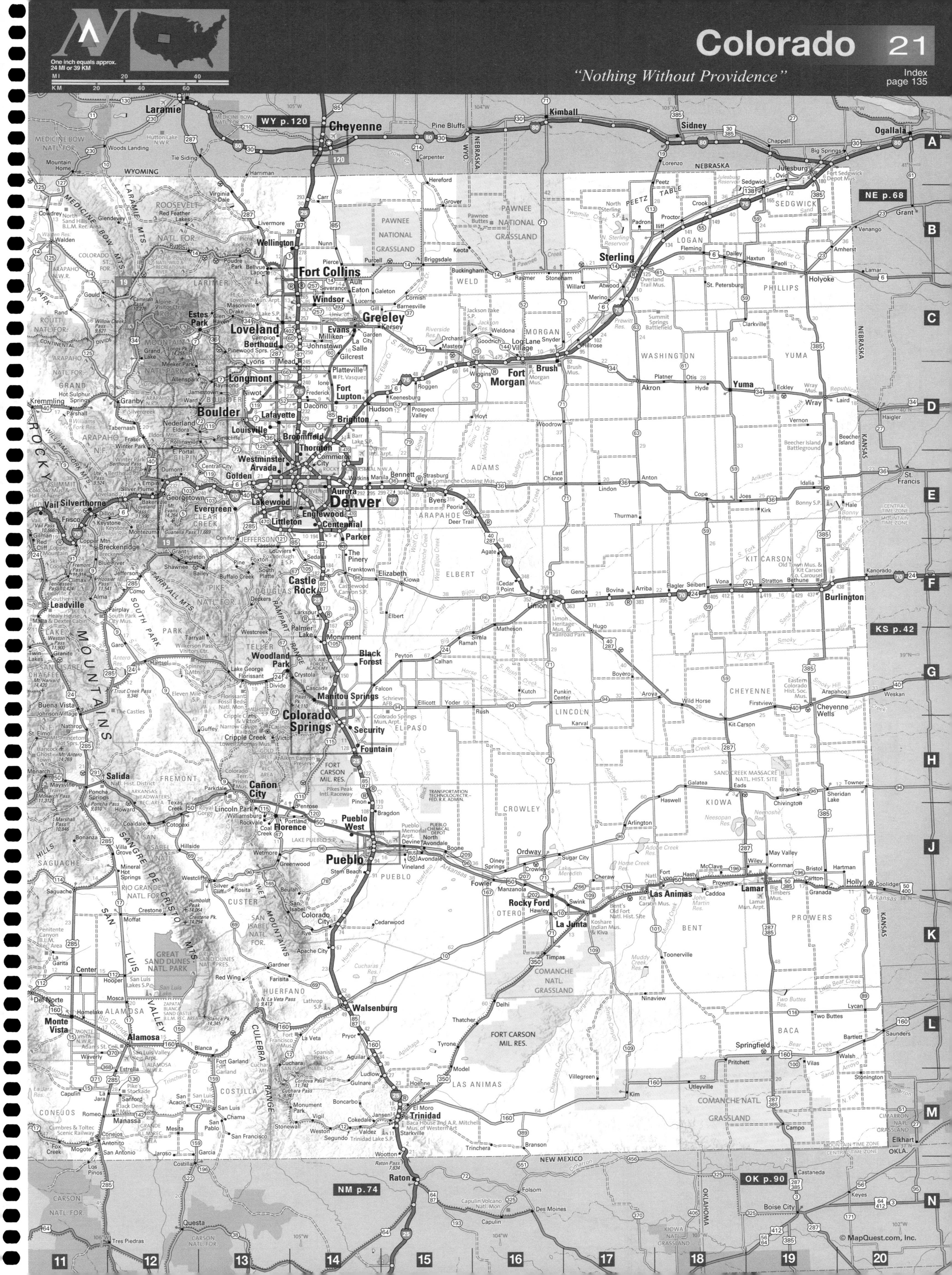

Colorado
21
"Nothing Without Providence"
Index page 135
One inch equals approx. 24 MI or 39 KM
MI 20 40
KM 20 40 60
WY p.120
NE p.68
KS p.42
OK p.90
NM p.74
WYOMING
NEBRASKA
KANSAS
NEW MEXICO
OKLAHOMA
Cheyenne
Laramie
Kimball
Sidney
Ogallala
Julesburg
Sterling
Fort Collins
Greeley
Loveland
Longmont
Boulder
Denver
Aurora
Lakewood
Littleton
Castle Rock
Colorado Springs
Pueblo
Cañon City
Walsenburg
Trinidad
Raton
Alamosa
Monte Vista
Salida
Leadville
Vail
Limon
Burlington
Yuma
Wray
Holyoke
Fort Morgan
Brush
Akron
Lamar
La Junta
Rocky Ford
Las Animas
Springfield
Kit Carson
Cheyenne Wells
ROCKY MOUNTAINS
PAWNEE NATIONAL GRASSLAND
COMANCHE NATL. GRASSLAND
GREAT SAND DUNES NATL. PARK
SANGRE DE CRISTO MTS.
WELD
MORGAN
LOGAN
SEDGWICK
PHILLIPS
WASHINGTON
YUMA
ADAMS
ARAPAHOE
ELBERT
KIT CARSON
LINCOLN
CHEYENNE
EL PASO
CROWLEY
KIOWA
OTERO
BENT
PROWERS
PUEBLO
LAS ANIMAS
BACA
COSTILLA
CONEJOS
FREMONT
CUSTER
HUERFANO
© MapQuest.com, Inc.

Index page 135

	BRIDGEPORT	DANBURY	HARTFORD	MERIDEN	MIDDLETOWN	NEW HAVEN	NEW LONDON	NEW YORK, NY	NORWICH	PROVIDENCE, RI	PUTNAM	SPRINGFIELD, MA	STAMFORD	STORRS	TORRINGTON	WATERBURY	WILLIMANTIC	WINDSOR LOCKS
BRIDGEPORT		31	56	37	44	19	64	60	72	118	100	81	21	75	54	33	79	68
HARTFORD	56	57		21	16	39	46	115	38	73	46	25	77	21	25	30	25	13
NEW LONDON	64	81	46	50	40	46		124	15	58	51	71	85	41	72	65	29	59
TORRINGTON	54	40	25	40	40	50	72	107	64	98	71	50	74	46		21	51	38
WATERBURY	33	31	30	20	25	30	65	99	60	118	76	55	53	51	21		56	43

DRIVING DISTANCES IN MILES

SEE ALSO MILEAGE AND DRIVING TIME MAP ON PAGE 144

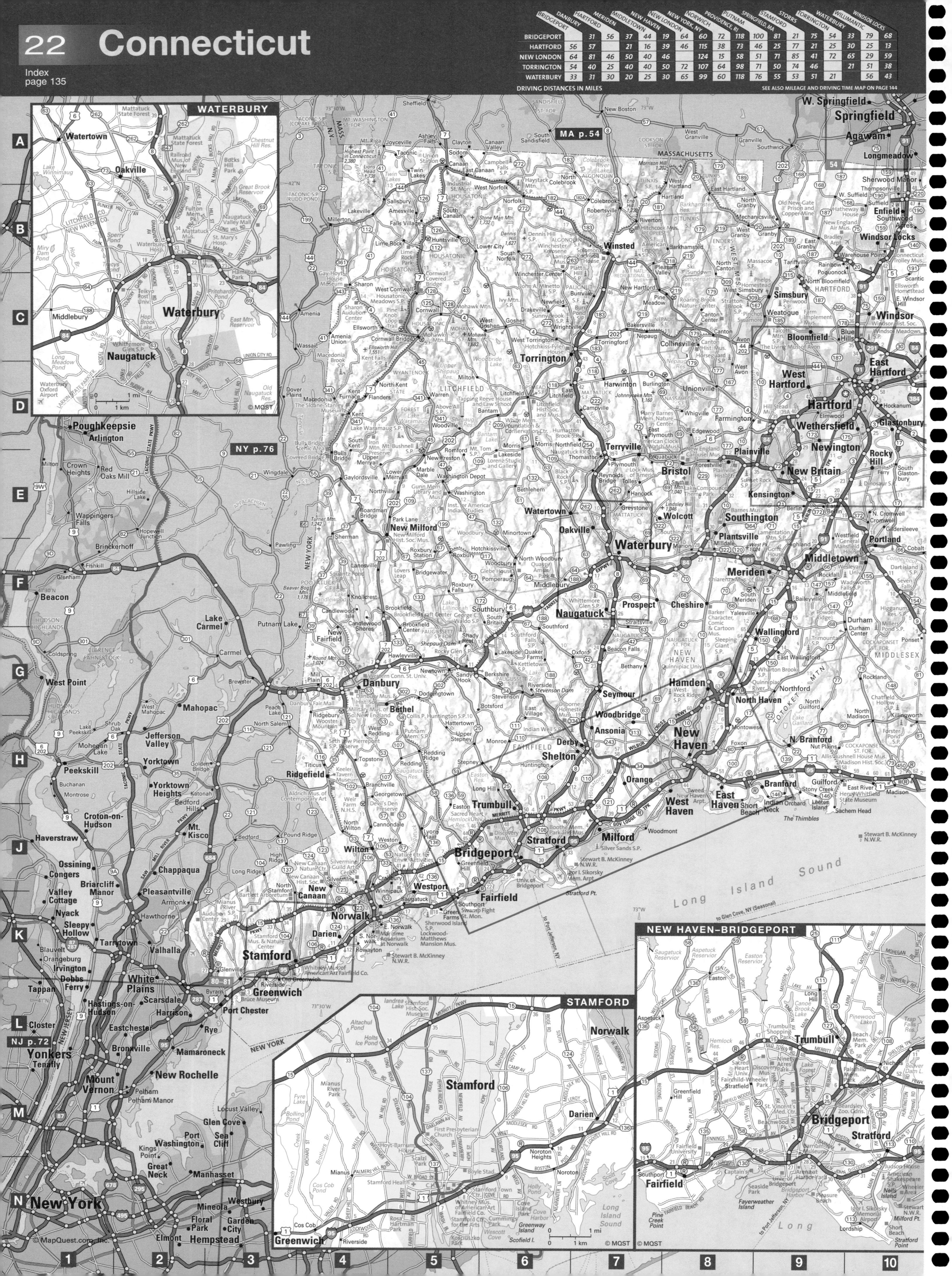

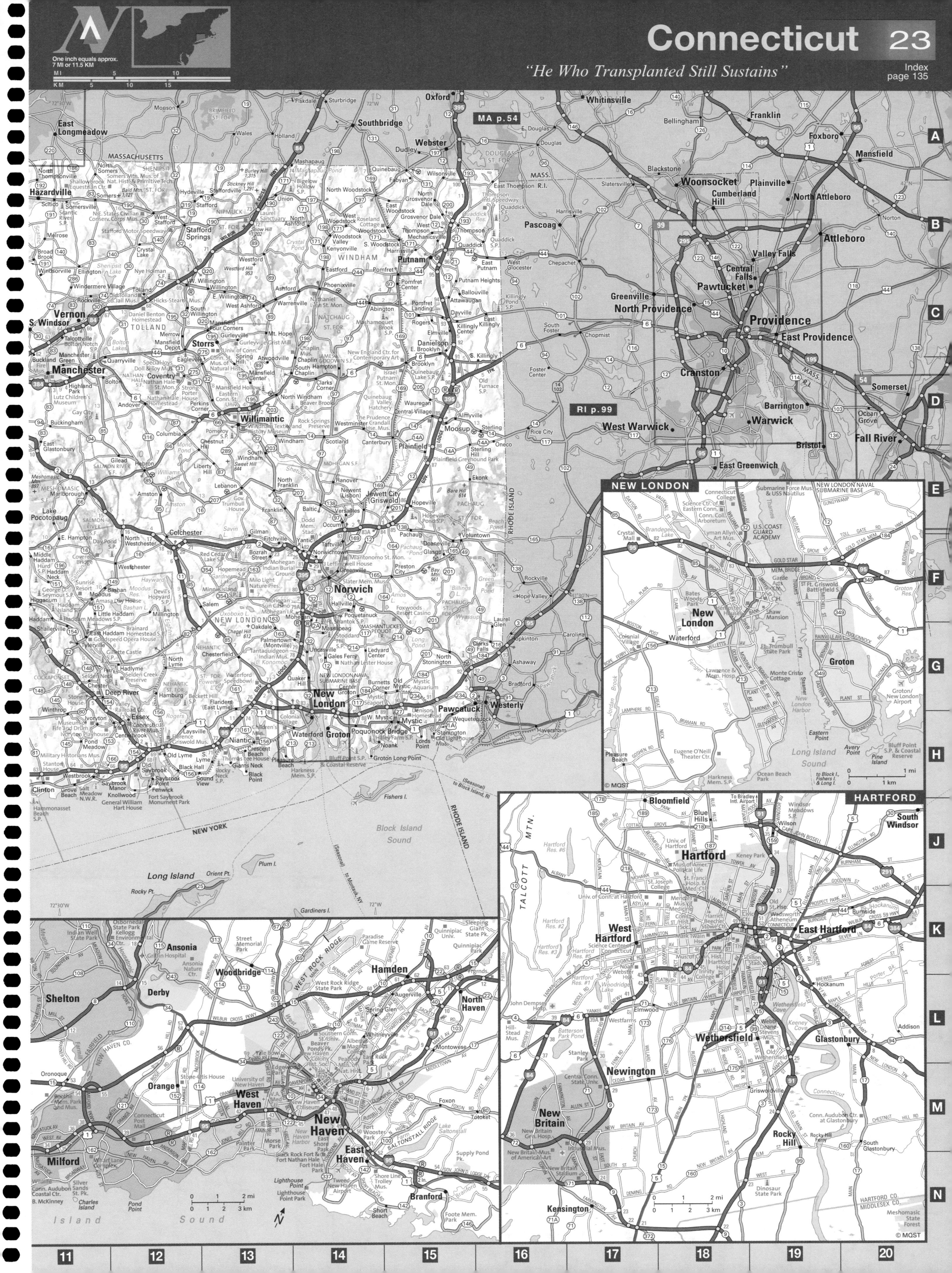

Connecticut 23
"He Who Transplanted Still Sustains"
Index page 135
One inch equals approx. 7 MI or 11.5 KM
MI 5 10
KM 5 10 15
MA p.54
RI p.99
NEW LONDON
HARTFORD
MASSACHUSETTS
RHODE ISLAND
NEW YORK
Long Island Sound
Block Island Sound
Fishers I.
Plum I.
Gardiners I.
Orient Pt.
Rocky Pt.
East Longmeadow
Hazardville
Somers
Stafford Springs
Vernon
S. Windsor
Manchester
Storrs
Coventry
Willimantic
Putnam
Danielson
Moosup
Plainfield
Jewett City (Griswold)
Norwich
Colchester
Salem
Deep River
Essex
Old Saybrook
Clinton
Niantic
New London
Groton
Mystic
Pawcatuck
Westerly
Hope Valley
Oxford
Southbridge
Webster
Whitinsville
Franklin
Foxboro
Mansfield
Woonsocket
Cumberland Hill
Plainville
North Attleboro
Attleboro
Pascoag
Greenville
North Providence
Pawtucket
Central Falls
Valley Falls
Providence
East Providence
Cranston
Warwick
West Warwick
Barrington
Bristol
East Greenwich
Somerset
Fall River
Ocean Grove
Carolina
Hopkinton
Ashaway
Bradford
Shelton
Ansonia
Derby
Woodbridge
Hamden
North Haven
Orange
West Haven
New Haven
East Haven
Branford
Milford
Bloomfield
Blue Hills
Hartford
West Hartford
East Hartford
South Windsor
Wethersfield
Glastonbury
Newington
New Britain
Rocky Hill
Kensington
© MQST
A B C D E F G H J K L M N
11 12 13 14 15 16 17 18 19 20

Delaware

Index page 135

"Liberty and Independence"

	BETHANY BEACH	DOVER	GEORGETOWN	HARRINGTON	LEWES	MILFORD	NEWARK	PHILADELPHIA, PA	REHOBOTH BEACH	SALISBURY, MD	SEAFORD	WILMINGTON
DOVER	55		38	17	42	21	41	74	43	56	36	44
NEWARK	94	41	78	57	81	60		44	83	97	76	14
REHOBOTH BEACH	13	43	18	31	10	24	83	116		46	35	86
SEAFORD	37	36	17	19	34	26	76	110	35	21		80
WILMINGTON	98	44	81	61	85	64	14	30	86	101	80	

DRIVING DISTANCES IN MILES

SEE ALSO MILEAGE AND DRIVING TIME MAP ON PAGE 144

One inch equals approx. 9 MI or 14 KM

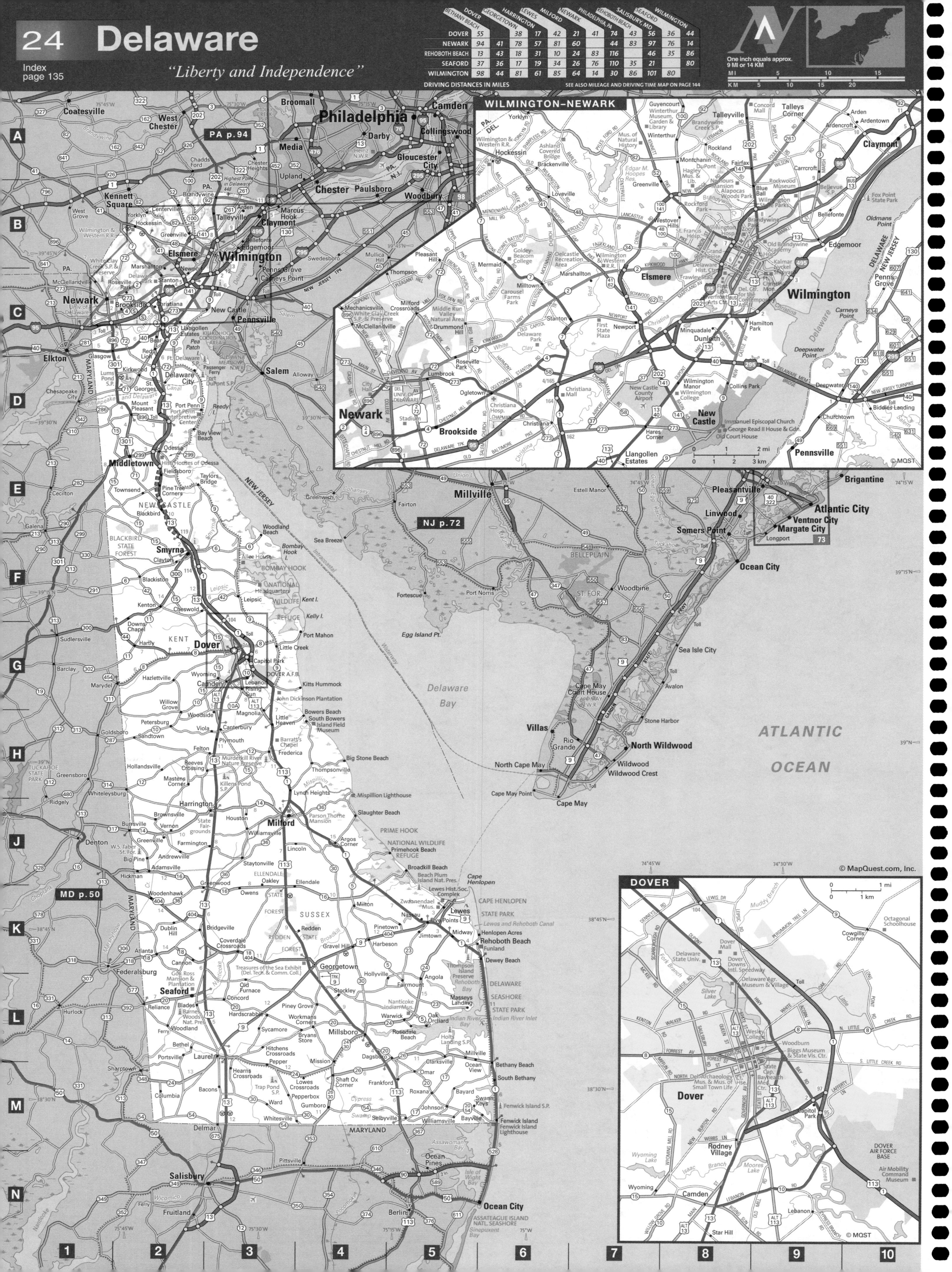

TAMPA–ST. PETERSBURG AREA
MIAMI AREA
DOWNTOWN MIAMI
GULF OF MEXICO
ATLANTIC OCEAN
Tampa Bay
Tarpon Springs
Palm Harbor
Dunedin
Oldsmar
Safety Harbor
Clearwater
Largo
Pinellas Park
Seminole
Lealman
St. Petersburg
Gulfport
St. Pete Beach
Treasure Island
South Pasadena
Tampa
Carrollwood
Town 'n' Country
Temple Terrace
Lutz
Brandon
Plant City
Lakeland
Gibsonia
Kathleen
Winston
Medulla
Apollo Beach
Ruskin
Sun City Center
Palmetto
Memphis
Ellenton
Bradenton
Samoset
Oneco
Longboat Key
Sarasota
Fruitville
Kensington Park
Bee Ridge
Siesta Key
Osprey
Venice
Nokomis
Venice Gardens
South Venice
North Port
Warm Mineral Springs
Jupiter
Palm Beach Gardens
North Palm Beach
Riviera Bch.
West Palm Beach
Royal Palm Beach
Wellington
Greenacres
Palm Springs
Lake Worth
Lantana
Boynton Beach
Delray Beach
Boca Raton
Deerfield Beach
Coconut Creek
Parkland
Coral Springs
Margate
North Lauderdale
Tamarac
Lauderhill
Lauderdale Lakes
Oakland Park
Sunrise
Plantation
Fort Lauderdale
Weston
Davie
Cooper City
Southwest Ranches
Pembroke Pines
Hollywood
Hallandale Beach
Miramar
Aventura
North Miami Beach
North Miami
Carol City
Miami Lakes
Opa-Locka
Hialeah Gardens
Hialeah
Miami Shores
Miami Springs
Miami
Miami Beach
Sweetwater
West Miami
Westwood Lake
South Miami
Coral Gables
Key Biscayne
Kendall
Pinecrest
Richmond Hts.
Palmetto Bay-Chicken Key
Perrine
S. Miami Hts.
Cutler Ridge
BISCAYNE NATIONAL PARK
ARTHUR R. MARSHALL LOXAHATCHEE NATIONAL WILDLIFE REFUGE
OVERTOWN
LITTLE HAVANA
DOWNTOWN
FINANCIAL DISTRICT
© MQST

Index page 135

	DAYTONA BEACH	FORT MYERS	FORT PIERCE	FORT WALTON BEACH	GAINESVILLE	JACKSONVILLE	LAKE CITY	LAKELAND	MELBOURNE	MIAMI	OCALA	ORLANDO	PANAMA CITY	PENSACOLA	ST. AUGUSTINE	TALLAHASSEE	TAMPA	TITUSVILLE
JACKSONVILLE	91	295	223	328	70		62	197	175	345	101	141	267	363	41	166	196	133
ORLANDO	56	155	120	425	117	141	157	56	72	232	80		364	460	103	262	82	40
PENSACOLA	455	589	567	39	349	363	306	471	526	681	383	460	102		405	200	474	497
TALLAHASSEE	258	392	369	166	152	166	109	274	329	483	186	262	104	200	207		277	300
TAMPA	138	123	172	440	132	196	172	37	142	274	95	82	378	474	185	277		121

DRIVING DISTANCES IN MILES

SEE ALSO MILEAGE AND DRIVING TIME MAP ON PAGE 144

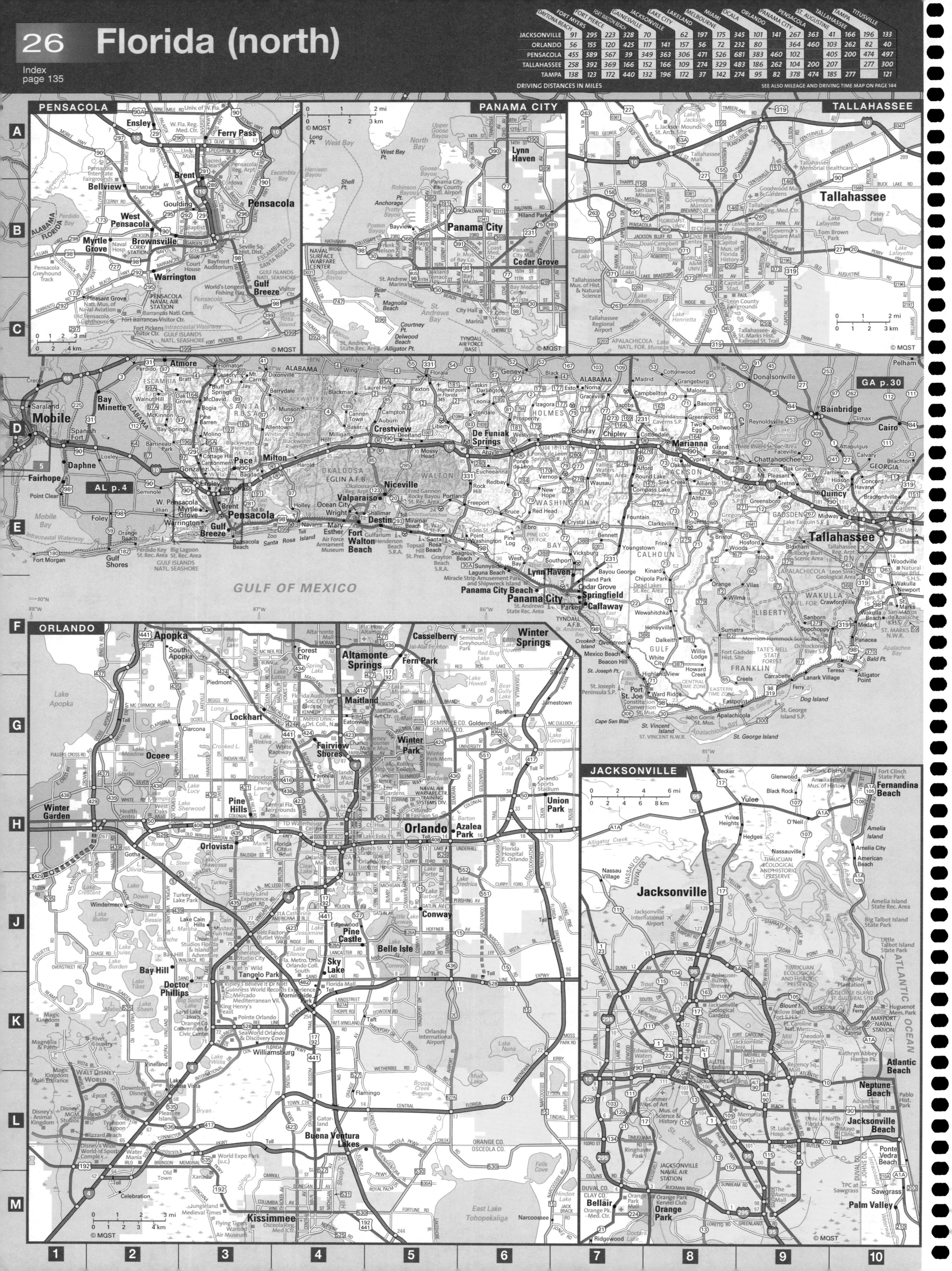

One inch equals approx. 23 MI or 37.5 KM

MI 20 40

KM 20 40 60

GAINESVILLE

Gainesville, Gainesville Regional Airport, Devil's Millhopper State Geological Site, Univ. of Florida, Morningside Nature Center, Paynes Prairie State Preserve, Arredondo, Alachua Sink, Bivans Arm, Lake Kanapaha

© MQST

DAYTONA BEACH

Ormond Beach, Holly Hill, Daytona Beach, Daytona Beach Shores, South Daytona, Port Orange, Ponce Inlet, Wilbur-by-the-Sea, Allandale, Tiger Bay St. Forest, Daytona International Speedway

ATLANTIC OCEAN

© MQST

MELBOURNE-KENNEDY SPACE CENTER

Mims, Titusville, Port St. John, Cocoa, Cocoa West, Merritt Island, Cape Canaveral, Cocoa Beach, Rockledge, Viera, South Patrick Shores, Satellite Beach, Indian Harbour Beach, Indialantic, Melbourne, W. Melbourne, Melbourne Beach, Palm Bay, Malabar, John F. Kennedy Space Center, Cape Canaveral Air Station, Patrick Air Force Base

ATLANTIC OCEAN

© MQST

Jacksonville, Tallahassee region: Thomasville, Valdosta, Quitman, Adel, Madison, Monticello, Live Oak, Lake City, Perry, Mayo, Fernandina Beach, St. Marys, Kingsland, Atlantic Beach, Neptune Beach, Jacksonville Beach, Palm Valley, Orange Park, Middleburg, Green Cove Sprs., St. Augustine, St. Augustine Beach, Palatka, Palm Coast, Flagler Beach, Starke, Alachua, Gainesville, High Sprs., Newberry, Ocala, Silver Sprs., Ormond-by-the-Sea, Ormond Beach, Daytona Beach, New Smyrna Beach, Edgewater, DeLand, Deltona, Sanford, Orange City, De Bary, Lady Lake, Leesburg, Eustis, Mt. Dora, Tavares, Apopka, Winter Park, Orlando, Kissimmee, St. Cloud, Clermont, Inverness, Crystal River, Beverly Hills, Homosassa Springs, Brooksville, Spring Hill, Hudson, New Port Richey, Bayonet Point, Tarpon Sprs., Palm Harbor, Dunedin, Clearwater, Largo, Pinellas Park, St. Petersburg, Tampa, Brandon, Plant City, Lakeland, Winter Haven, Bartow, Haines City, Lake Wales, Titusville, Cocoa, Merritt Island, Cocoa Beach, Melbourne, Palm Bay, Sebastian, Vero Bch.

Okefenokee N.W.R., Osceola N.F., Ocala National Forest, Withlacoochee St. For.

GA p.30

ATLANTIC OCEAN

GULF OF MEXICO

© MapQuest.com, Inc.

A B C D E F G H J K L M

11 12 13 14 15 16 17 18 19 20

"In God We Trust"

	FORT LAUDERDALE	FORT MYERS	FORT PIERCE	KEY WEST	LAKELAND	MELBOURNE	MIAMI	ORLANDO	ST. PETERSBURG	SARASOTA	TAMPA	WEST PALM BEACH
FORT MYERS	139		126	308	113	178	155	155	108	74	123	125
FORT PIERCE	102	126		288	122	57	122	120	197	150	172	57
MIAMI	23	155	122	168	236	179		232	259	225	274	67
ORLANDO	216	155	120	398	56	72	232		107	130	82	169
TAMPA	257	123	172	426	37	142	274	82	25	60		223

DRIVING DISTANCES IN MILES
SEE ALSO MILEAGE AND DRIVING TIME MAP ON PAGE 144

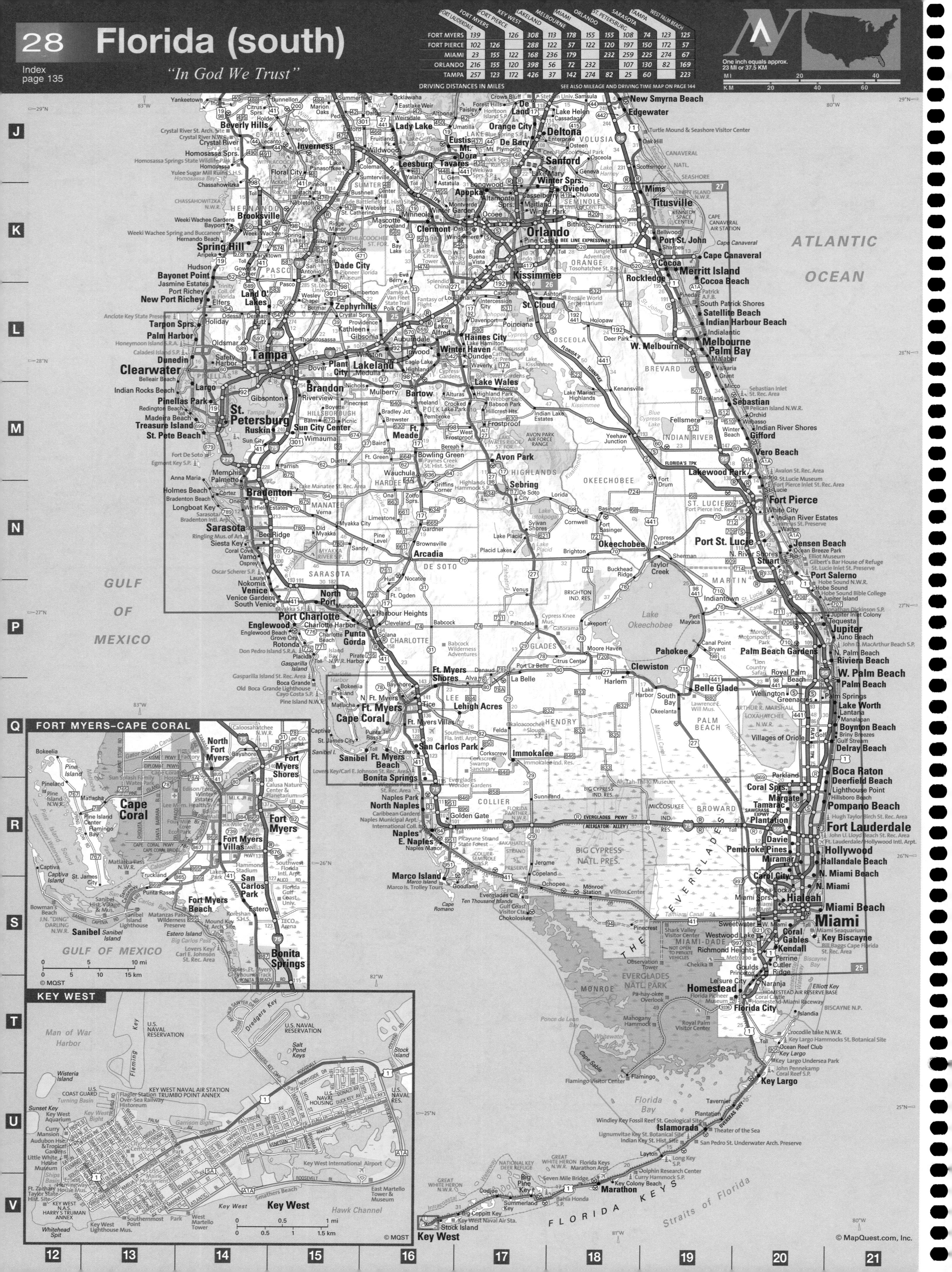

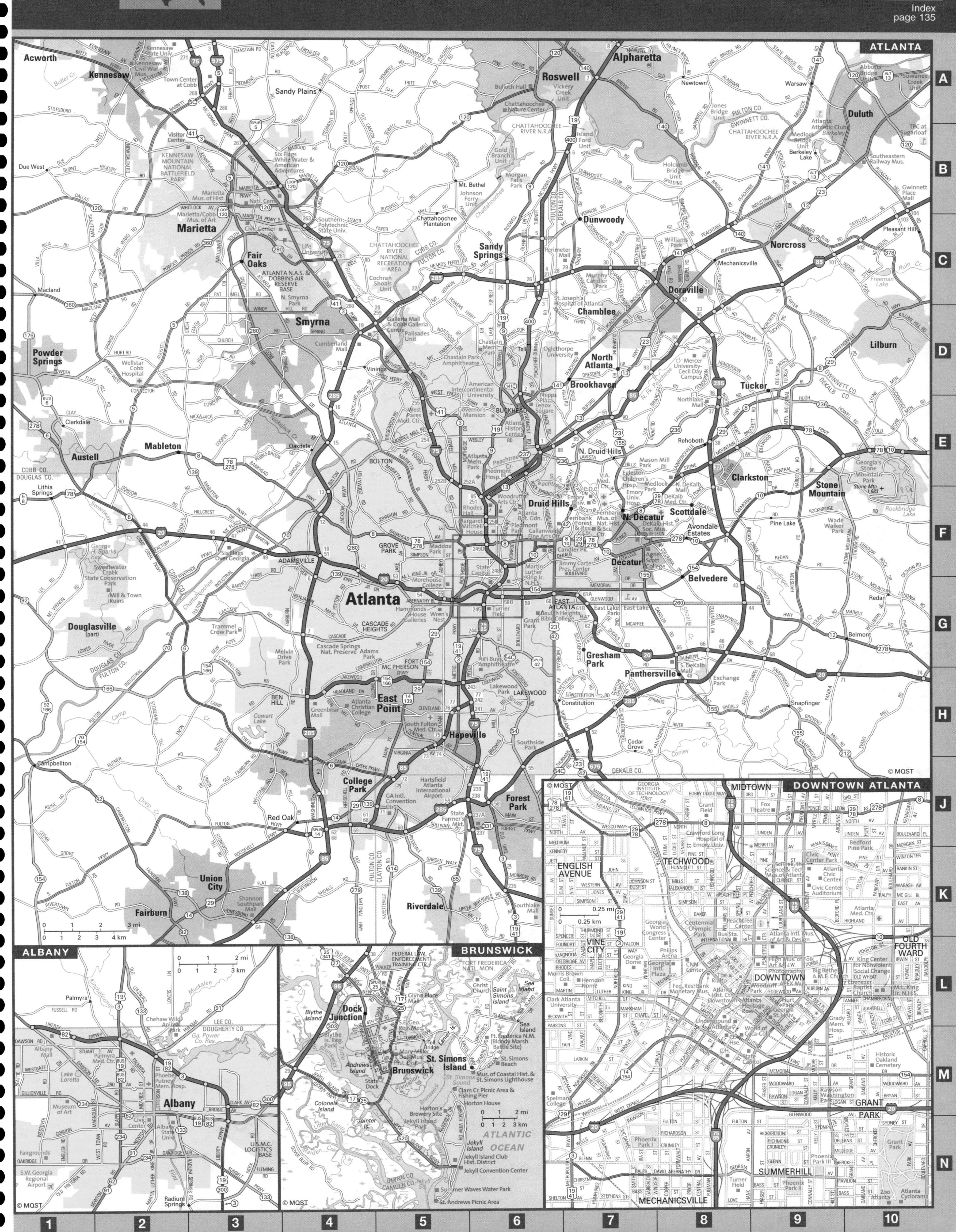
ATLANTA
Acworth
Kennesaw
Roswell
Alpharetta
Duluth
Marietta
Smyrna
Sandy Springs
Dunwoody
Norcross
Doraville
Chamblee
North Atlanta
Brookhaven
Tucker
Lilburn
Powder Springs
Austell
Mableton
Clarkston
Stone Mountain
Druid Hills
N. Decatur
Scottdale
Decatur
Belvedere
Atlanta
East Point
Hapeville
College Park
Forest Park
Riverdale
Union City
Fairburn
Douglasville (part)
Gresham Park
Panthersville
Red Oak
Campbellton
Macland
Due West
Sandy Plains
Fair Oaks
Vinings
Redan
Belmont
ALBANY
Albany
Palmyra
BRUNSWICK
Dock Junction
Brunswick
St. Simons Island
ATLANTIC OCEAN
DOWNTOWN ATLANTA
MIDTOWN
TECHWOOD
ENGLISH AVENUE
VINE CITY
DOWNTOWN
OLD FOURTH WARD
GRANT PARK
SUMMERHILL
MECHANICSVILLE
© MQST
1
2
3
4
5
6
7
8
9
10
A
B
C
D
E
F
G
H
J
K
L
M
N

Georgia

Index
page 135

	ALBANY	AMERICUS	ATHENS	ATLANTA	AUGUSTA	BAINBRIDGE	BRUNSWICK	CHATTANOOGA, TN	COLUMBUS	DUBLIN	GAINESVILLE	LA GRANGE	MACON	ROME	SAVANNAH	STATESBORO	VALDOSTA	WAYCROSS
ATLANTA	180	129	70		149	236	308	113	106	139	56	69	84	66	249	211	228	253
AUGUSTA	226	206	97	149		282	194	266	249	95	136	212	123	219	135	81	274	184
MACON	102	83	89	84	123	159	225	201	95	55	142	114		154	165	127	151	159
SAVANNAH	246	226	225	249	135	248	78	366	244	114	307	279	165	319		53	168	106
VALDOSTA	90	119	239	228	274	80	120	346	183	139	287	226	151	298	168	173		62

DRIVING DISTANCES IN MILES

SEE ALSO MILEAGE AND DRIVING TIME MAP ON PAGE 144

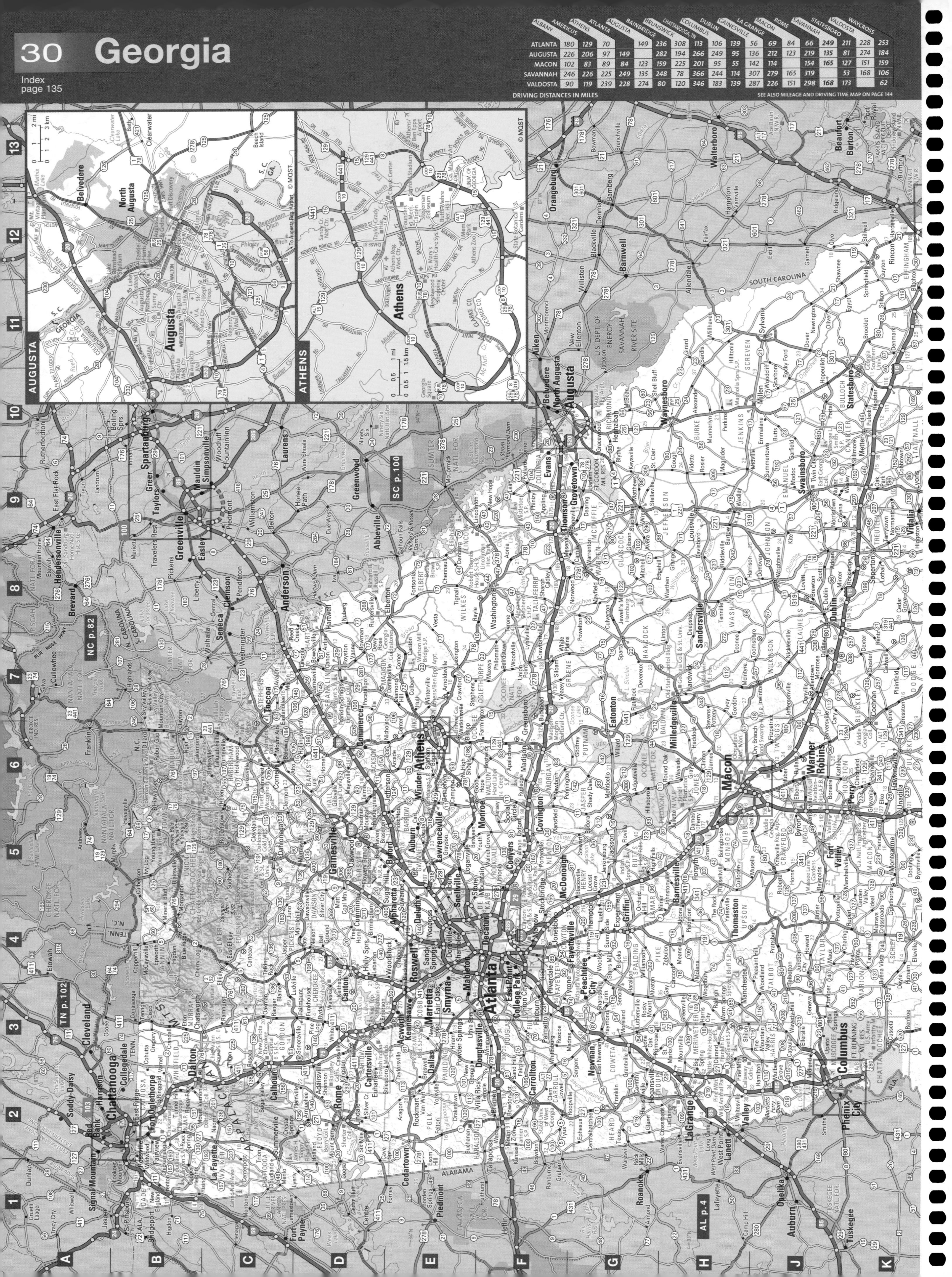

One inch equals approx. 22 MI or 36 KM

MI 20 40

KM 20 40 60

SAVANNAH

MACON

COLUMBUS

AL p. 4

FL p. 26

ATLANTIC OCEAN

Hawaii

"The Life of the Land Is Perpetuated in Righteousness"

	HANA	HILO	HONOLULU	HOOLEHUA	KAHULUI	KAILUA	KAILUA-KONA	LAHAINA	LANAI CITY	LIHUE	WAHIAWA	WAIMEA
HILO	149*		217*	169*	121*	235*	88	142*	155*	319*	234*	54
HONOLULU	129*	217*		54*	101*	14	185*	92*	74*	102*	23	172*
KAHULUI	42	121*	101*	76		119*	109*	23	57	202*	118*	79*
KAILUA-KONA	137*	88	185*	157*	109*	203*		132*	143*	285*	202*	39
LIHUE	230*	319*	102*	156*	202*	120*	285*	225*	176*		119*	174*

DISTANCES IN MILES

* DISTANCE INCLUDES AIR TRAVEL

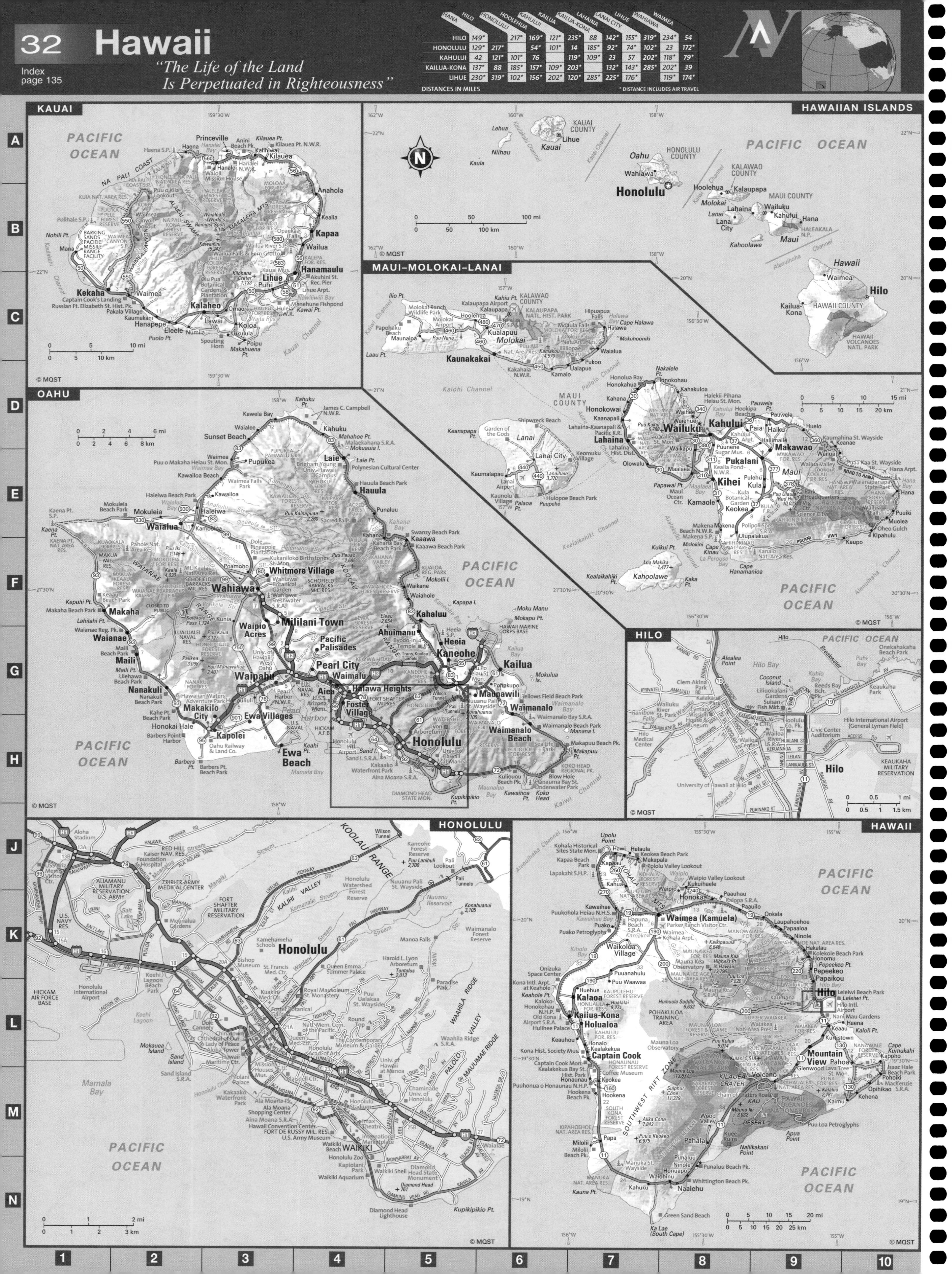

"It Is Perpetual"

Index page 135

	BOISE	COEUR D'ALENE	GRANGEVILLE	IDAHO FALLS	KETCHUM	LEWISTON	MISSOULA, MT	MOUNTAIN HOME	POCATELLO	SALMON	SANDPOINT	TWIN FALLS
BOISE		406	202	288	163	270	374	49	241	247	452	134
COEUR D'ALENE	406	476	186	476	485	118	167	499	526	307	48	584
IDAHO FALLS	288	118	483		153	532	311	240	53	168	523	162
LEWISTON	270	526	74	532	477		221	363	555	337	166	448
POCATELLO	241		440	53	190	555	360	193		217	572	116

DRIVING DISTANCES IN MILES

SEE ALSO MILEAGE AND DRIVING TIME MAP ON PAGE 144

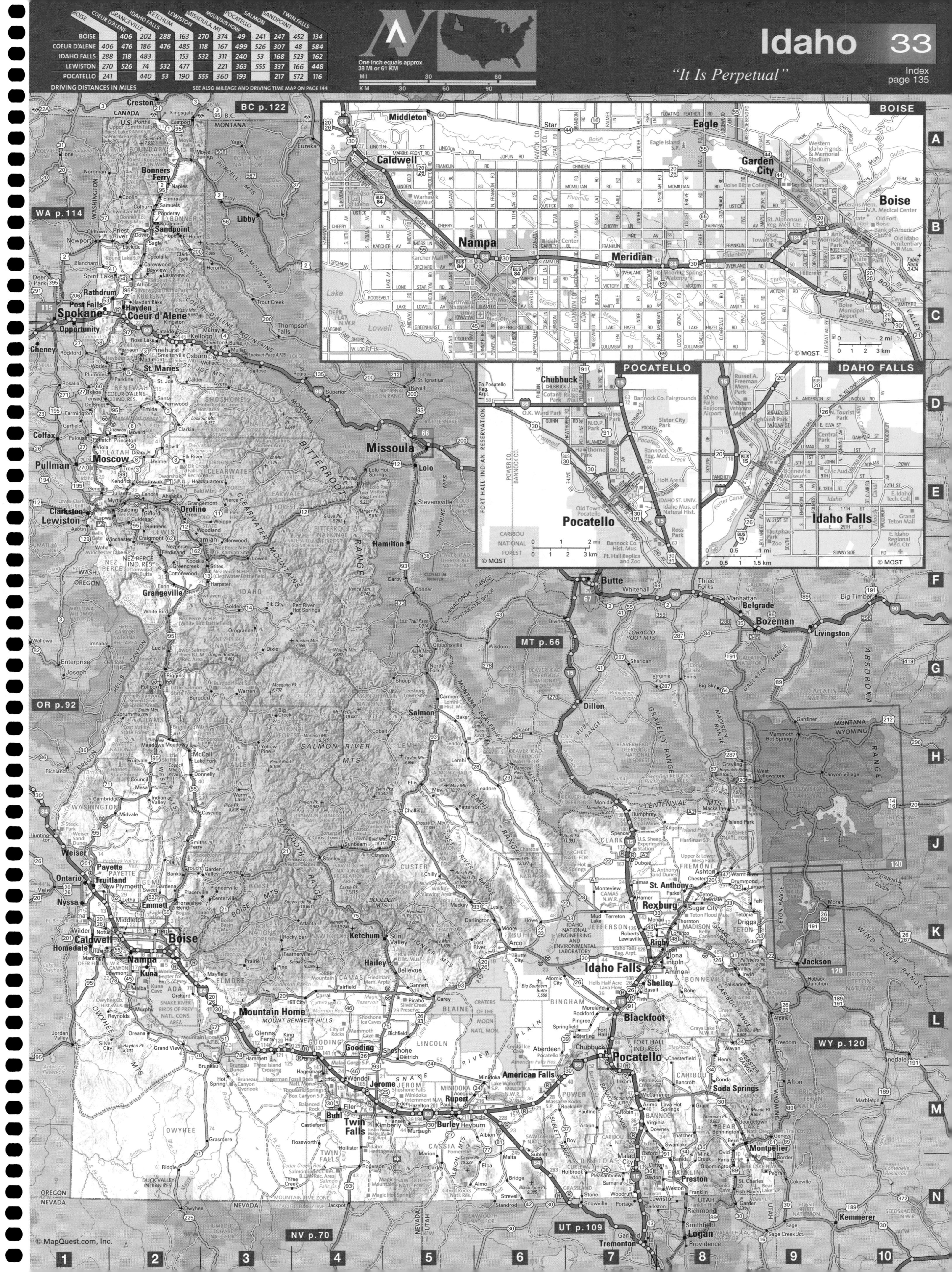

Index page 135

	BLOOMINGTON	CAIRO	CARBONDALE	CHAMPAIGN	CHICAGO	DECATUR	DUBUQUE, IA	EFFINGHAM	GALESBURG	JOLIET	KANKAKEE	MOUNT VERNON	PEORIA	QUINCY	ROCKFORD	ROCK ISLAND	ST. LOUIS, MO	SPRINGFIELD
CHAMPAIGN	54	241	199		141	52	263	77	141	115	79	145	94	197	189	191	179	87
CHICAGO	135	376	334	141		186	180	212	198	40	61	280	168	306	86	169	294	197
ROCKFORD	134	424	382	189	86	184	93	260	153	99	139	328	135	272		124	293	196
ST. LOUIS, MO	160	156	105	179	294	116	342	103	220	257	252	81	172	131	293	270		97
SPRINGFIELD	63	254	182	87	197	40	245	89	123	160	152	158	75	110	196	173	97	

DRIVING DISTANCES IN MILES

SEE ALSO MILEAGE AND DRIVING TIME MAP ON PAGE 144

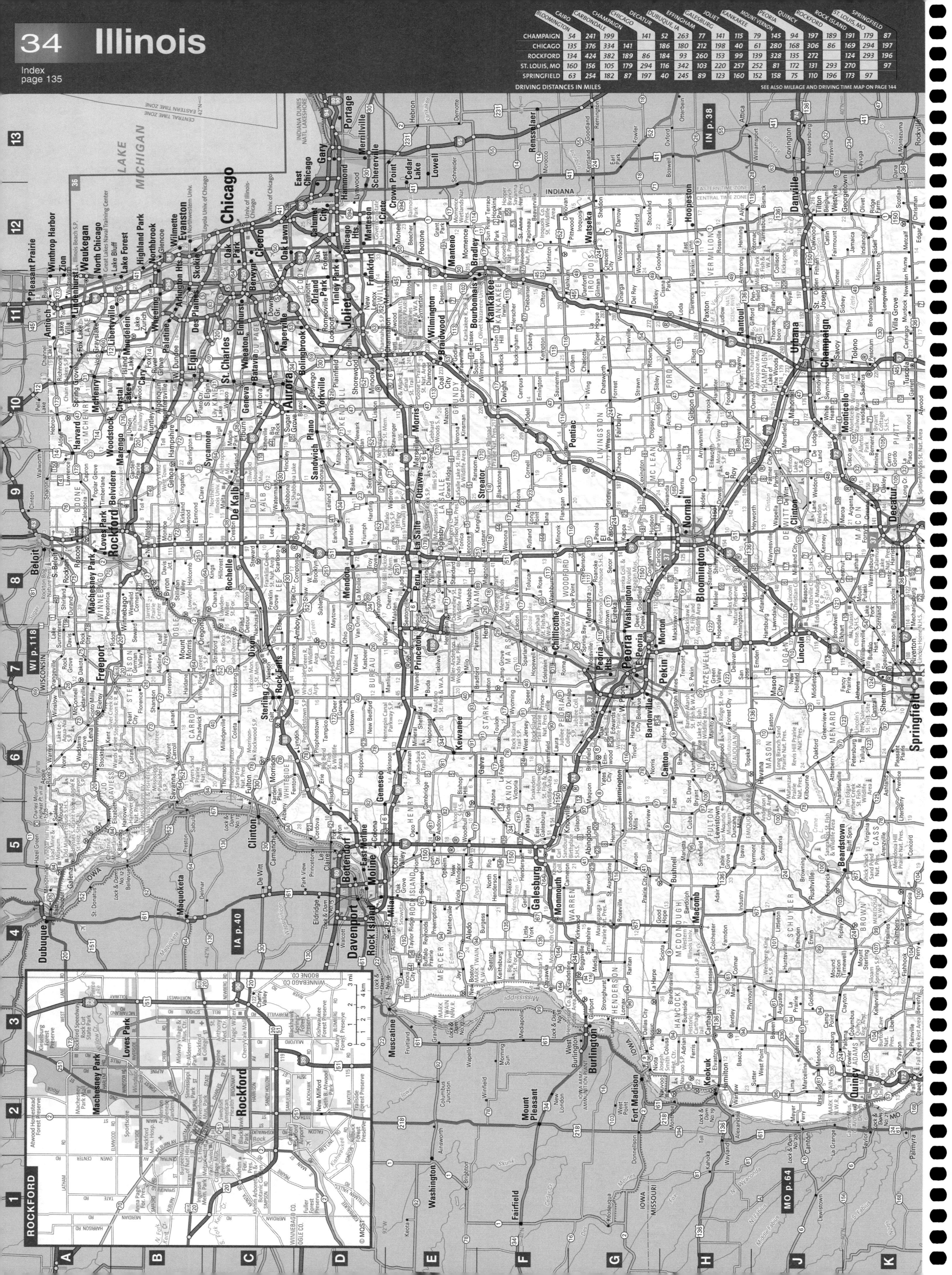

"State Sovereignty—National Unity"

Index page 135

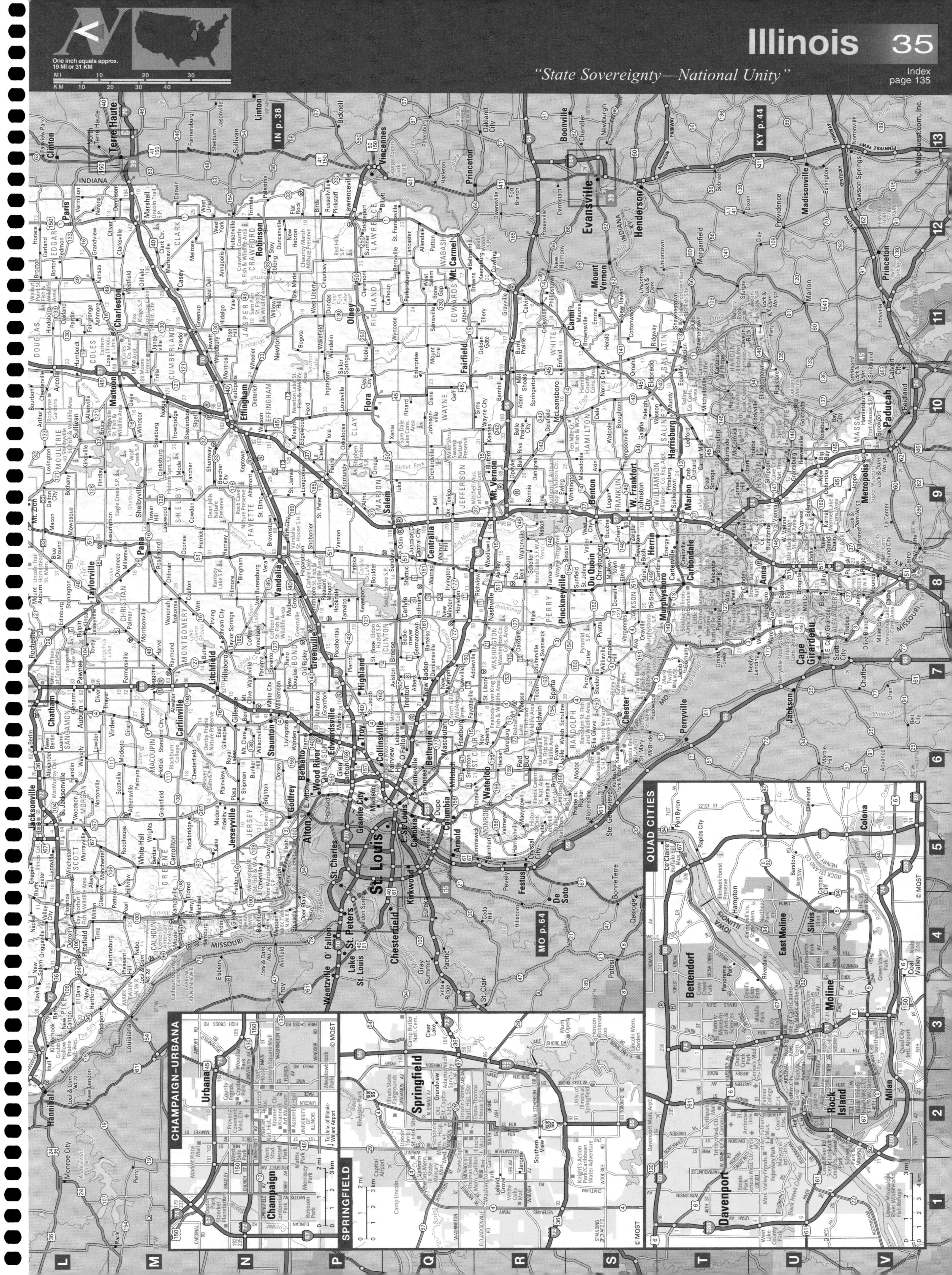

Index page 135

One inch equals approx. 5 MI or 8 KM

MI 4 8

KM 4 8 12

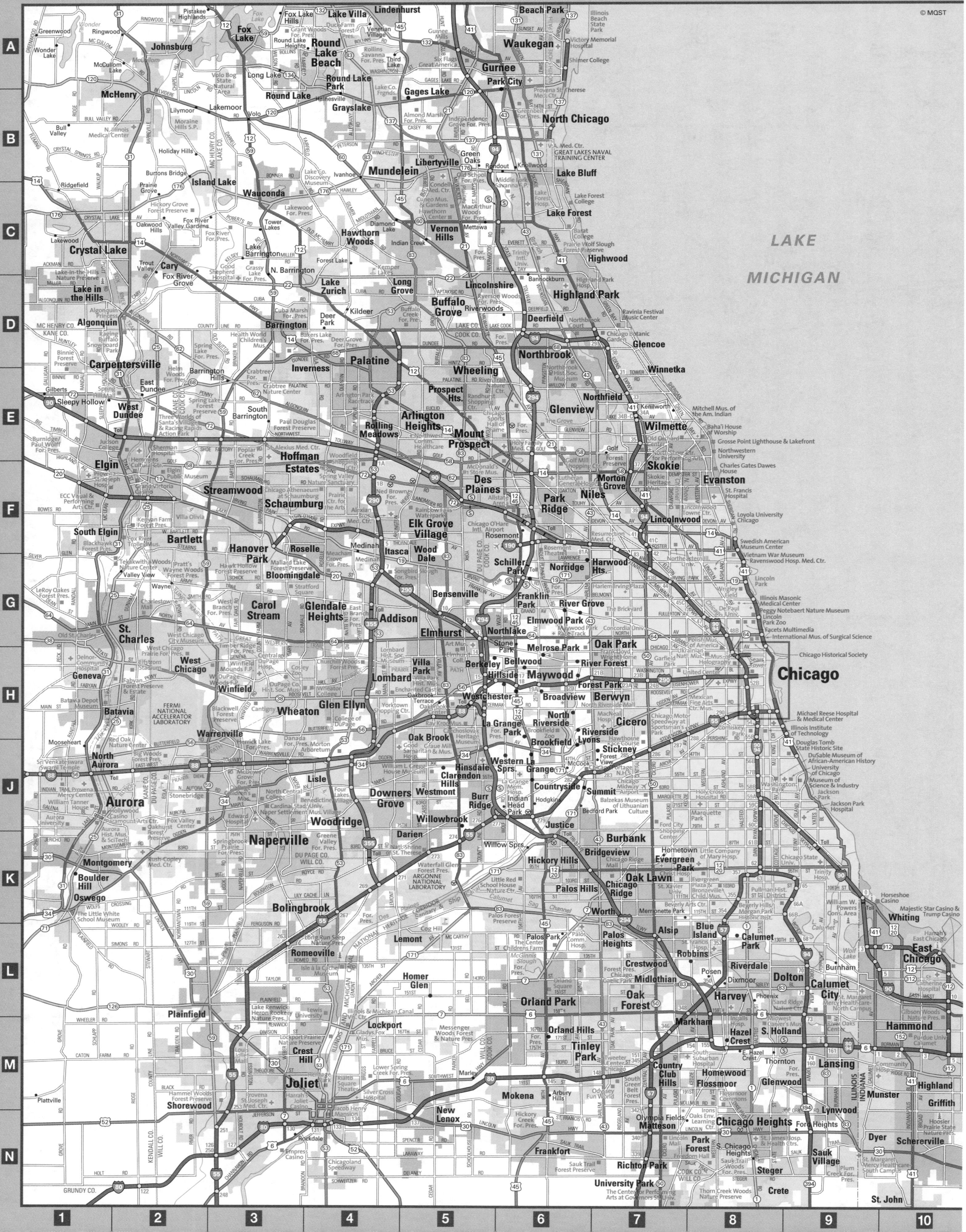

© MQST

LAKE MICHIGAN

Chicago

A B C D E F G H J K L M N

1 2 3 4 5 6 7 8 9 10

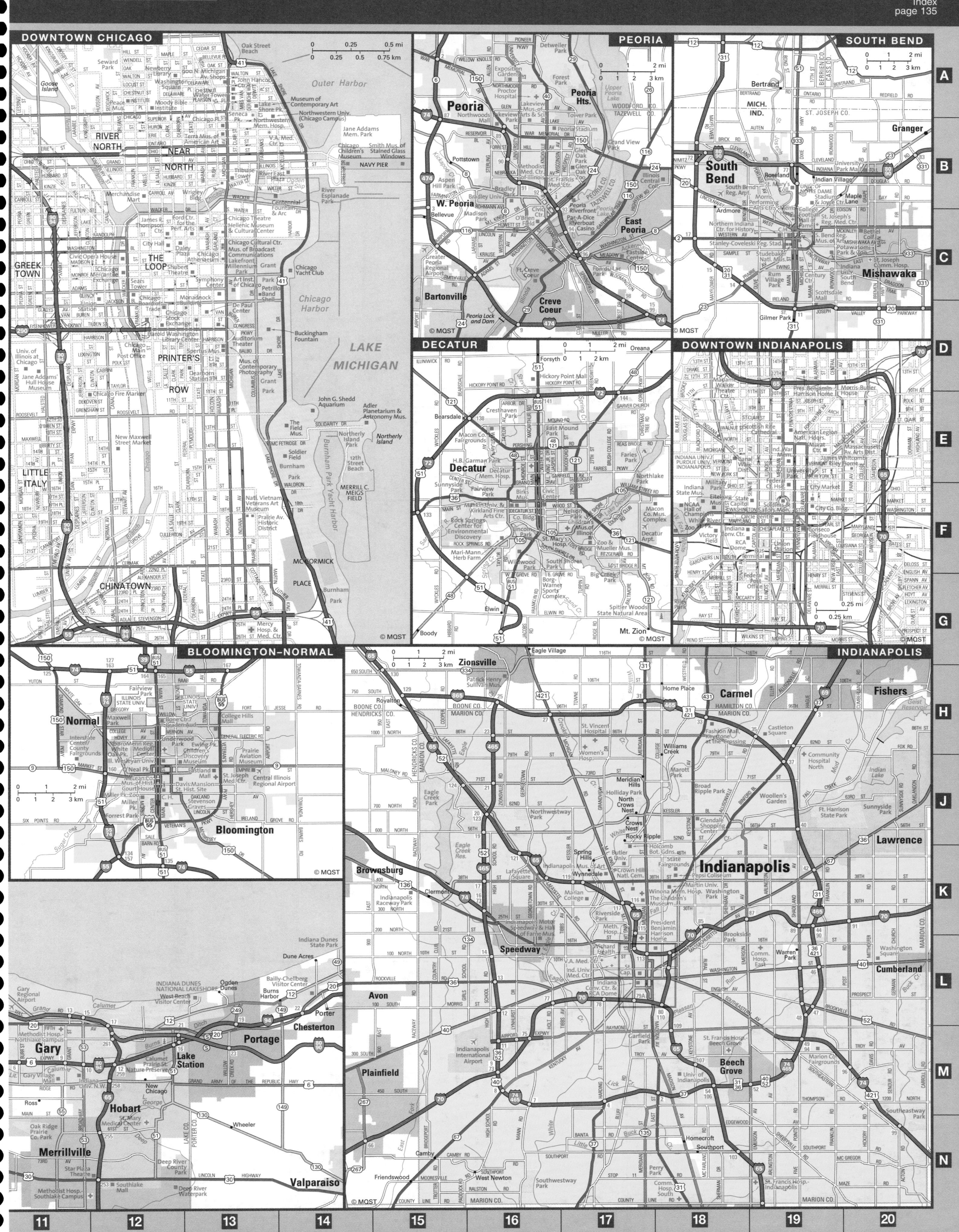
DOWNTOWN CHICAGO
PEORIA
SOUTH BEND
DECATUR
DOWNTOWN INDIANAPOLIS
BLOOMINGTON–NORMAL
INDIANAPOLIS
RIVER NORTH
NEAR NORTH
GREEK TOWN
THE LOOP
PRINTER'S ROW
LITTLE ITALY
CHINATOWN
LAKE MICHIGAN
Outer Harbor
Chicago Harbor
NAVY PIER
MC CORMICK PLACE
Burnham Park
Grant Park
John Hancock Ctr.
Sears Tower
Buckingham Fountain
John G. Shedd Aquarium
Adler Planetarium & Astronomy Mus.
The Field Mus.
Soldier Field
Northerly Island
MERRILL C. MEIGS FIELD
Burnham Park Yacht Harbor
Chicago Yacht Club
Museum of Contemporary Art
Navy Pier
Oak Street Beach
Goose Island
Peoria
Peoria Hts.
W. Peoria
East Peoria
Bartonville
Creve Coeur
Bellevue
Pottstown
Peoria Lock and Dam
Greater Peoria Regional Airport
South Bend
Mishawaka
Granger
Roseland
Bertrand
Ardmore
Gilmer Park
MICH.
IND.
Decatur
Bearsdale
Forsyth
Oreana
Elwin
Boody
Mt. Zion
Normal
Bloomington
Central Illinois Regional Airport
ILLINOIS STATE UNIV.
Indianapolis
Carmel
Fishers
Zionsville
Brownsburg
Speedway
Avon
Plainfield
Lawrence
Cumberland
Beech Grove
Castleton
Williams Creek
Clermont
Southport
Homecroft
Friendswood
West Newton
Indianapolis International Airport
Gary
Hobart
Lake Station
Portage
Chesterton
Porter
Merrillville
Valparaiso
Ogden Dunes
Dune Acres
Burns Harbor
New Chicago
Wheeler
INDIANA DUNES NATIONAL LAKESHORE
Indiana Dunes State Park
Gary Regional Airport
© MQST
A B C D E F G H I J K L M N
11 12 13 14 15 16 17 18 19 20

Index page 136

	ANDERSON	BLOOMINGTON	COLUMBUS	CRAWFORDSVILLE	EVANSVILLE	FORT WAYNE	GARY	GREENSBURG	INDIANAPOLIS	KOKOMO	LAFAYETTE	LOUISVILLE, KY	MUNCIE	PLYMOUTH	RICHMOND	SOUTH BEND	TERRE HAUTE	VINCENNES
EVANSVILLE	211	117	175	164		296	324	195	166	219	194	114	228	281	241	305	107	51
FORT WAYNE	86	175	169	163	296		143	149	128	85	116	236	75	65	95	79	207	253
GARY	180	192	200	122	324	143		210	153	127	91	268	198	66	226	62	161	268
INDIANAPOLIS	43	47	45	47	166	128	153	55		52	66	112	61	114	74	138	77	123
SOUTH BEND	129	187	187	136	305	79	62	187	138	86	104	255	141	24	172		217	263

DRIVING DISTANCES IN MILES

SEE ALSO MILEAGE AND DRIVING TIME MAP ON PAGE 144

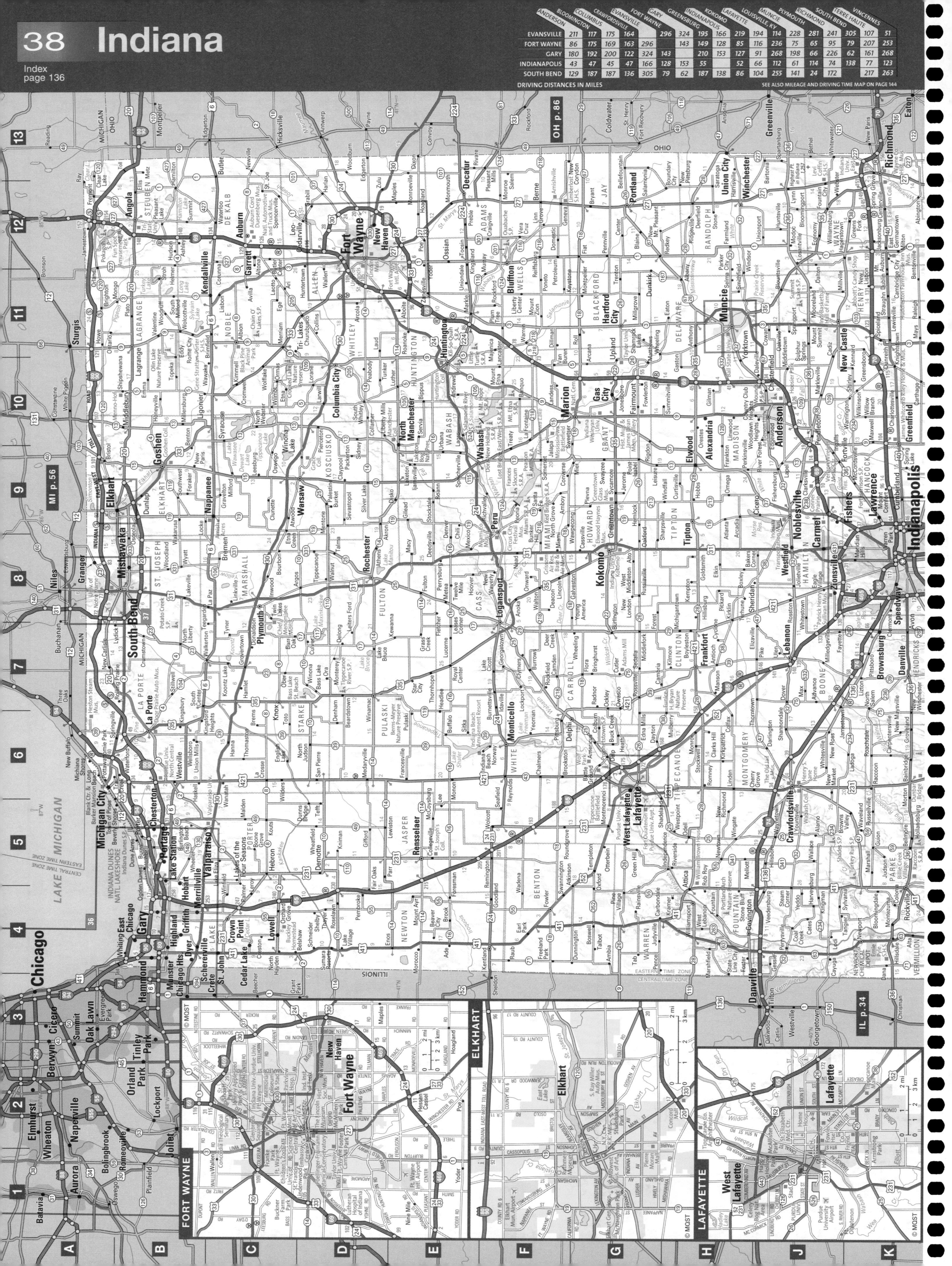

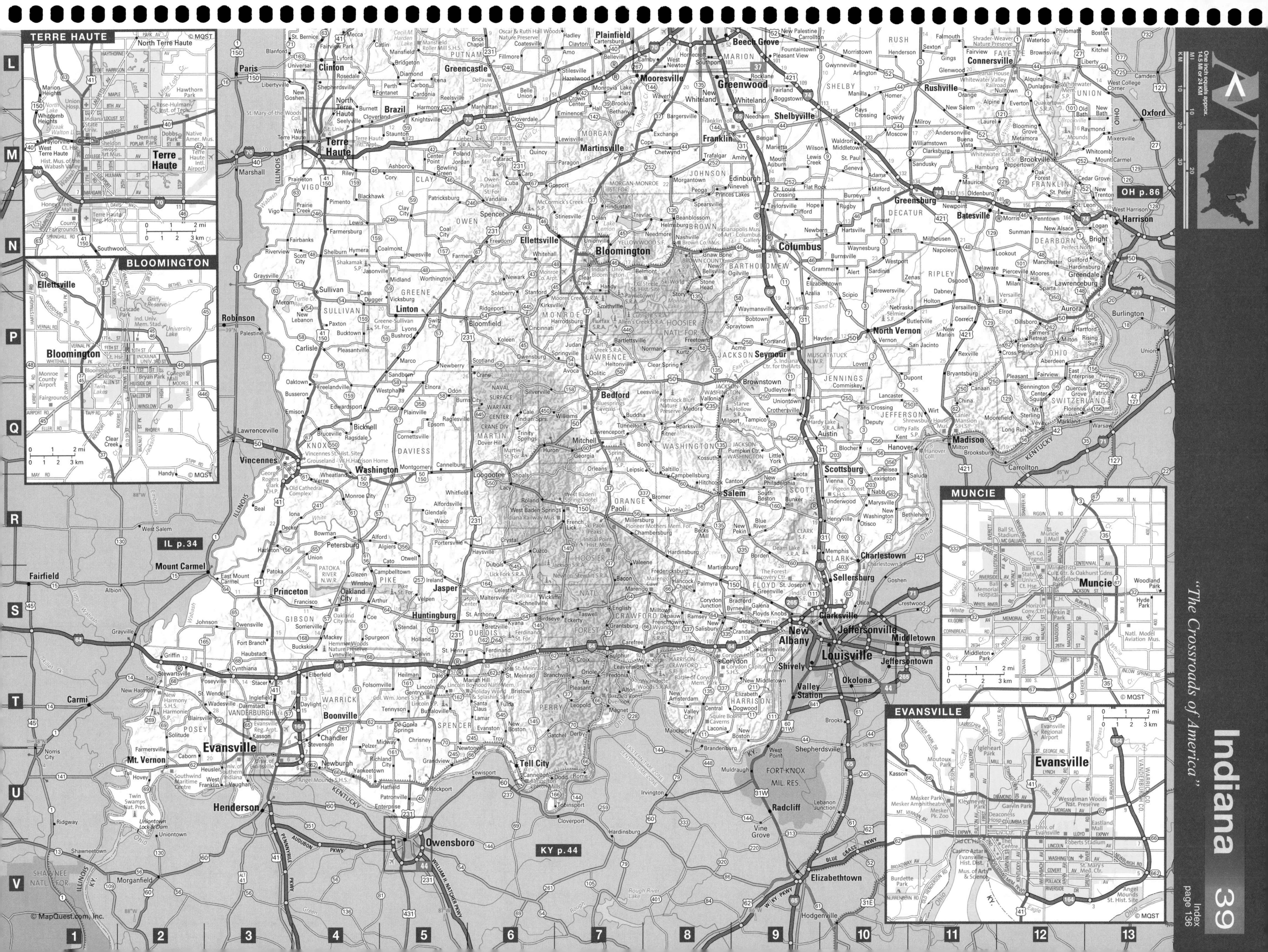
Indiana 39
"The Crossroads of America"
Index page 136
One inch equals approx. 14.5 MI or 24 KM
TERRE HAUTE
BLOOMINGTON
MUNCIE
EVANSVILLE
OH p.86
KY p.44
IL p.34
Indianapolis
Terre Haute
Bloomington
Columbus
Evansville
Louisville
New Albany
Jeffersonville
Madison
Owensboro
Henderson
Vincennes
Washington
Bedford
Seymour
Greenwood
Shelbyville
Greensburg
Connersville
Rushville
Batesville
Martinsville
Franklin
Jasper
Princeton
Mt. Vernon
Tell City
Boonville
Elizabethtown
© MapQuest.com, Inc.
© MQST

Index page 136

	AMES	BURLINGTON	CARROLL	CEDAR RAPIDS	COUNCIL BLUFFS	CRESTON	DAVENPORT	DECORAH	DES MOINES	DUBUQUE	FORT DODGE	IOWA CITY	MARSHALLTOWN	MASON CITY	OTTUMWA	SIOUX CITY	SPENCER	WATERLOO
COUNCIL BLUFFS	165	323	101	261		99	303	347	130	327	160	245	181	258	216	101	157	238
DES MOINES	34	157	90	129	130	81	171	215		196	94	113	49	126	86	202	188	106
IOWA CITY	136	82	195	28	245	195	59	131	113	84	196		98	157	83	316	267	78
SIOUX CITY	171	394	105	332	101	189	375	303	202	321	120	316	252	218	287		103	228
WATERLOO	95	157	160	53	238	189	137	79	106	93	108	78	58	79	125	228	189	

DRIVING DISTANCES IN MILES

SEE ALSO MILEAGE AND DRIVING TIME MAP ON PAGE 144

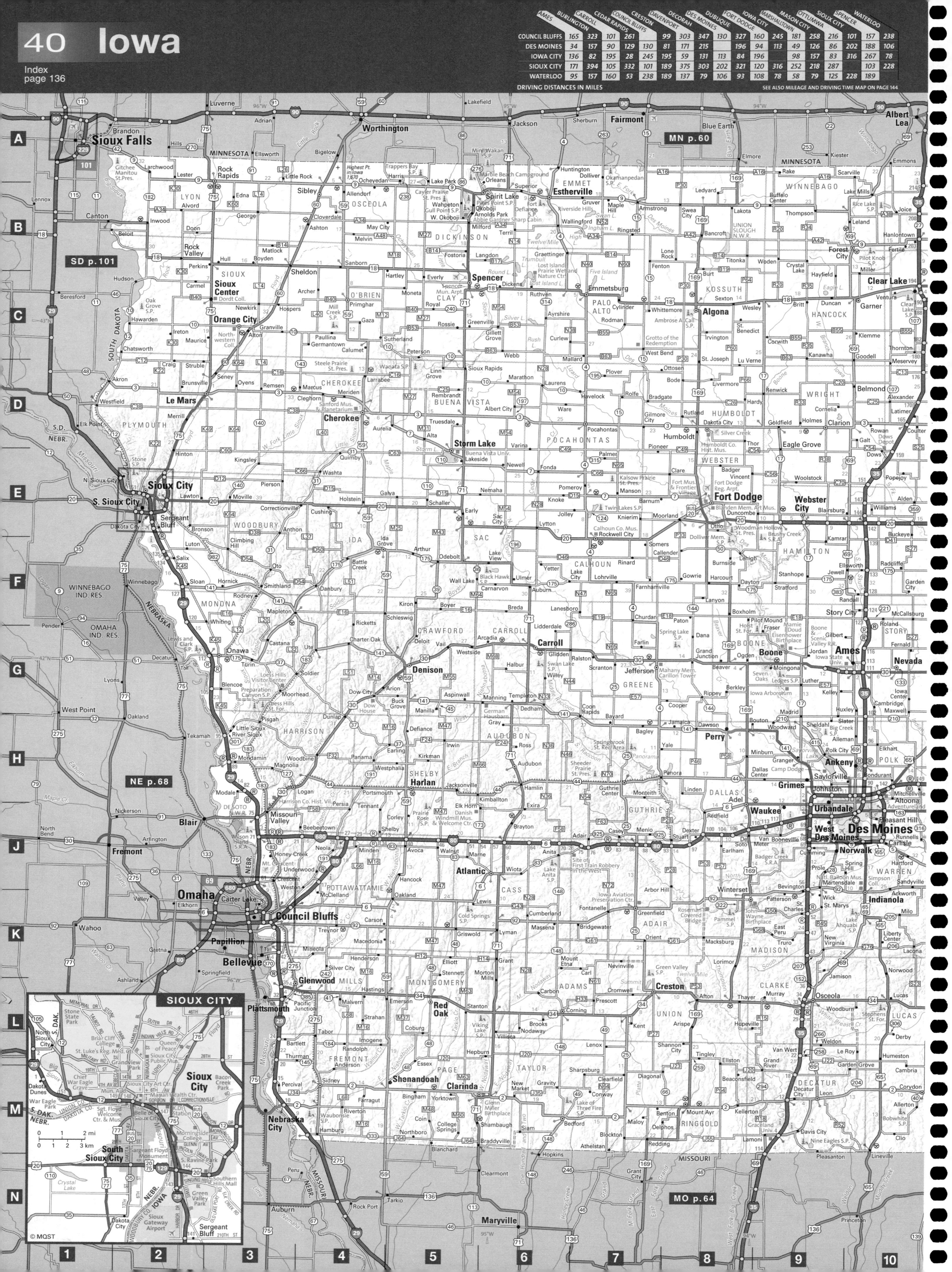

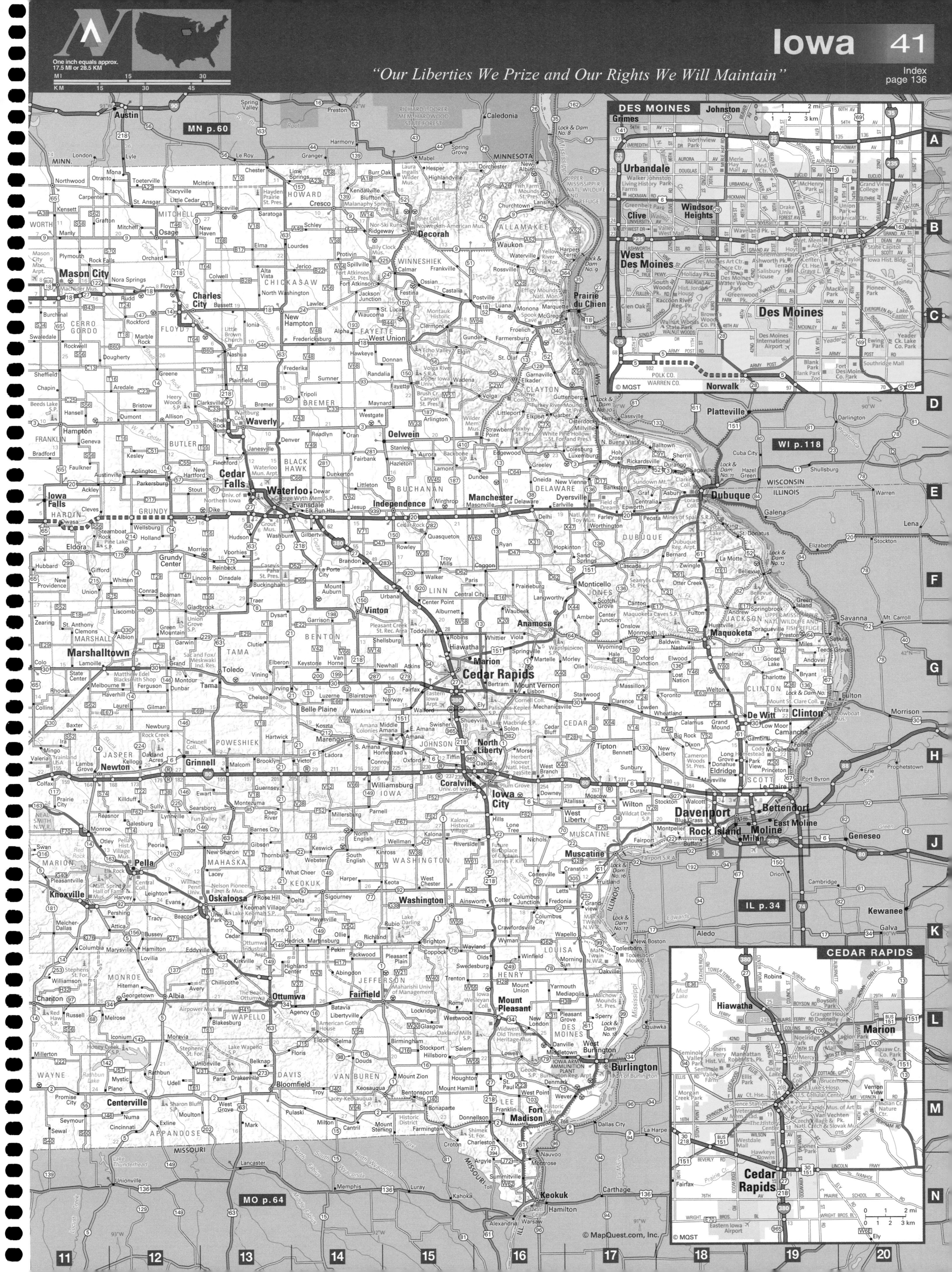

Iowa
41
"Our Liberties We Prize and Our Rights We Will Maintain"
Index page 136
One inch equals approx. 17.5 MI or 28.5 KM
MN p.60
WI p.118
IL p.34
MO p.64
DES MOINES
CEDAR RAPIDS
Mason City
Charles City
Decorah
Cedar Falls
Waterloo
Waverly
Oelwein
Independence
Manchester
Dubuque
Iowa Falls
Marshalltown
Cedar Rapids
Marion
Anamosa
Maquoketa
Clinton
De Witt
Toledo
Tama
Grinnell
Newton
Iowa City
Coralville
North Liberty
Davenport
Bettendorf
Rock Island
Moline
East Moline
Muscatine
Pella
Knoxville
Oskaloosa
Washington
Fairfield
Ottumwa
Mount Pleasant
Burlington
Fort Madison
Keokuk
Centerville
Albia
Chariton
Bloomfield
Austin
Prairie du Chien
Platteville
Galena
Urbandale
Clive
Windsor Heights
West Des Moines
Des Moines
Norwalk
Johnston
Grimes
Hiawatha
© MapQuest.com, Inc.
© MQST

Index page 136

	ARKANSAS CITY	ATCHISON	COLBY	DODGE CITY	EMPORIA	GARDEN CITY	GREAT BEND	HAYS	HUTCHINSON	INDEPENDENCE	IOLA	KANSAS CITY	LAWRENCE	LIBERAL	MANHATTAN	SALINA	TOPEKA	WICHITA
DODGE CITY	141	107	315		238	52	83	106	120	270	264	333	298	83	232	164	271	153
KANSAS CITY	247	50	369	333	106	373	250	261	240	162	105		35	402	117	172	61	192
SALINA	151	160	200	164	118	204	81	93	68	206	187	172	137	247	72		111	92
TOPEKA	193	49	308	271	58	311	188	200	178	135	100	61	26	347	55	111		137
WICHITA	61	186	289	153	85	205	119	181	51	118	112	192	159	210	131	92	137	

DRIVING DISTANCES IN MILES

SEE ALSO MILEAGE AND DRIVING TIME MAP ON PAGE 144

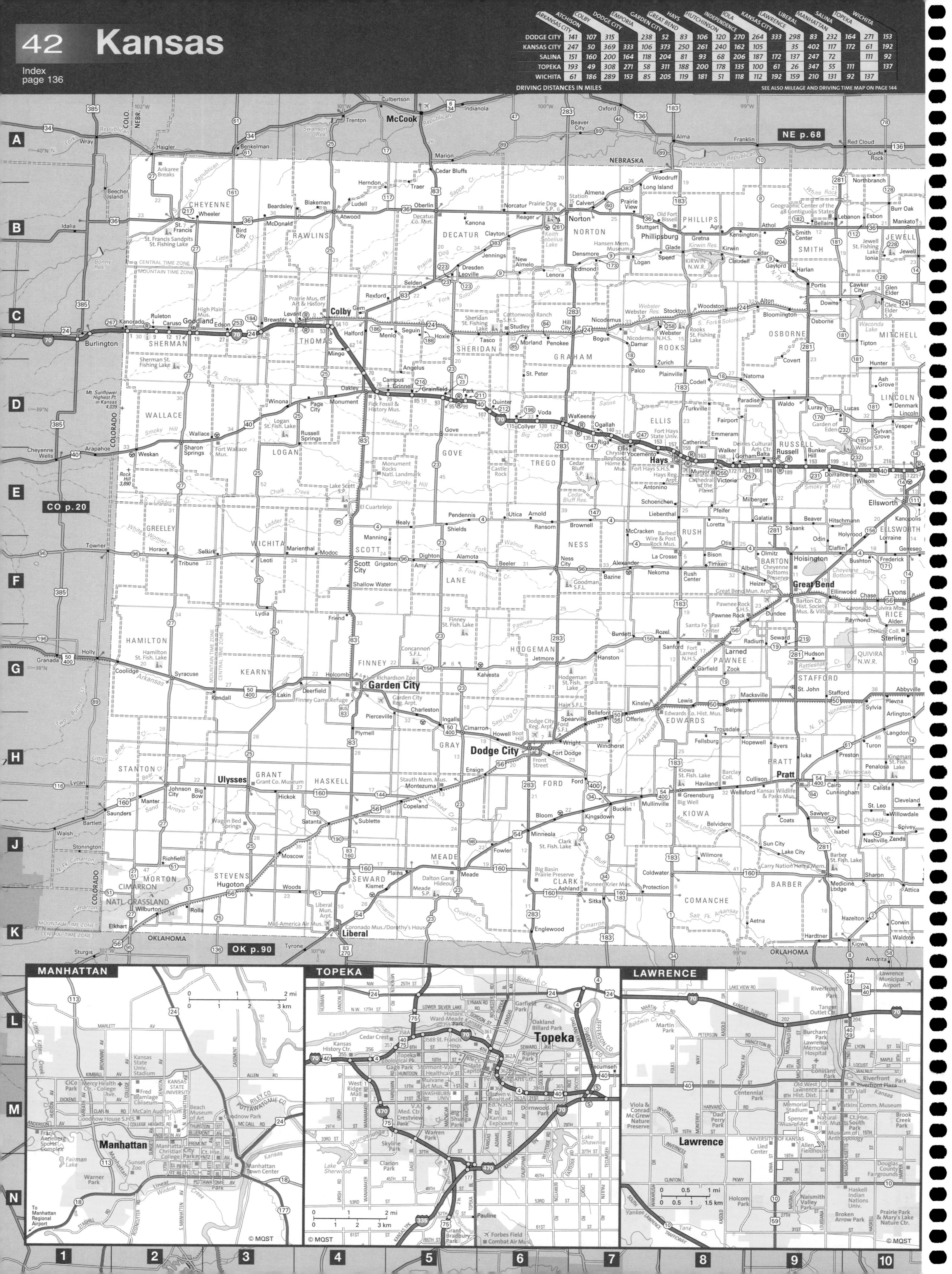

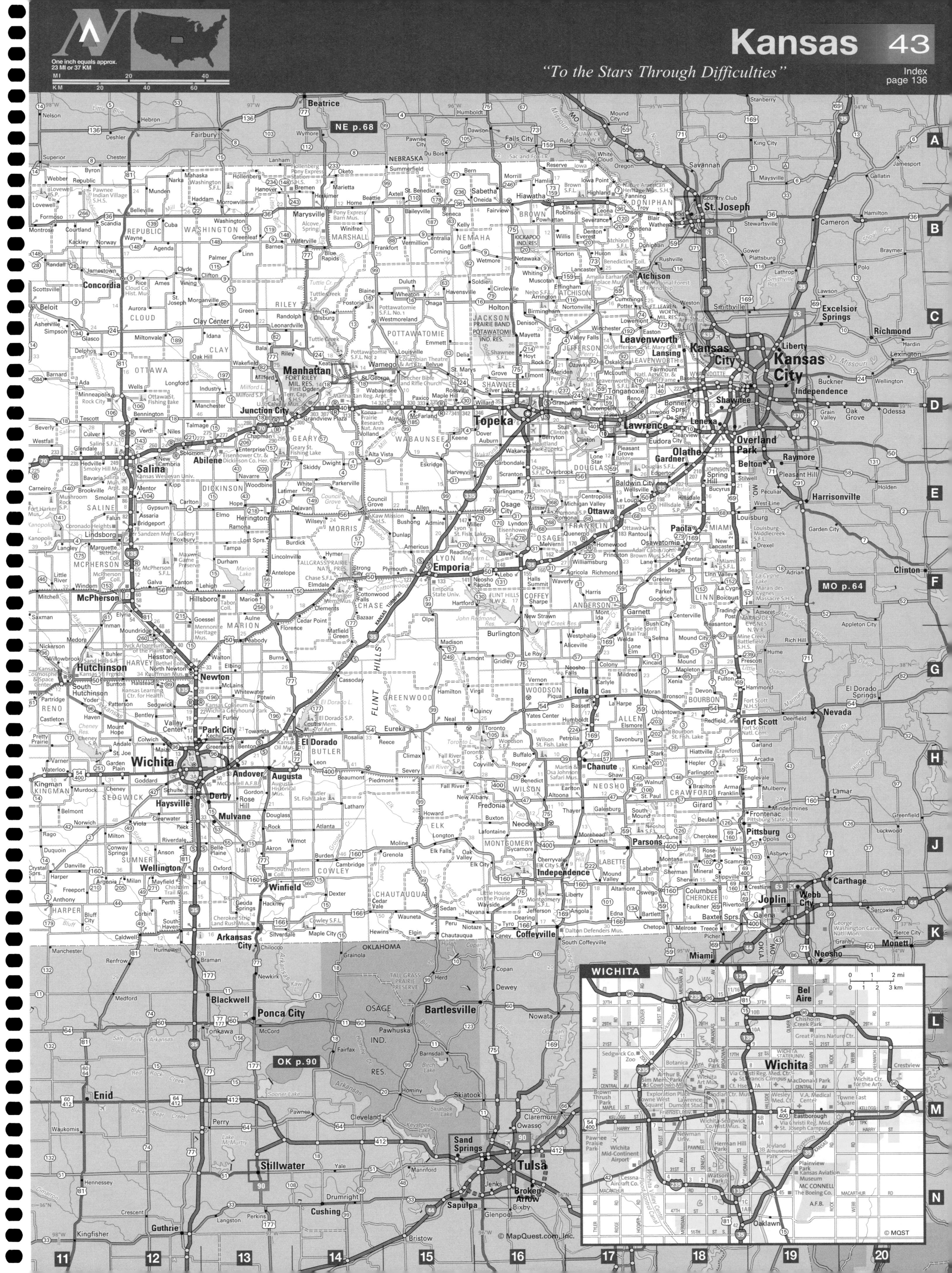

Kansas
43
"To the Stars Through Difficulties"
Index
page 136
One inch equals approx.
23 MI or 37 KM
MI
KM
NE p.68
MO p.64
OK p.90
NEBRASKA
OKLAHOMA
WICHITA
© MapQuest.com, Inc.
© MQST
Topeka
Wichita
Kansas City
Lawrence
Manhattan
Salina
Hutchinson
Emporia
Junction City
Abilene
Newton
McPherson
Concordia
Leavenworth
Atchison
Olathe
Overland Park
Lenexa
Shawnee
Ottawa
Paola
Iola
Chanute
Parsons
Pittsburg
Independence
Coffeyville
Winfield
Arkansas City
Wellington
El Dorado
Augusta
Andover
Derby
Haysville
Mulvane
Park City
Fort Scott
Joplin
St. Joseph
Beatrice
Ponca City
Bartlesville
Enid
Stillwater
Tulsa
Sand Springs
Broken Arrow
Sapulpa
Cushing
Guthrie
Blackwell
Miami
Carthage
Nevada
Clinton
Harrisonville
Independence
Liberty
Excelsior Springs
Richmond
A
B
C
D
E
F
G
H
J
K
L
M
N
11
12
13
14
15
16
17
18
19
20

Index page 136

	ASHLAND	BOWLING GREEN	CINCINNATI, OH	ELIZABETHTOWN	FRANKFORT	GLASGOW	HAZARD	HENDERSON	HOPKINSVILLE	LEXINGTON	LONDON	LOUISVILLE	MAYFIELD	MAYSVILLE	MIDDLESBORO	OWENSBORO	PADUCAH	PIKEVILLE
BOWLING GREEN	274		212	70	161	36	200	107	63	157	145	112	146	222	203	76	135	265
LEXINGTON	119	157	85	89	29	138	120	201	215		77	80	273	67	136	183	262	142
LOUISVILLE	194	112	100	44	54	92	194	123	170	80	156		228	141	214	109	217	217
OWENSBORO	300	76	206	95	161	111	275	30	80	183	221	109	138	248	279		127	323
PADUCAH	379	135	317	175	266	173	337	121	72	262	283	217	24	327	373	127		402

DRIVING DISTANCES IN MILES

SEE ALSO MILEAGE AND DRIVING TIME MAP ON PAGE 144

"United We Stand, Divided We Fall"

Index page 136

One inch equals approx. 17 MI or 27.5 KM

MI 10 20 30

KM 10 20 30 40

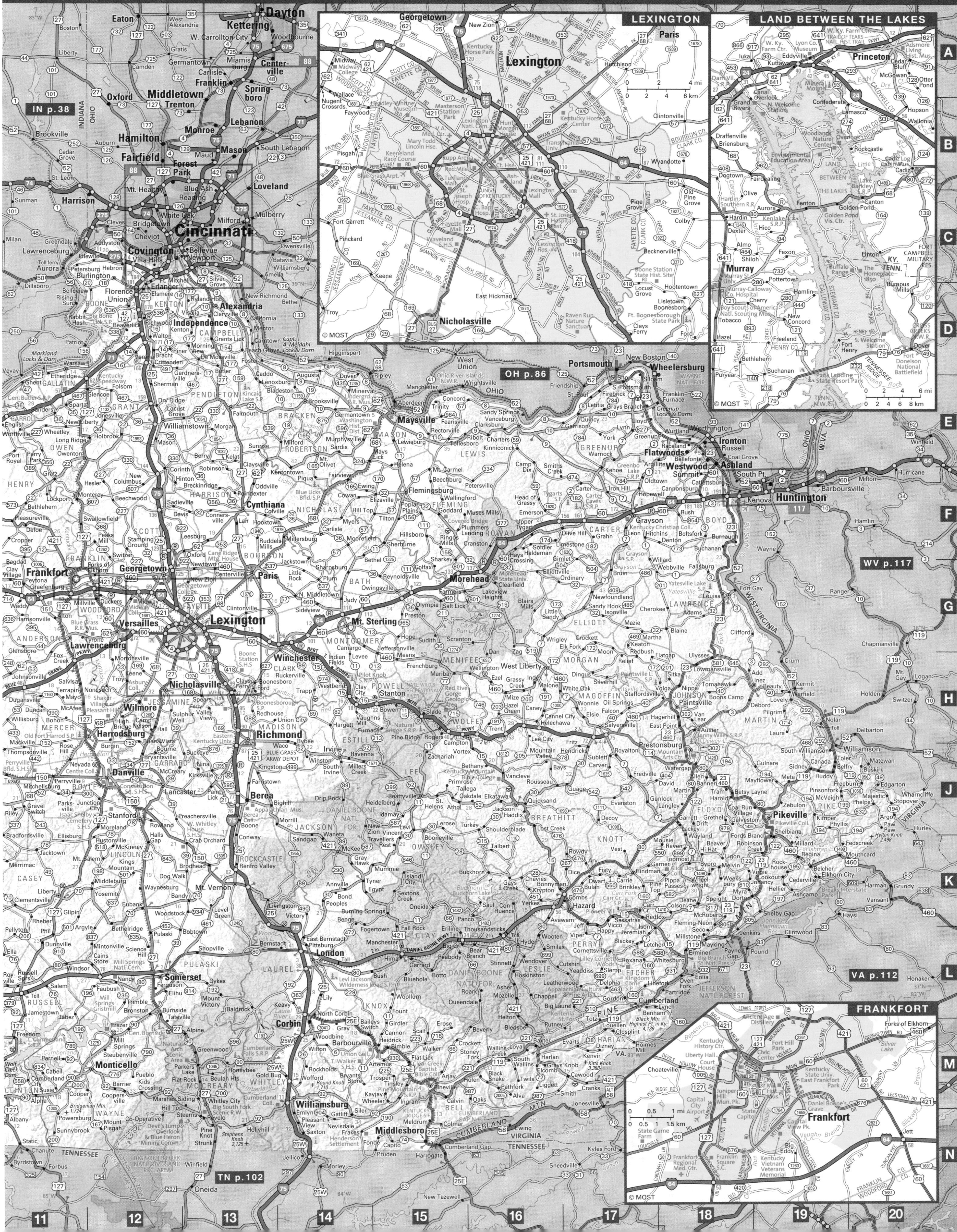

LEXINGTON

LAND BETWEEN THE LAKES

FRANKFORT

IN p. 38

OH p. 86

WV p. 117

VA p. 112

TN p. 102

© MQST

Index page 136

	ALEXANDRIA	BATON ROUGE	DE RIDDER	FERRIDAY	HAMMOND	HOUMA	LAFAYETTE	LAKE CHARLES	MONROE	NATCHITOCHES	NEW IBERIA	NEW ORLEANS	OPELOUSAS	RUSTON	SHREVEPORT	SLIDELL	TALLULAH	WINNFIELD
BATON ROUGE	140		176	104	51	101	60	132	188	195	79	91	80	233	261	97	163	188
LAFAYETTE	87	60	119	152	106	101		76	183	142	20	147	27	180	208	152	214	135
MONROE	96	188	170	85	248	283	183	196		100	202	302	156	37	103	298	55	64
NEW ORLEANS	227	91	262	191	57	57	147	219	302	282	166		167	339	348	31	247	275
SHREVEPORT	121	261	137	188	308	309	208	186	103	73	227	348	182	71		354	158	105

DRIVING DISTANCES IN MILES

SEE ALSO MILEAGE AND DRIVING TIME MAP ON PAGE 144

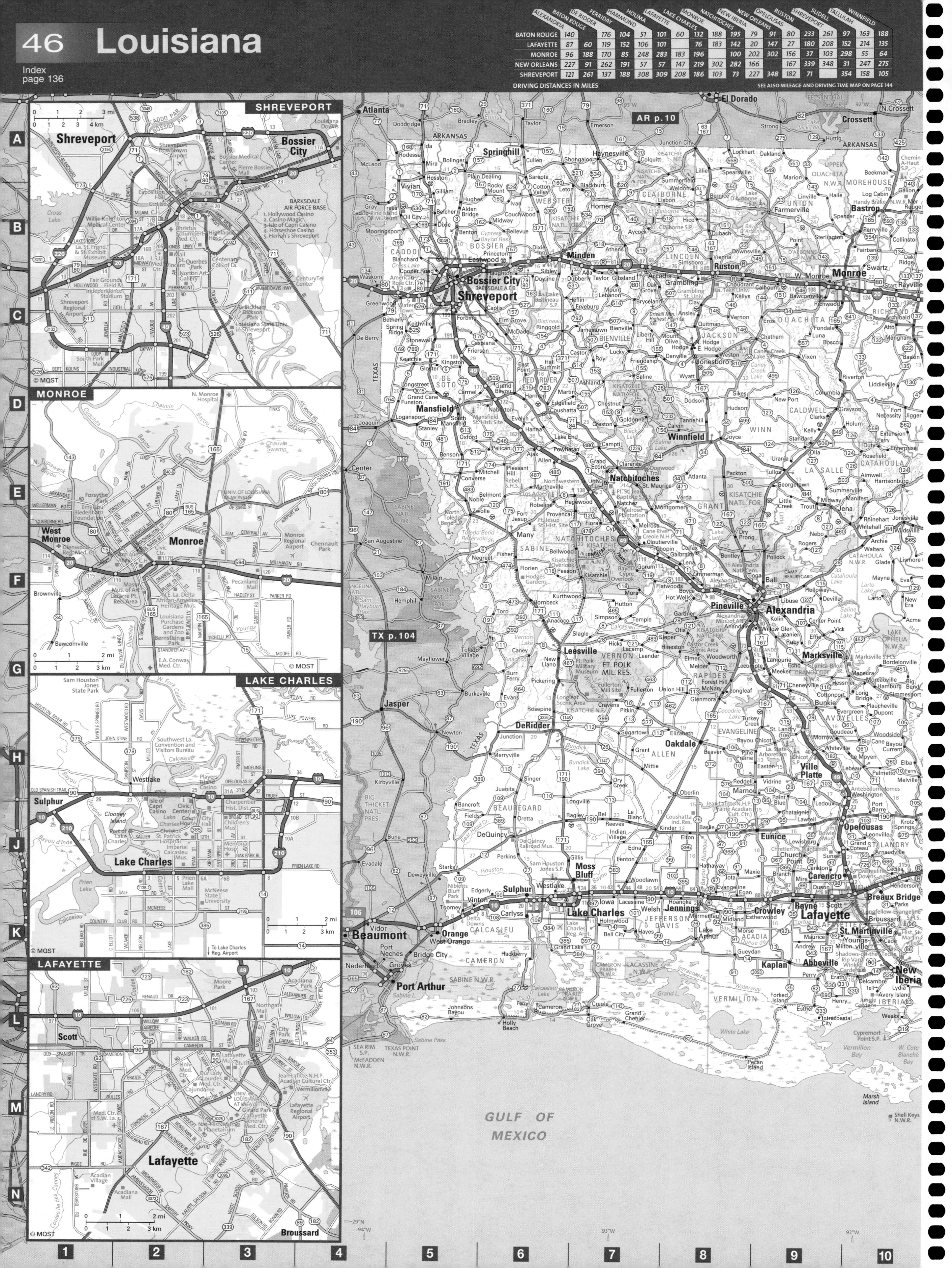

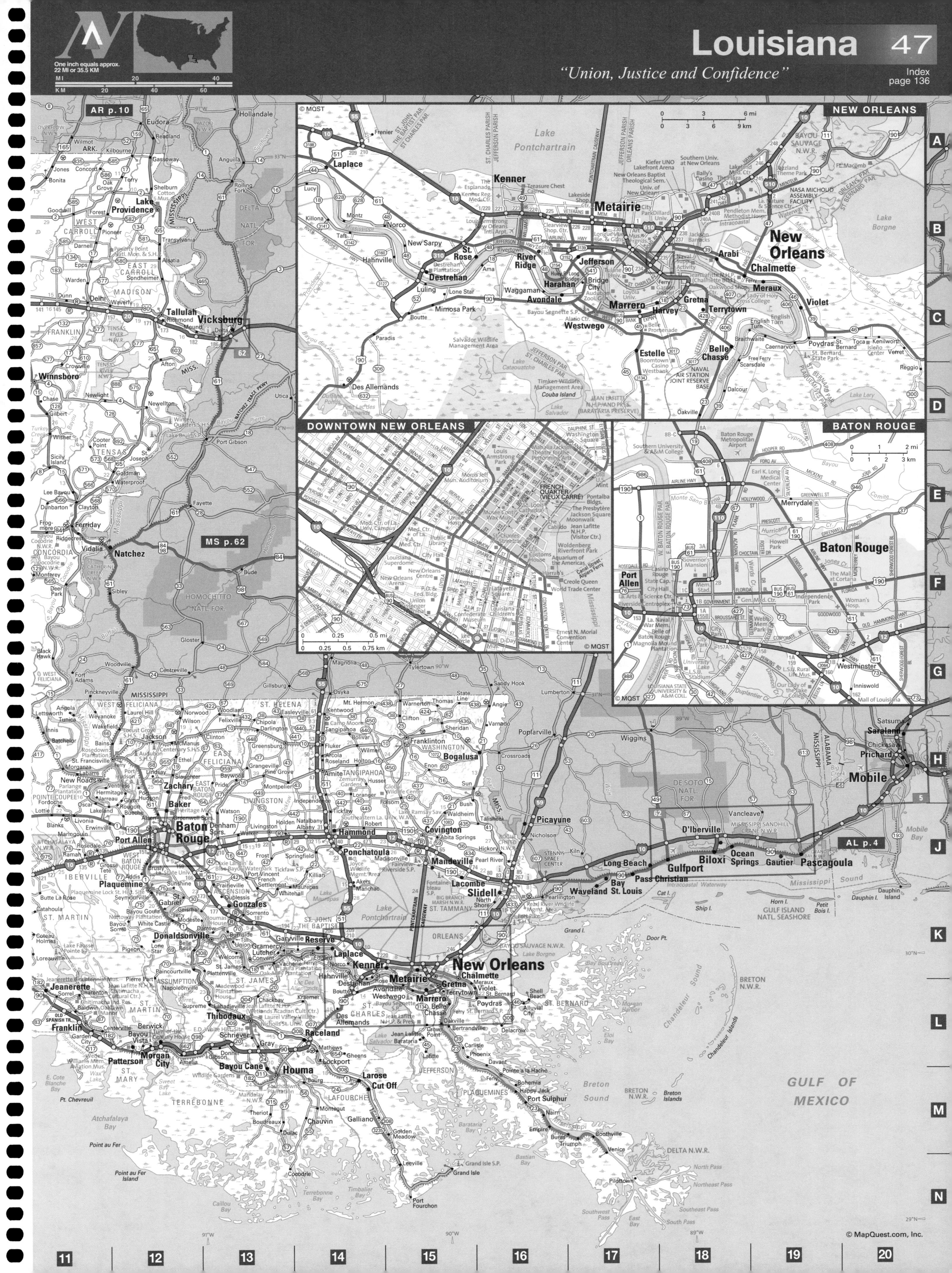

Louisiana
47
"Union, Justice and Confidence"
Index page 136
One inch equals approx. 22 MI or 35.5 KM
MI 20 40
KM 20 40 60
AR p.10
MS p.62
AL p.4
NEW ORLEANS
DOWNTOWN NEW ORLEANS
BATON ROUGE
© MQST
Lake Pontchartrain
Lake Borgne
Metairie
New Orleans
Kenner
Laplace
Chalmette
Arabi
Meraux
Violet
Gretna
Harvey
Marrero
Westwego
Terrytown
Belle Chasse
Destrehan
Luling
Hahnville
Harahan
Jefferson
River Ridge
Avondale
Estelle
NAVAL AIR STATION JOINT RESERVE BASE
FRENCH QUARTER (VIEUX CARRÉ)
Louisiana Superdome
Baton Rouge
Port Allen
Baton Rouge Metropolitan Airport
Southern University & A&M College
LOUISIANA STATE UNIVERSITY & A&M COLL.
Shreveport
Vicksburg
Natchez
Tallulah
Winnsboro
Ferriday
Vidalia
Lake Providence
Zachary
Baker
Hammond
Ponchatoula
Covington
Mandeville
Slidell
Bogalusa
Picayune
Gonzales
Donaldsonville
Thibodaux
Houma
Morgan City
Franklin
Jeanerette
Patterson
Raceland
Larose
Cut Off
Golden Meadow
Grand Isle
Port Fourchon
Venice
Port Sulphur
Gulfport
Biloxi
Ocean Springs
Pascagoula
Mobile
Bay St. Louis
Waveland
Long Beach
Pass Christian
D'Iberville
Gautier
Prichard
Saraland
Atchafalaya Bay
GULF OF MEXICO
Breton Sound
Chandeleur Sound
Mississippi Sound
HOMOCHITTO NATL. FOR.
DE SOTO NATL. FOR.
© MapQuest.com, Inc.

Index page 137

	AUGUSTA	BANGOR	BAR HARBOR	BRUNSWICK	CALAIS	FARMINGTON	FORT KENT	GREENVILLE	HOULTON	LEWISTON	MACHIAS	MILLINOCKET	PORTLAND	PORTSMOUTH, NH	PRESQUE ISLE	ROCKLAND	SACO	WATERVILLE
AUGUSTA		77	120	32	173	65	269	99	196	35	161	149	58	110	236	43	74	20
BANGOR	77		45	106	97	80	195	74	122	108	85	75	131	184	162	58	147	56
CALAIS	173	97	112	203		177	189	160	91	205	55	112	228	281	133	155	244	153
HOULTON	196	122	166	226	91	200	98	155		228	126	73	251	304	42	182	267	176
PORTLAND	58	131	175	27	228	81	324	153	251	36	216	203		53	291	78	16	84

DRIVING DISTANCES IN MILES

SEE ALSO MILEAGE AND DRIVING TIME MAP ON PAGE 144

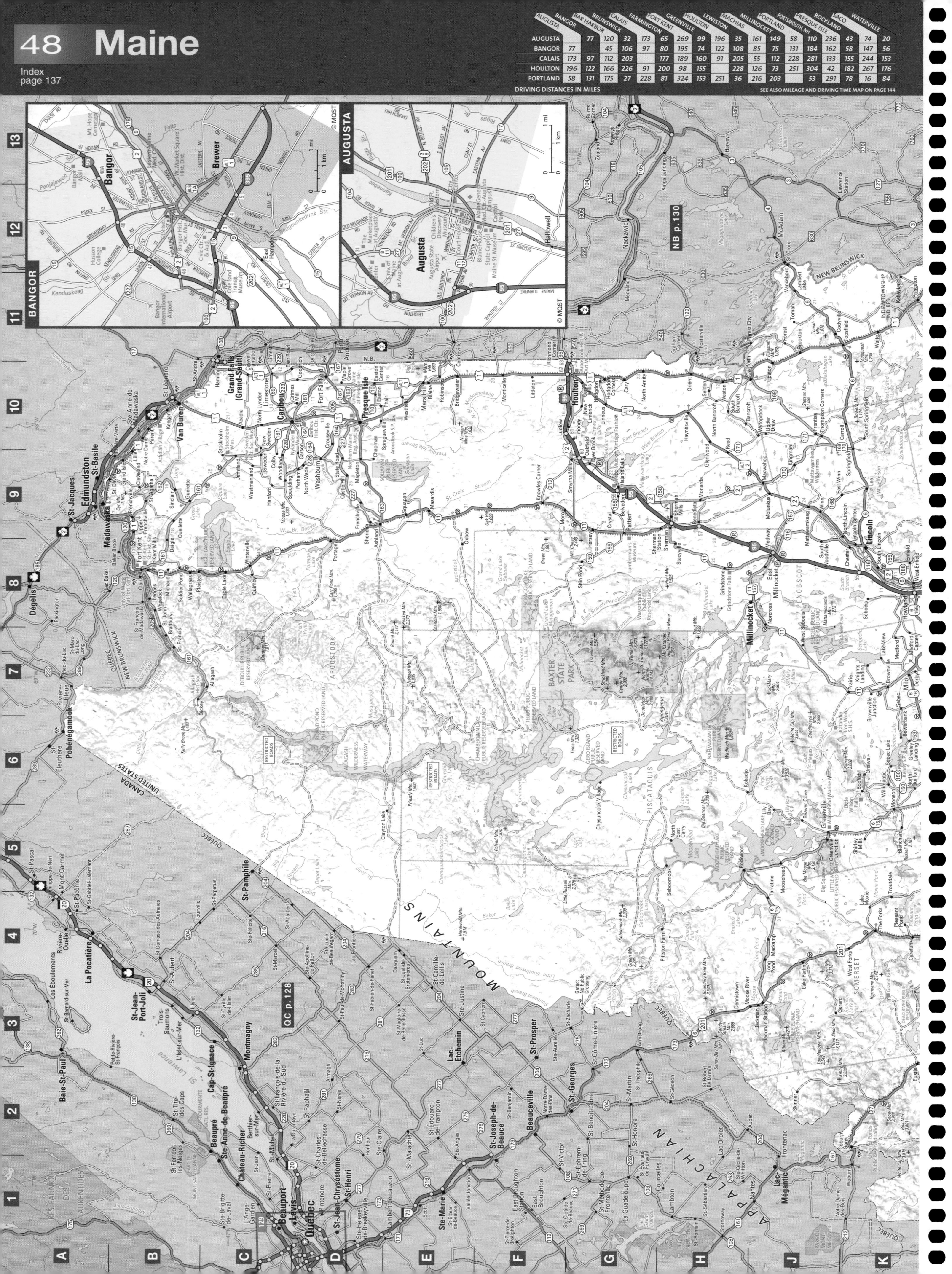

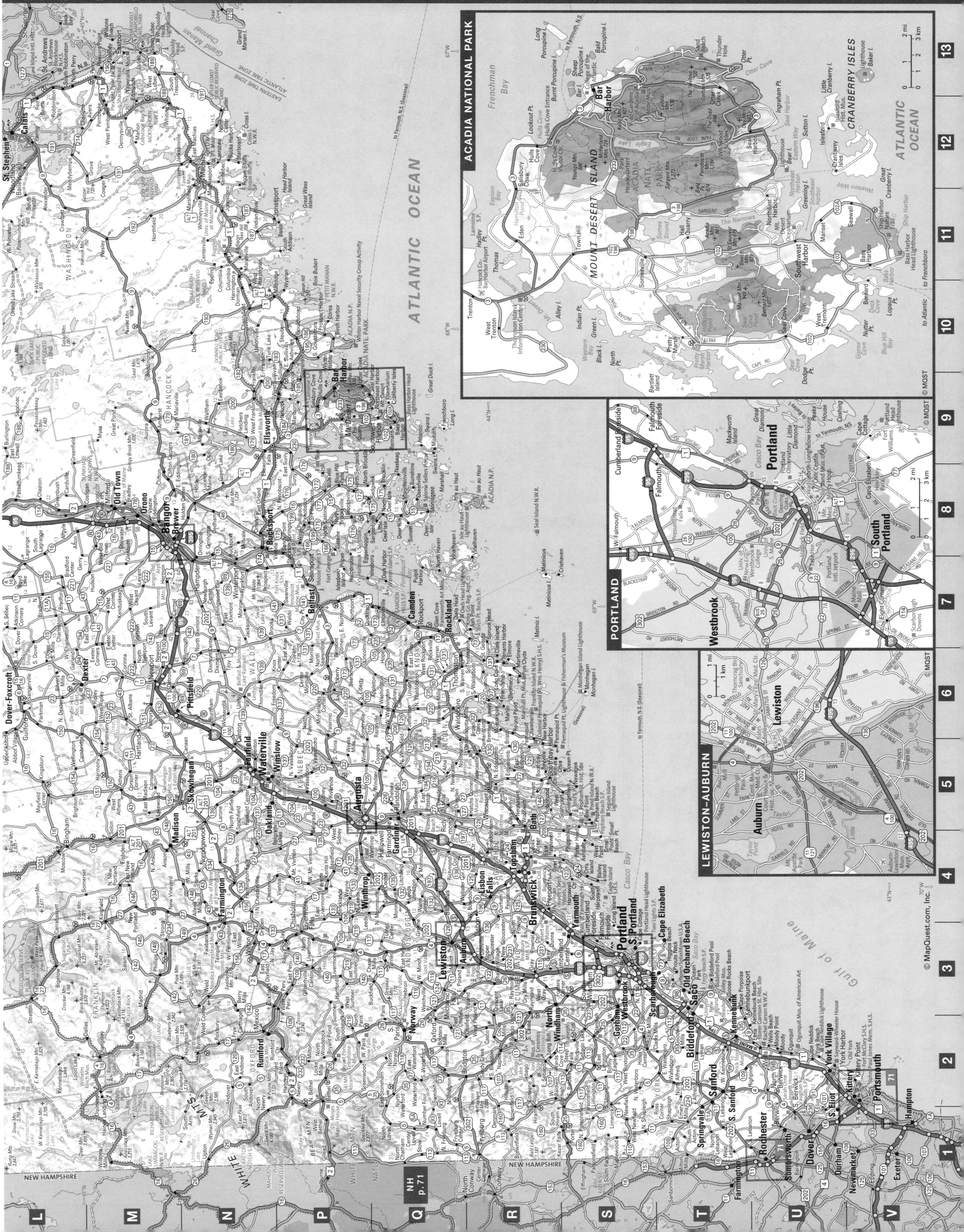

One inch equals approx. 15.5 MI or 25.5 KM

MI 10 20 30
KM 10 20 30 40

ACADIA NATIONAL PARK

PORTLAND

LEWISTON-AUBURN

ATLANTIC OCEAN

NEW HAMPSHIRE

NH p.71

Index page 137

	ABERDEEN	ANNAPOLIS	BALTIMORE	CAMBRIDGE	CHESTERTOWN	CUMBERLAND	EASTON	FREDERICK	HAGERSTOWN	HANCOCK	LEXINGTON PARK	OCEAN CITY	POCOMOKE CITY	ROCKVILLE	ST. CHARLES	SALISBURY	WASHINGTON, DC	WESTMINSTER
ANNAPOLIS	54		25	55	45	162	38	73	98	124	66	108	112	47	47	83	31	56
BALTIMORE	35	25		78	68	140	61	51	76	102	95	131	135	45	57	106	38	39
HAGERSTOWN	109	98	76	153	143	67	136	28		29	142	206	211	54	103	182	70	50
SALISBURY	124	83	106	32	81	246	47	156	182	207	149	30	29	130	130		115	138
WASHINGTON, DC	71	31	38	87	76	134	70	44	70	96	63	139	144	19	25	115		53

DRIVING DISTANCES IN MILES

SEE ALSO MILEAGE AND DRIVING TIME MAP ON PAGE 144

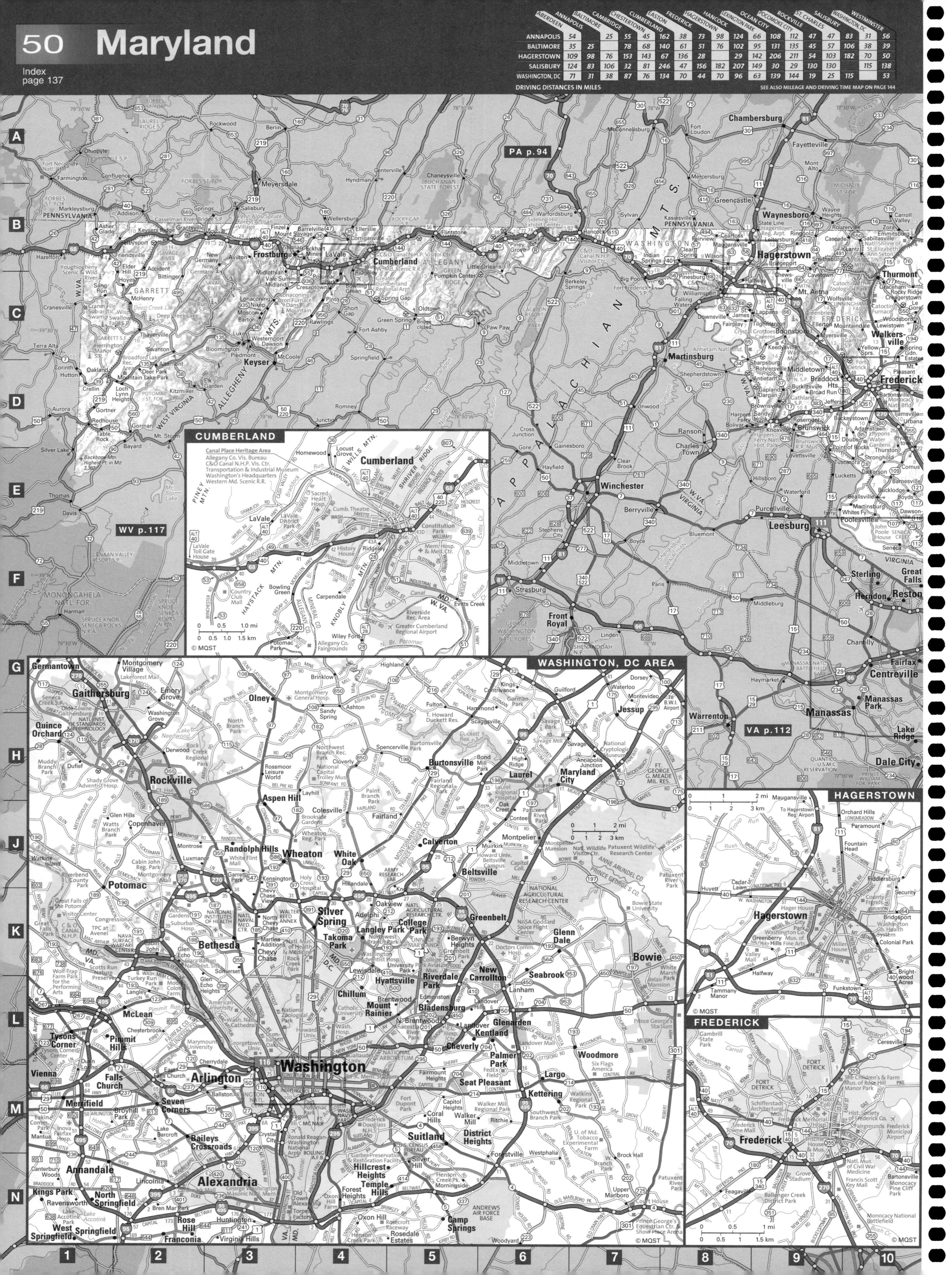

"Manly Deeds, Womanly Words"

Index page 137

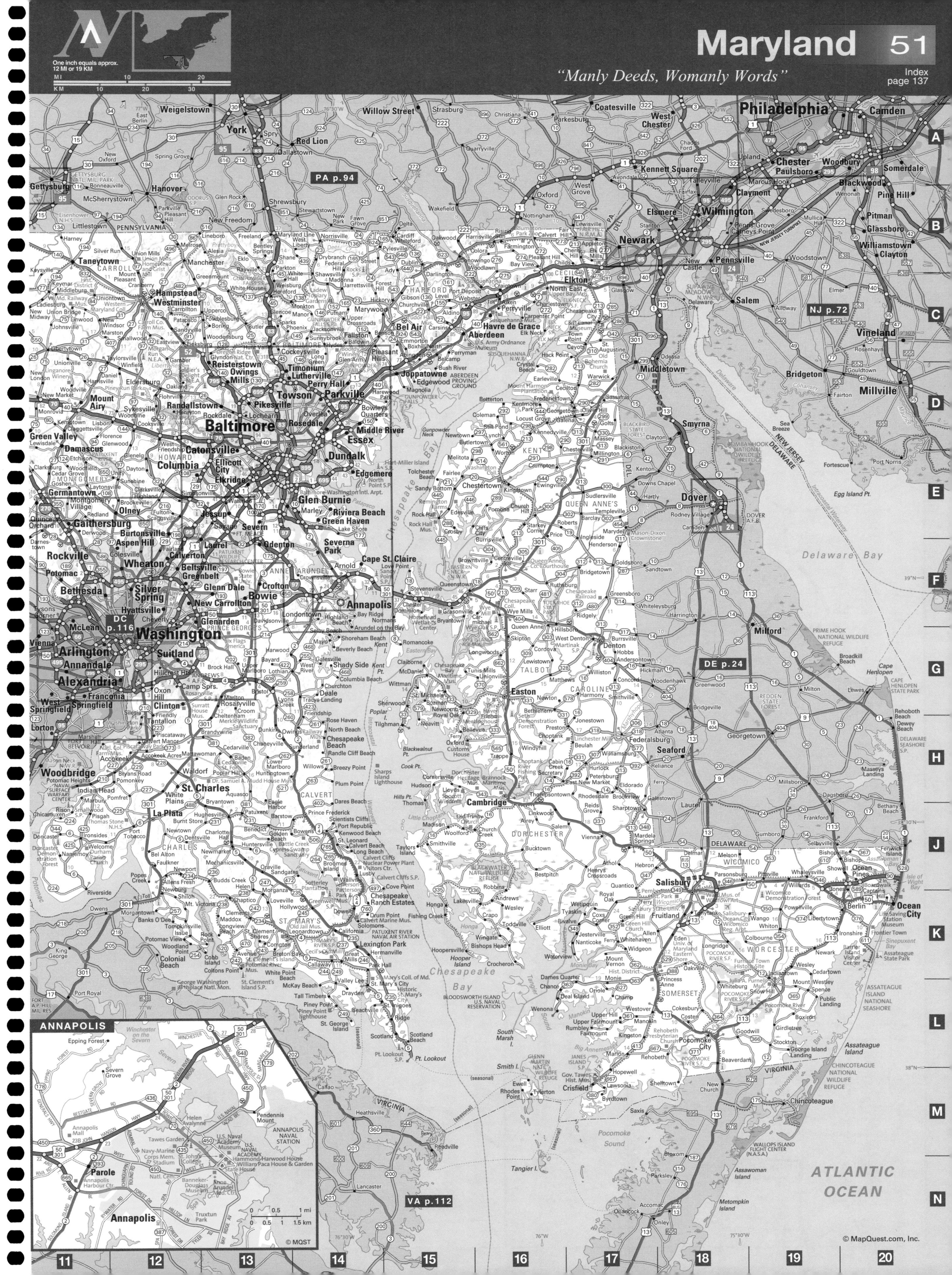

Index page 137

One inch equals approx. 3 MI or 4.5 KM

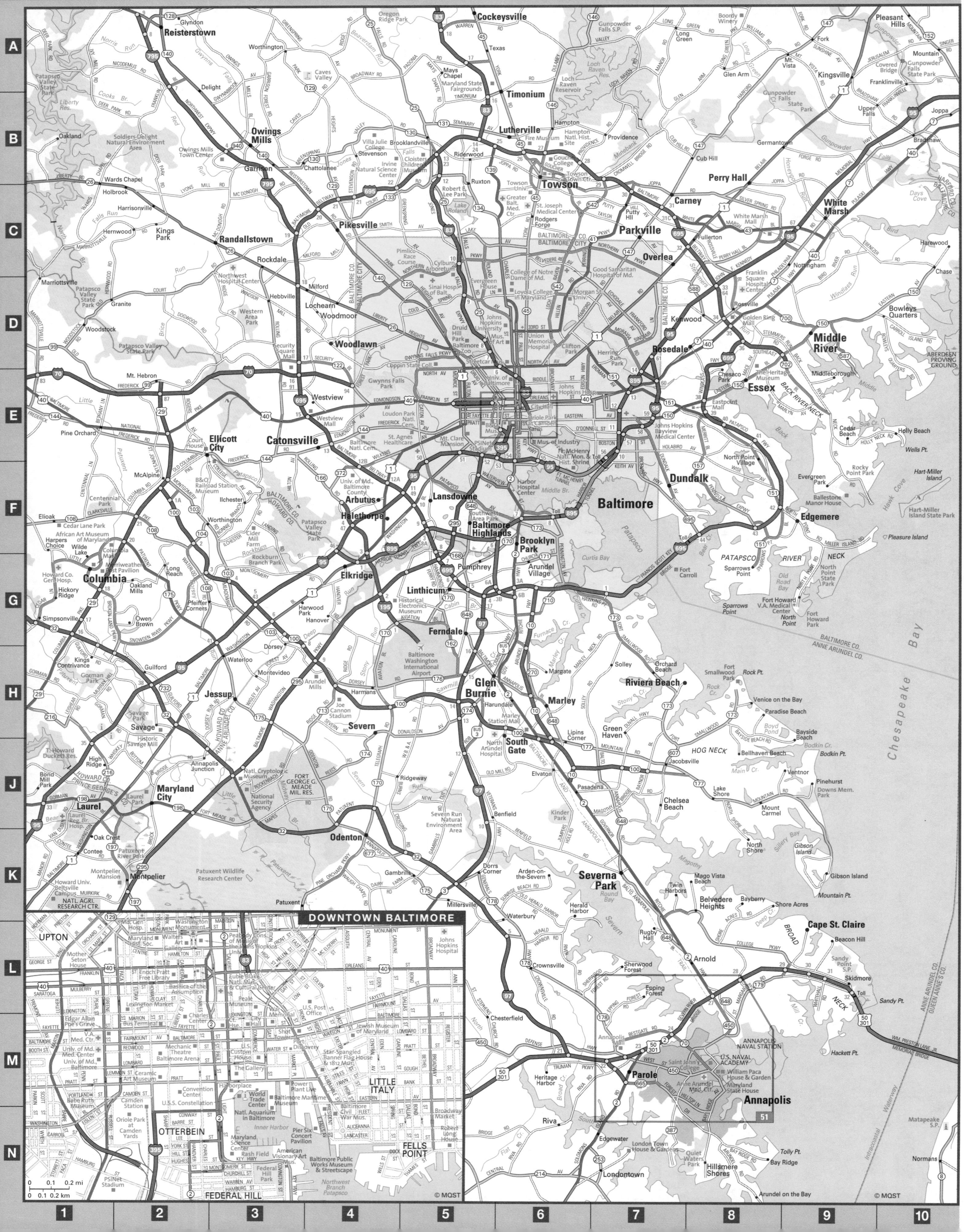

MI 2 4

KM 2 4 6

A B C D E F G H J K L M N

Reisterstown
Glyndon
Worthington
Cockeysville
Texas
Timonium
Lutherville
Towson
Hampton
Providence
Perry Hall
Carney
Parkville
Overlea
White Marsh
Kingsville
Fork
Glen Arm
Long Green
Pleasant Hills
Joppa
Bradshaw
Owings Mills
Garrison
Pikesville
Randallstown
Rockdale
Milford
Lochearn
Woodmoor
Woodlawn
Catonsville
Westview
Ellicott City
Arbutus
Halethorpe
Lansdowne
Baltimore Highlands
Brooklyn Park
Pumphrey
Elkridge
Linthicum
Ferndale
Glen Burnie
Marley
South Gate
Severn
Jessup
Savage
Maryland City
Laurel
Columbia
Odenton
Severna Park
Arnold
Annapolis
Parole
Riva
Londontown
Pasadena
Riviera Beach
Dundalk
Baltimore
Essex
Middle River
Rosedale
Edgemere
Cape St. Claire
Chesapeake Bay
Patapsco River
Baltimore Washington International Airport
Fort George G. Meade Mil. Res.
Patuxent Wildlife Research Center

DOWNTOWN BALTIMORE

Upton
Otterbein
Little Italy
Fells Point
Federal Hill
Inner Harbor

0 0.1 0.2 mi
0 0.1 0.2 km

© MQST

1 2 3 4 5 6 7 8 9 10

One inch equals approx. 2.5 MI or 4 KM

MI 0 2 4
KM 0 2 4 6

DOWNTOWN BOSTON

TRAVEL NOTE: Some road patterns may change near I-93 in downtown Boston due to construction through the year 2004.

0 0.1 0.2 mi
0 0.1 0.2 0.3 km

ATLANTIC OCEAN

Boston, Cambridge, Somerville, Brookline, Newton, Watertown, Waltham, Belmont, Arlington, Medford, Malden, Everett, Chelsea, Revere, Melrose, Saugus, Lynn, Swampscott, Marblehead, Salem, Peabody, Beverly, Lynnfield, Wakefield, Reading, Stoneham, Woburn, Winchester, Burlington, Lexington, Bedford, Wilmington, Weston, Wellesley, Needham, Dedham, Milton, Quincy, Braintree, Weymouth, Hingham, Hull, Winthrop, Nahant, Randolph, Holbrook, Stoughton, Avon, Brockton, Abington, Rockland, Whitman, Hanson

A B C D E F G H J K L M N

1 2 3 4 5 6 7 8 9 10

Massachusetts

Index page 137

	BOSTON	BROCKTON	FALL RIVER	FALMOUTH	FITCHBURG	GLOUCESTER	GREENFIELD	HYANNIS	LOWELL	NEW BEDFORD	NORTH ADAMS	NORTHAMPTON	PITTSFIELD	PLYMOUTH	PROVIDENCE, RI	PROVINCETOWN	SPRINGFIELD	WORCESTER
BOSTON		26	53	72	49	35	93	72	31	60	133	105	140	41	52	117	95	46
NEW BEDFORD	60	38	16	41	101	95	136	45	86		189	137	172	43	33	91	127	78
PITTSFIELD	140	153	153	189	101	174	52	193	142	172	17	41		166	138	239	55	101
SPRINGFIELD	95	108	92	143	85	129	40	148	96	127	72	18	55	120	75	193		55
WORCESTER	46	59	58	95	31	80	58	99	44	78	97	65	101	72	43	144	55	

DRIVING DISTANCES IN MILES

SEE ALSO MILEAGE AND DRIVING TIME MAP ON PAGE 144

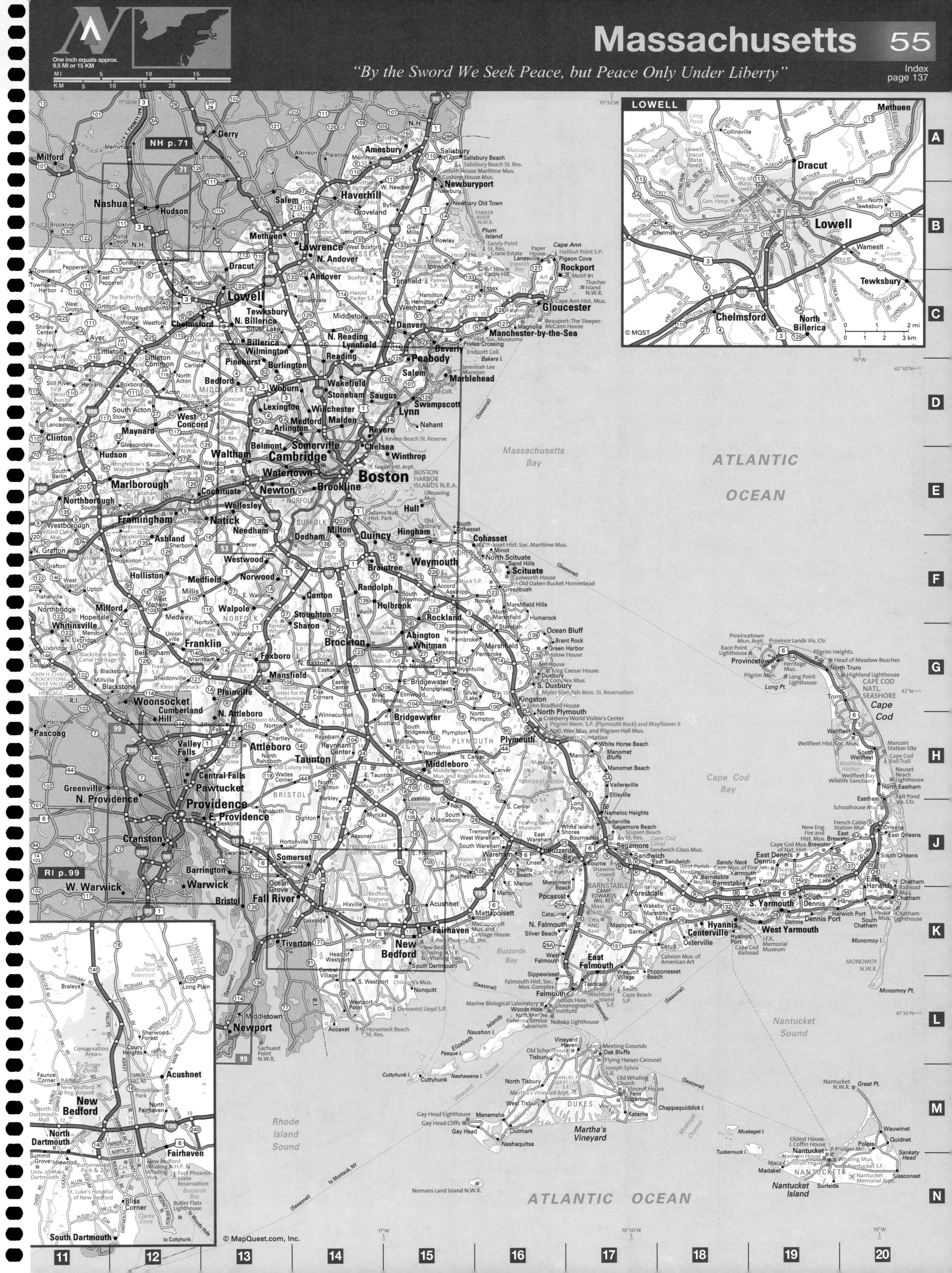

Massachusetts 55
"By the Sword We Seek Peace, but Peace Only Under Liberty"
Index page 137
One inch equals approx. 9.5 MI or 15 KM
NH p.71
RI p.99
LOWELL
Methuen
Dracut
Lowell
Tewksbury
Chelmsford
North Billerica
© MQST
ATLANTIC OCEAN
Massachusetts Bay
Cape Cod Bay
Buzzards Bay
Nantucket Sound
Rhode Island Sound
Vineyard Sound
Martha's Vineyard
Nantucket Island
Cape Cod
Boston
Cambridge
Providence
Worcester
Lowell
Lawrence
Haverhill
Newburyport
Gloucester
Salem
Lynn
Quincy
Brockton
Plymouth
Taunton
Fall River
New Bedford
Newport
Woonsocket
Pawtucket
Cranston
Warwick
Hyannis
Falmouth
Provincetown
Nantucket
Edgartown
Nashua
Hudson
Framingham
Marlborough
Attleboro
Middleboro
Barnstable
A
B
C
D
E
F
G
H
J
K
L
M
N
11
12
13
14
15
16
17
18
19
20
© MapQuest.com, Inc.

Index
page 137

	ALPENA	ANN ARBOR	BENTON HARBOR	CADILLAC	DETROIT	ESCANABA	FLINT	GRAND RAPIDS	HOUGHTON	KALAMAZOO	LANSING	MACKINAW CITY	MARQUETTE	MUSKEGON	PORT HURON	SAGINAW	SAULT STE MARIE	TRAVERSE CITY
DETROIT	242	42	186	209		438	62	153	556	136	86	291	455	191	58	97	346	257
GRAND RAPIDS	261	129	78	99	153	391	112		510	53	67	244	405	40	176	144	299	141
LANSING	230	63	126	131	86	375	53	67	493	76		228	391	105	117	86	282	173
MACKINAW CITY	94	281	323	145	291	149	230	244	268	302	228		166	248	293	198	57	106
MARQUETTE	257	444	487	309	455	65	393	408	102	466	391	166		412	457	361	163	269

DRIVING DISTANCES IN MILES

SEE ALSO MILEAGE AND DRIVING TIME MAP ON PAGE 144

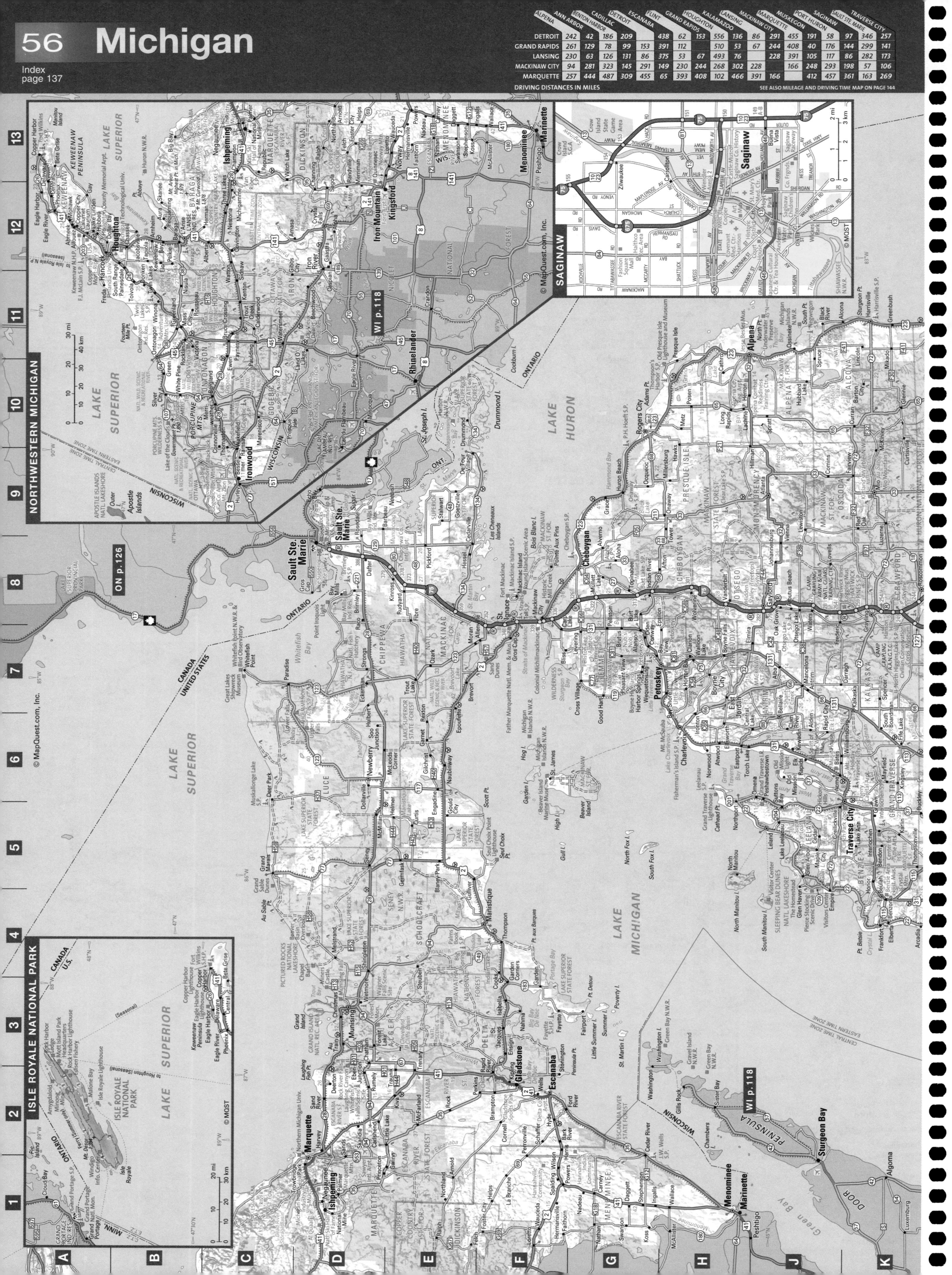

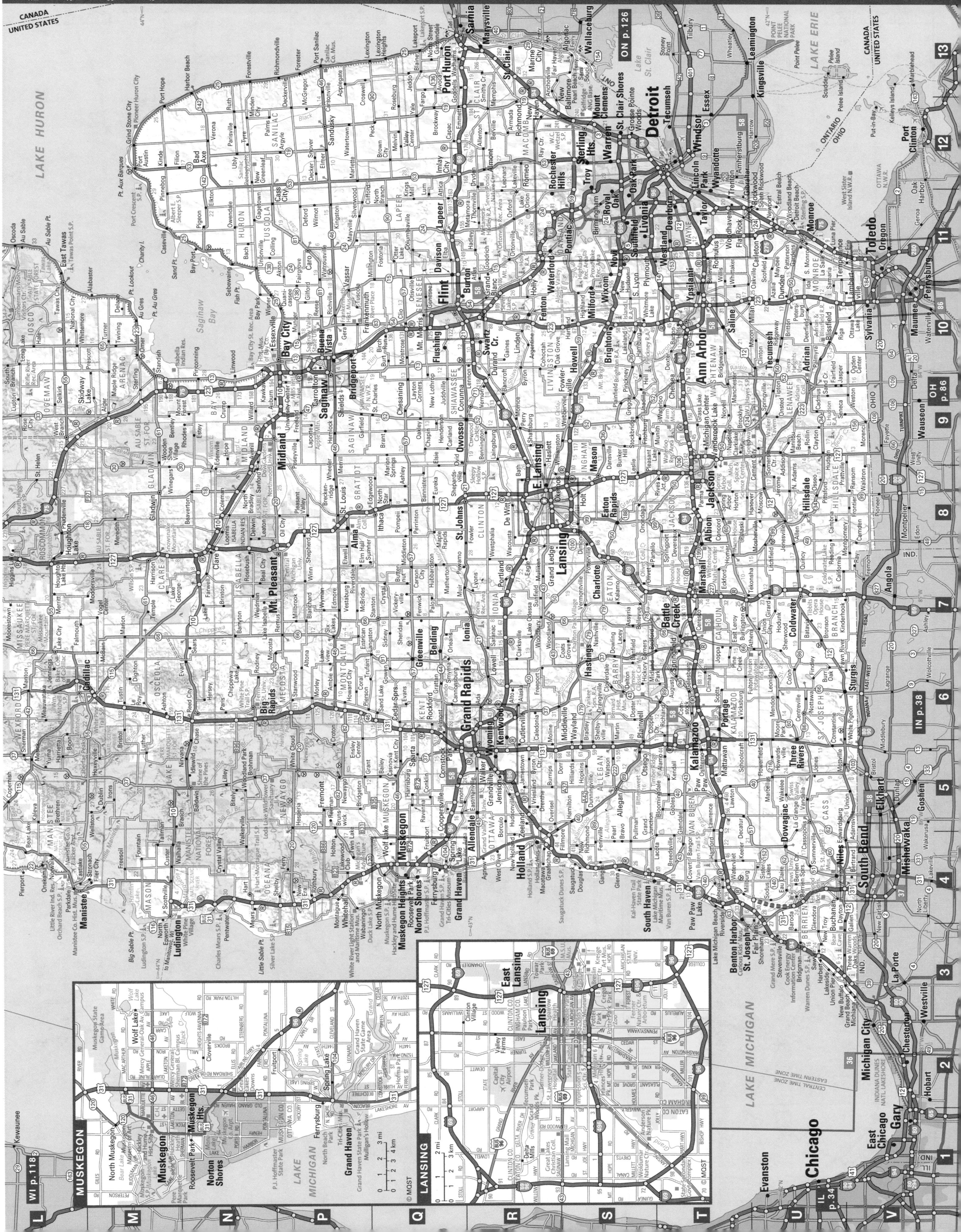

"If You Seek a Pleasant Peninsula, Look About You"

One inch equals approx. 20.5 MI or 33 KM

MI 15 30

KM 15 30 45

MUSKEGON

LANSING

GRAND RAPIDS

KALAMAZOO

BATTLE CREEK

FLINT

DETROIT

ANN ARBOR

DOWNTOWN DETROIT

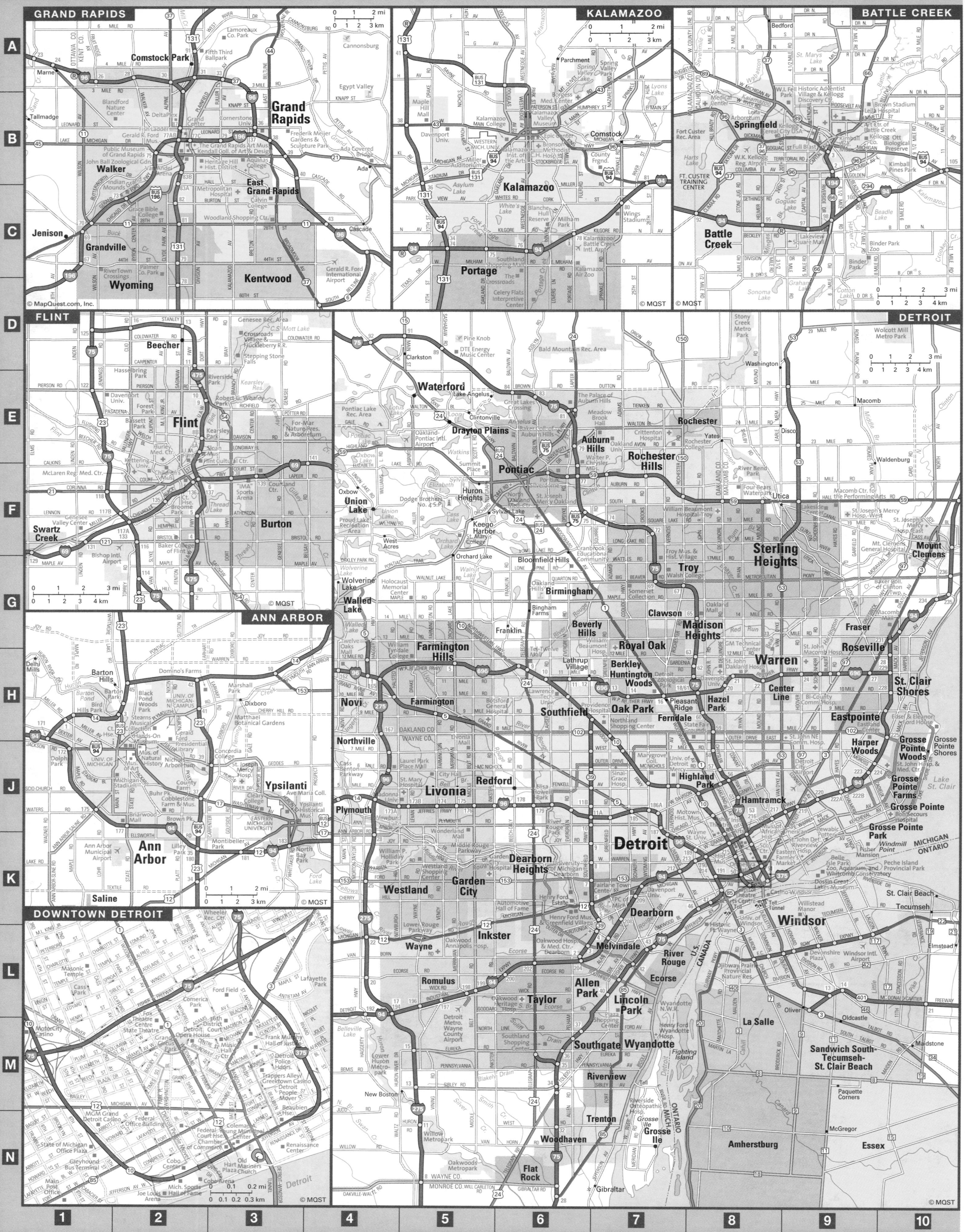

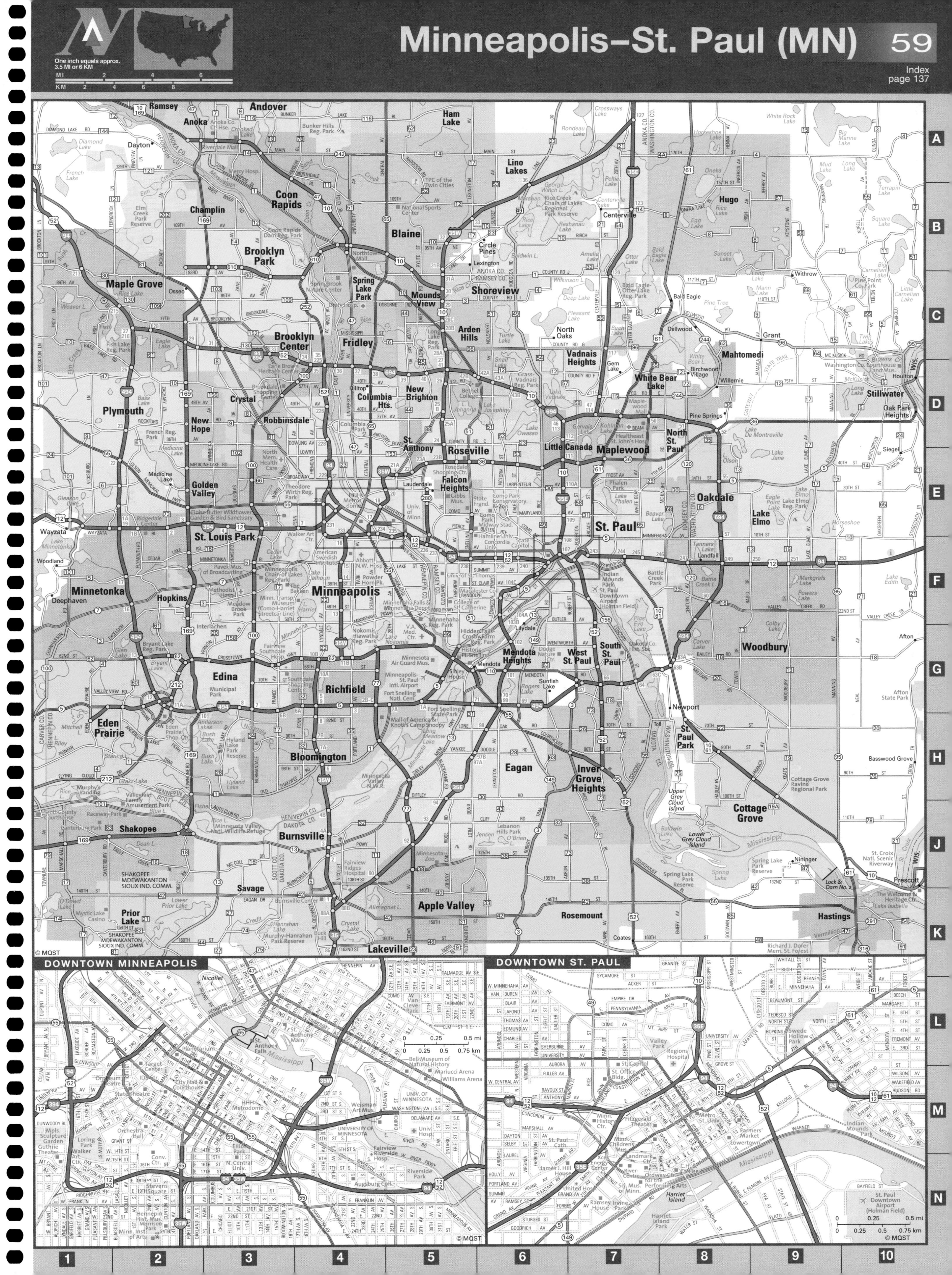
Minneapolis–St. Paul (MN)
59
Index page 137
One inch equals approx. 3.5 MI or 6 KM
DOWNTOWN MINNEAPOLIS
DOWNTOWN ST. PAUL
Ramsey
Anoka
Andover
Ham Lake
Dayton
Champlin
Coon Rapids
Lino Lakes
Hugo
Blaine
Centerville
Brooklyn Park
Circle Pines
Lexington
Maple Grove
Osseo
Spring Lake Park
Mounds View
Shoreview
Brooklyn Center
Fridley
Arden Hills
North Oaks
Vadnais Heights
Mahtomedi
White Bear Lake
Grant
Crystal
Plymouth
New Hope
Robbinsdale
Columbia Hts.
New Brighton
Roseville
Little Canada
Maplewood
North St. Paul
Stillwater
Oak Park Heights
St. Anthony
Golden Valley
Falcon Heights
Lauderdale
Oakdale
Lake Elmo
Wayzata
St. Louis Park
St. Paul
Minneapolis
Minnetonka
Hopkins
Deephaven
Woodland
Mendota Heights
West St. Paul
South St. Paul
Woodbury
Lilydale
Edina
Richfield
Sunfish Lake
Eden Prairie
Newport
St. Paul Park
Bloomington
Eagan
Inver Grove Heights
Cottage Grove
Shakopee
Burnsville
Savage
Prior Lake
Apple Valley
Rosemount
Hastings
Lakeville
Coates
Prescott
Afton
© MQST

Index page 137

	ALBERT LEA	BEMIDJI	BRAINERD	DULUTH	FERGUS FALLS	GRAND FORKS, ND	INTERNATIONAL FALLS	MANKATO	MARSHALL	MINNEAPOLIS	MOORHEAD	ROCHESTER	ST. CLOUD	ST. PAUL	VIRGINIA	WILLMAR	WINONA	WORTHINGTON
DULUTH	251	153	116		210	264	157	239	274	158	257	239	149	154	61	206	216	362
MINNEAPOLIS	96	225	129	158	176	312	290	78	148		230	88	64	10	193	92	120	207
MOORHEAD	325	133	141	257	55	80	242	294	220	230		317	172	239	229	168	351	298
ROCHESTER	62	311	215	239	262	399	371	80	185	88	317		151	80	274	177	51	174
ST. CLOUD	159	157	62	149	117	254	251	128	131	64	172	151		73	184	63	185	201

DRIVING DISTANCES IN MILES

SEE ALSO MILEAGE AND DRIVING TIME MAP ON PAGE 144

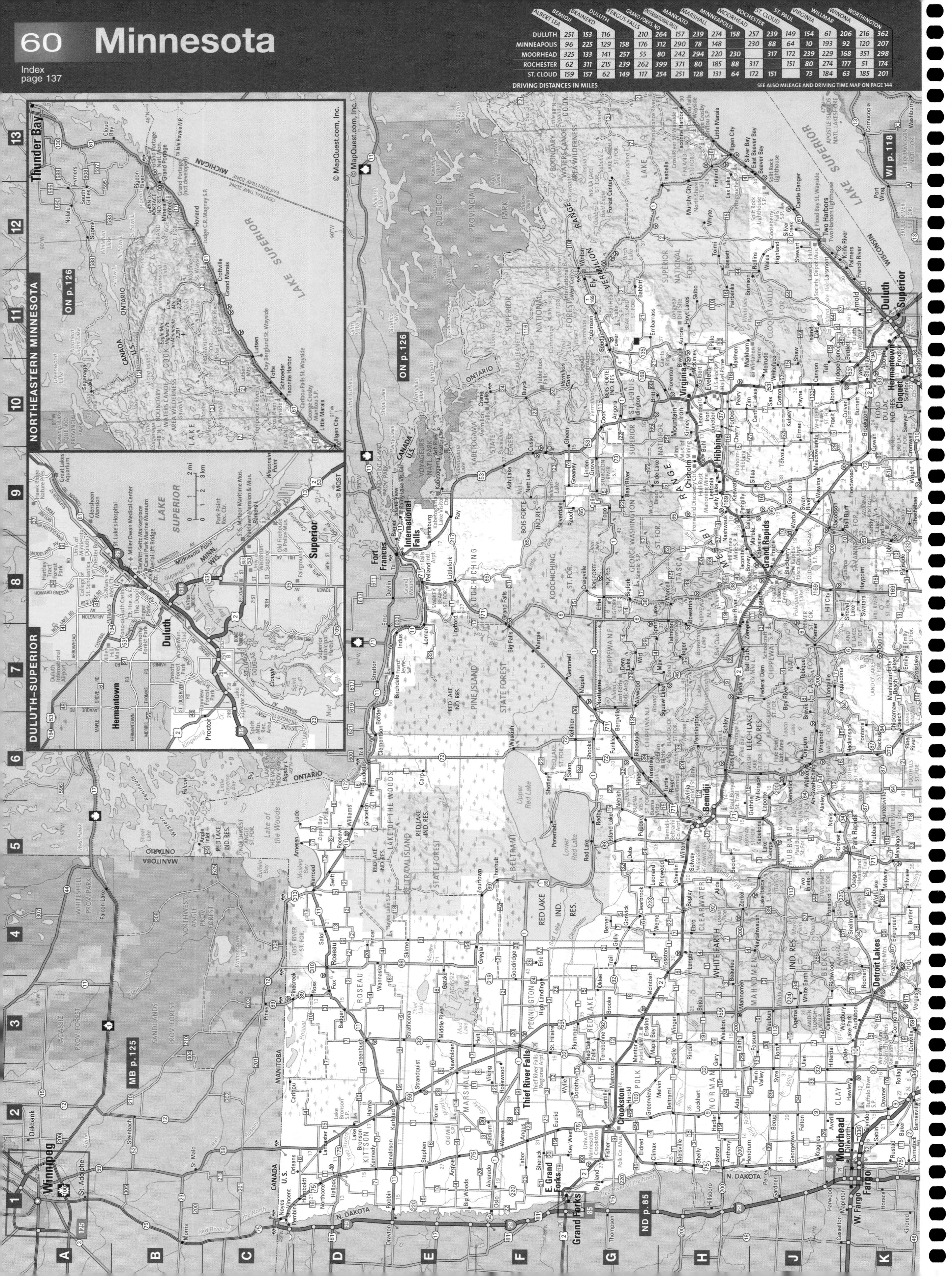

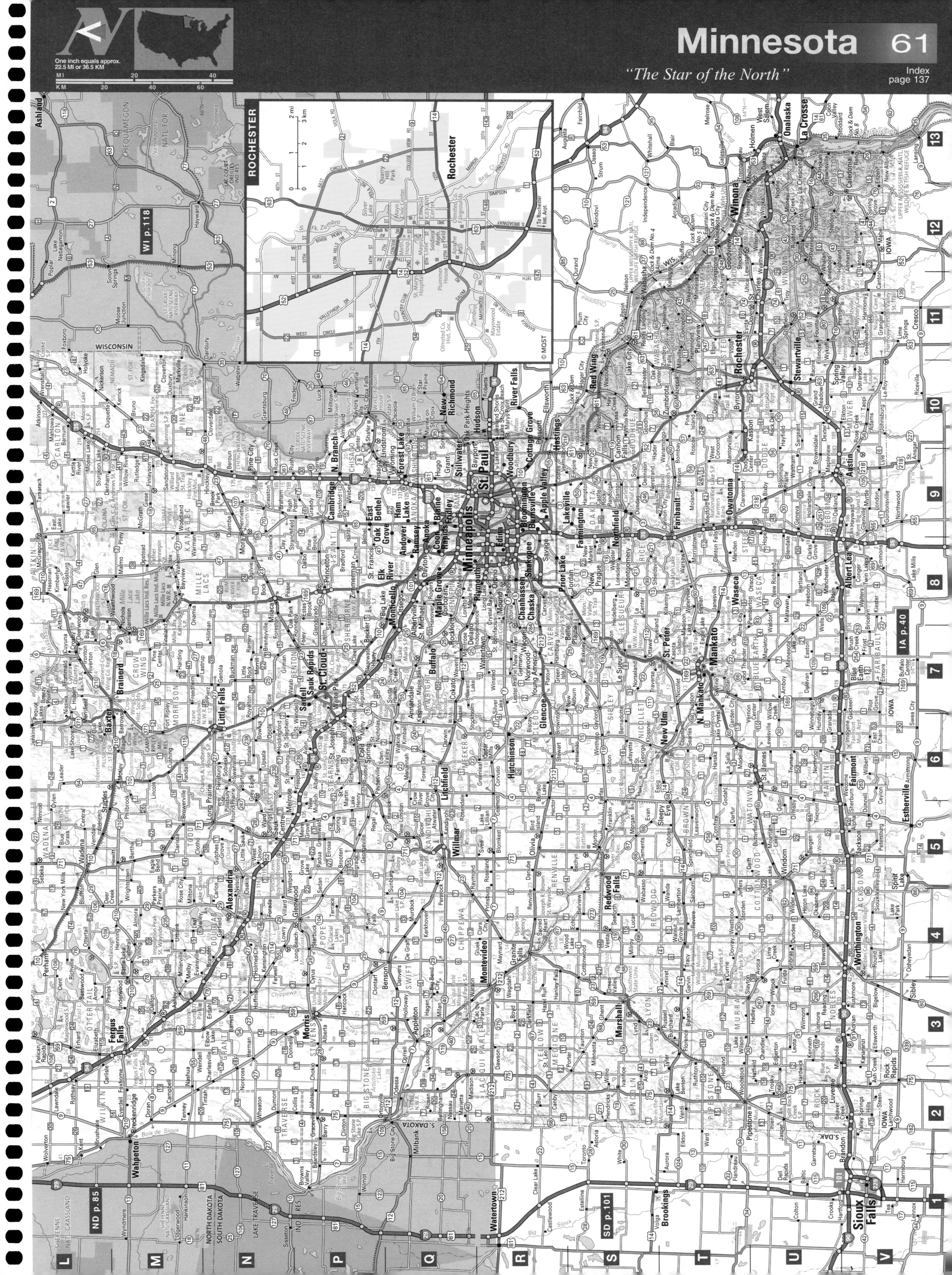
One inch equals approx. 22.5 MI or 36.5 KM
MI 20 40
KM 20 40 60
ROCHESTER
WI p.118
WISCONSIN
ND p.85
SD p.101
IA p.40
NORTH DAKOTA
SOUTH DAKOTA
S.DAKOTA
IOWA
Minneapolis
St. Paul
Rochester
Duluth
St. Cloud
Mankato
Winona
La Crosse
Onalaska
Sioux Falls
Brookings
Watertown
Wahpeton
Breckenridge
Fergus Falls
Alexandria
Brainerd
Baxter
Little Falls
Willmar
Hutchinson
Marshall
Worthington
Albert Lea
Austin
Owatonna
Faribault
Northfield
Red Wing
Hastings
Stillwater
Hudson
River Falls
New Ulm
Redwood Falls
Montevideo
Morris
Litchfield
Glencoe
Fairmont
Estherville
Ashland
Cambridge
Monticello
Buffalo
Waseca
St. Peter
Lakeville
Farmington
Cresco
Stewartville
Spirit Lake
Sibley
Luverne
Pipestone
Wadena
Perham
Staples
Milbank
Appleton
Windom
Jackson
L M N P Q R S T U V
1 2 3 4 5 6 7 8 9 10 11 12 13
© MOST

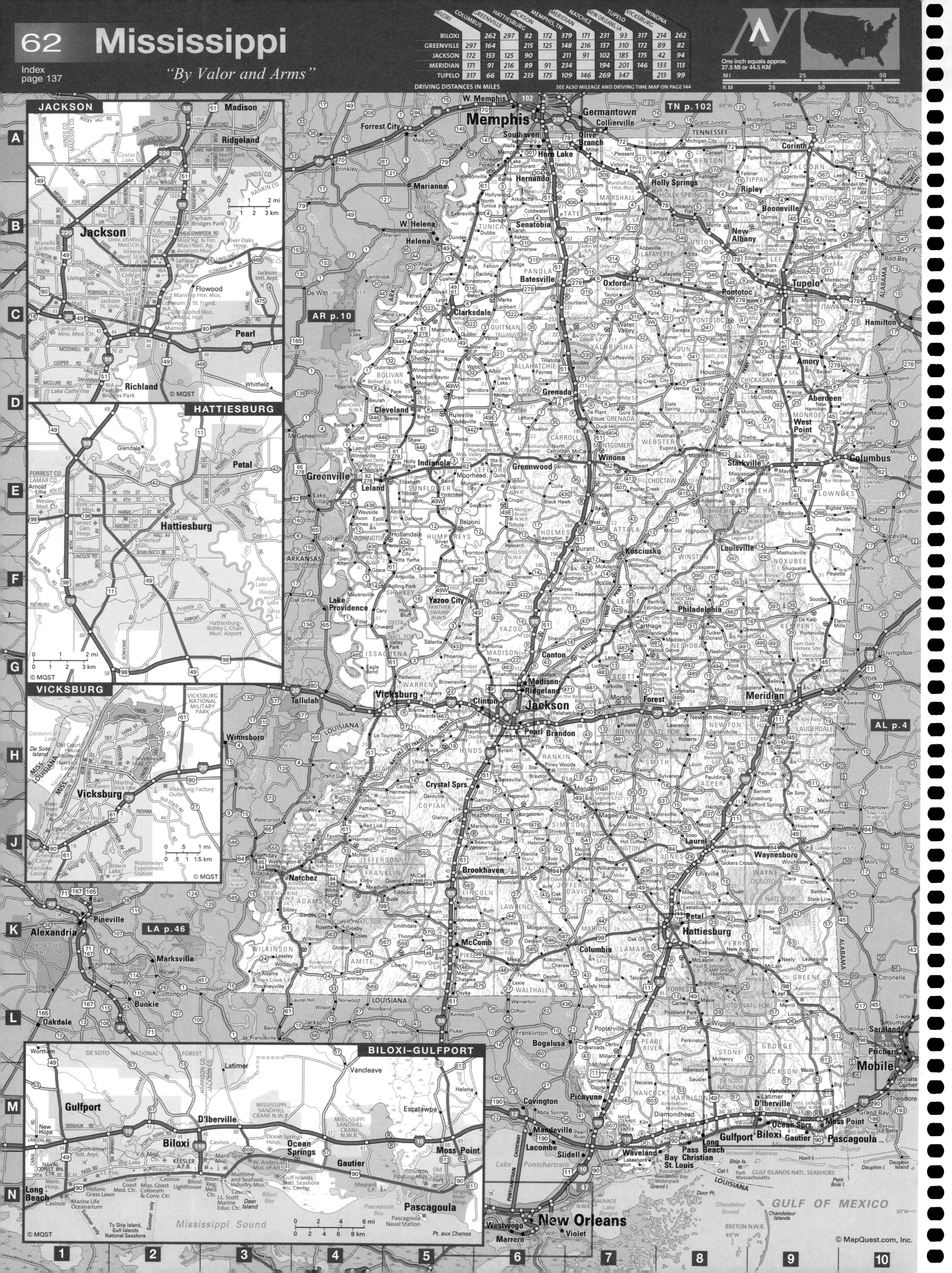

	BILOXI	COLUMBUS	GREENVILLE	HATTIESBURG	JACKSON	MEMPHIS, TN	MERIDIAN	NATCHEZ	NEW ORLEANS, LA	TUPELO	VICKSBURG	WINONA
BILOXI		262	297	82	172	379	171	231	93	317	214	262
GREENVILLE	297	164		215	125	148	216	157	310	172	89	82
JACKSON	172	153	125	90		211	91	102	185	175	42	94
MERIDIAN	171	91	216	89	91	234		194	201	146	133	113
TUPELO	317	66	172	235	175	109	146	269	347		213	99

Index page 138

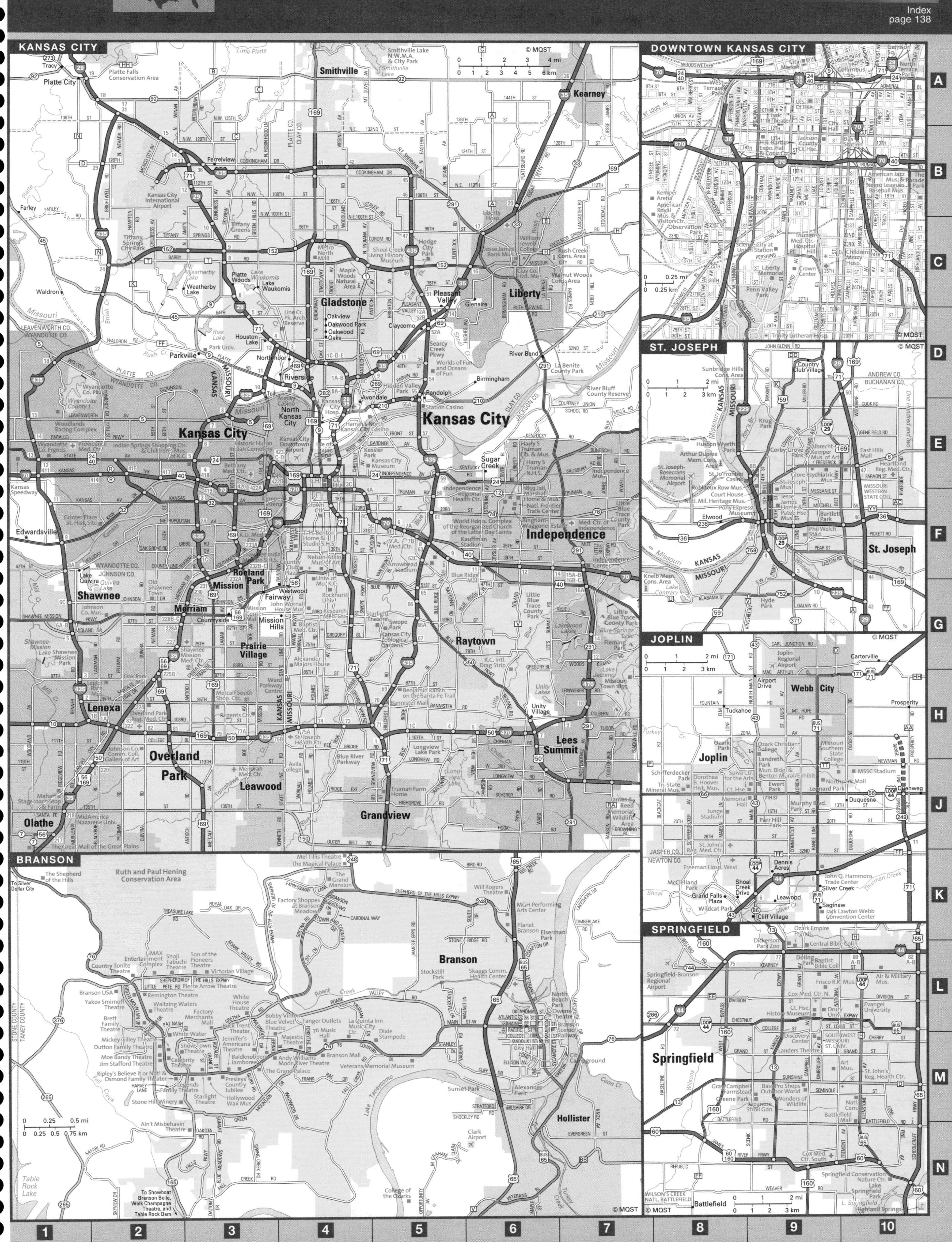

Index page 138

	BRANSON	CAPE GIRARDEAU	CHILLICOTHE	COLUMBIA	HANNIBAL	JEFFERSON CITY	JOPLIN	KANSAS CITY	KIRKSVILLE	NEVADA	POPLAR BLUFF	ROLLA	ST. JOSEPH	ST. LOUIS	SEDALIA	SIKESTON	SPRINGFIELD	WEST PLAINS
CAPE GIRARDEAU	347		357	234	228	243	382	363	322	374	75	205	419	120	303	36	307	175
COLUMBIA	203	234	124		101	32	238	129	89	206	269	97	185	123	69	265	163	194
KANSAS CITY	210	363	92	129	230	161	165		161	104	398	226	56	252	97	394	169	278
ST. LOUIS	249	120	247	123	117	132	284	252	212	276	156	107	308		192	151	209	204
SPRINGFIELD	41	307	200	163	241	131	70	169	251	95	191	110	225	209	108	238		109

DRIVING DISTANCES IN MILES

SEE ALSO MILEAGE AND DRIVING TIME MAP ON PAGE 144

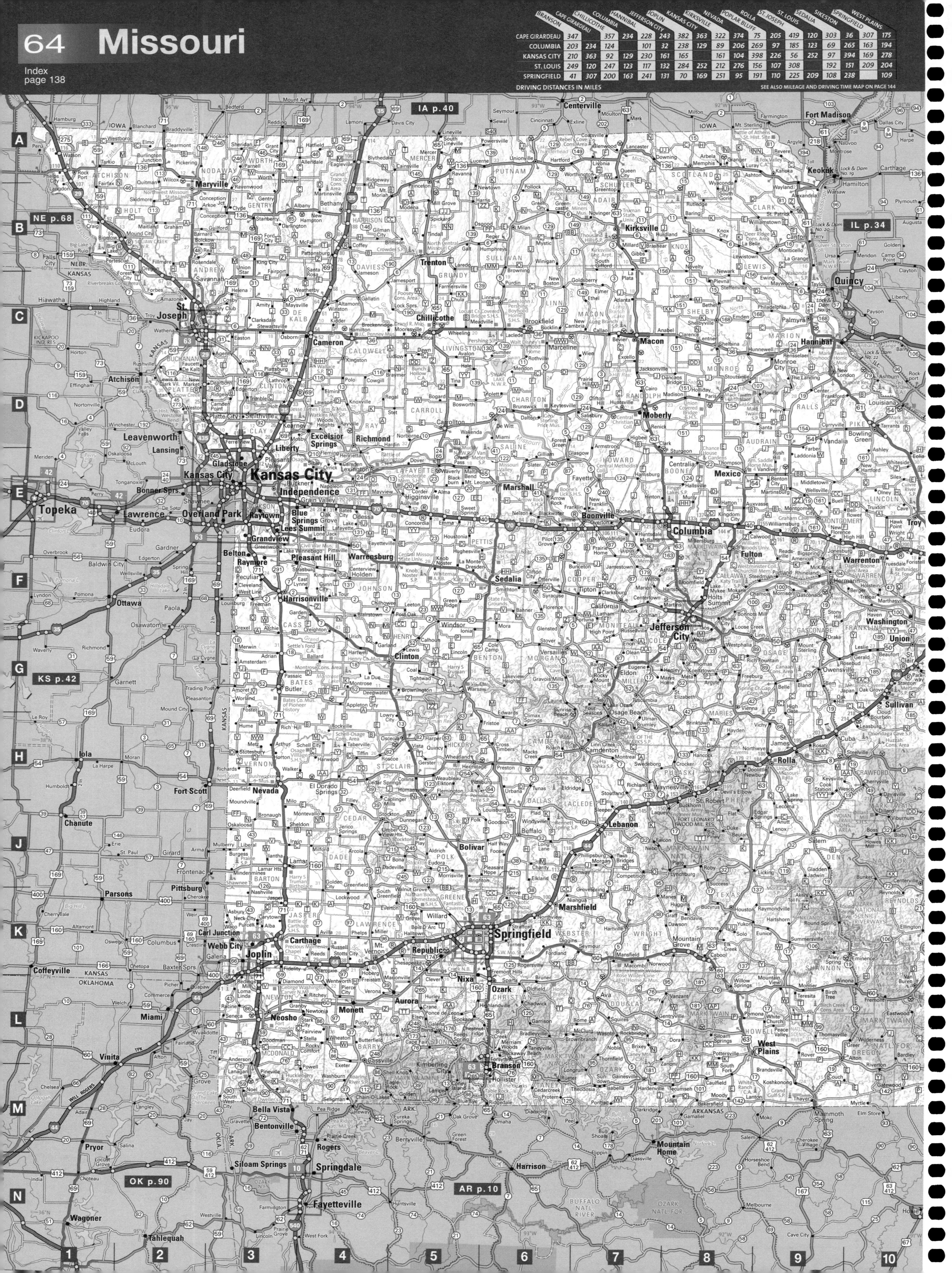

One inch equals approx. 25 MI or 40 KM

MI 20 40
KM 20 40 60

"The Welfare of the People Shall Be the Supreme Law"

Index page 138

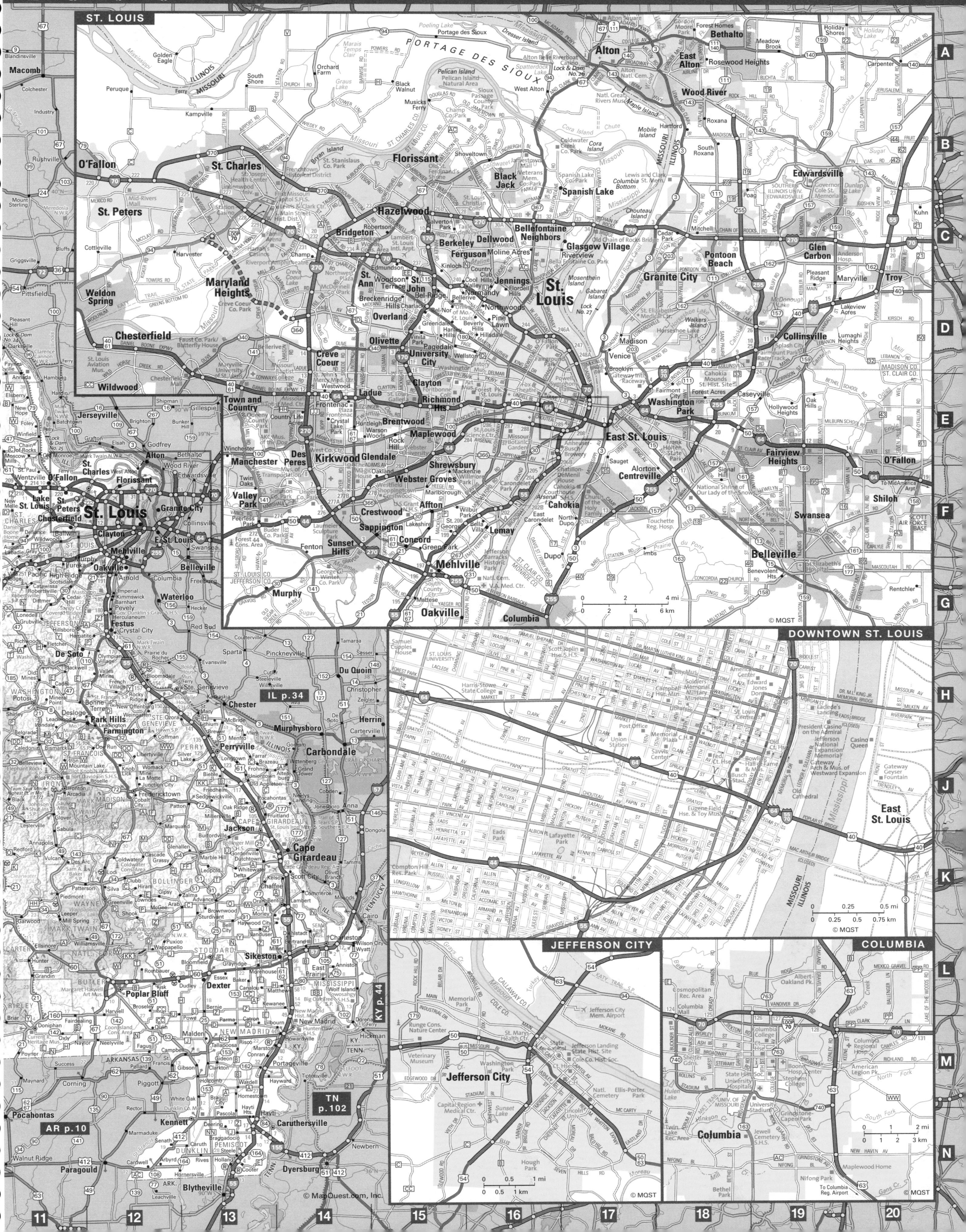

ST. LOUIS

DOWNTOWN ST. LOUIS

JEFFERSON CITY

COLUMBIA

IL p.34

KY p. 44

TN p.102

AR p.10

Montana

Index page 138

	BILLINGS	BOZEMAN	BROWNING	BUTTE	DILLON	GLASGOW	GLENDIVE	GREAT FALLS	HAVRE	HELENA	KALISPELL	LEWISTOWN	MILES CITY	MISSOULA	SHELBY	SHERIDAN, WY	WEST GLACIER	WEST YELLOWSTONE
BILLINGS		141	346	223	253	277	217	222	249	235	454	125	144	340	304	131	474	232
BUTTE	223	81	241		63	430	439	153	271	71	232	247	367	118	235	354	252	162
GREAT FALLS	222	176	124	153	215	277	351		118	85	222	109	329	199	82	353	192	257
HELENA	235	94	174	71	132	362	452	85	203		195	192	379	114	168	366	216	174
MISSOULA	340	199	201	118	171	476	557	199	317	114	116	306	484		227	471	136	279

DRIVING DISTANCES IN MILES

SEE ALSO MILEAGE AND DRIVING TIME MAP ON PAGE 144

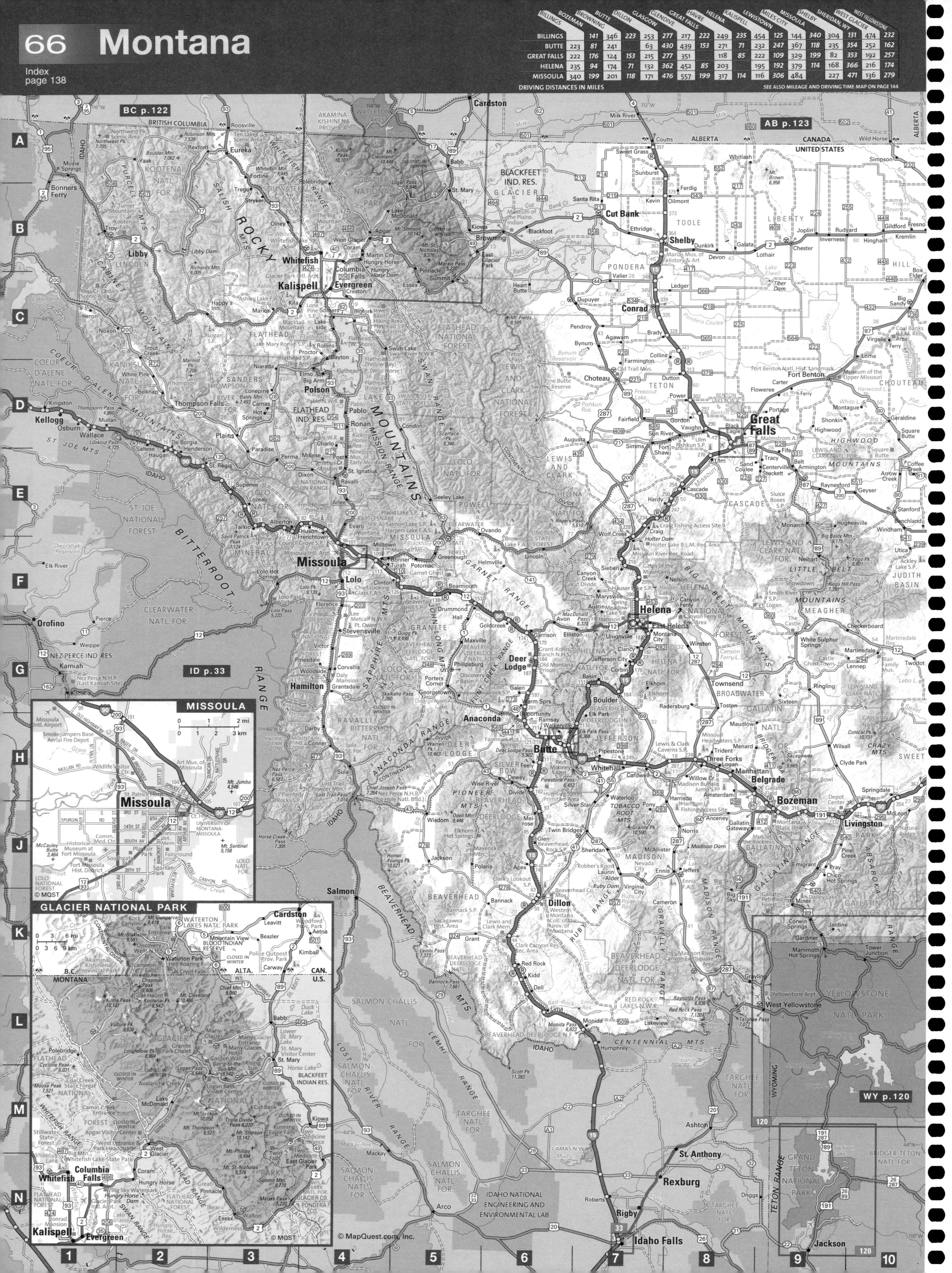

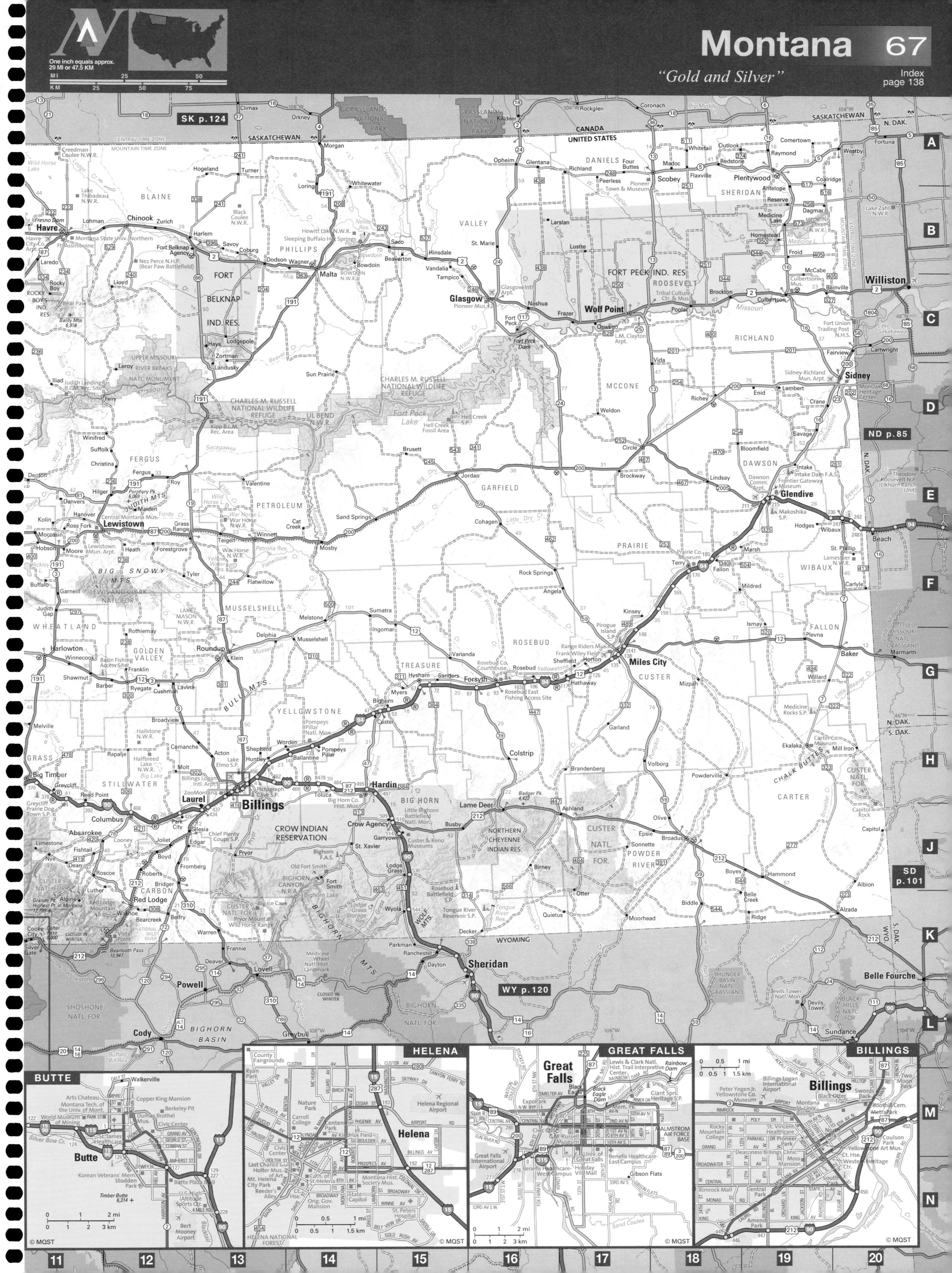

Montana 67
"Gold and Silver"
Index page 138
One inch equals approx. 29 MI or 47.5 KM
SK p.124
ND p.85
SD p.101
WY p.120
SASKATCHEWAN
CANADA
UNITED STATES
N. DAK.
S. DAK.
WYOMING
CENTRAL TIME ZONE
MOUNTAIN TIME ZONE
BLAINE
PHILLIPS
VALLEY
DANIELS
SHERIDAN
ROOSEVELT
RICHLAND
MCCONE
DAWSON
GARFIELD
PRAIRIE
WIBAUX
FALLON
CUSTER
CARTER
ROSEBUD
TREASURE
PETROLEUM
FERGUS
MUSSELSHELL
WHEATLAND
GOLDEN VALLEY
YELLOWSTONE
STILLWATER
CARBON
BIG HORN
POWDER RIVER
SWEET GRASS
FORT BELKNAP IND. RES.
FORT PECK IND. RES.
CROW INDIAN RESERVATION
NORTHERN CHEYENNE INDIAN RES.
CHARLES M. RUSSELL NATIONAL WILDLIFE REFUGE
UPPER MISSOURI RIVER BREAKS NAT'L MONUMENT
CUSTER NATL. FOR.
LEWIS AND CLARK NATL. FOR.
SHOSHONE NATL. FOR.
BIGHORN NATL. FOR.
BIGHORN CANYON N.R.A.
Fort Peck Lake
Havre
Chinook
Malta
Glasgow
Wolf Point
Williston
Sidney
Glendive
Miles City
Lewistown
Roundup
Billings
Laurel
Hardin
Big Timber
Columbus
Red Lodge
Sheridan
Powell
Cody
Baker
Plentywood
Scobey
Jordan
Forsyth
Circle
Ekalaka
Broadus
Lame Deer
Crow Agency
Belle Fourche
HELENA
Helena
GREAT FALLS
Great Falls
BILLINGS
Billings
BUTTE
Butte
© MQST
11
12
13
14
15
16
17
18
19
20
A
B
C
D
E
F
G
H
J
K
L
M
N

Index
page 138

	ALLIANCE	BEATRICE	CHADRON	COLUMBUS	GRAND ISLAND	HASTINGS	KEARNEY	LINCOLN	MC COOK	NEBRASKA CITY	NORFOLK	NORTH PLATTE	OGALLALA	OMAHA	O'NEILL	SCOTTSBLUFF	SOUTH SIOUX CITY	VALENTINE
GRAND ISLAND	317	135	373	64		23	49	95	147	144	105	143	196	150	111	318	179	210
LINCOLN	397	40	453	77	95	102	129		226	49	119	223	275	58	207	397	154	302
NORTH PLATTE	174	262	230	207	143	150	98	223	67	271	248		53	278	203	175	374	131
OMAHA	452	97	508	84	150	157	184	58	281	50	115	278	330		188	452	99	298
SCOTTSBLUFF	55	437	96	382	318	325	273	397	242	446	423	175	122	452	324		549	214

DRIVING DISTANCES IN MILES

SEE ALSO MILEAGE AND DRIVING TIME MAP ON PAGE 144

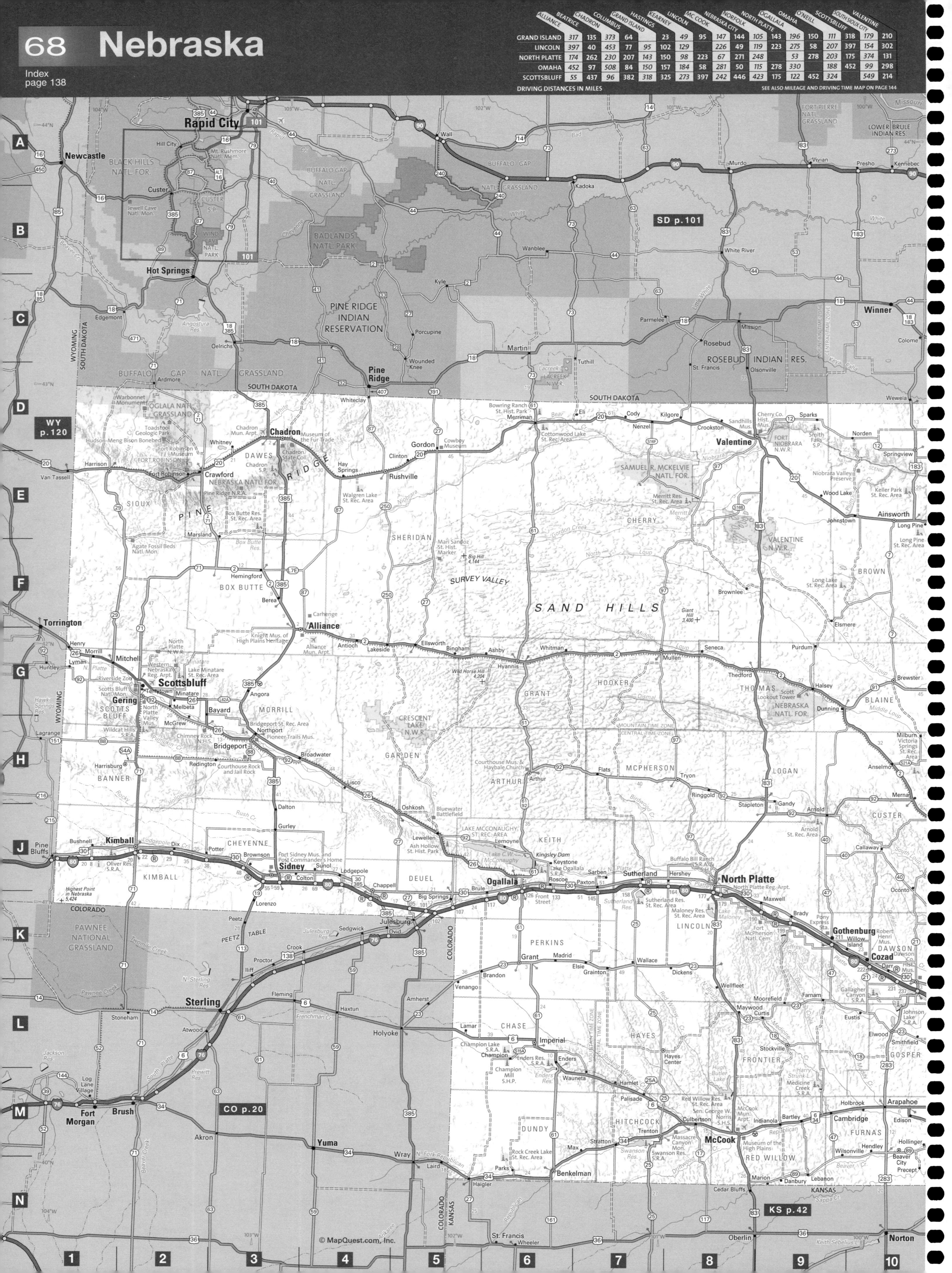

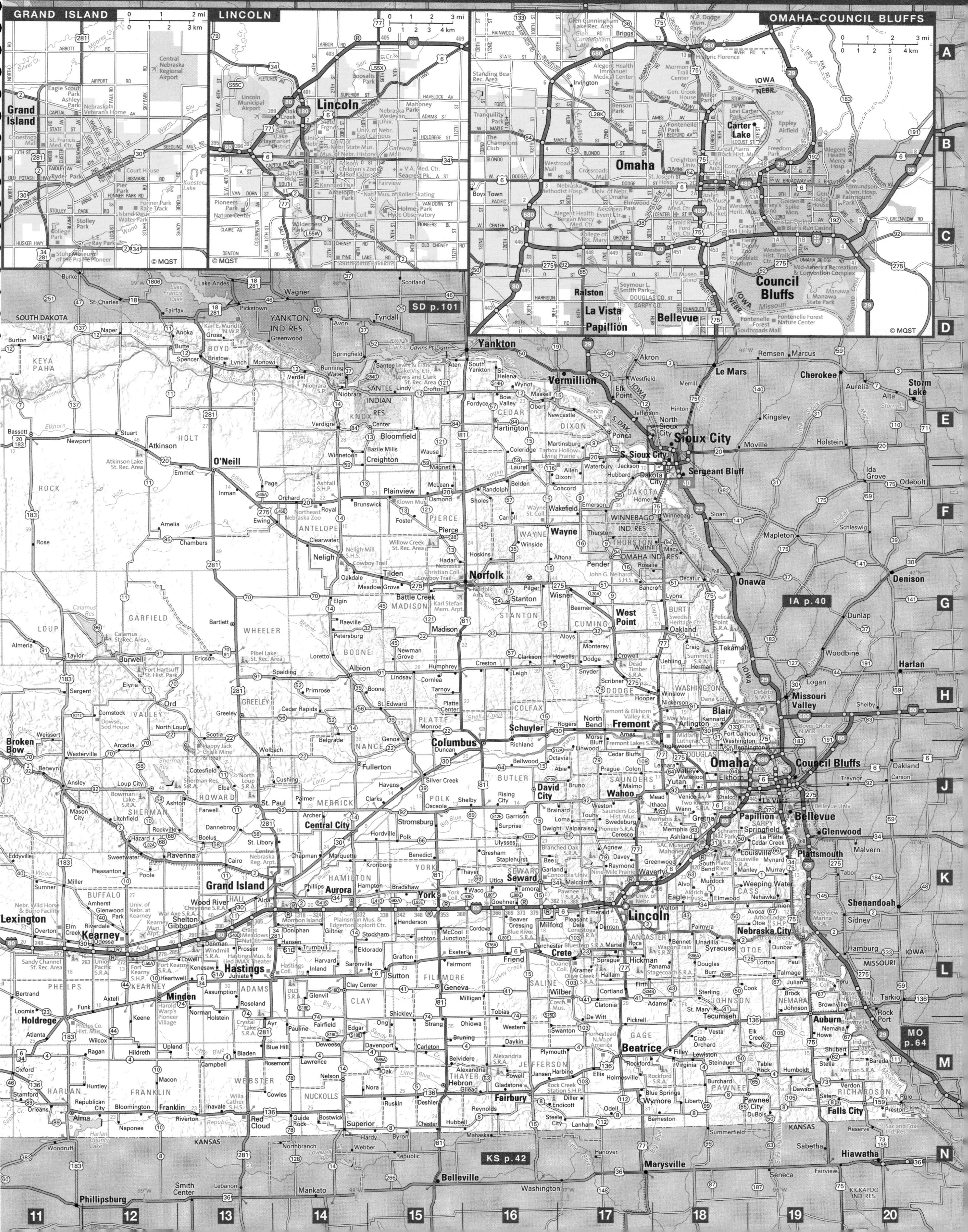

One inch equals approx. 22.5 MI or 36 KM

MI 20 40

KM 20 40 60

GRAND ISLAND

LINCOLN

OMAHA–COUNCIL BLUFFS

© MQST

SD p.101

IA p.40

MO p.64

KS p.42

SOUTH DAKOTA

IOWA

MISSOURI

KANSAS

A B C D E F G H J K L M N

11 12 13 14 15 16 17 18 19 20

Index page 138

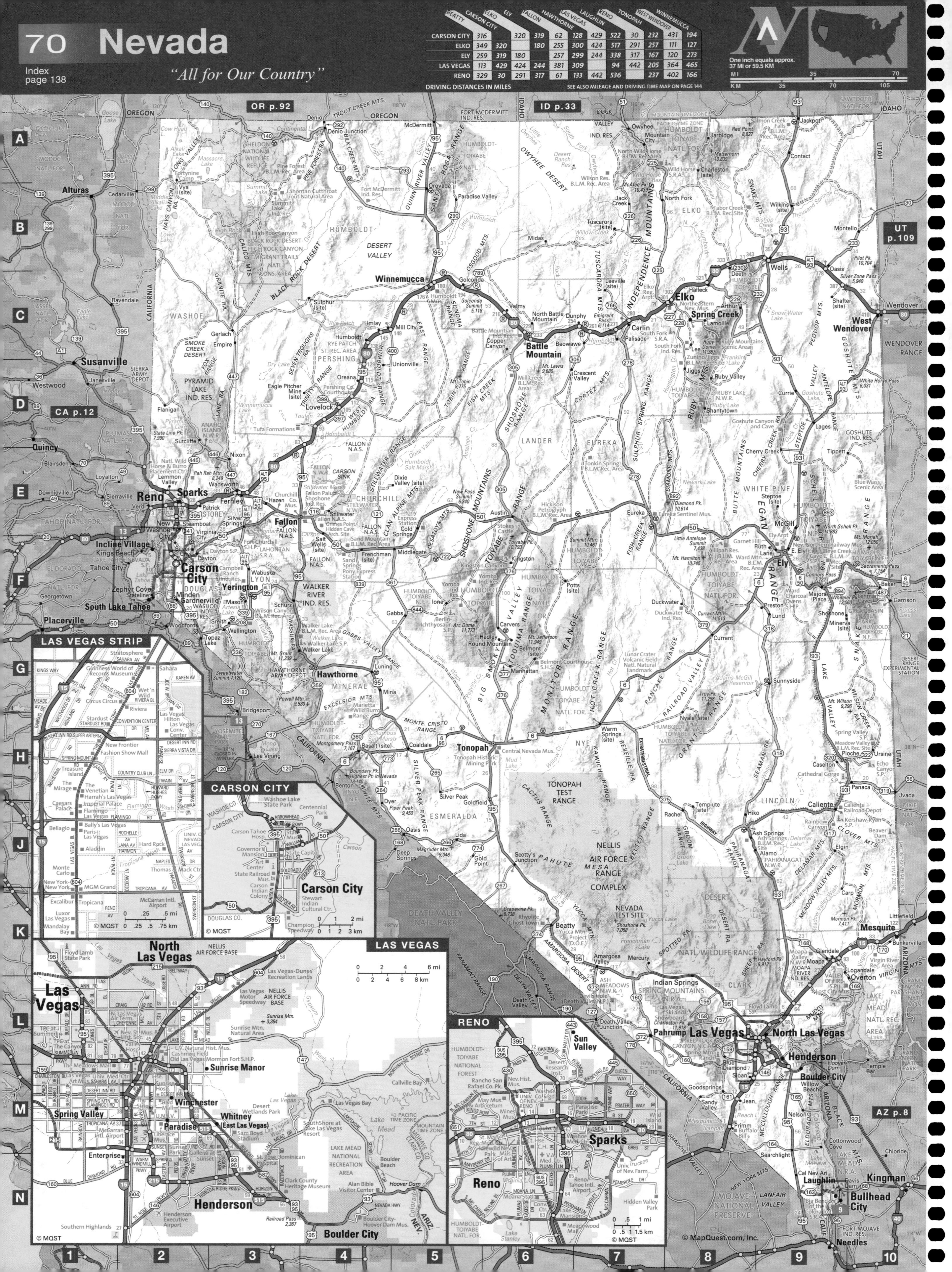

DRIVING DISTANCES IN MILES

	BEATTY	CARSON CITY	ELKO	ELY	FALLON	HAWTHORNE	LAS VEGAS	LAUGHLIN	RENO	TONOPAH	WEST WENDOVER	WINNEMUCCA
CARSON CITY	316		320	319	62	128	429	522	30	232	431	194
ELKO	349	320		180	255	300	424	517	291	257	111	127
ELY	259	319	180		257	299	244	338	317	167	120	273
LAS VEGAS	113	429	424	244	381	309		94	442	205	364	465
RENO	329	30	291	317	61	133	442	536		237	402	166

SEE ALSO MILEAGE AND DRIVING TIME MAP ON PAGE 144

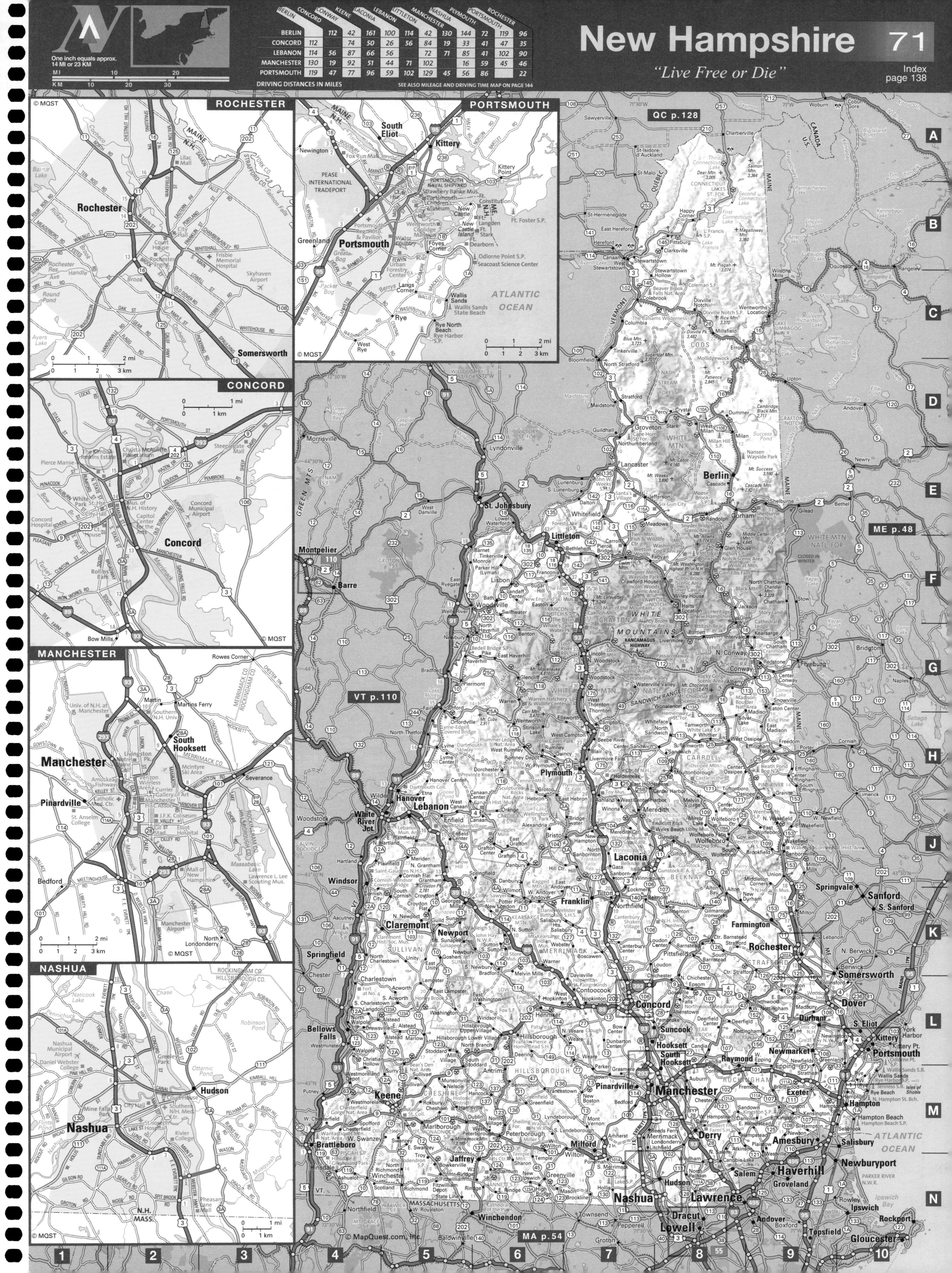

	BERLIN	CONCORD	CONWAY	KEENE	LACONIA	LEBANON	LITTLETON	MANCHESTER	NASHUA	PLYMOUTH	PORTSMOUTH	ROCHESTER
BERLIN		112	42	161	100	114	42	130	144	72	119	96
CONCORD	112		74	50	26	56	84	19	33	41	47	35
LEBANON	114	56	87	66	56		72	71	85	41	102	90
MANCHESTER	130	19	92	51	44	71	102		16	59	45	46
PORTSMOUTH	119	47	77	96	59	102	129	45	56	86		22

DRIVING DISTANCES IN MILES

SEE ALSO MILEAGE AND DRIVING TIME MAP ON PAGE 144

Index page 138

	ATLANTIC CITY	CAMDEN	CAPE MAY	HACKENSACK	JERSEY CITY	LONG BRANCH	MORRISTOWN	NEW BRUNSWICK	NEW YORK, NY	NEWARK	NEWTON	PATERSON	PHILADELPHIA, PA	PHILLIPSBURG	TOMS RIVER	TRENTON	VINELAND	WILMINGTON, DE
ATLANTIC CITY		61	41	133	120	82	126	94	125	114	159	128	62	120	54	77	47	86
NEW YORK, NY	125	92	155	12	5	55	32	34		11	54	16	91	67	75	55	119	120
NEWARK	114	82	144	15	5	45	18	23	11		51	18	80	57	65	45	109	109
PHILADELPHIA, PA	62	2	92	98	86	77	82	55	91	80	94	94		58	58	34	36	30
TRENTON	77	35	107	63	50	53	47	22	55	45	63	58	34	50	48		68	68

DRIVING DISTANCES IN MILES

SEE ALSO MILEAGE AND DRIVING TIME MAP ON PAGE 144

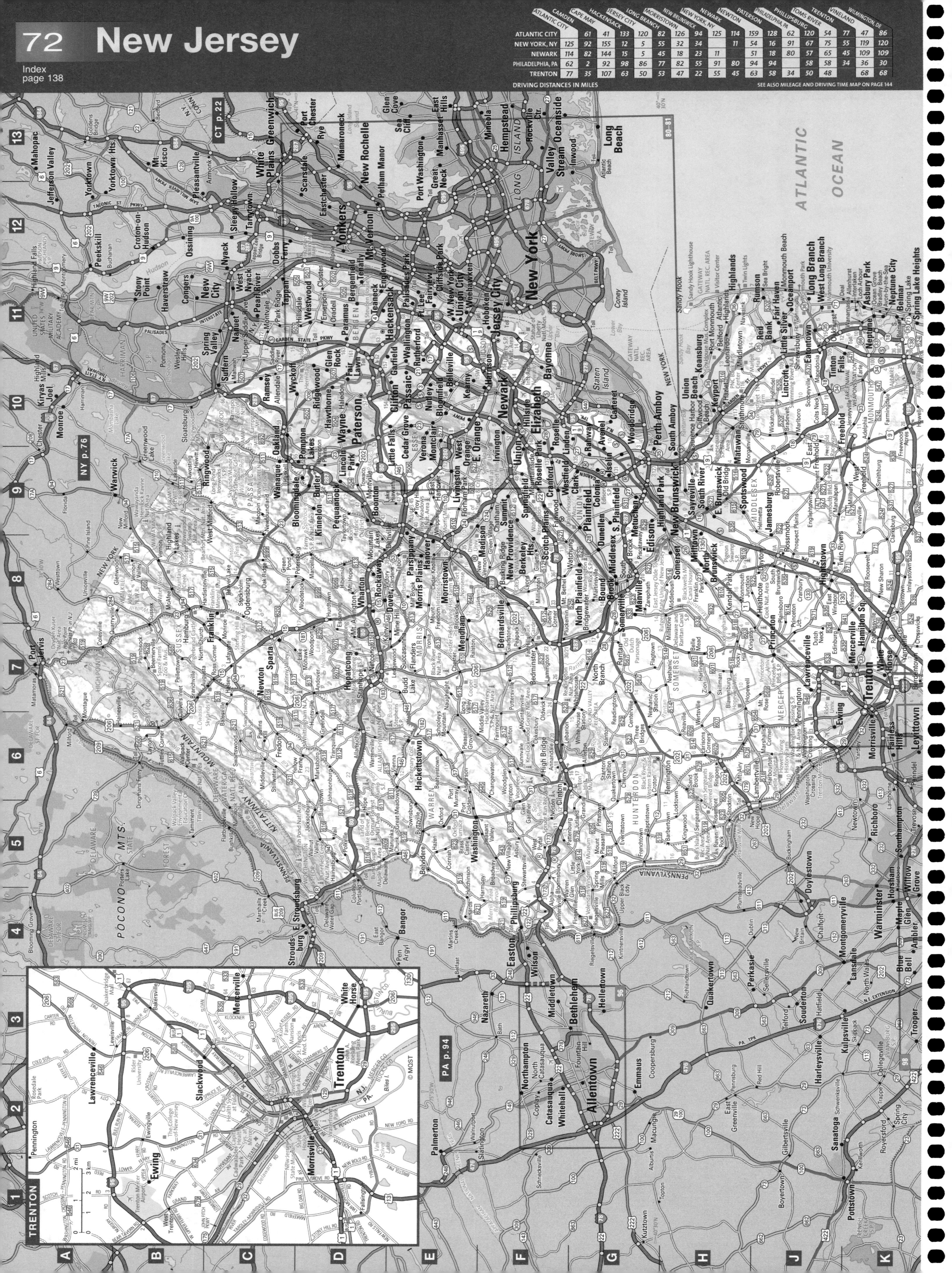

One inch equals approx. 8.5 MI or 13.5 KM

MI 5 10 15
KM 5 10 15 20

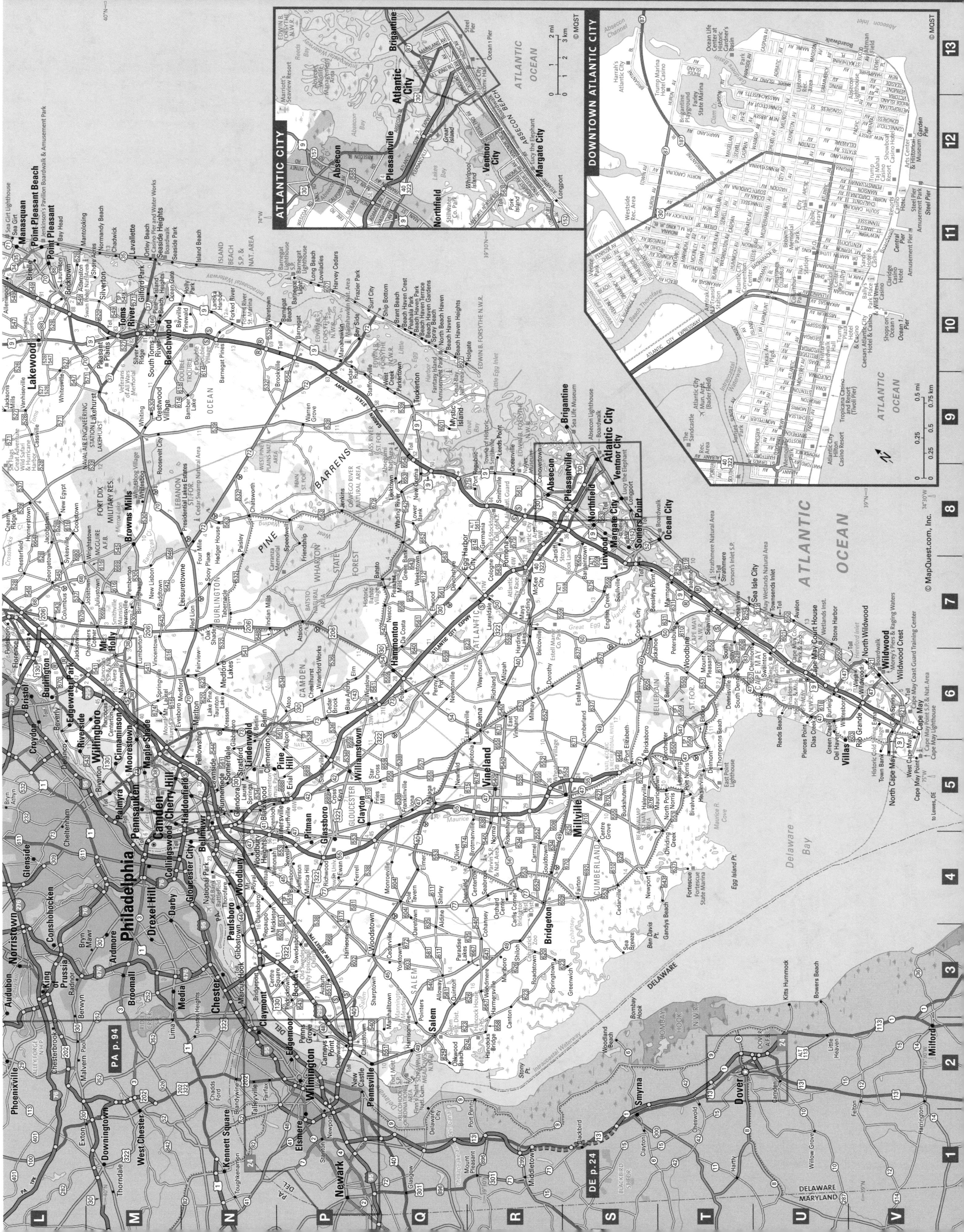

ATLANTIC CITY
DOWNTOWN ATLANTIC CITY
ATLANTIC OCEAN
Delaware Bay
PINE BARRENS
PA p. 94
DE p. 24
© MapQuest.com, Inc.

Index page 138

	ALAMOGORDO	ALBUQUERQUE	CARLSBAD	CLOVIS	EL PASO TX	FARMINGTON	GALLUP	HOBBS	LAS CRUCES	LAS VEGAS	LOS ALAMOS	RATON	ROSWELL	SANTA FE	SILVER CITY	SOCORRO	TAOS	TUCUMCARI
ALBUQUERQUE	213		275	220	263	181	141	316	220	115	92	221	199	55	234	77	123	174
FARMINGTON	399	181	455	401	450		120	496	407	264	196	300	379	205	361	263	211	355
LAS CRUCES	65	220	203	293	42	407	338	250		335	312	441	182	275	111	146	343	394
ROSWELL	117	199	76	110	203	379	340	117	182	178	228	284		191	293	164	248	161
SANTA FE	220	55	267	213	319	205	197	308	275	65	37	171	191		290	132	68	167

DRIVING DISTANCES IN MILES

SEE ALSO MILEAGE AND DRIVING TIME MAP ON PAGE 144

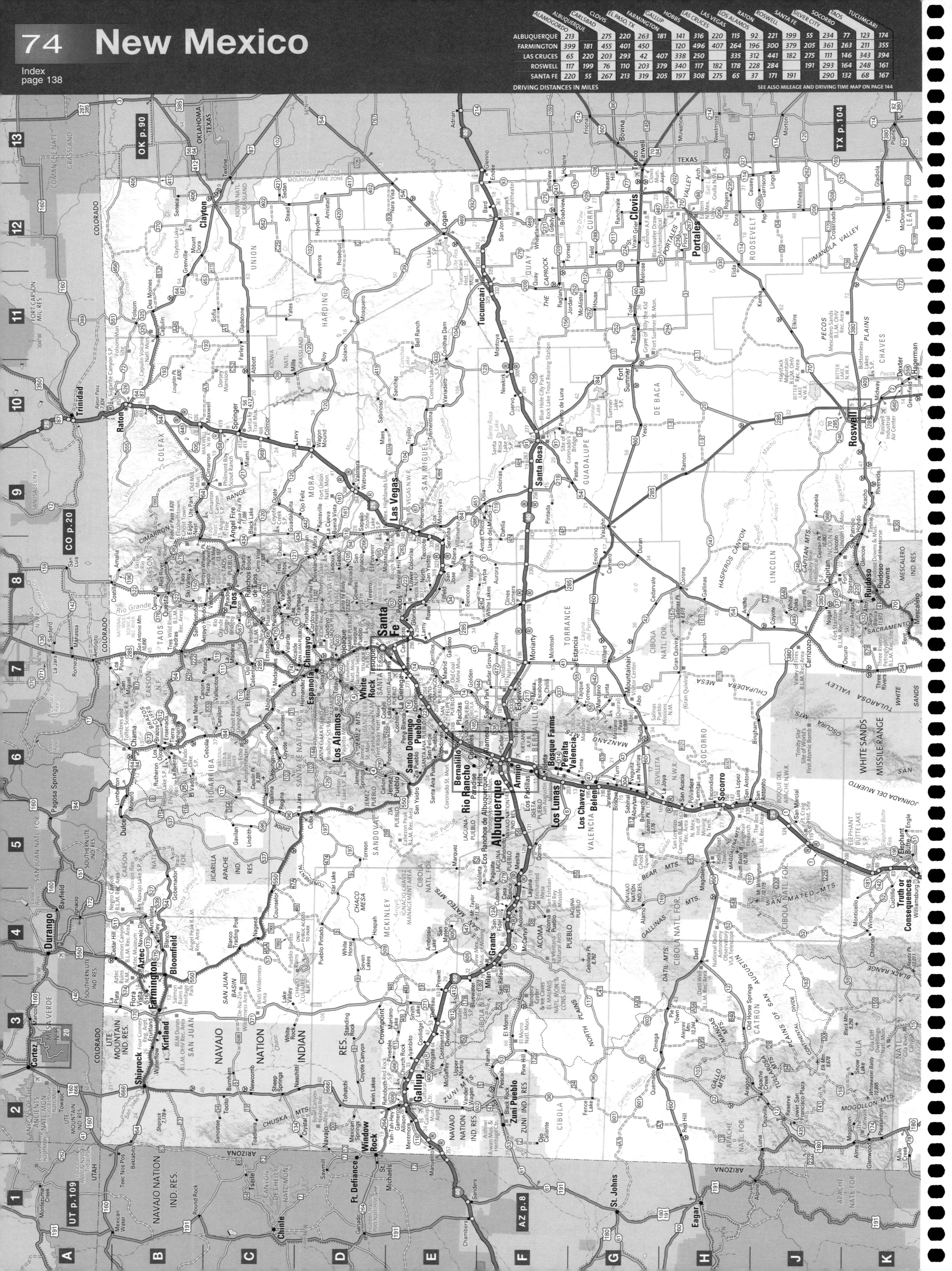

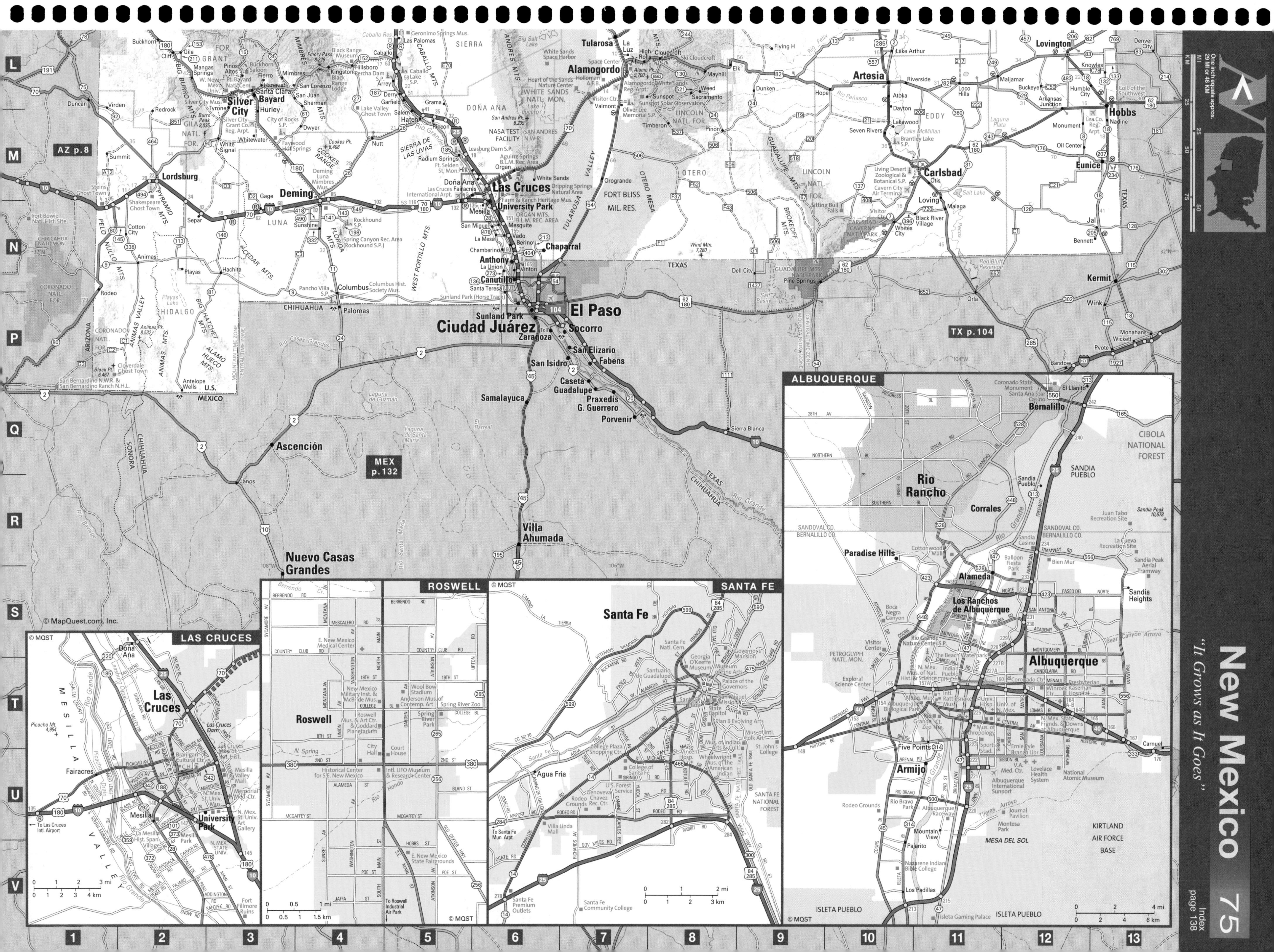
One inch equals approx. 29 MI or 46 KM
MI 25 50
KM 25 50 75
ALBUQUERQUE
SANTA FE
ROSWELL
LAS CRUCES
Albuquerque
Rio Rancho
Corrales
Bernalillo
Alameda
Los Ranchos de Albuquerque
Paradise Hills
Five Points
Armijo
KIRTLAND AIR FORCE BASE
SANDIA PUEBLO
ISLETA PUEBLO
CIBOLA NATIONAL FOREST
PETROGLYPH NATL. MON.
MESA DEL SOL
Santa Fe
Agua Fria
SANTA FE NATIONAL FOREST
Roswell
Las Cruces
Mesilla
University Park
Doña Ana
Fairacres
MESILLA VALLEY
El Paso
Ciudad Juárez
Socorro
San Elizario
Fabens
San Isidro
Caseta
Guadalupe
Praxedis G. Guerrero
Porvenir
Villa Ahumada
Samalayuca
Ascención
Nuevo Casas Grandes
Janos
Sunland Park
Anthony
Canutillo
Chaparral
Alamogordo
Tularosa
Carlsbad
Artesia
Hobbs
Lovington
Eunice
Kermit
Deming
Lordsburg
Silver City
Bayard
Hurley
Columbus
FORT BLISS MIL. RES.
TX p.104
MEX p.132
AZ p.8
TEXAS
CHIHUAHUA
SONORA
ARIZONA
MEXICO
CENTRAL TIME ZONE
MOUNTAIN TIME ZONE
© MapQuest.com, Inc.
© MQST

New York (north)

Index page 138

	ALBANY	BINGHAMTON	BUFFALO	COOPERSTOWN	GENEVA	ITHACA	JAMESTOWN	KINGSTON	LAKE PLACID	NEW YORK	NIAGARA FALLS	OLEAN	PLATTSBURGH	ROCHESTER	SARATOGA SPRINGS	SYRACUSE	UTICA	WATERTOWN
ALBANY		135	292	89	197	186	361	56	138	151	306	297	160	228	32	146	94	179
BINGHAMTON	135		225	78	97	53	214	125	253	176	239	164	276	161	160	76	95	139
BUFFALO	292	225		239	103	153	74	346	337	400	20	74	374	74	293	152	199	210
ROCHESTER	228	161	74	175	39	89	142	282	273	336	88	113	310		229	88	135	146
SYRACUSE	146	76	152	93	56	59	220	201	192	250	166	163	228	88	147		53	65

DRIVING DISTANCES IN MILES

SEE ALSO MILEAGE AND DRIVING TIME MAP ON PAGE 144

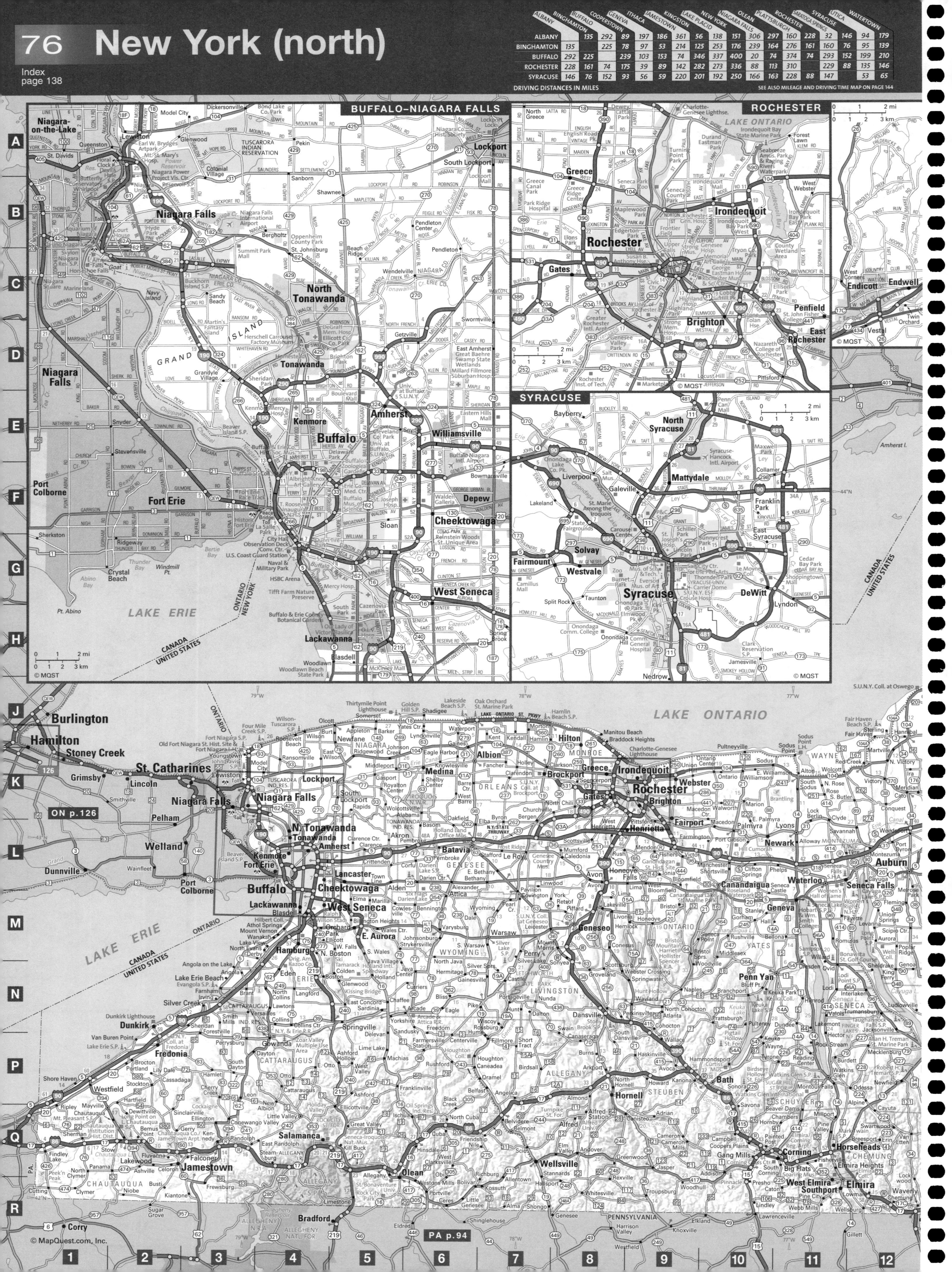

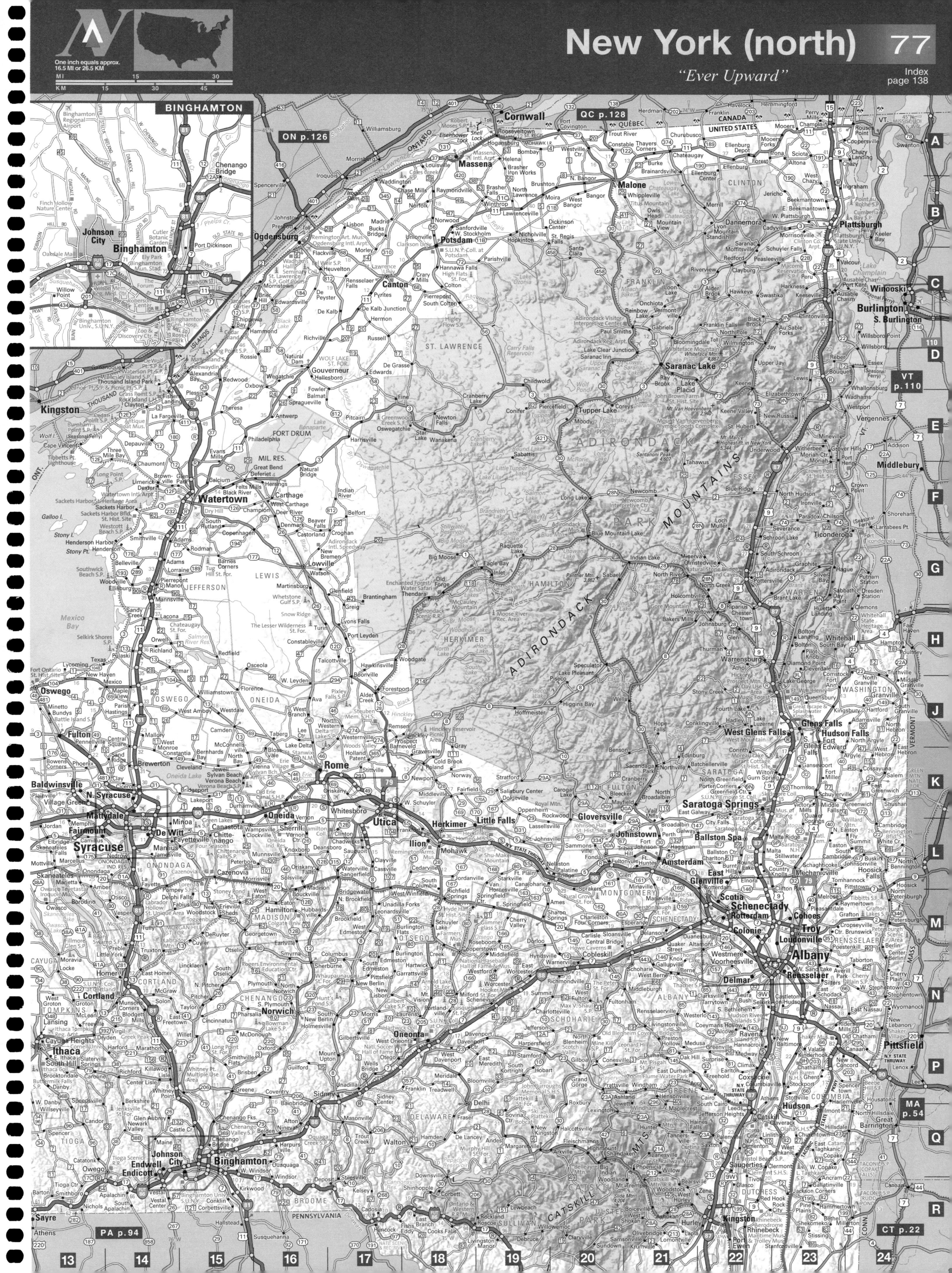

One inch equals approx. 16.5 MI or 26.5 KM
MI 15 30
KM 15 30 45
BINGHAMTON
Johnson City
Binghamton
Chenango Bridge
Port Dickinson
ON p.126
QC p.128
QUÉBEC
CANADA
UNITED STATES
Cornwall
Massena
Malone
Ogdensburg
Potsdam
Canton
Plattsburgh
Burlington
S. Burlington
Winooski
Kingston
Watertown
Saranac Lake
Lake Placid
Tupper Lake
ADIRONDACK PARK MOUNTAINS
ADIRONDACK
ST. LAWRENCE
FRANKLIN
CLINTON
ESSEX
HAMILTON
WARREN
HERKIMER
LEWIS
JEFFERSON
OSWEGO
ONEIDA
ONONDAGA
MADISON
CORTLAND
CHENANGO
OTSEGO
DELAWARE
SCHOHARIE
ALBANY
GREENE
ULSTER
SULLIVAN
BROOME
TIOGA
TOMPKINS
CAYUGA
FULTON
MONTGOMERY
SARATOGA
SCHENECTADY
RENSSELAER
COLUMBIA
DUTCHESS
WASHINGTON
FORT DRUM
MIL. RES.
Middlebury
Ticonderoga
VT p.110
Oswego
Fulton
Syracuse
N. Syracuse
Mattydale
Baldwinsville
Fairmount
De Witt
Oneida
Rome
Utica
Ilion
Herkimer
Little Falls
Gloversville
Johnstown
Amsterdam
Saratoga Springs
Ballston Spa
Glens Falls
Hudson Falls
West Glens Falls
Schenectady
Scotia
Glenville
Rotterdam
Colonie
Cohoes
Troy
Loudonville
Albany
Rensselaer
Delmar
Pittsfield
MA p.54
Hudson
Catskill
Saugerties
Kingston
Rhinebeck
Great Barrington
CATSKILL MTS.
CATSKILL PARK
Oneonta
Norwich
Cortland
Ithaca
Cayuga Heights
Sidney
Endicott
Endwell
Johnson City
Binghamton
Owego
Sayre
Athens
PENNSYLVANIA
PA p.94
CT p.22
VERMONT
MASS
CONN.
N.Y. STATE THRUWAY
A
B
C
D
E
F
G
H
J
K
L
M
N
P
Q
R
13
14
15
16
17
18
19
20
21
22
23
24

Index page 138

	ALBANY	BINGHAMTON	BUFFALO	HEMPSTEAD	KINGSTON	MIDDLETOWN	MONTAUK	MONTICELLO	NEWBURGH	NEW YORK	PEEKSKILL	PORT JEFFERSON	PORT JERVIS	POUGHKEEPSIE	RIVERHEAD	ROCHESTER	SYRACUSE	WHITE PLAINS
ALBANY		135	292	182	56	105	276	103	89	151	107	214	121	79	234	228	146	148
BINGHAMTON	135		225	203	125	116	296	87	134	176	144	235	117	127	254	161	76	167
KINGSTON	56	125	346	132		55	225	53	39	101	57	164	71	20	183	282	201	98
NEWBURGH	89	134	357	74	39	26	167	47		56	18	106	42	22	125	294	208	42
NEW YORK	151	176	400	26	101	72	120	95	56		45	58	87	96	78	336	250	29

DRIVING DISTANCES IN MILES

SEE ALSO MILEAGE AND DRIVING TIME MAP ON PAGE 144

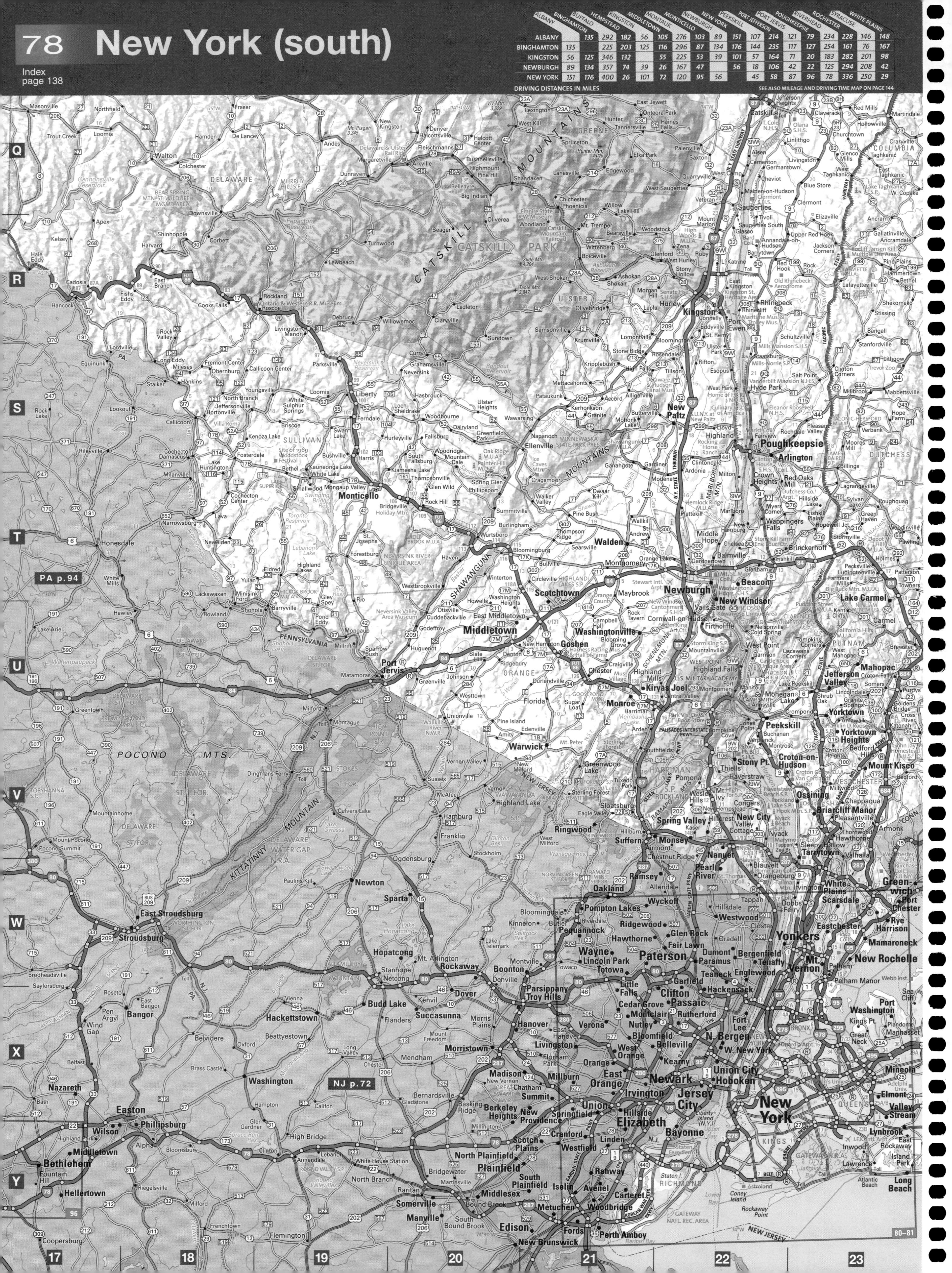

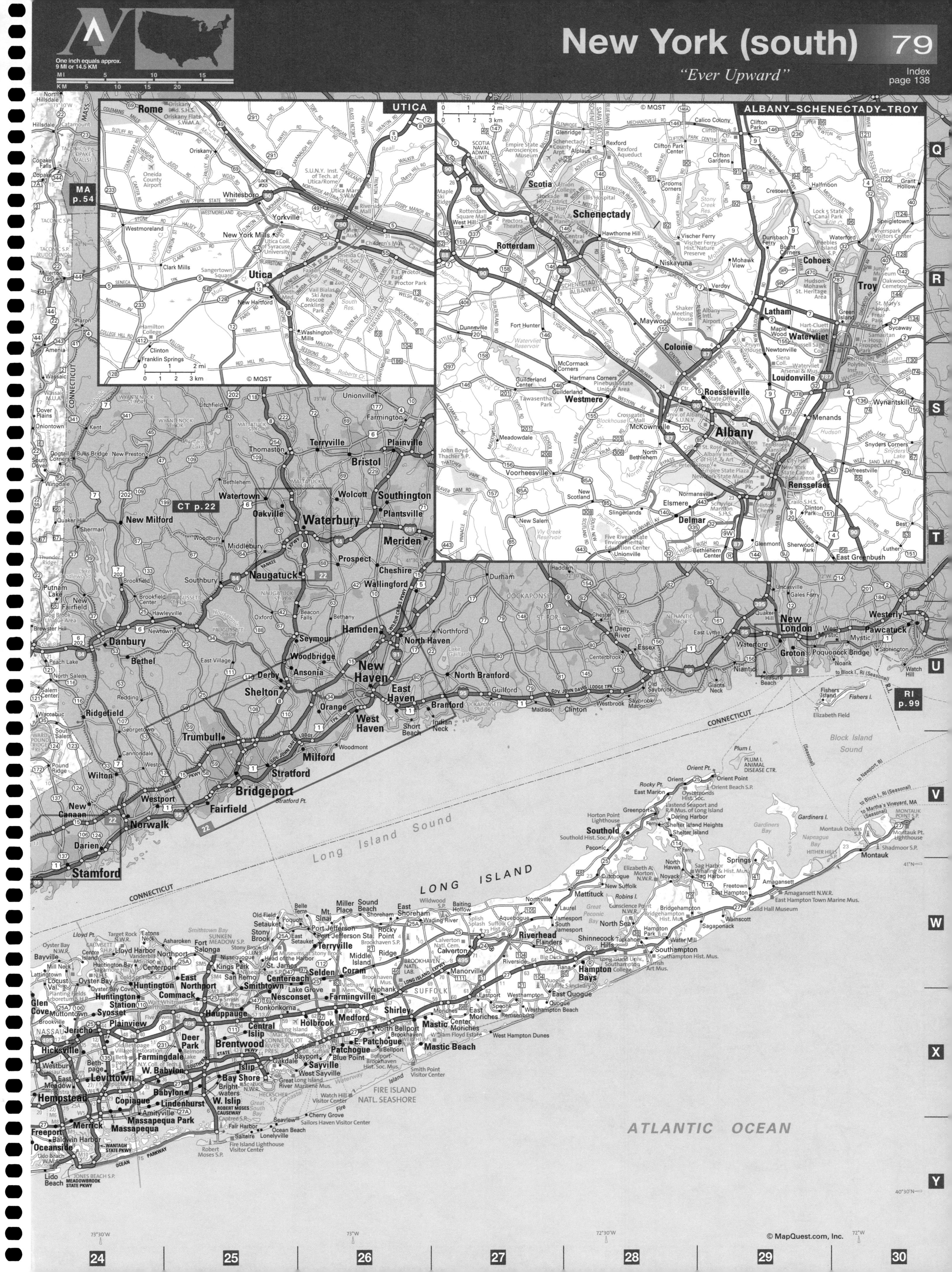
New York (south)
79
"Ever Upward"
Index
page 138
One inch equals approx.
9 MI or 14.5 KM
UTICA
ALBANY-SCHENECTADY-TROY
© MQST
Rome
Oriskany
Whitesboro
Yorkville
New York Mills
Utica
Clark Mills
New Hartford
Washington Mills
Clinton
Franklin Springs
Hamilton College
Oneida County Airport
Scotia
Schenectady
Rotterdam
Glenville
Niskayuna
Latham
Cohoes
Troy
Colonie
Watervliet
Loudonville
Roessleville
Westmere
Albany
Menands
Rensselaer
Delmar
Elsmere
Voorheesville
Guilderland
McKownville
Wynantskill
Sycaway
Halfmoon
MA p.54
CT p.22
RI p.99
Q
R
S
T
U
V
W
X
Y
Danbury
New Milford
Watertown
Waterbury
Naugatuck
Southington
Bristol
Meriden
Wallingford
Cheshire
Hamden
New Haven
East Haven
Branford
West Haven
Orange
Milford
Stratford
Bridgeport
Fairfield
Trumbull
Shelton
Derby
Ansonia
Seymour
Westport
Norwalk
Wilton
Ridgefield
Bethel
New Canaan
Darien
Stamford
Clinton
Madison
Guilford
North Branford
Old Saybrook
Essex
Deep River
Chester
Niantic
Waterford
New London
Groton
Mystic
Westerly
Pawcatuck
Long Island Sound
CONNECTICUT
LONG ISLAND
Block Island Sound
ATLANTIC OCEAN
Orient Point
Greenport
Southold
Mattituck
Riverhead
Southampton
Hampton Bays
East Hampton
Montauk
Sag Harbor
Shirley
Mastic
Mastic Beach
Medford
Patchogue
Holbrook
Hauppauge
Brentwood
Central Islip
Bay Shore
West Islip
Babylon
Lindenhurst
Copiague
Massapequa
Massapequa Park
Farmingdale
Levittown
Hicksville
Hempstead
Merrick
Freeport
Oceanside
Jericho
Plainview
Syosset
Huntington
Huntington Station
Commack
Smithtown
East Northport
Centereach
Selden
Coram
Port Jefferson
Terryville
Sayville
FIRE ISLAND NATL. SEASHORE
© MapQuest.com, Inc.
24
25
26
27
28
29
30

Index page 138

One inch equals approx. 3 MI or 4.5 KM

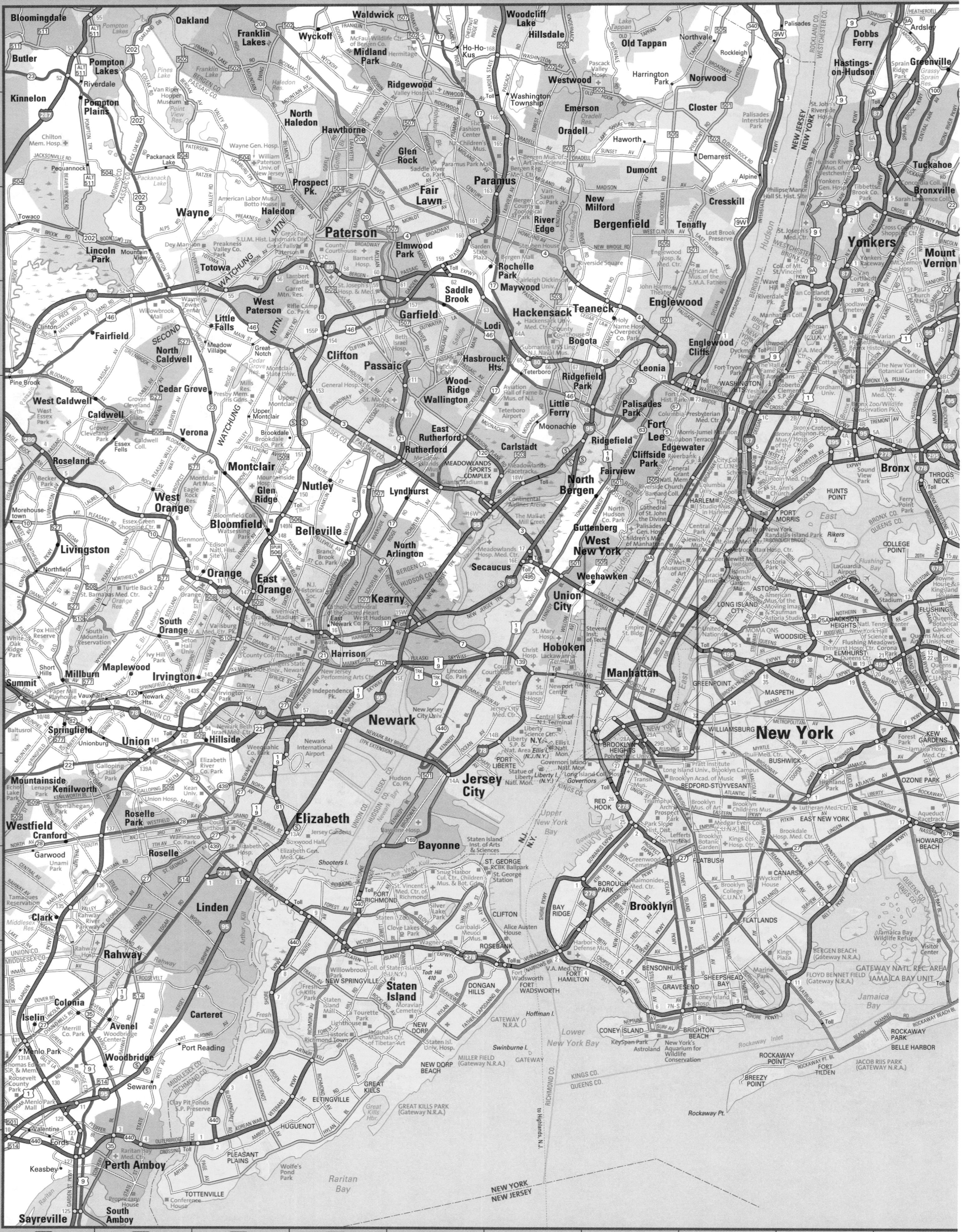

MI 2 4

KM 2 4 6

Bloomingdale
Oakland
Waldwick
Woodcliff Lake
Hillsdale
Wyckoff
Franklin Lakes
Midland Park
Ho-Ho-Kus
Old Tappan
Northvale
Rockleigh
Palisades
Dobbs Ferry
Ardsley
Butler
Pompton Lakes
Riverdale
Westwood
Norwood
Harrington Park
Hastings-on-Hudson
Greenville
Kinnelon
Pompton Plains
Ridgewood
Washington Township
Emerson
Closter
North Haledon
Hawthorne
Oradell
Haworth
Demarest
Glen Rock
Paramus
Dumont
Tuckahoe
Prospect Pk.
Fair Lawn
New Milford
Cresskill
Bronxville
Wayne
Haledon
River Edge
Bergenfield
Tenafly
Paterson
Elmwood Park
Yonkers
Mount Vernon
Lincoln Park
Totowa
Rochelle Park
Maywood
Saddle Brook
Englewood
West Paterson
Garfield
Hackensack
Teaneck
Little Falls
Lodi
Bogota
Englewood Cliffs
Fairfield
North Caldwell
Clifton
Passaic
Hasbrouck Hts.
Leonia
Cedar Grove
Ridgefield Park
West Caldwell
Wood-Ridge
Wallington
Little Ferry
Palisades Park
Caldwell
Moonachie
Fort Lee
Verona
East Rutherford
Rutherford
Ridgefield
Edgewater
Roseland
Montclair
Carlstadt
Cliffside Park
Nutley
Fairview
North Bergen
Bronx
Glen Ridge
Lyndhurst
West Orange
Bloomfield
Belleville
Guttenberg
West New York
Livingston
North Arlington
Secaucus
Weehawken
Orange
East Orange
Union City
Kearny
Harrison
Hoboken
South Orange
Manhattan
Maplewood
Irvington
Millburn
Summit
Newark
Springfield
Union
Hillside
Jersey City
New York
Kenilworth
Mountainside
Roselle Park
Elizabeth
Bayonne
Westfield
Cranford
Roselle
Garwood
Linden
Brooklyn
Clark
Rahway
Staten Island
Carteret
Colonia
Iselin
Avenel
Woodbridge
Menlo Park
Sewaren
Perth Amboy
Sayreville
South Amboy
Tottenville
Huguenot
Eltingville
Great Kills
New Dorp Beach
Coney Island
Brighton Beach
Rockaway Point
Breezy Point
Rockaway Park
Belle Harbor
Jamaica Bay
Lower New York Bay
Upper New York Bay
Raritan Bay
Newark Bay
Gateway Natl. Rec. Area Jamaica Bay Unit
New York / New Jersey

A B C D E F G H J K L M N

1 2 3 4 5 6 7 8 9 10

Index
page 138

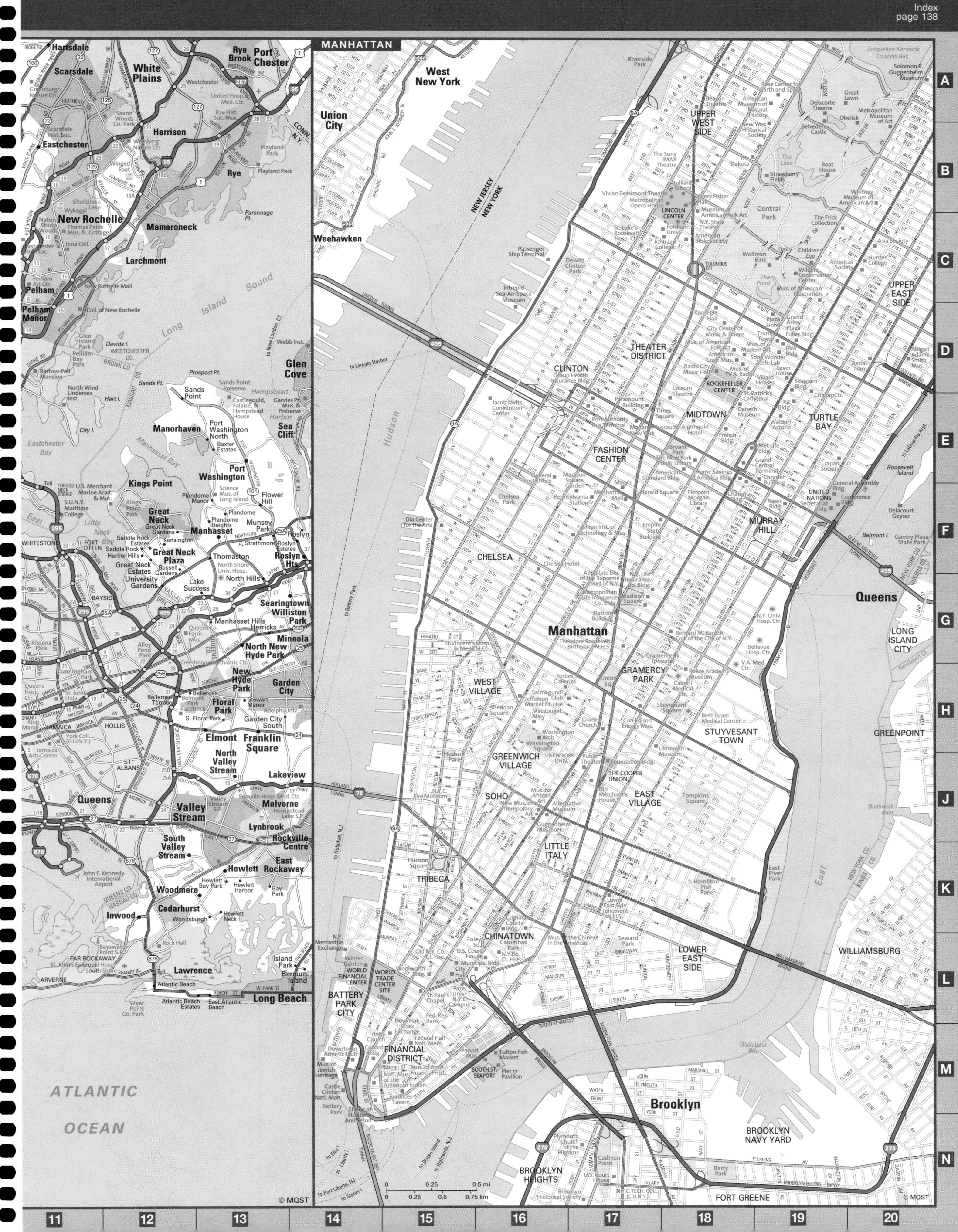

Index
page 139

	ASHEVILLE	BOONE	CHARLOTTE	DURHAM	ELIZABETH CITY	FAYETTEVILLE	GREENSBORO	GREENVILLE	HICKORY	JACKSONVILLE	KINSTON	MOREHEAD CITY	NAGS HEAD	RALEIGH	ROCKINGHAM	ROCKY MOUNT	WILMINGTON	WINSTON-SALEM
ASHEVILLE		198	116	224	404	264	176	324	78	354	316	383	444	242	190	297	368	146
CHARLOTTE	116	95		139	319	139	91	239	48	269	232	298	359	158	74	213	205	79
GREENSBORO	176	117	91	49	228	90		148	98	179	141	207	268	67	83	122	193	30
RALEIGH	242	183	158	24	160	62	67	80	164	113	76	142	200		96	54	127	96
WILMINGTON	368	309	205	150	211	92	193	123	290	52	93	95	241	127	131	153		222

DRIVING DISTANCES IN MILES

SEE ALSO MILEAGE AND DRIVING TIME MAP ON PAGE 144

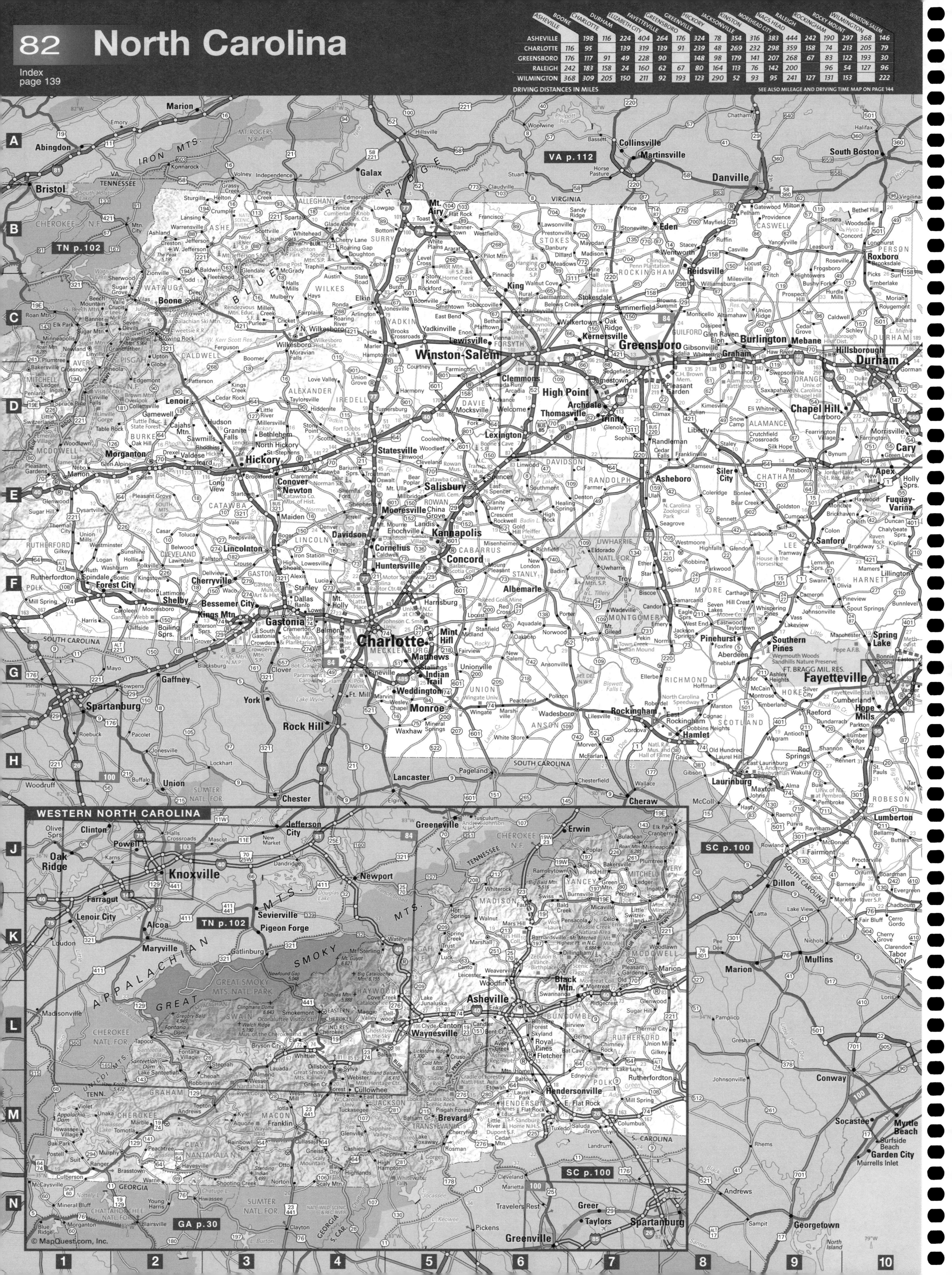

"To Be, Rather than to Seem"

Index page 139

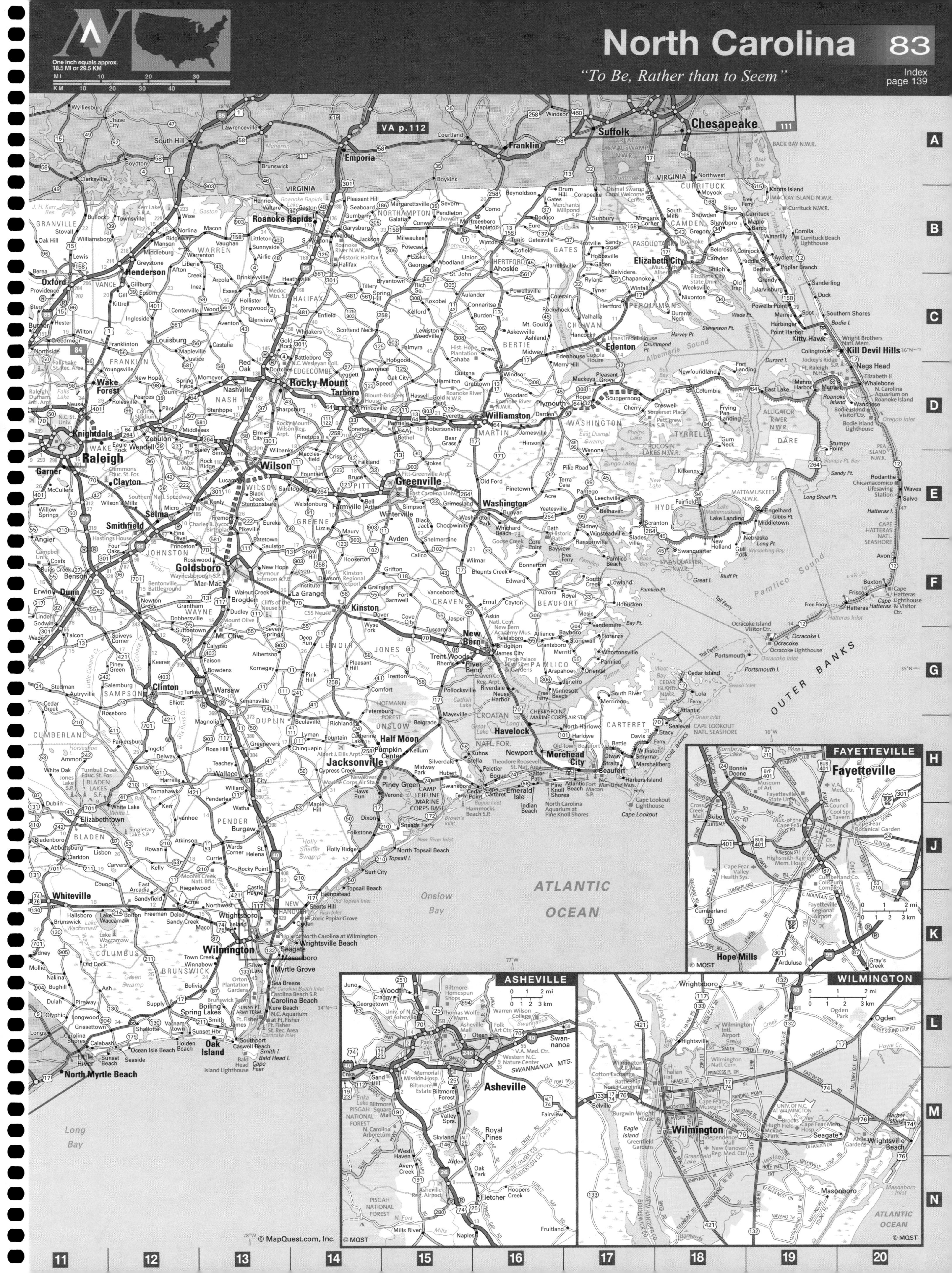

North Carolina (cities)

Index page 139

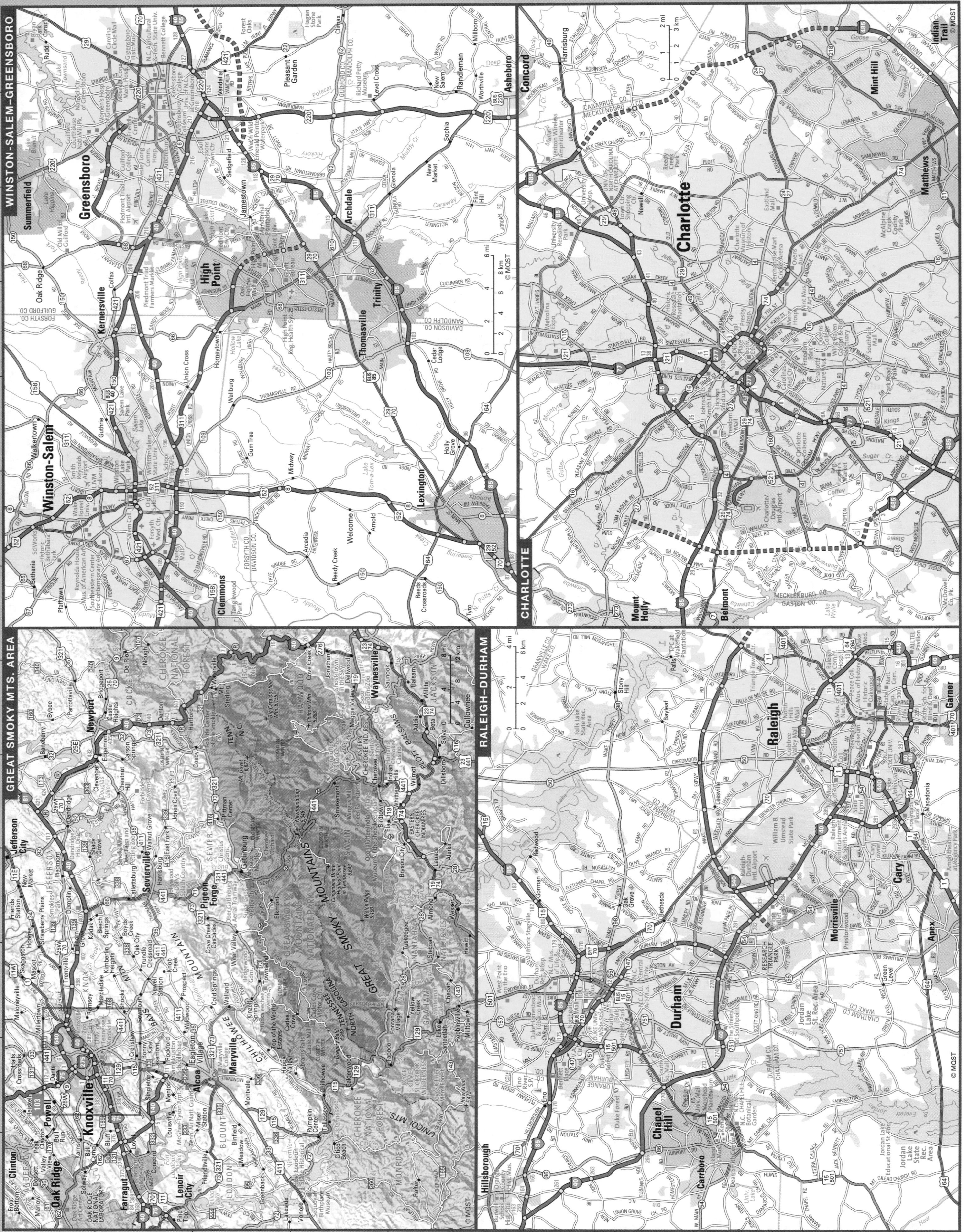

WINSTON-SALEM–GREENSBORO

CHARLOTTE

GREAT SMOKY MTS. AREA

RALEIGH-DURHAM

"Liberty and Union, Now and Forever, One and Inseparable"

Index page 139

	BISMARCK	DEVILS LAKE	DICKINSON	FARGO	GRAND FORKS	JAMESTOWN	MINOT	PEMBINA	RUGBY	VALLEY CITY	WAHPETON	WILLISTON
BISMARCK		186	97	199	274	105	116	347	153	141	249	229
DICKINSON	97	278		291	367	197	178	440	245	234	341	133
FARGO	199	163	291		79	97	268	152	221	58	55	424
GRAND FORKS	274	91	367	79		173	212	77	148	133	130	340
MINOT	116	122	178	268	212	171		238	64	210	318	128

DRIVING DISTANCES IN MILES

SEE ALSO MILEAGE AND DRIVING TIME MAP ON PAGE 144

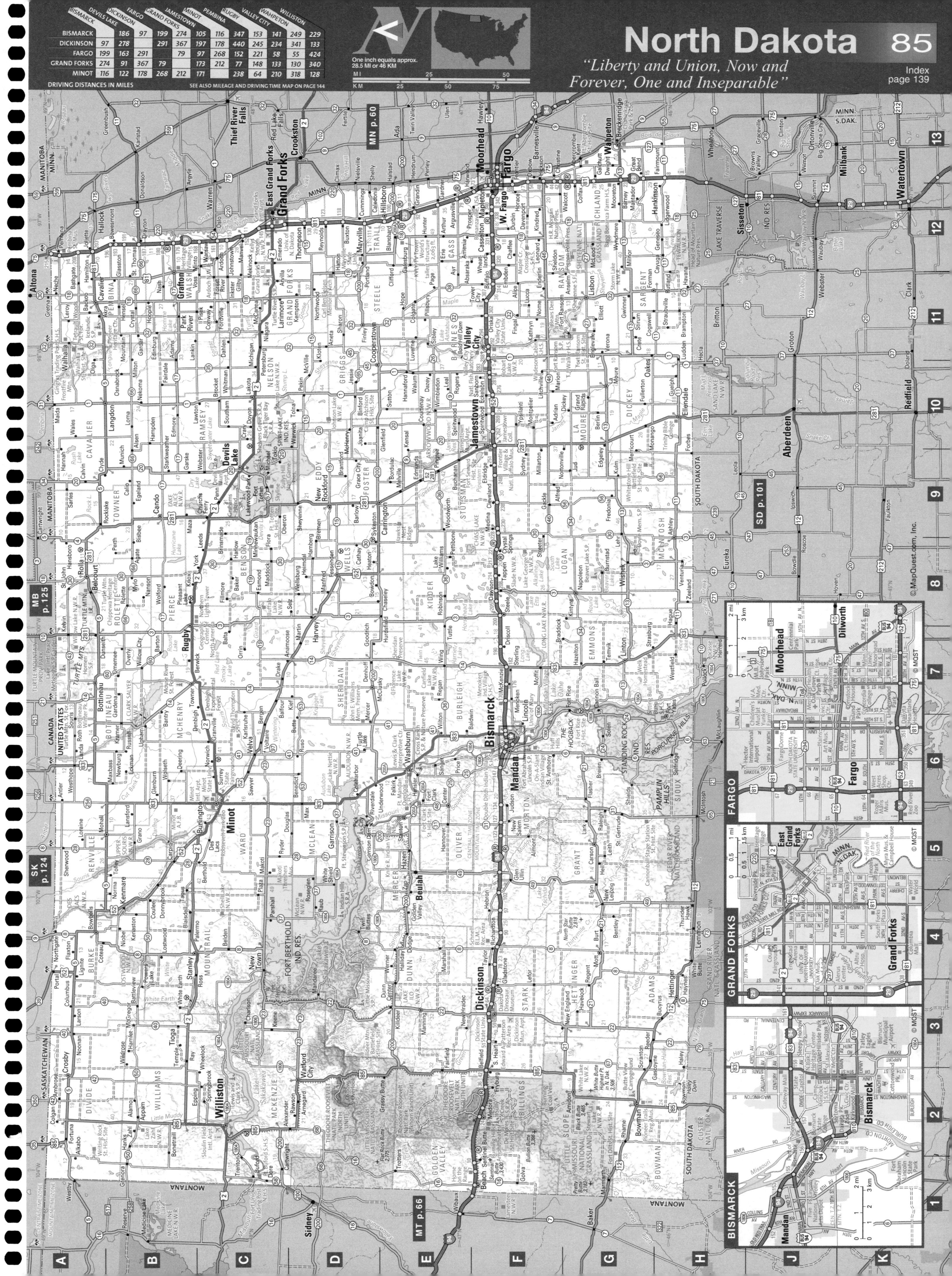

Index page 139

	AKRON	CAMBRIDGE	CANTON	CHILLICOTHE	CINCINNATI	CLEVELAND	COLUMBUS	DAYTON	DEFIANCE	FINDLAY	LIMA	MANSFIELD	MARION	NEW PHILADELPHIA	SANDUSKY	SPRINGFIELD	TOLEDO	YOUNGSTOWN
AKRON		83	23	184	243	38	129	198	186	140	157	66	101	46	84	172	142	49
CAMBRIDGE	83		61	98	187	124	80	155	228	178	175	108	126	37	169	128	228	129
CLEVELAND	38	124	64	199	259		144	213	163	126	163	81	116	87	61	187	119	75
COLUMBUS	129	80	143	47	110	144		70	146	101	96	67	50	117	119	44	148	175
TOLEDO	142	228	168	189	209	119	148	156	63	51	83	105	100	191	62	169		179

DRIVING DISTANCES IN MILES

SEE ALSO MILEAGE AND DRIVING TIME MAP ON PAGE 144

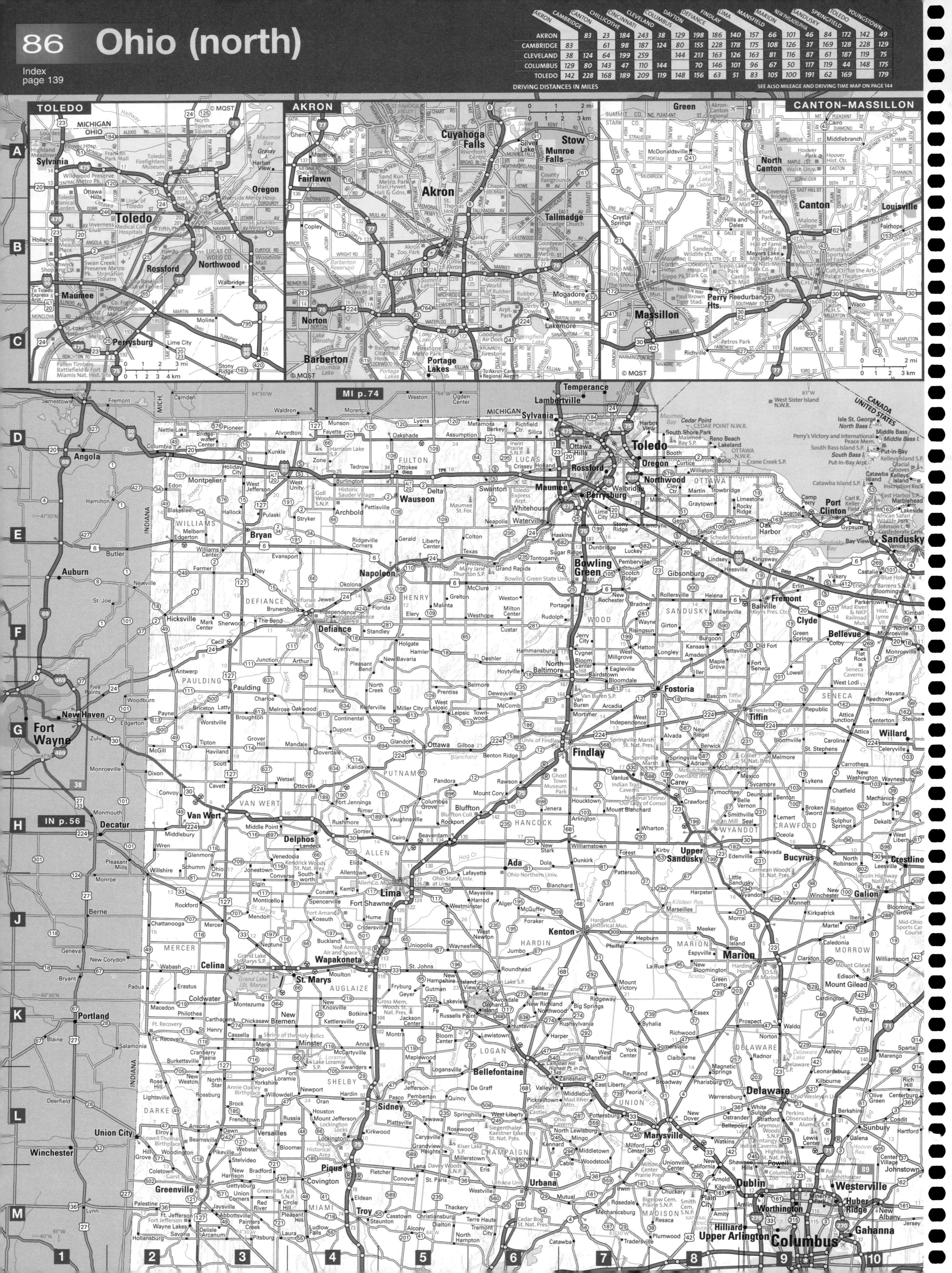

One inch equals approx. 12.5 MI or 20 KM

MI 0 10 20
KM 0 10 20 30

Ohio (north)

"With God All Things Are Possible"

Index page 139

CLEVELAND

LAKE ERIE

Cleveland

© MOST

DOWNTOWN CLEVELAND

LAKE ERIE

© MOST

© MapQuest.com, Inc.

LAKE ERIE

PA p.94

WV p.117

11 12 13 14 15 16 17 18 19 20

A B C D E F G H J K L M

Index page 139

	AKRON	ATHENS	CAMBRIDGE	CHILLICOTHE	CINCINNATI	CLEVELAND	COLUMBUS	DAYTON	GALLIPOLIS	HILLSBORO	HUNTINGTON, WV	LANCASTER	MARIETTA	PORTSMOUTH	SPRINGFIELD	TOLEDO	WHEELING, WV	ZANESVILLE
CAMBRIDGE	83	81		98	187	124	80	155	128	145	185	63	49	142	128	228	50	23
CHILLICOTHE	184	57	98		108	199	47	77	69	40	89	35	107	44	85	189	147	75
CINCINNATI	243	152	187	108		259	110	53	154	61	148	134	236	104	79	209	236	164
COLUMBUS	129	74	80	47	110	144		70	114	69	135	30	129	91	44	148	130	58
DAYTON	198	146	155	77	53	213	70		145	57	160	102	204	116	26	156	204	132

DRIVING DISTANCES IN MILES

SEE ALSO MILEAGE AND DRIVING TIME MAP ON PAGE 144

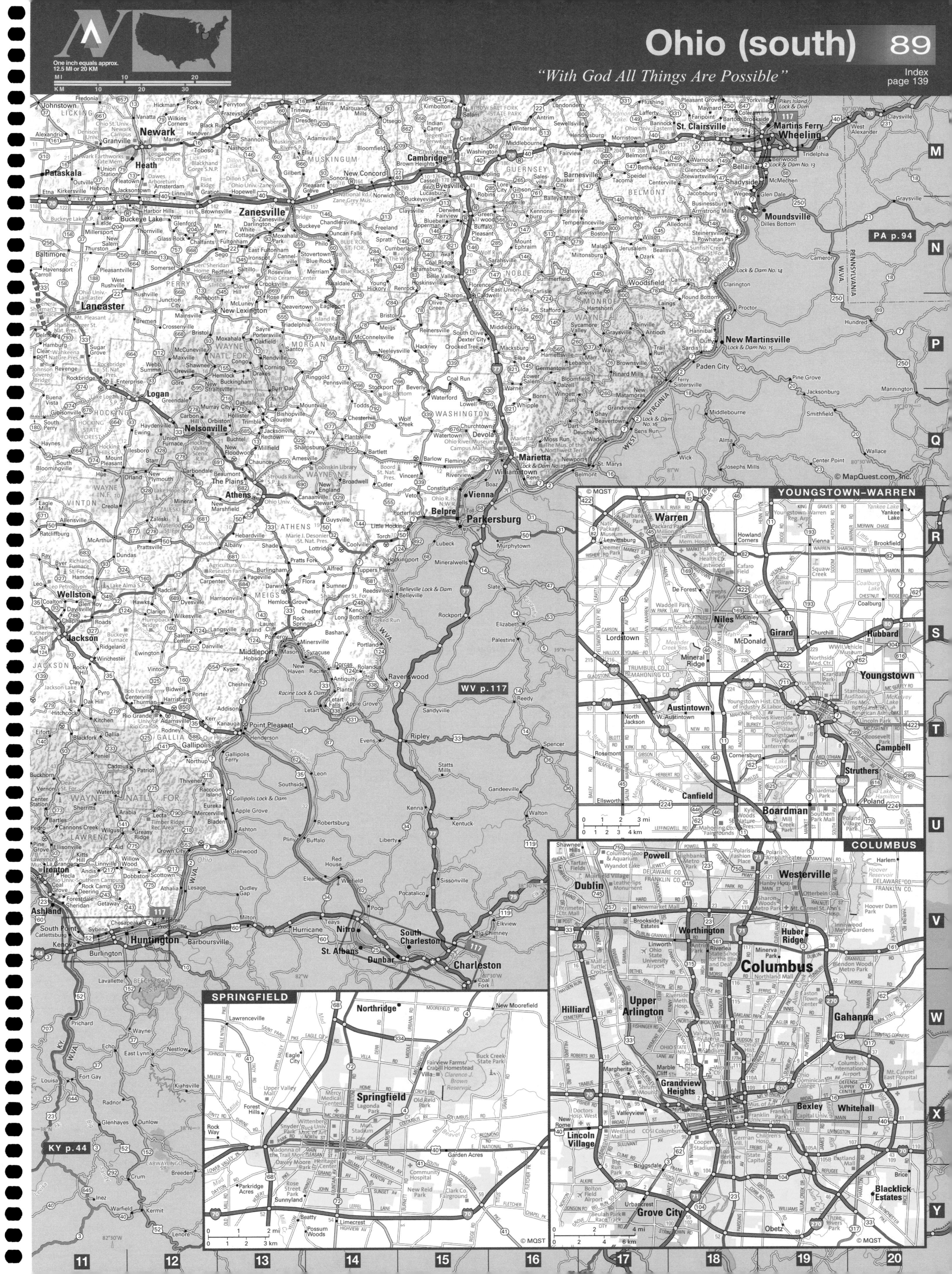
Ohio (south)
89
"With God All Things Are Possible"
Index
page 139
One inch equals approx. 12.5 MI or 20 KM
MI 10 20
KM 10 20 30
PA p.94
WV p.117
KY p.44
YOUNGSTOWN-WARREN
COLUMBUS
SPRINGFIELD
© MapQuest.com, Inc.
© MQST
Newark
Zanesville
Cambridge
St. Clairsville
Wheeling
Martins Ferry
Moundsville
Lancaster
Logan
Nelsonville
Athens
Marietta
Parkersburg
Belpre
Vienna
New Martinsville
Wellston
Jackson
Gallipolis
Point Pleasant
Ironton
Ashland
Huntington
Charleston
South Charleston
Warren
Niles
Youngstown
Austintown
Boardman
Canfield
Columbus
Dublin
Westerville
Worthington
Upper Arlington
Hilliard
Gahanna
Bexley
Whitehall
Grandview Heights
Grove City
Springfield
Northridge
M
N
P
Q
R
S
T
U
V
W
X
Y
11
12
13
14
15
16
17
18
19
20

Index page 139

	ARDMORE	BARTLESVILLE	DALLAS, TX	DURANT	ELK CITY	ENID	FORT SMITH, AR	GUYMON	HUGO	LAWTON	MC ALESTER	MIAMI	MUSKOGEE	OKLAHOMA CITY	PONCA CITY	STILLWATER	TULSA	WOODWARD
ENID	183	141	292	238	148		242	219	282	142	210	207	168	84	69	66	117	88
LAWTON	103	243	197	158	115	142	270	297	224		211	283	223	85	192	152	194	175
MC ALESTER	117	141	169	77	245	210	114	407	75	211		160	68	133	186	154	93	276
OKLAHOMA CITY	99	157	209	154	112	84	191	274	205	85	133	198	144		107	67	109	143
TULSA	206	48	259	168	221	117	125	336	165	194	93	91	52	109	93	71		205

DRIVING DISTANCES IN MILES

SEE ALSO MILEAGE AND DRIVING TIME MAP ON PAGE 144

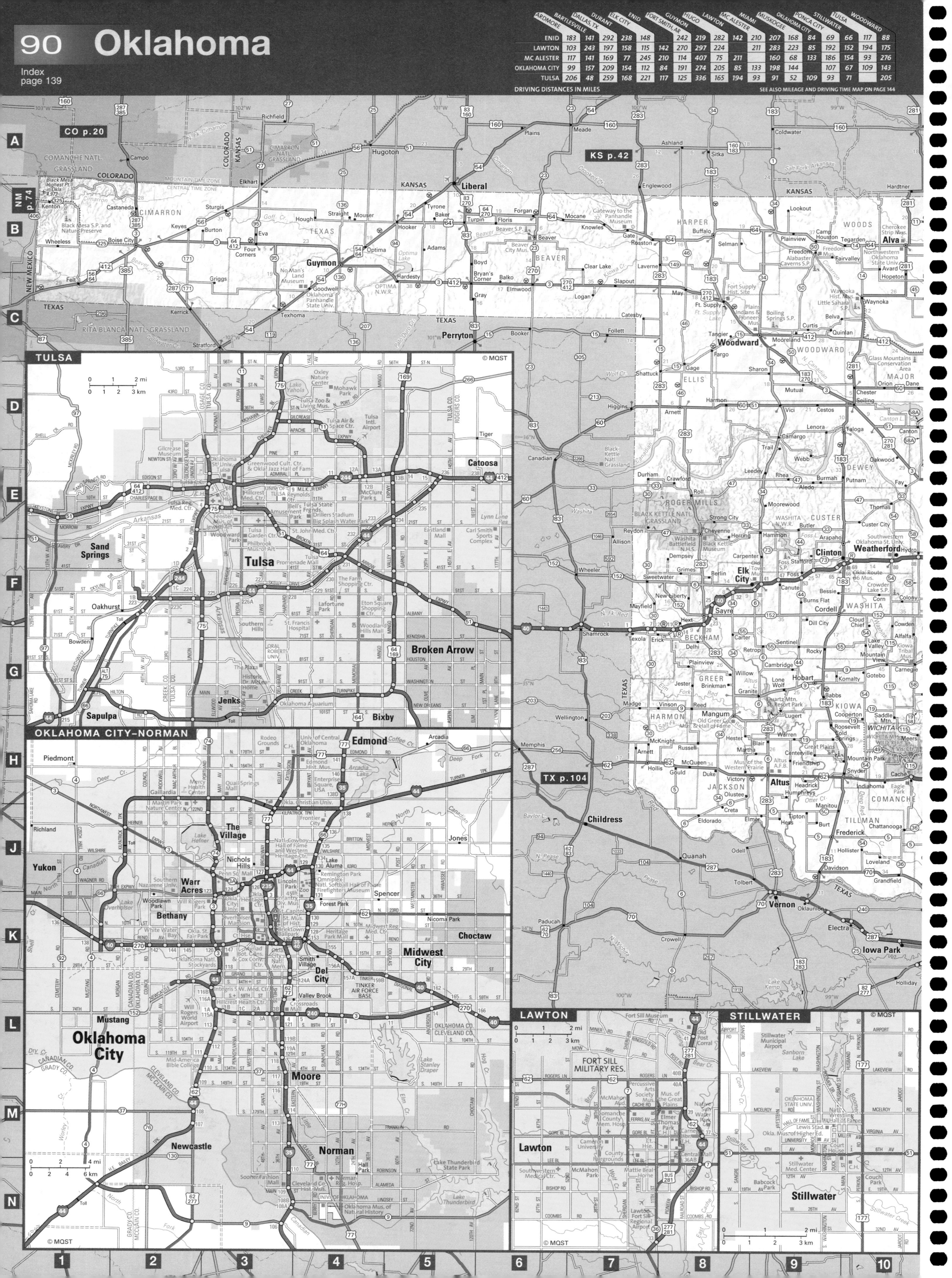

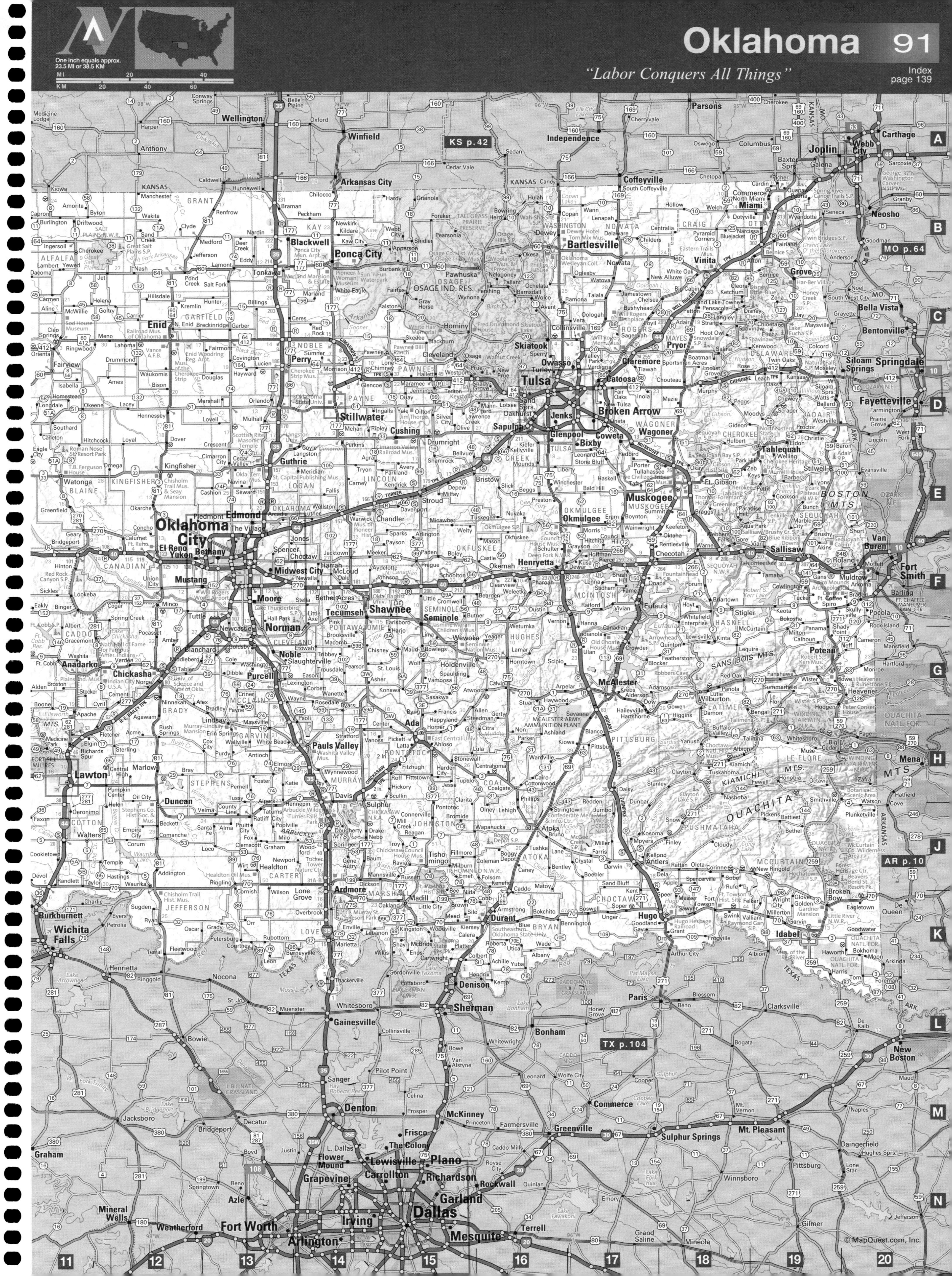

Oklahoma
91
"Labor Conquers All Things"
Index page 139
One inch equals approx. 23.5 MI or 38.5 KM
MI 20 40
KM 20 40 60
KS p.42
MO p.64
AR p.10
TX p.104
KANSAS
MO.
ARKANSAS
TEXAS
ARK.
A
B
C
D
E
F
G
H
J
K
L
M
N
11
12
13
14
15
16
17
18
19
20
Wellington
Winfield
Independence
Coffeyville
Parsons
Joplin
Carthage
Webb City
Neosho
Blackwell
Ponca City
Bartlesville
Miami
Vinita
Grove
Bella Vista
Bentonville
Springdale
Siloam Springs
Fayetteville
Enid
Perry
Stillwater
Cushing
Guthrie
Tulsa
Owasso
Claremore
Pryor
Jenks
Broken Arrow
Sapulpa
Bixby
Wagoner
Tahlequah
Muskogee
Okmulgee
Henryetta
Edmond
Oklahoma City
El Reno
Yukon
Bethany
Mustang
Midwest City
Moore
Norman
Shawnee
Tecumseh
Sallisaw
Fort Smith
Van Buren
Poteau
Eufaula
McAlester
Ada
Anadarko
Chickasha
Purcell
Pauls Valley
Lawton
Duncan
Ardmore
Durant
Hugo
Idabel
Mena
Wichita Falls
Burkburnett
Sherman
Denison
Gainesville
Paris
Bonham
Denton
McKinney
Frisco
Plano
Lewisville
Carrollton
Richardson
Grapevine
Garland
Dallas
Irving
Arlington
Fort Worth
Mesquite
Rockwall
Greenville
Sulphur Springs
Mt. Pleasant
Commerce
New Boston
Weatherford
Mineral Wells
Graham
© MapQuest.com, Inc.

Index page 140

	ASTORIA	BAKER CITY	BEND	BURNS	COOS BAY	CORVALLIS	CRATER LAKE N.P.	EUGENE	GRANTS PASS	KLAMATH FALLS	LAKEVIEW	MEDFORD	NEWPORT	ONTARIO	PENDLETON	PORTLAND	SALEM	THE DALLES
BEND	252	228		142	227	128	110	115	196	139	177	178	183	272	246	158	134	137
EUGENE	216	423	115	257	105	46	146		137	175	265	164	101	491	328	112	65	198
MEDFORD	375	406	178	311	170	205	80	164	28	76	171		260	441	487	271	224	357
PENDLETON	307	96	246	195	440	298	355	328	460	385	335	487	328	164		212	265	131
PORTLAND	97	307	158	299	224	82	253	112	244	282	335	271	116	375	212		48	82

DRIVING DISTANCES IN MILES

SEE ALSO MILEAGE AND DRIVING TIME MAP PAGE 144

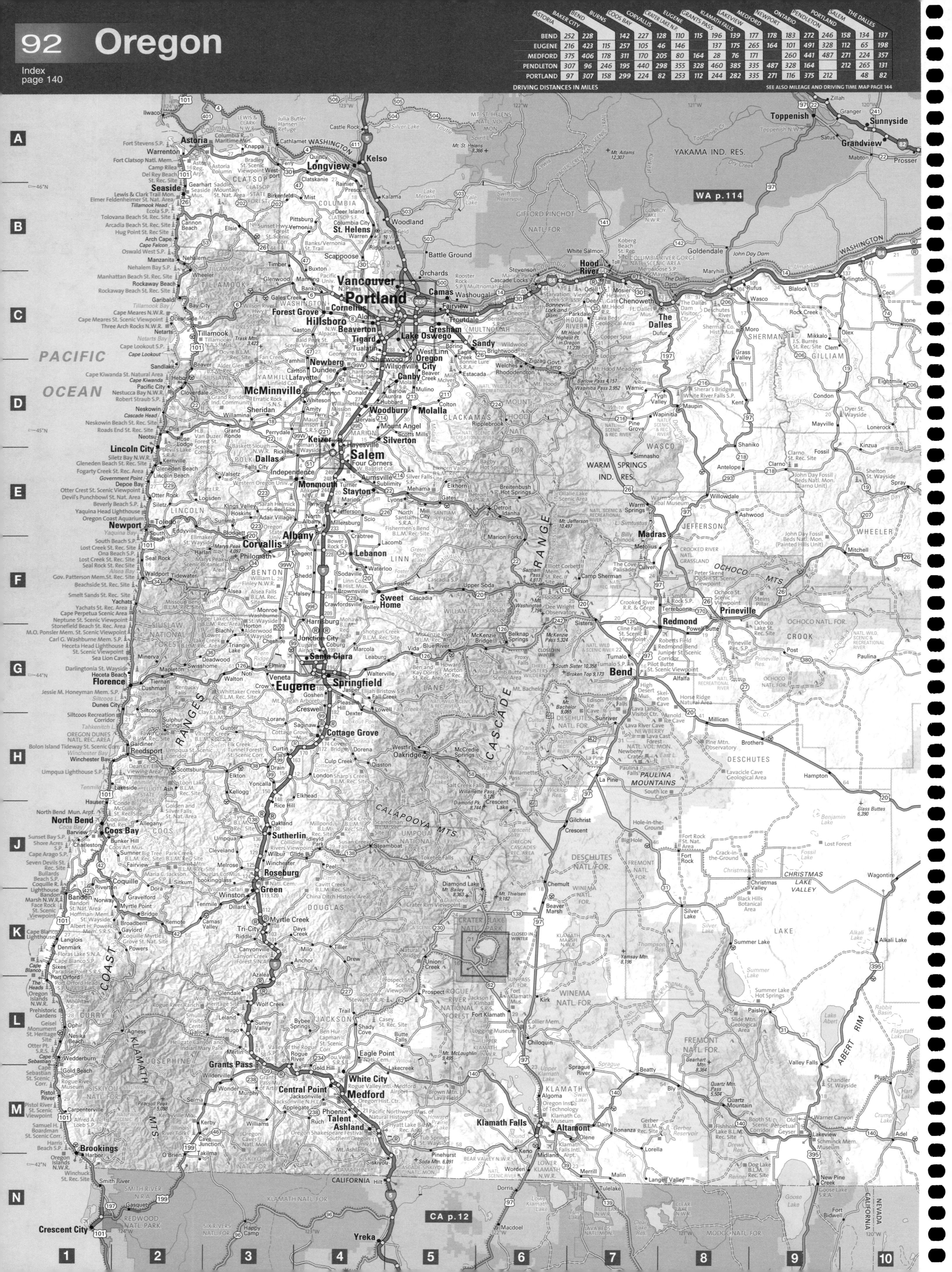

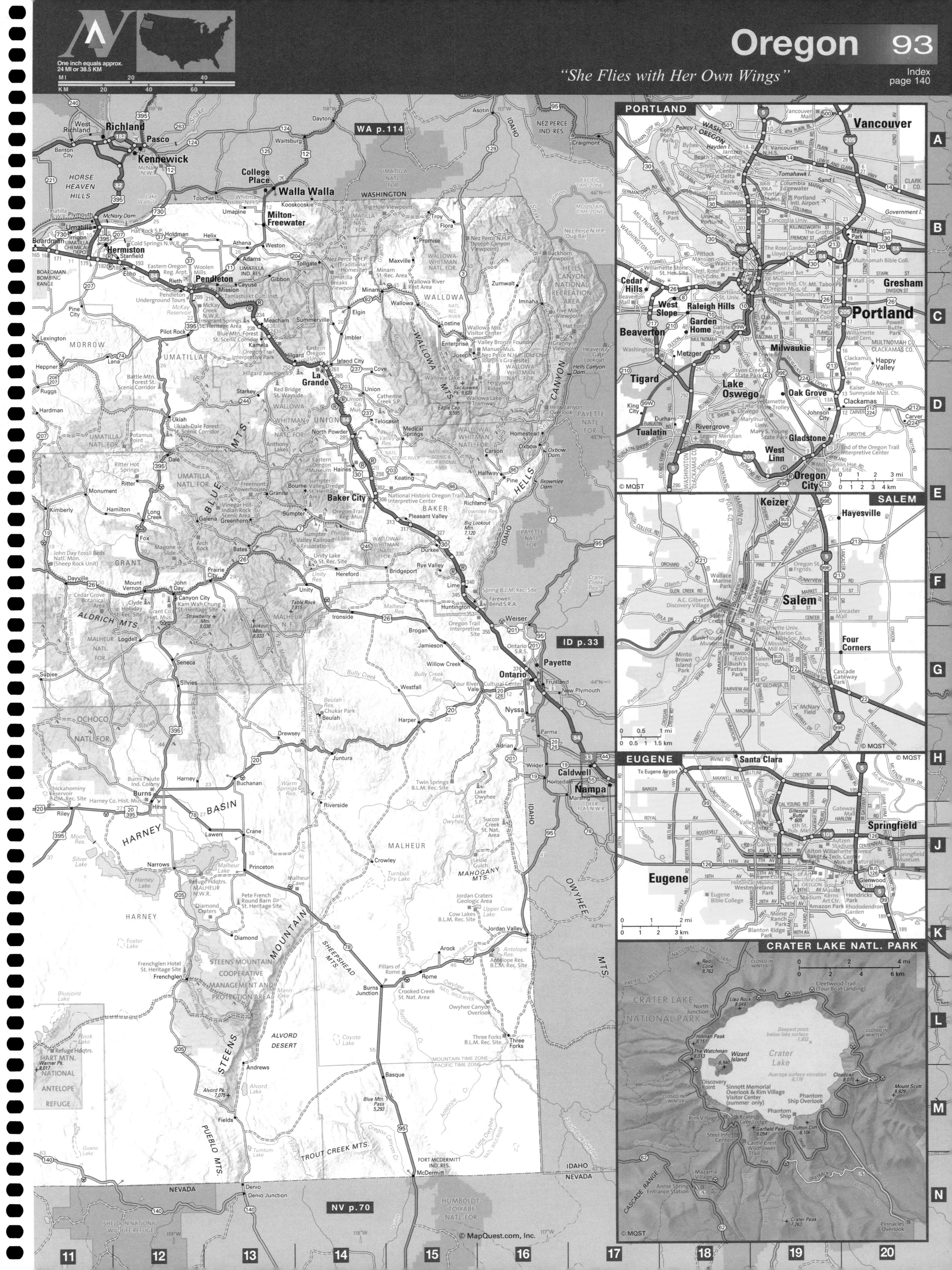

Oregon
93
"She Flies with Her Own Wings"
Index page 140
One inch equals approx. 24 MI or 38.5 KM
MI 20 40
KM 20 40 60
WA p.114
ID p.33
NV p.70
PORTLAND
SALEM
EUGENE
CRATER LAKE NATL. PARK
Richland
Pasco
Kennewick
College Place
Walla Walla
Milton-Freewater
Hermiston
Pendleton
La Grande
Baker City
Ontario
Nampa
Caldwell
Payette
Burns
Hines
Vancouver
Gresham
Portland
Beaverton
Tigard
Lake Oswego
Oak Grove
Milwaukie
Tualatin
West Linn
Oregon City
Keizer
Salem
Santa Clara
Springfield
Eugene
WALLOWA MTS.
BLUE MTS.
HELLS CANYON
HARNEY BASIN
STEENS MOUNTAIN
ALVORD DESERT
ALDRICH MTS.
OWYHEE MTS.
PUEBLO MTS.
TROUT CREEK MTS.
MALHEUR
HARNEY
GRANT
BAKER
UNION
WALLOWA
UMATILLA
MORROW
IDAHO
NEVADA
WASHINGTON
Crater Lake
Wizard Island
© MapQuest.com, Inc.
11 12 13 14 15 16 17 18 19 20
A B C D E F G H J K L M N

Index page 140

	ALLENTOWN	ALTOONA	CHAMBERSBURG	ERIE	HARRISBURG	INDIANA	JOHNSTOWN	LEWISTOWN	MEADVILLE	NEW CASTLE	PHILADELPHIA	PITTSBURGH	SCRANTON	STATE COLLEGE	UNIONTOWN	WARREN	WASHINGTON	WILLIAMSPORT
ALTOONA	218		95	205	140	55	48	71	168	129	241	99	185	40	109	147	123	99
ERIE	361	205	282		298	150	195	242	40	95	405	126	317	210	183	66	153	259
HARRISBURG	82	140	54	298		179	138	58	261	250	109	205	119	88	200	224	213	83
PITTSBURGH	284	99	160	126	205	56	73	155	88	49	306		301	139	48	145	30	215
STATE COLLEGE	165	40	105	210	88	95	87	32	172	167	195	139	149		148	136	163	63

DRIVING DISTANCES IN MILES

SEE ALSO MILEAGE AND DRIVING TIME MAP ON PAGE 144

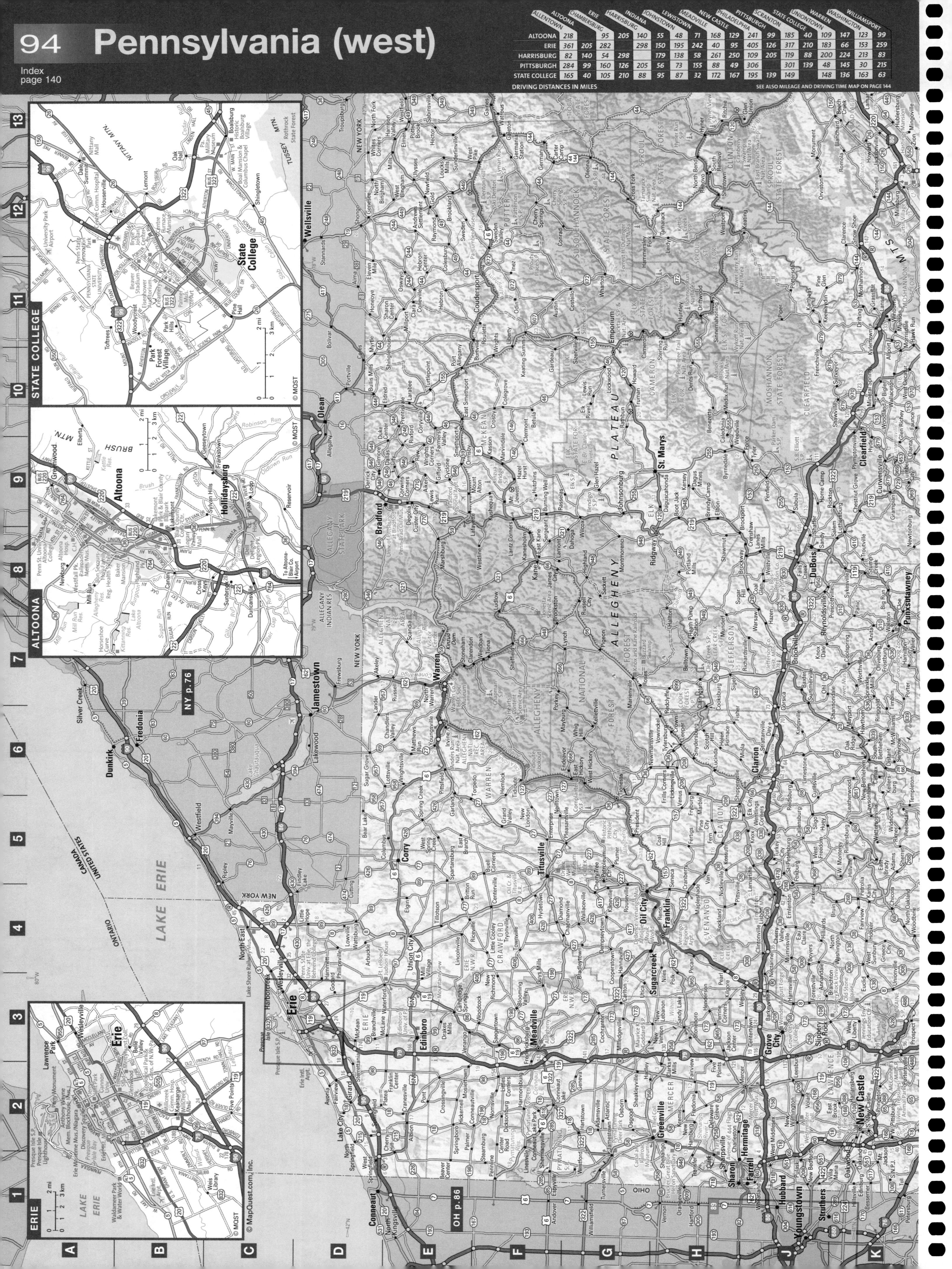

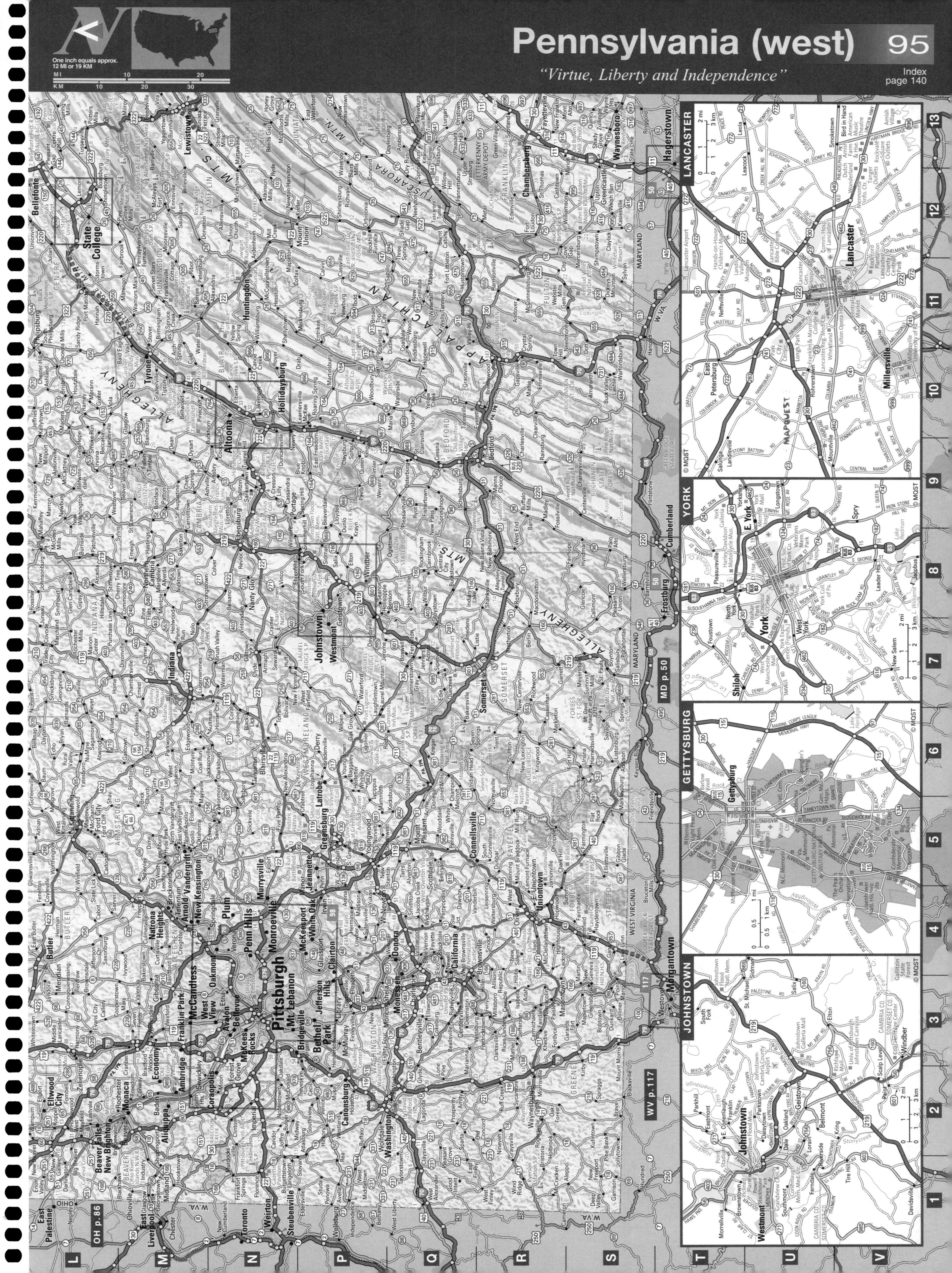

Pennsylvania (west)
95
"Virtue, Liberty and Independence"
Index page 140
One inch equals approx. 12 MI or 19 KM
MI 10 20
KM 10 20 30
LANCASTER
YORK
GETTYSBURG
JOHNSTOWN
© MQST
MD p. 50
WV p. 117
OH p. 86
MARYLAND
WEST VIRGINIA
W.VA.
OHIO
APPALACHIAN
ALLEGHENY
TUSCARORA
MTS
Pittsburgh
Altoona
Johnstown
State College
Huntingdon
Hollidaysburg
Bedford
Somerset
Greensburg
Washington
Uniontown
Indiana
Kittanning
Butler
Chambersburg
Hagerstown
Cumberland
Morgantown
Frostburg
Lewistown
Bellefonte
Tyrone
Ebensburg
Latrobe
Connellsville
Waynesburg
Monroeville
McKeesport
Beaver Falls
New Brighton
Ellwood City
Aliquippa
Ambridge
Weirton
Steubenville
East Liverpool
East Palestine
Canonsburg
Bethel Park
Mt. Lebanon
Penn Hills
Plum
New Kensington
Murrysville
Jeannette
Monessen
Donora
California
Westmont
Gettysburg
Lancaster
Millersville
York
West York
Shiloh
Spry
Waynesboro
Hancock

Index page 140

	ALLENTOWN	ALTOONA	CHAMBERSBURG	EAST STROUDSBURG	ERIE	GETTYSBURG	HARRISBURG	LANCASTER	LEWISTOWN	PHILADELPHIA	PITTSBURGH	READING	SCRANTON	STATE COLLEGE	SUNBURY	WILKES-BARRE	WILLIAMSPORT	YORK
ALLENTOWN		218	133	39	361	125	82	71	137	63	284	37	76	165	93	64	116	91
HARRISBURG	82	140	54	121	298	42		44	58	109	205	65	119	88	52	105	83	25
PHILADELPHIA	63	241	154	87	405	131	109	79	164		306	63	128	195	144	117	169	100
SCRANTON	76	185	170	50	317	162	119	130	130	128	301	103		149	84	17	83	143
WILLIAMSPORT	116	99	134	118	259	125	83	124	83	169	215	110	83	63	34	66		108

DRIVING DISTANCES IN MILES

SEE ALSO MILEAGE AND DRIVING TIME MAP ON PAGE 144

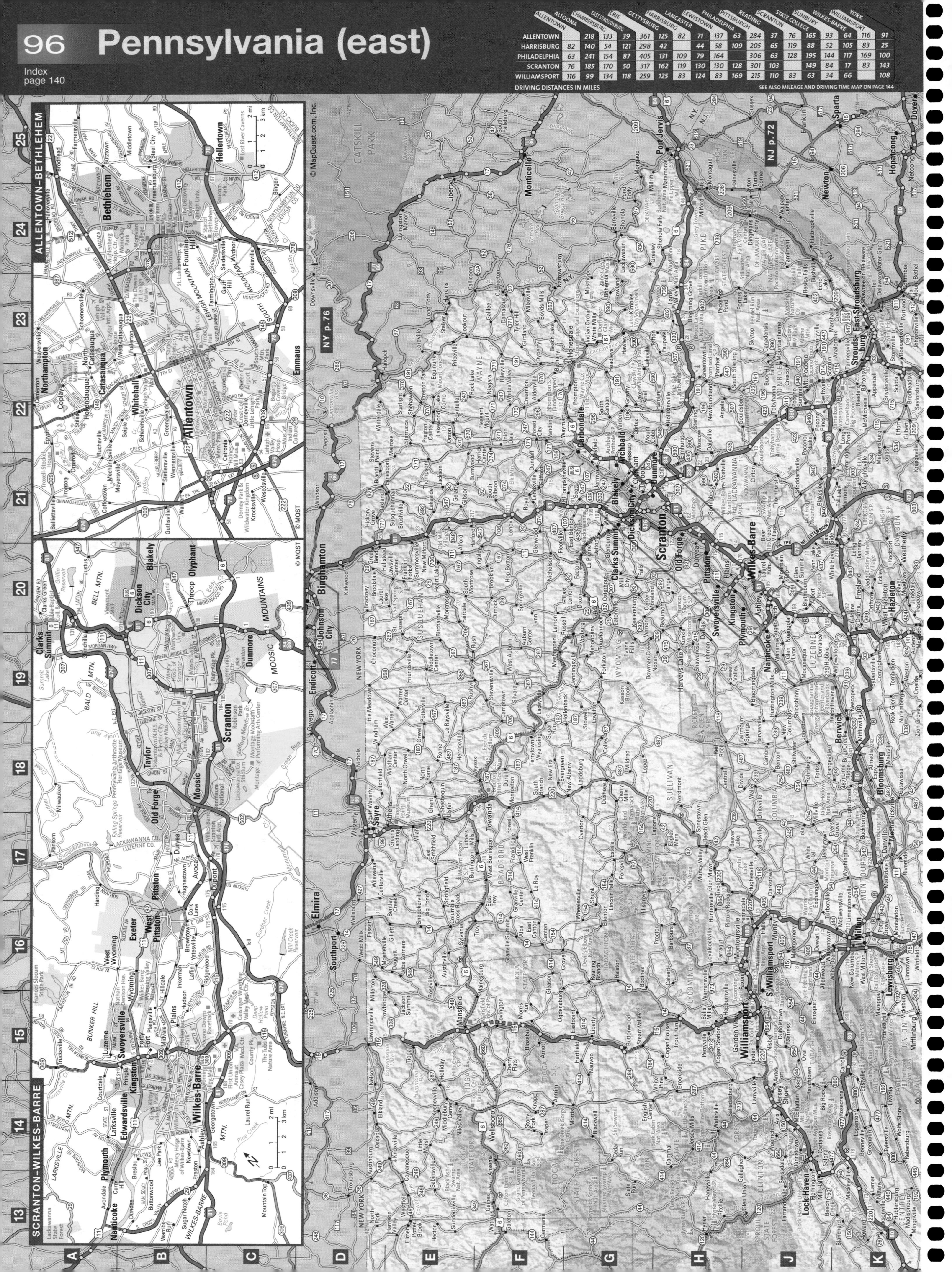

"Virtue, Liberty and Independence"

Index page 140

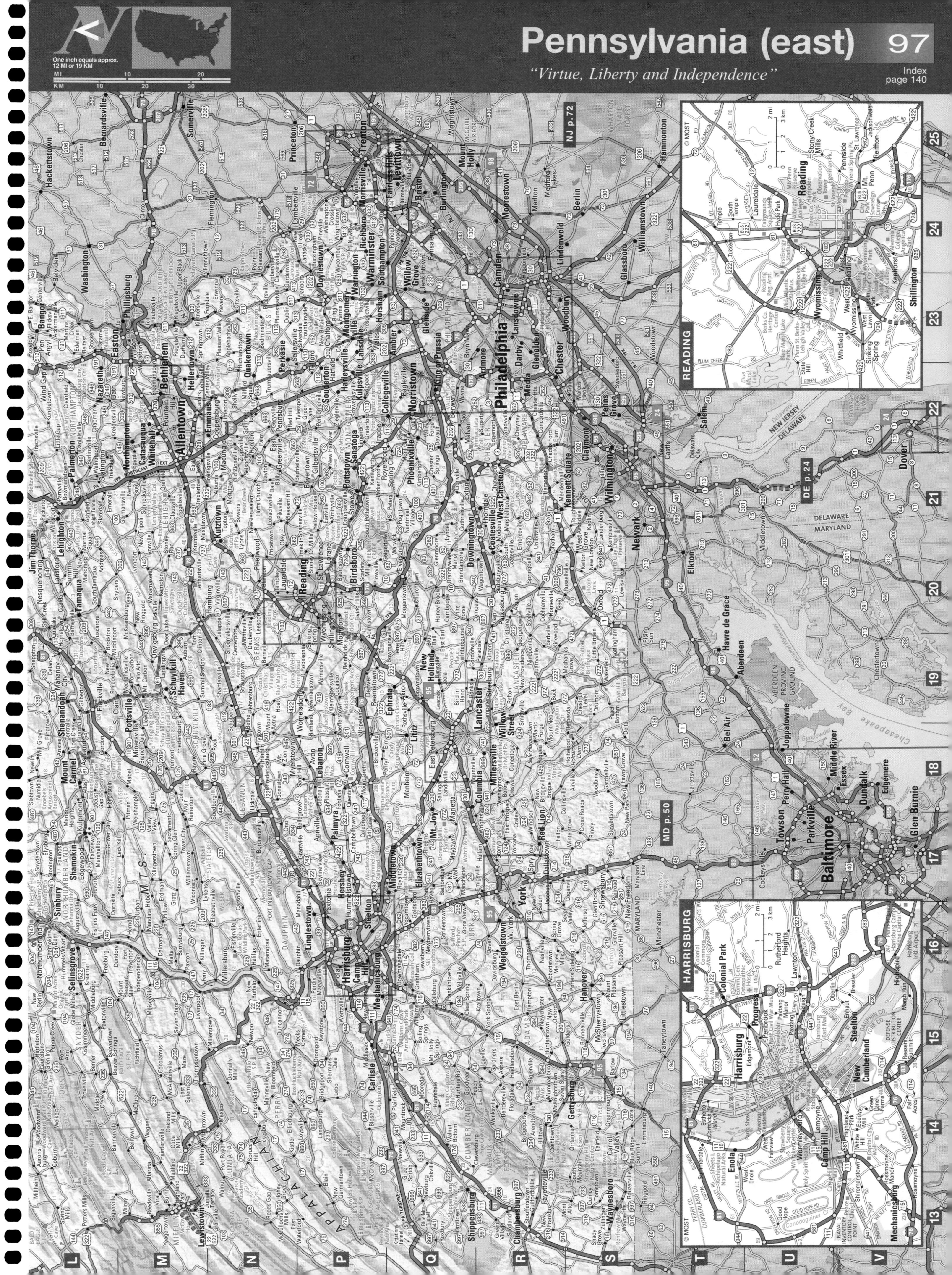

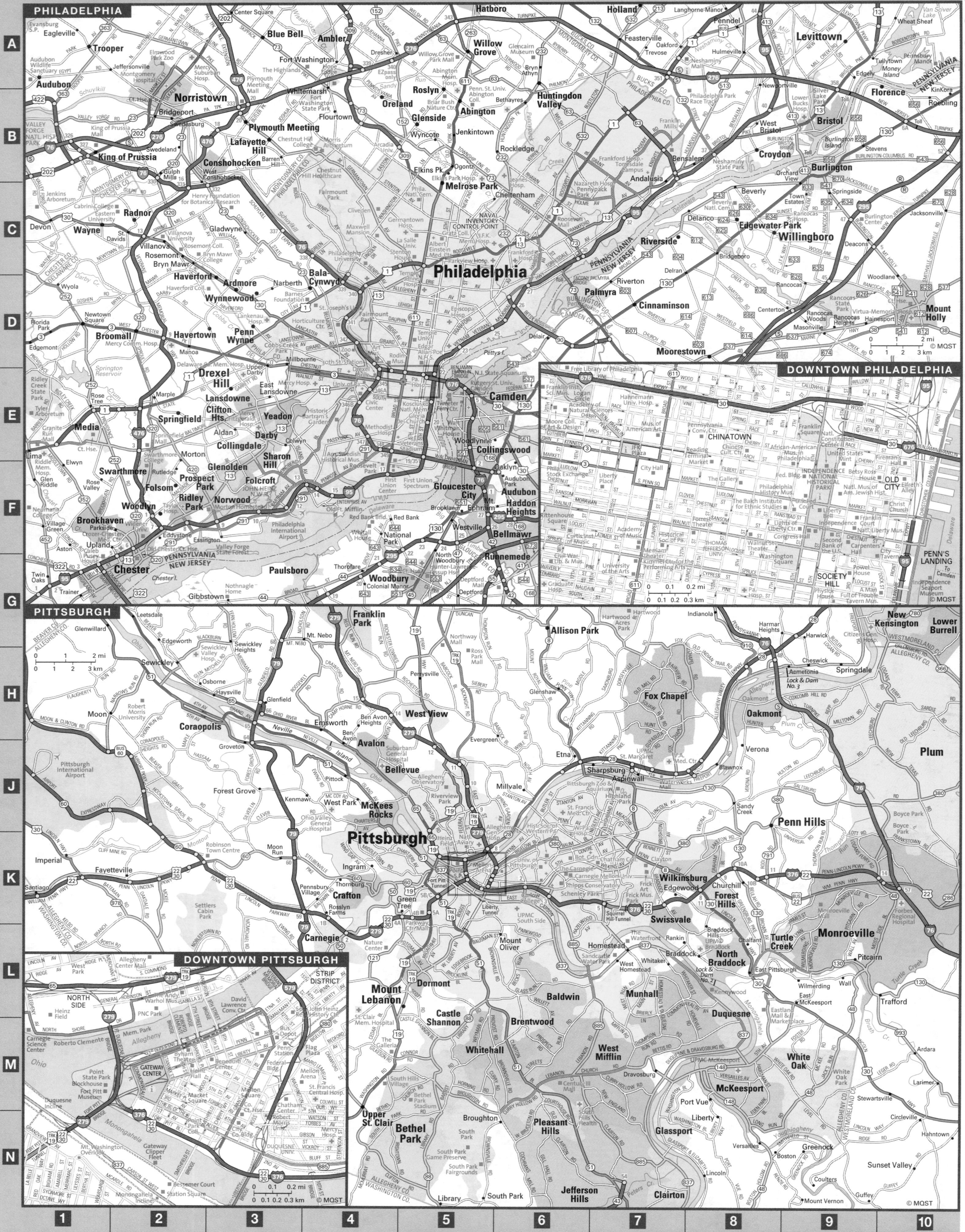

Index page 140

PHILADELPHIA

Hatboro, Holland, Langhorne Manor, Levittown, Blue Bell, Ambler, Willow Grove, Trooper, Eagleville, Audubon, Norristown, Bridgeport, Plymouth Meeting, Fort Washington, Oreland, Roslyn, Glenside, Abington, Huntingdon Valley, Penndel, Bristol, Florence, Roebling, King of Prussia, Conshohocken, Lafayette Hill, Jenkintown, Rockledge, Bensalem, Croydon, Burlington, Elkins Pk., Melrose Park, Cheltenham, Andalusia, Beverly, Edgewater Park, Willingboro, Radnor, Wayne, Devon, Villanova, Rosemont, Bryn Mawr, Gladwyne, Haverford, Ardmore, Wynnewood, Narberth, Bala-Cynwyd, Philadelphia, Riverside, Delanco, Riverton, Palmyra, Cinnaminson, Moorestown, Mount Holly, Broomall, Havertown, Penn Wynne, Drexel Hill, Lansdowne, Upper Darby, East Lansdowne, Camden, Springfield, Clifton Hts., Yeadon, Media, Aldan, Darby, Collingdale, Sharon Hill, Collingswood, Swarthmore, Glenolden, Prospect Park, Folcroft, Gloucester City, Audubon, Haddon Heights, Folsom, Ridley Park, Norwood, Woodlyn, Brookhaven, Bellmawr, Runnemede, Chester, Paulsboro, Woodbury, National Park, Westville

DOWNTOWN PHILADELPHIA

Chinatown, Independence National Historical Park, Old City, Society Hill, Penn's Landing

PITTSBURGH

Franklin Park, Allison Park, New Kensington, Lower Burrell, Sewickley, Fox Chapel, Oakmont, Moon, Coraopolis, West View, Avalon, Bellevue, Plum, Etna, Sharpsburg, Aspinwall, Millvale, McKees Rocks, Pittsburgh, Penn Hills, Wilkinsburg, Edgewood, Forest Hills, Swissvale, Crafton, Green Tree, Carnegie, Mount Oliver, Monroeville, Turtle Creek, North Braddock, Mount Lebanon, Dormont, Castle Shannon, Baldwin, Munhall, Duquesne, Brentwood, Whitehall, West Mifflin, White Oak, McKeesport, Upper St. Clair, Bethel Park, Pleasant Hills, Glassport, Jefferson Hills, Clairton

DOWNTOWN PITTSBURGH

North Side, Strip District, Gateway Center, Point State Park

© MQST

A B C D E F G H J K L M N

1 2 3 4 5 6 7 8 9 10

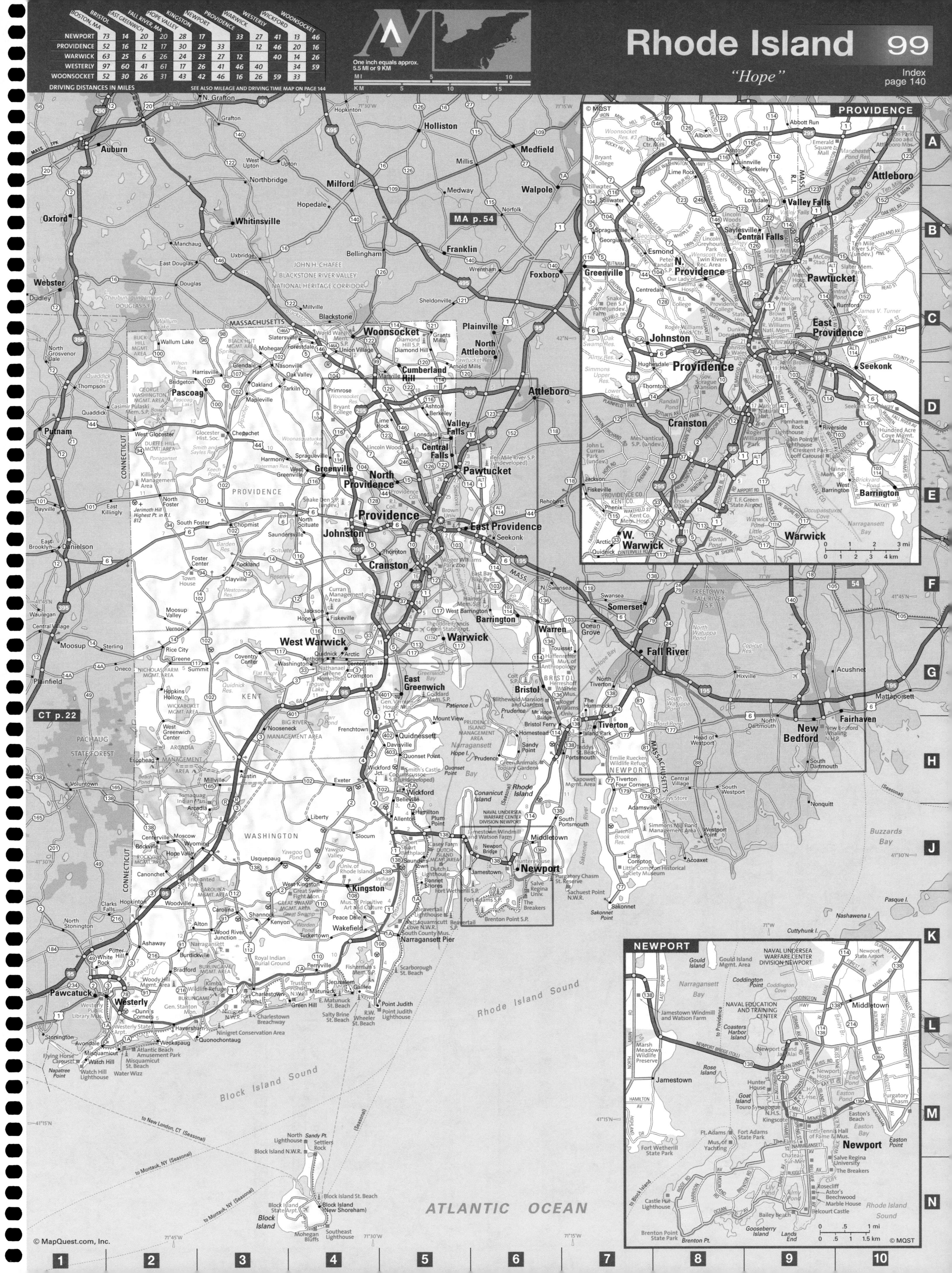

	BOSTON, MA	BRISTOL	EAST GREENWICH	FALL RIVER, MA	HOPE VALLEY	KINGSTON	NEWPORT	PROVIDENCE	WARWICK	WESTERLY	WICKFORD	WOONSOCKET
NEWPORT	73	14	20	20	28	17		33	27	41	13	46
PROVIDENCE	52	16	12	17	30	29	33		12	46	20	16
WARWICK	63	25	6	26	24	23	27	12		40	14	26
WESTERLY	97	60	41	61	17	26	41	46	40		34	59
WOONSOCKET	52	30	26	31	43	42	46	16	26	59	33	

Index page 140

"While I Breathe, I Hope"

	AUGUSTA, GA	CHARLOTTE, NC	CHARLESTON	COLUMBIA	FLORENCE	GREENVILLE	HILTON HEAD ISLAND	MYRTLE BEACH	ROCK HILL	SAVANNAH, GA	SPARTANBURG	SUMTER
CHARLESTON	142	204		110	127	205	95	92	183	107	200	100
COLUMBIA	70	91	110		80	97	152	146	70	159	92	45
FLORENCE	147	107	127	80		174	170	66	115	176	169	39
GREENVILLE	110	96	205	97	174		248	241	88	255	30	142
MYRTLE BEACH	213	173	92	146	66	241	190		181	197	235	93

DRIVING DISTANCES IN MILES

SEE ALSO MILEAGE AND DRIVING TIME MAP ON PAGE 144

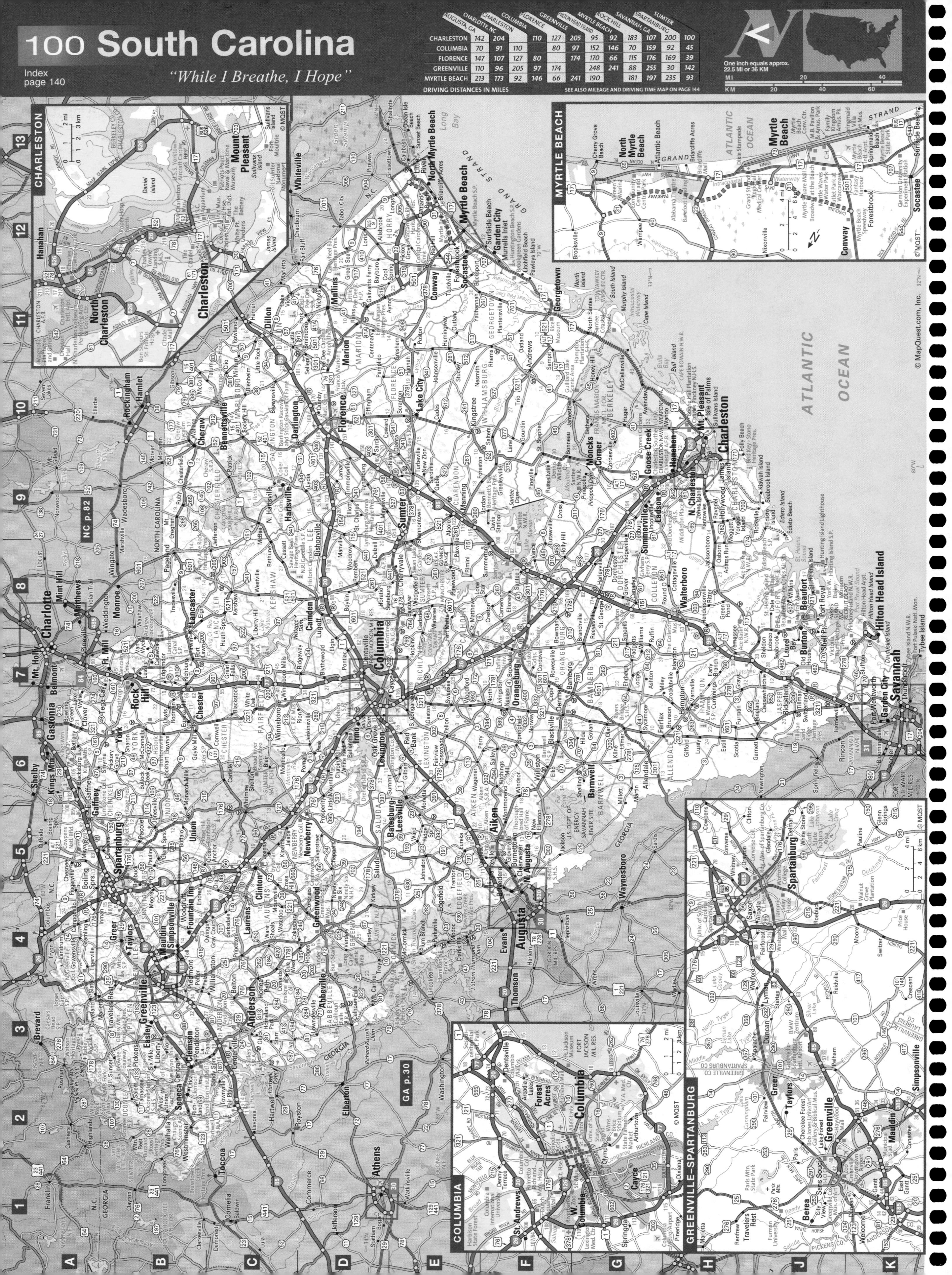

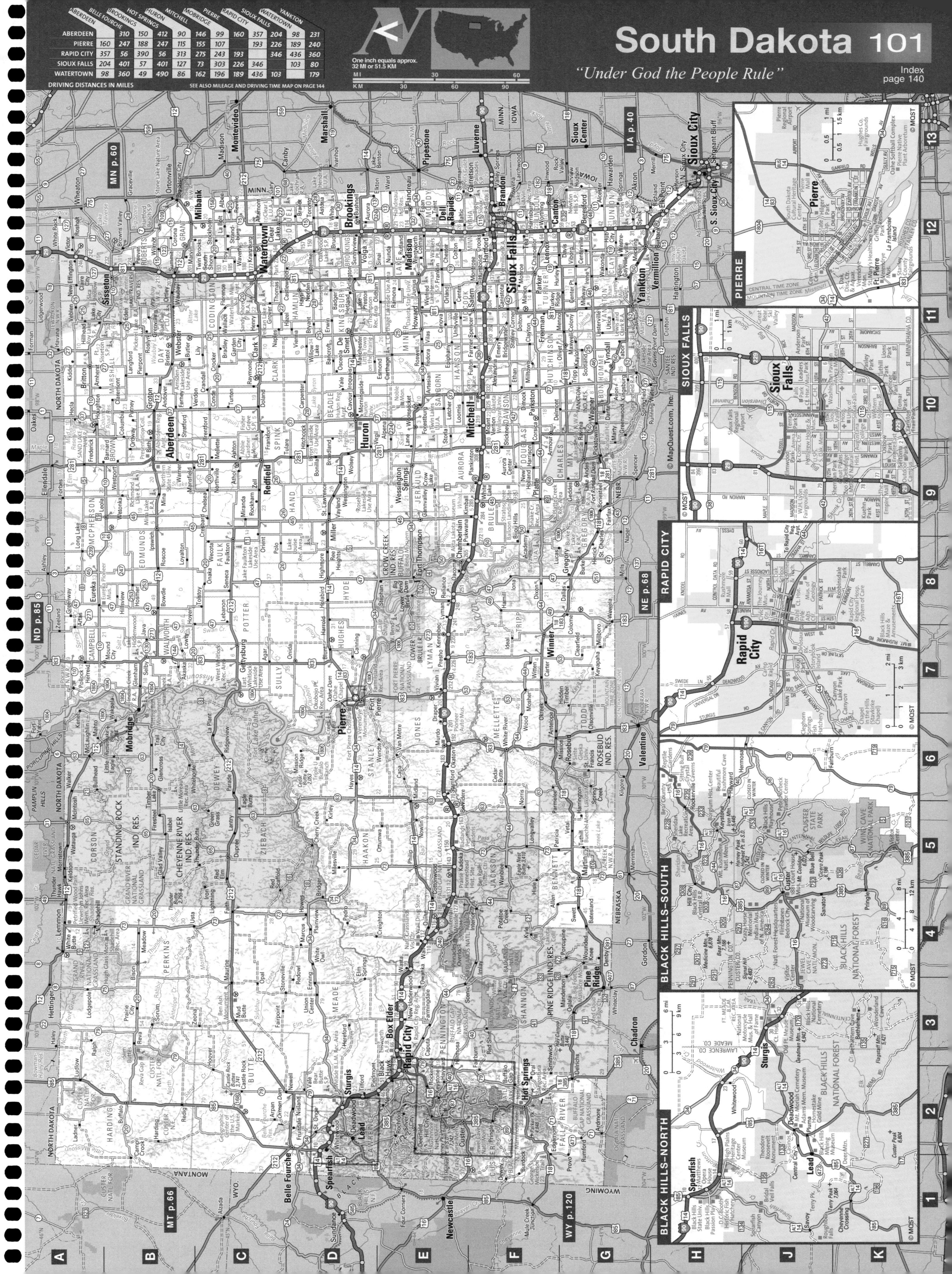

South Dakota 101
"Under God the People Rule"
Index page 140
One inch equals approx. 32 MI or 51.5 KM
DRIVING DISTANCES IN MILES
SEE ALSO MILEAGE AND DRIVING TIME MAP ON PAGE 144

	ABERDEEN	BELLE FOURCHE	BROOKINGS	HOT SPRINGS	HURON	MITCHELL	MOBRIDGE	PIERRE	RAPID CITY	SIOUX FALLS	WATERTOWN	YANKTON
ABERDEEN		310	150	412	90	146	99	160	357	204	98	231
PIERRE	160	247	188	247	115	155	107		193	226	189	240
RAPID CITY	357	56	390	56	313	275	243	193		346	436	360
SIOUX FALLS	204	401	57	401	127	73	303	226	346		103	80
WATERTOWN	98	360	49	490	86	162	196	189	436	103		179

MN p. 60
IA p. 40
ND p. 85
NE p. 68
MT p. 66
WY p. 120
PIERRE
SIOUX FALLS
RAPID CITY
BLACK HILLS–SOUTH
BLACK HILLS–NORTH
© MapQuest.com, Inc.
© MOST
Aberdeen
Watertown
Brookings
Sioux Falls
Mitchell
Huron
Pierre
Rapid City
Yankton
Vermillion
Spearfish
Sturgis
Hot Springs
Mobridge
Winner
Lemmon
Belle Fourche

Index page 140

	BRISTOL	CHATTANOOGA	CLARKSVILLE	COLUMBIA	COOKEVILLE	DYERSBURG	FAYETTEVILLE	GATLINBURG	JACKSON	JOHNSON CITY	KNOXVILLE	MANCHESTER	MEMPHIS	MORRISTOWN	MURFREESBORO	NASHVILLE	OAK RIDGE	UNION CITY
CHATTANOOGA	233		177	158	89	308	97	156	262	222	116	69	346	164	102	131	110	311
JOHNSON CITY	24	222	336	337	213	469	317	108	423		107	289	507	69	285	290	126	471
KNOXVILLE	117	116	230	231	107	363	211	40	317	107		183	401	48	179	184	24	365
MEMPHIS	518	346	213	210	296	81	268	441	91	507	401	279		449	246	215	383	113
NASHVILLE	301	131	46	49	79	178	91	223	132	290	184	64	215	232	31		166	181

DRIVING DISTANCES IN MILES

SEE ALSO MILEAGE AND DRIVING TIME MAP ON PAGE 144

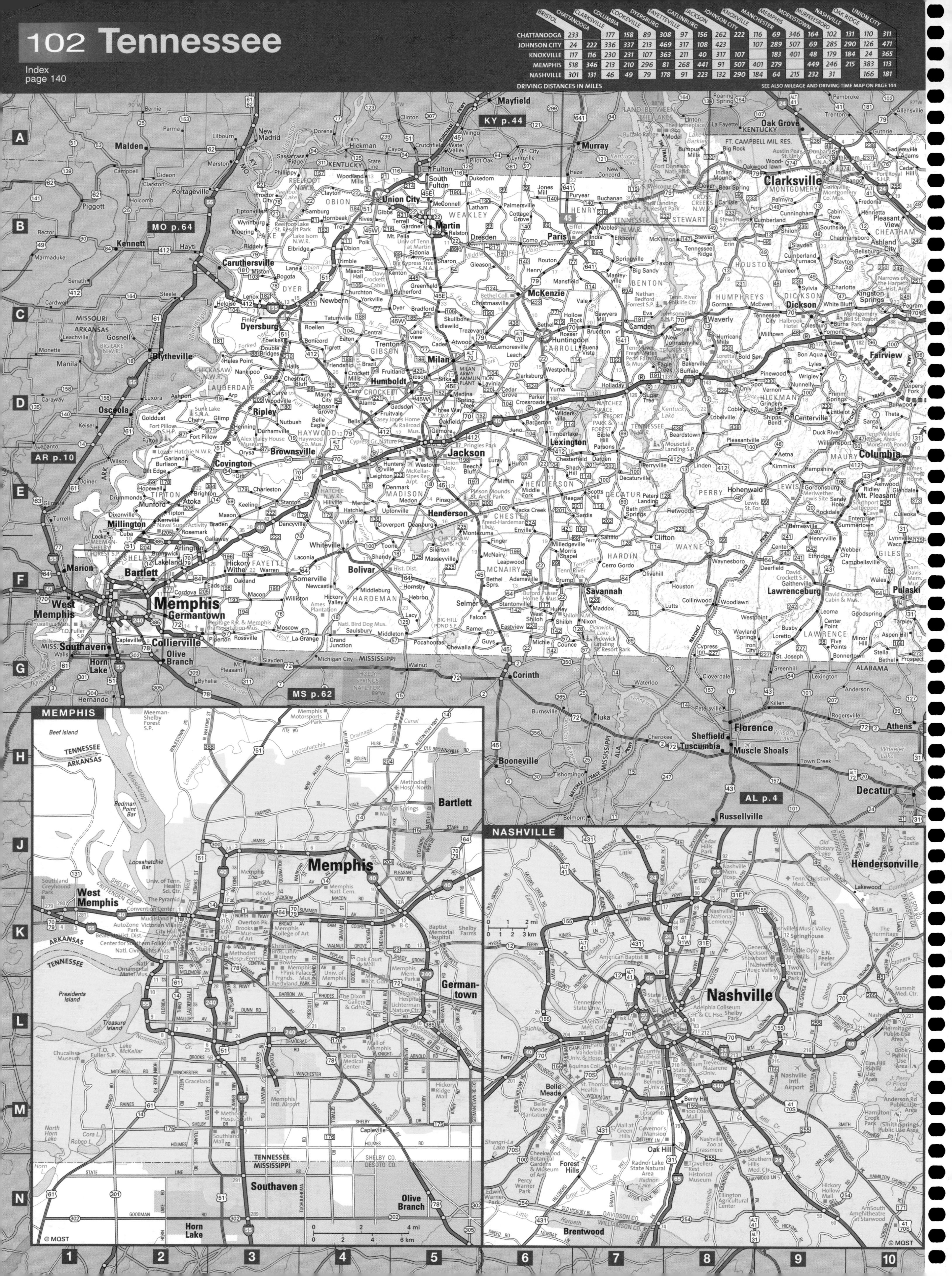

"Agriculture and Commerce"

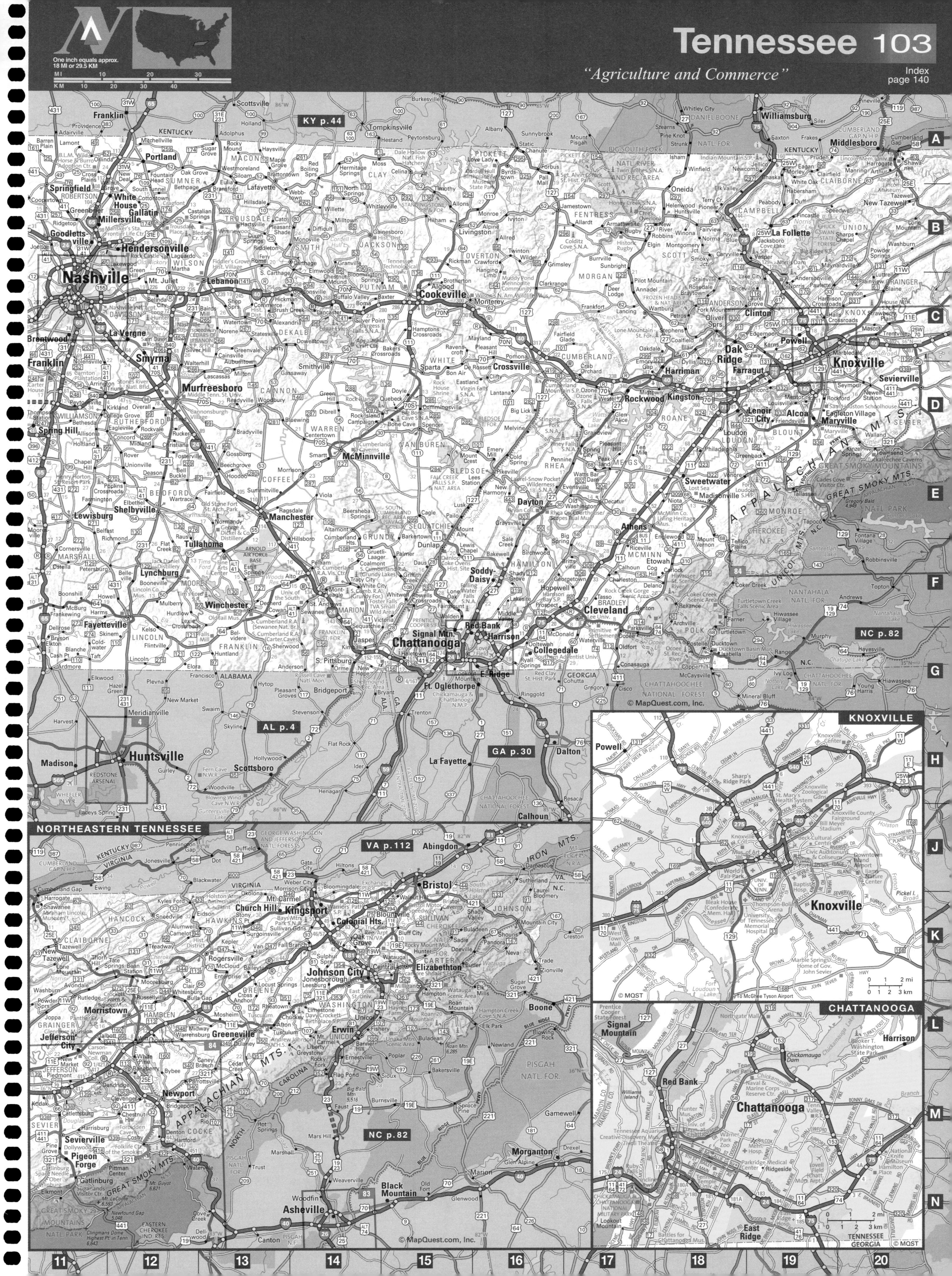

Index page 140

	ABILENE	ALPINE	AMARILLO	BIG BEND N.P.	BIG SPRING	CHILDRESS	DALHART	DALLAS	DEL RIO	EL PASO	FORT STOCKTON	LUBBOCK	ODESSA	PECOS	SAN ANGELO	SAN ANTONIO	VAN HORN	WICHITA FALLS
AMARILLO	290	414		472	230	118	87	470	462	438	349	124	266	340	308	513	427	228
EL PASO	459	232	438	329	347	558	420	647	425		241	341	285	209	416	556	122	596
LUBBOCK	166	291	124	349	106	144	211	354	338	341	226		142	217	185	389	303	207
ODESSA	176	151	266	209	65	276	353	364	246	285	86	142		76	134	342	163	314
SAN ANGELO	91	230	308	287	87	238	395	265	156	416	164	185	134	208		208	295	232

DRIVING DISTANCES IN MILES

SEE ALSO MILEAGE AND DRIVING TIME MAP ON PAGE 144

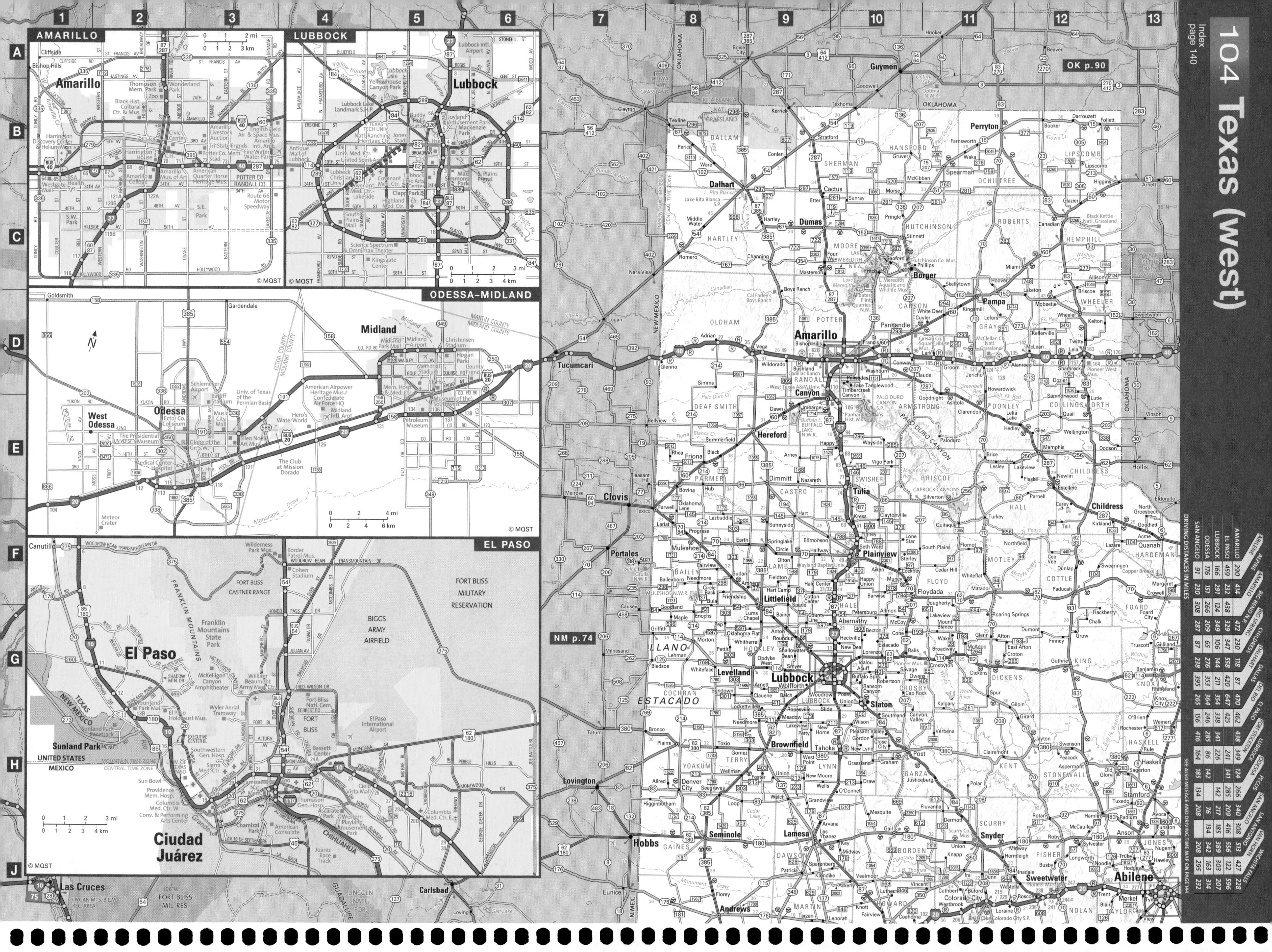

"Friendship"

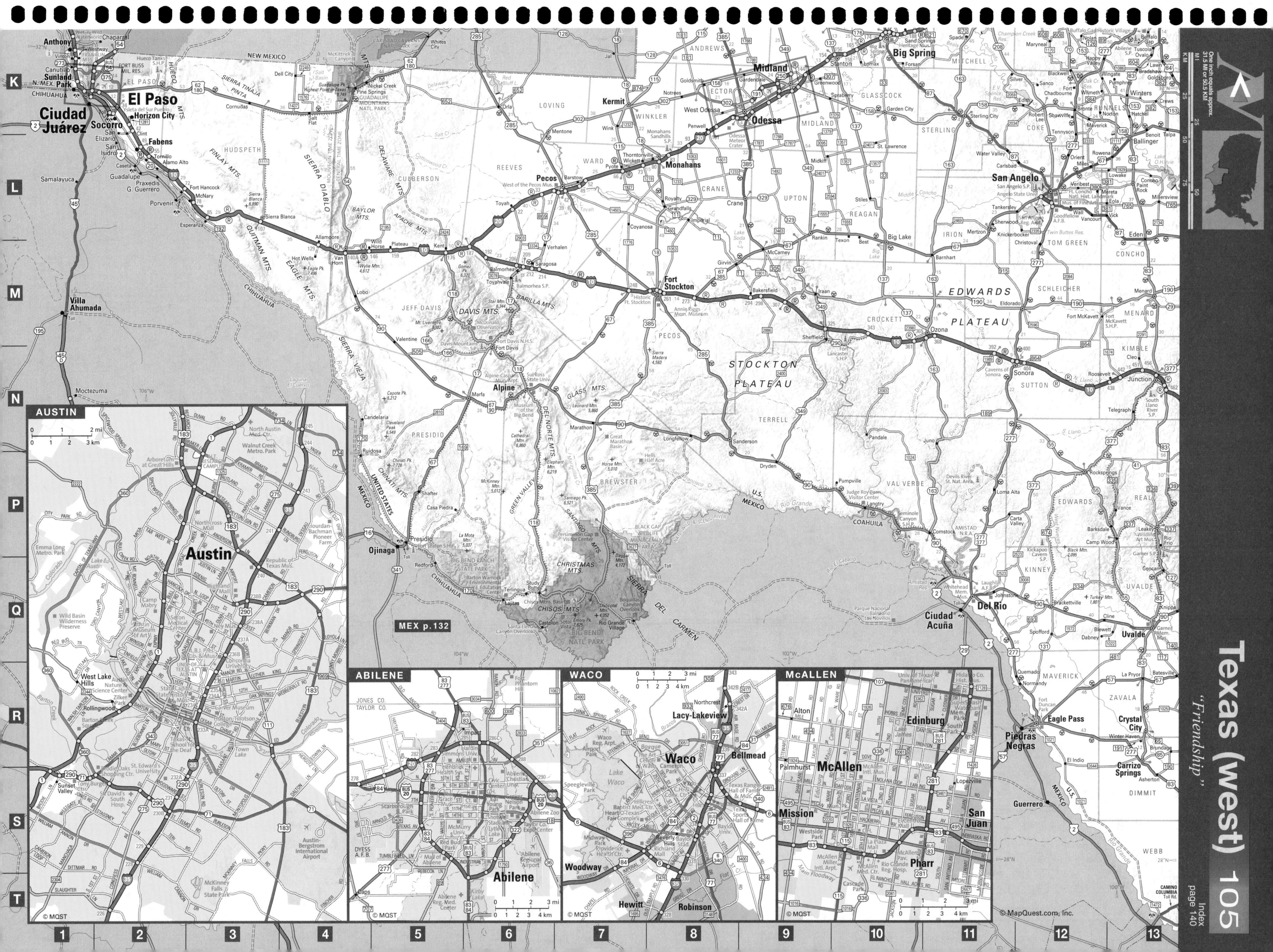
One inch equals approx. 31.5 MI or 50.5 KM
El Paso
Ciudad Juárez
Midland
Odessa
Big Spring
San Angelo
Fort Stockton
Pecos
Alpine
Del Rio
Eagle Pass
Piedras Negras
Ciudad Acuña
Uvalde
MEX p.132
AUSTIN
Austin
ABILENE
Abilene
WACO
Waco
McALLEN
McAllen
EDWARDS PLATEAU
STOCKTON PLATEAU
© MapQuest.com, Inc.

Index page 140

	ABILENE	AUSTIN	BEAUMONT	BROWNSVILLE	COLLEGE STATION	CORPUS CHRISTI	DALLAS	DEL RIO	FORT WORTH	HOUSTON	LAREDO	MC ALLEN	SAN ANGELO	SAN ANTONIO	TEXARKANA	TYLER	WACO	WICHITA FALLS
AUSTIN	217		250	350	108	217	195	229	187	166	238	313	207	78	375	229	105	301
CORPUS CHRISTI	411	217	293	157	254		411	272	403	211	141	152	362	147	591	445	321	517
DALLAS	191	195	323	544	184	411		422	32	241	432	507	265	271	179	100	94	141
HOUSTON	425	166	84	351	106	211	241	349	275		355	346	410	200	290	202	203	382
SAN ANTONIO	258	78	284	279	171	147	271	152	264	200	157	243	208		452	306	182	378

DRIVING DISTANCES IN MILES

SEE ALSO MILEAGE AND DRIVING TIME MAP ON PAGE 144

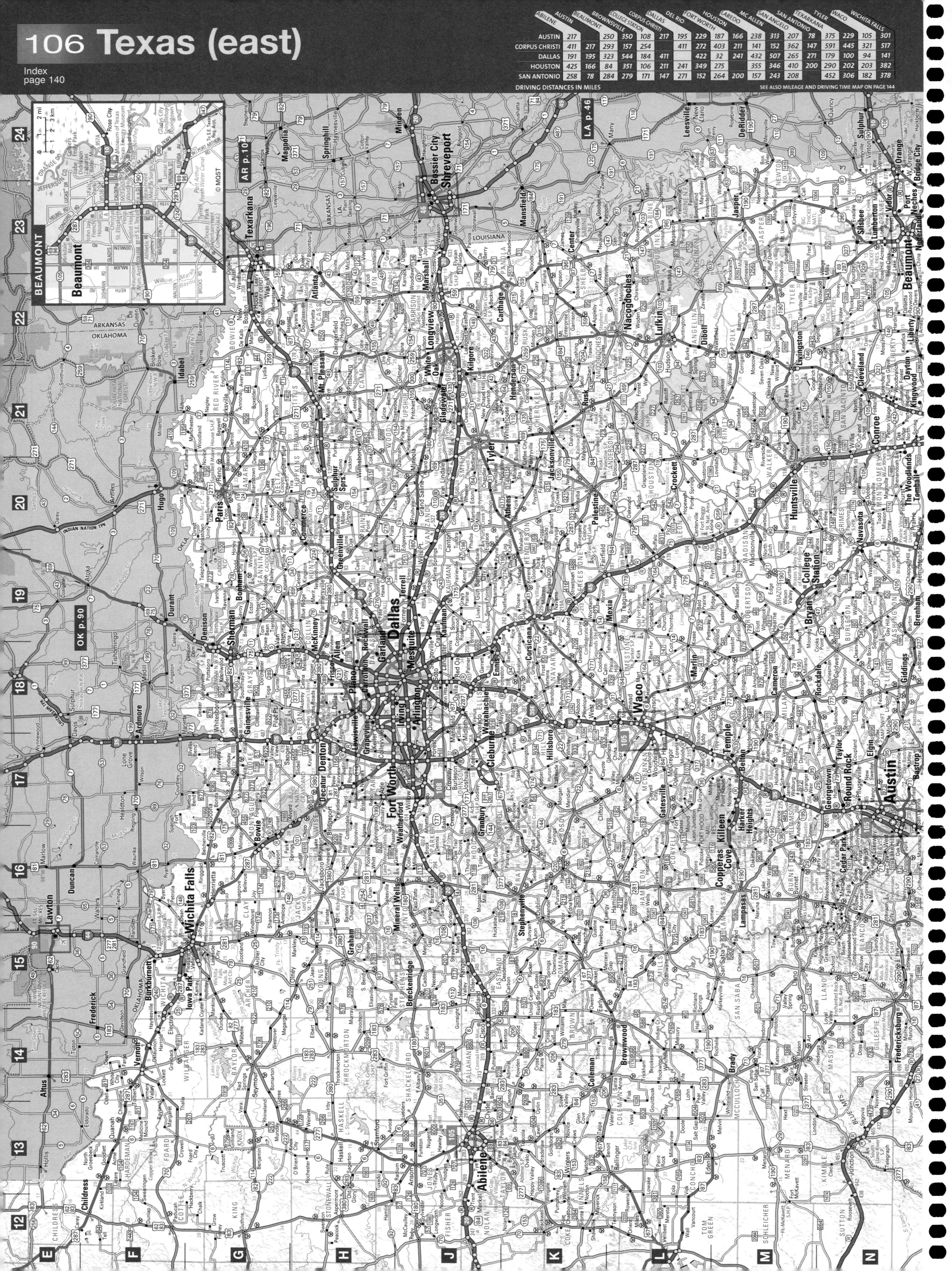

"Friendship"

Index page 140

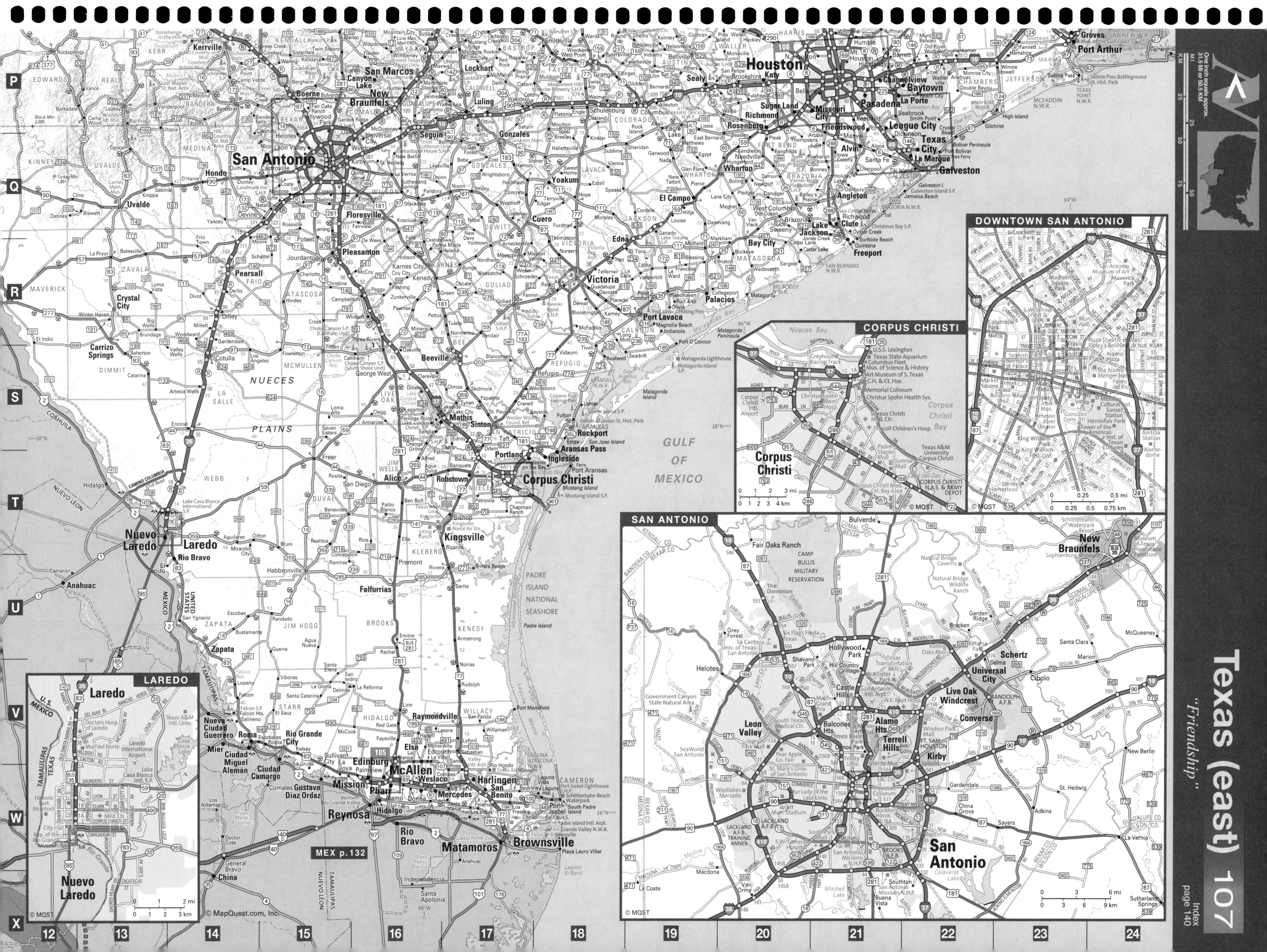

Index
page 140

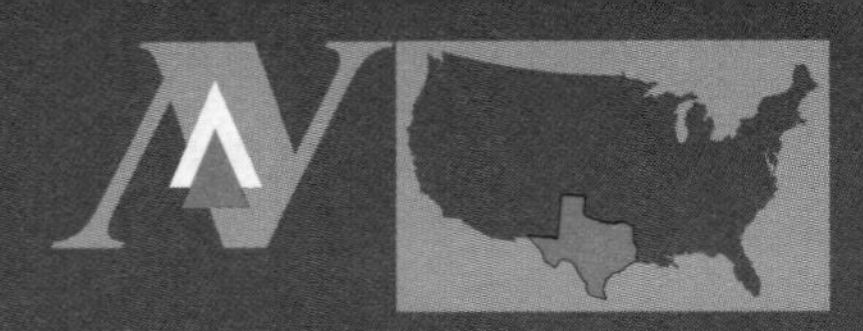

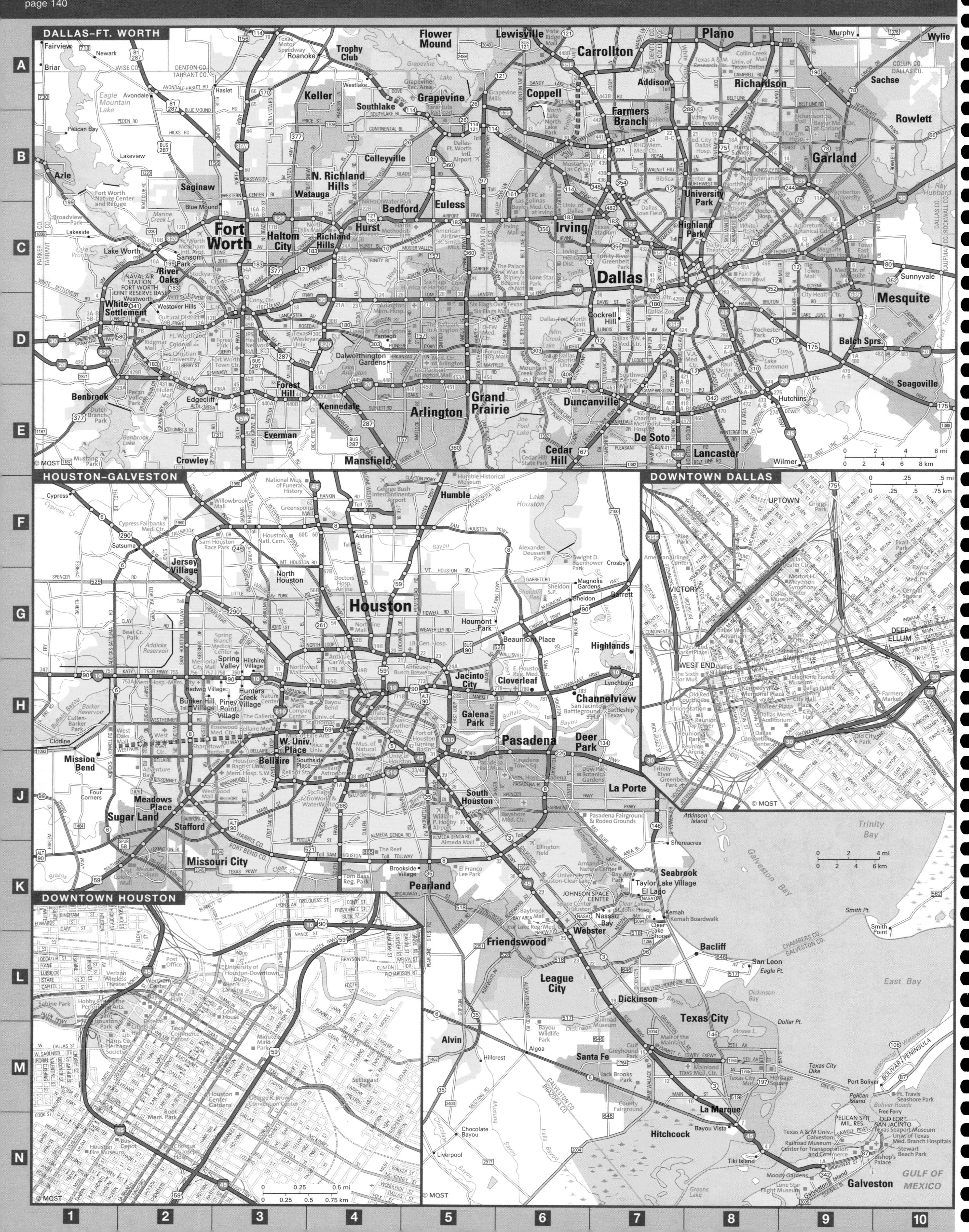

Index page 141

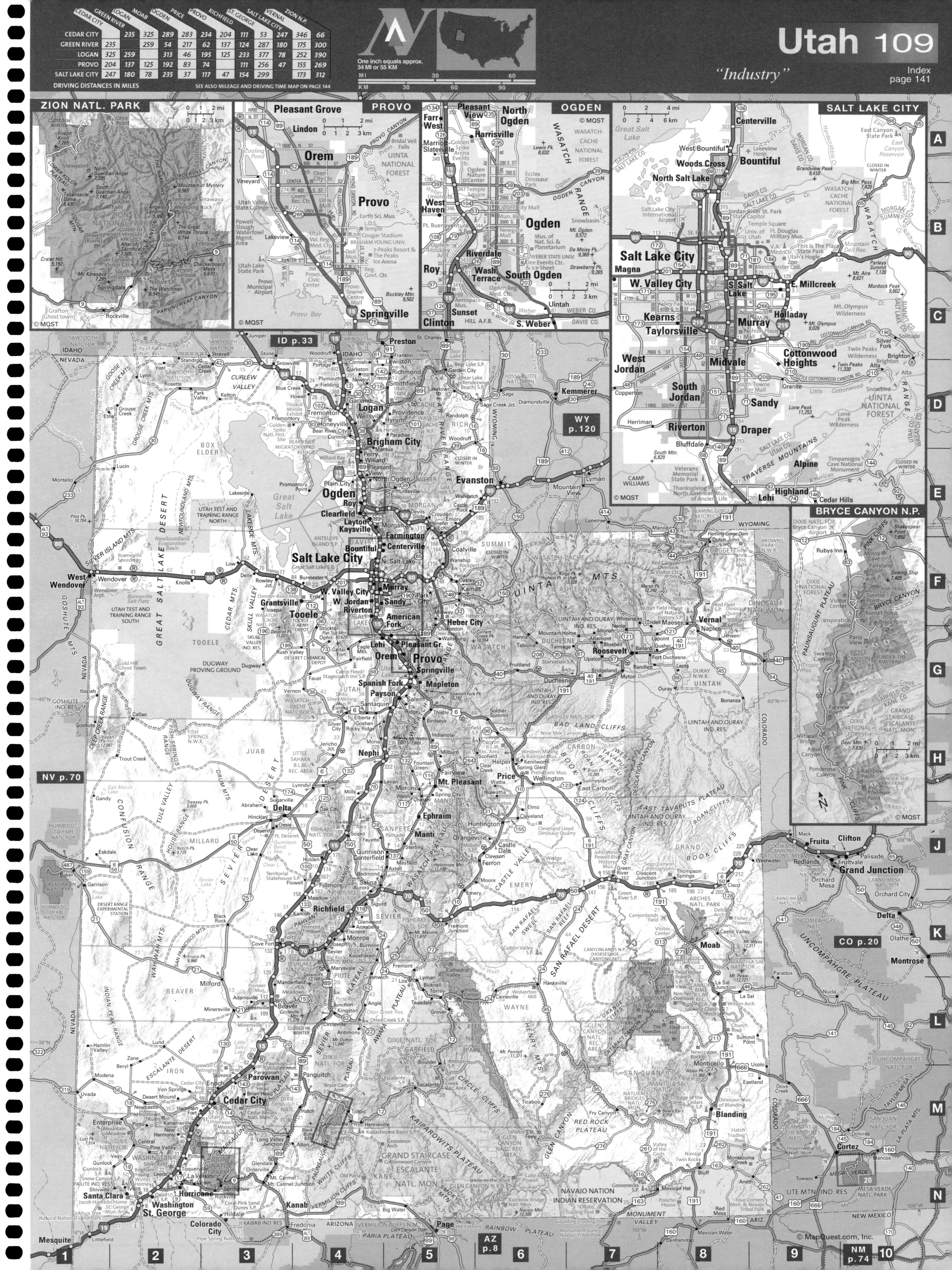

	CEDAR CITY	GREEN RIVER	LOGAN	MOAB	OGDEN	PRICE	PROVO	RICHFIELD	ST. GEORGE	SALT LAKE CITY	VERNAL	ZION N.P.
CEDAR CITY		235	325	289	283	234	204	111	53	247	346	66
GREEN RIVER	235		259	54	217	62	137	124	287	180	175	300
LOGAN	325	259		313	46	195	125	233	377	78	252	390
PROVO	204	137	125	192	83	74		111	256	47	155	269
SALT LAKE CITY	247	180	78	235	37	117	47	154	299		173	312

DRIVING DISTANCES IN MILES

SEE ALSO MILEAGE AND DRIVING TIME MAP ON PAGE 144

Index page 141

"Freedom and Unity"

	BENNINGTON	BRATTLEBORO	BURLINGTON	MIDDLEBURY	MONTPELIER	NEWPORT	RUTLAND	ST. ALBANS	ST. JOHNSBURY	SPRINGFIELD	VERGENNES	WHITE RIVER JCT.
BENNINGTON		38	127	91	124	200	58	150	161	63	105	98
BURLINGTON	127	148		36	39	81	69	23	76	120	22	91
MONTPELIER	124	112	39	56		64	66	60	37	84	58	54
RUTLAND	58	72	69	33	66	129		93	107	39	47	44
WHITE RIVER JCT.	98	62	91	66	54	104	44	112	65	34	80	

DRIVING DISTANCES IN MILES

SEE ALSO MILEAGE AND DRIVING TIME MAP ON PAGE 144

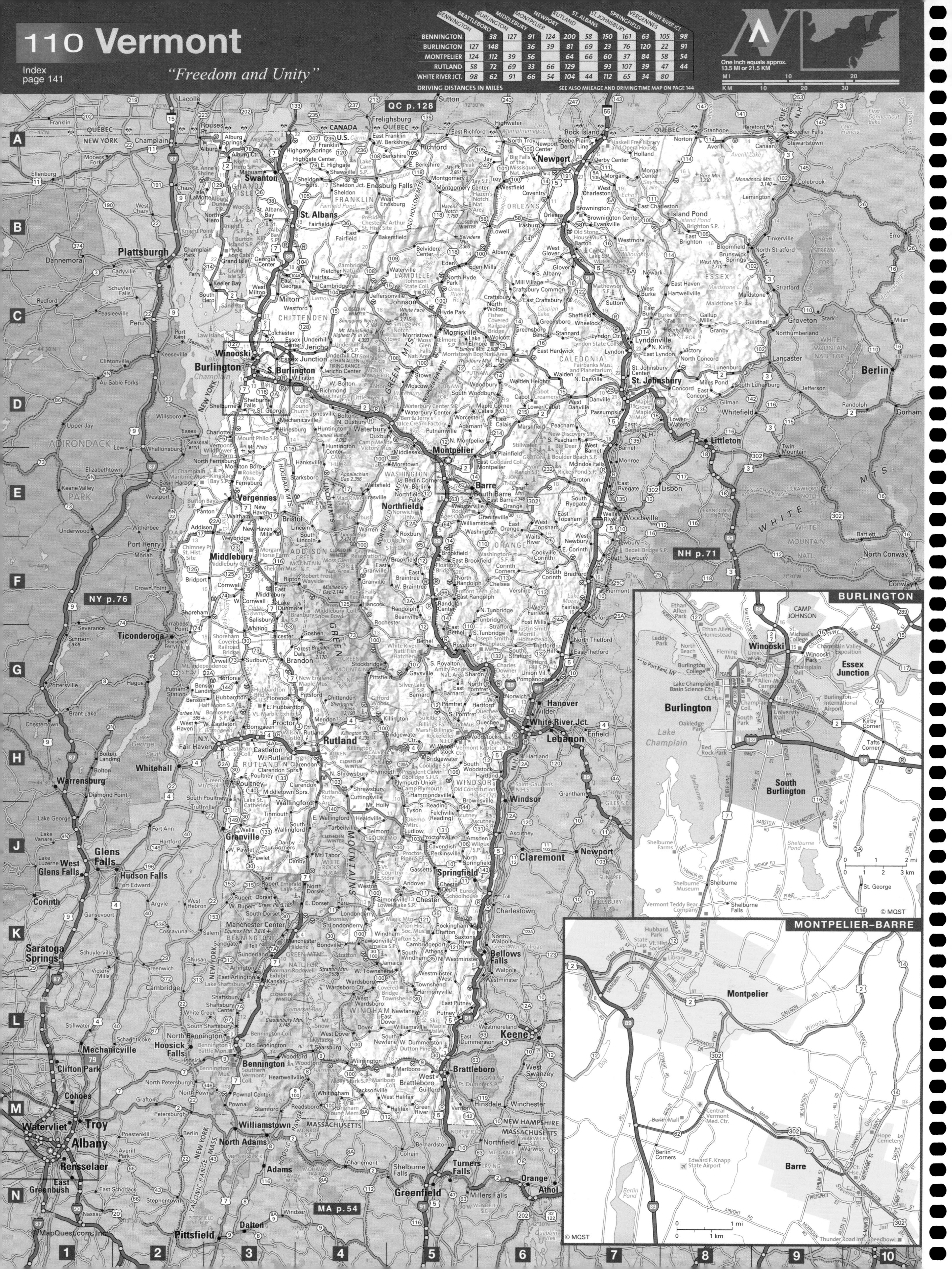

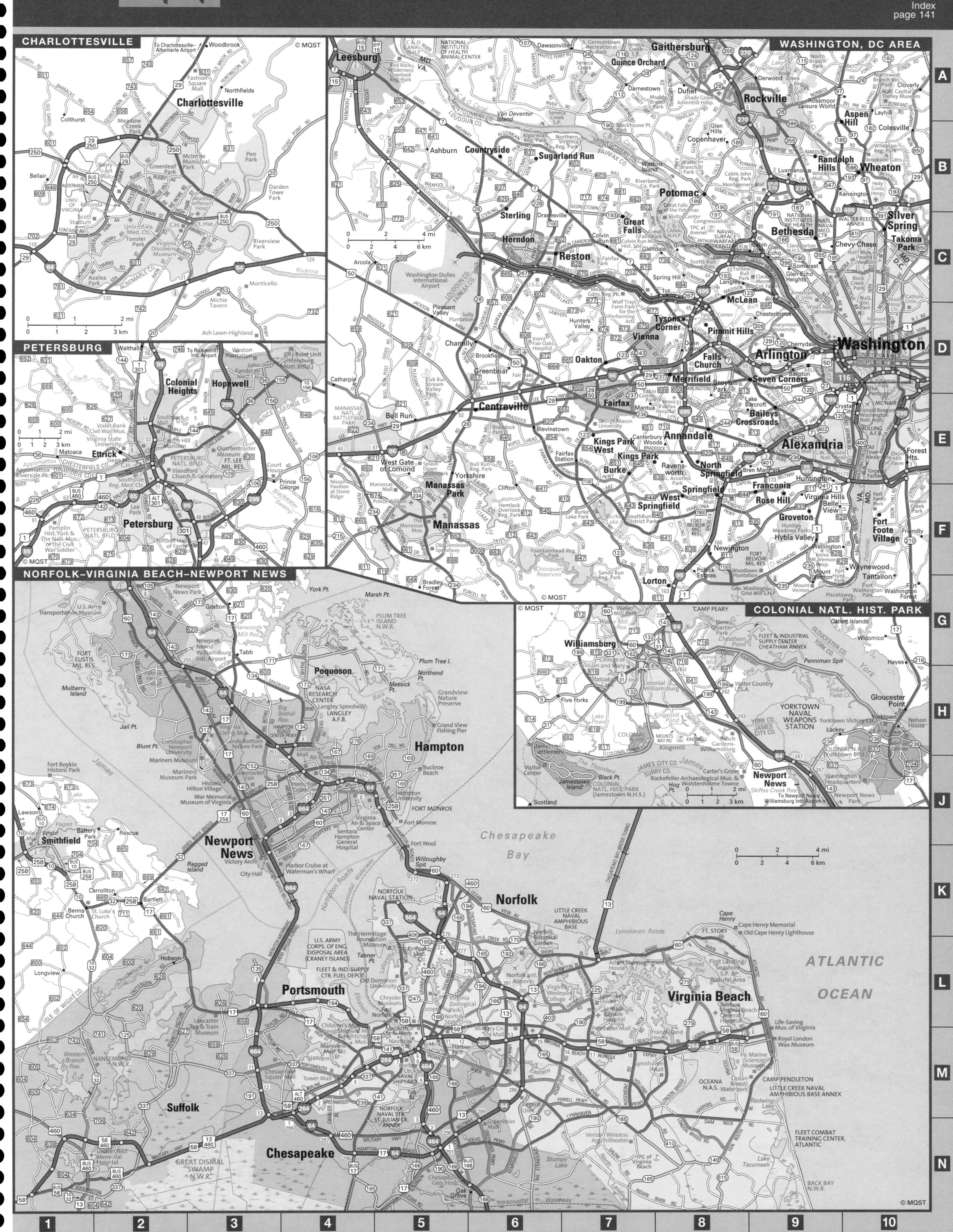

CHARLOTTESVILLE
© MQST
Charlottesville
Colthurst
Bellair
Meadow Creek Park
Fashion Square Mall
Northfields
McIntire Municipal Park
Pen Park
Darden Towe Park
Riverview Park
Greenleaf Park
Univ. of Virginia
Rotunda
Scott Stadium
Univ. of Va. Med. Ctr.
Tonsler Park
Azalea Park
Virginia Discovery Museum
Monticello
Michie Tavern
Ash Lawn-Highland
Rivanna
PETERSBURG
Walthall
Colonial Heights
Hopewell
City Point Unit Petersburg Natl. Btfld.
Weston Plantation
Ettrick
Matoaca
Virginia State University
Petersburg Natl. Btfld.
Quartermaster Museum
Ft. Lee Mil. Res.
Blandford Church & Cemetery
Prince George
Petersburg
Pamplin Hist. Park & The Natl. Mus. of The Civil War Soldier
Poplar Lawn
WASHINGTON, DC AREA
Leesburg
Gaithersburg
Quince Orchard
Rockville
Darnestown
Aspen Hill
Wheaton
Silver Spring
Takoma Park
Bethesda
Potomac
Great Falls
Countryside
Sugarland Run
Sterling
Herndon
Reston
Ashburn
Washington Dulles International Airport
Tysons Corner
McLean
Vienna
Oakton
Chantilly
Centreville
Fairfax
Falls Church
Arlington
Washington
Alexandria
Annandale
Springfield
Burke
Manassas
Manassas Park
Franconia
Rose Hill
Groveton
Hybla Valley
Fort Foote Village
Lorton
Mount Vernon
Woodbridge
COLONIAL NATL. HIST. PARK
Williamsburg
Colonial Williamsburg
Yorktown
Jamestown Island
Newport News
Busch Gardens Williamsburg
Kingsmill
YORKTOWN NAVAL WEAPONS STATION
CAMP PEARY
NORFOLK–VIRGINIA BEACH–NEWPORT NEWS
Poquoson
Hampton
Newport News
Smithfield
Norfolk
Portsmouth
Virginia Beach
Chesapeake
Suffolk
Chesapeake Bay
ATLANTIC OCEAN
FORT EUSTIS MIL. RES.
LANGLEY A.F.B.
FORT MONROE
NORFOLK NAVAL STATION
OCEANA N.A.S.
CAMP PENDLETON
GREAT DISMAL SWAMP N.W.R.
BACK BAY N.W.R.
A B C D E F G H J K L M N
1 2 3 4 5 6 7 8 9 10

Index page 141

	BRISTOL	CHARLOTTESVILLE	CHINCOTEAGUE	DANVILLE	EMPORIA	FREDERICKSBURG	HARRISONBURG	LEXINGTON	LYNCHBURG	NORFOLK	PETERSBURG	RICHMOND	ROANOKE	VIRGINIA BEACH	WASHINGTON, DC	WILLIAMSBURG	WINCHESTER	WYTHEVILLE
CHARLOTTESVILLE	258		255	131	140	70	62	69	67	164	95	71	123	180	118	122	100	187
NORFOLK	420	164	101	191	78	145	225	231	203		79	91	285	18	196	43	235	350
RICHMOND	327	71	182	160	69	57	131	138	114	91	24		192	107	108	49	147	256
ROANOKE	149	123	377	83	180	192	117	54	55	285	216	192		301	245	243	184	78
WASHINGTON, DC	380	118	158	268	177	54	131	191	183	196	133	108	245	212		153	92	309

DRIVING DISTANCES IN MILES

SEE ALSO MILEAGE AND DRIVING TIME MAP ON PAGE 144

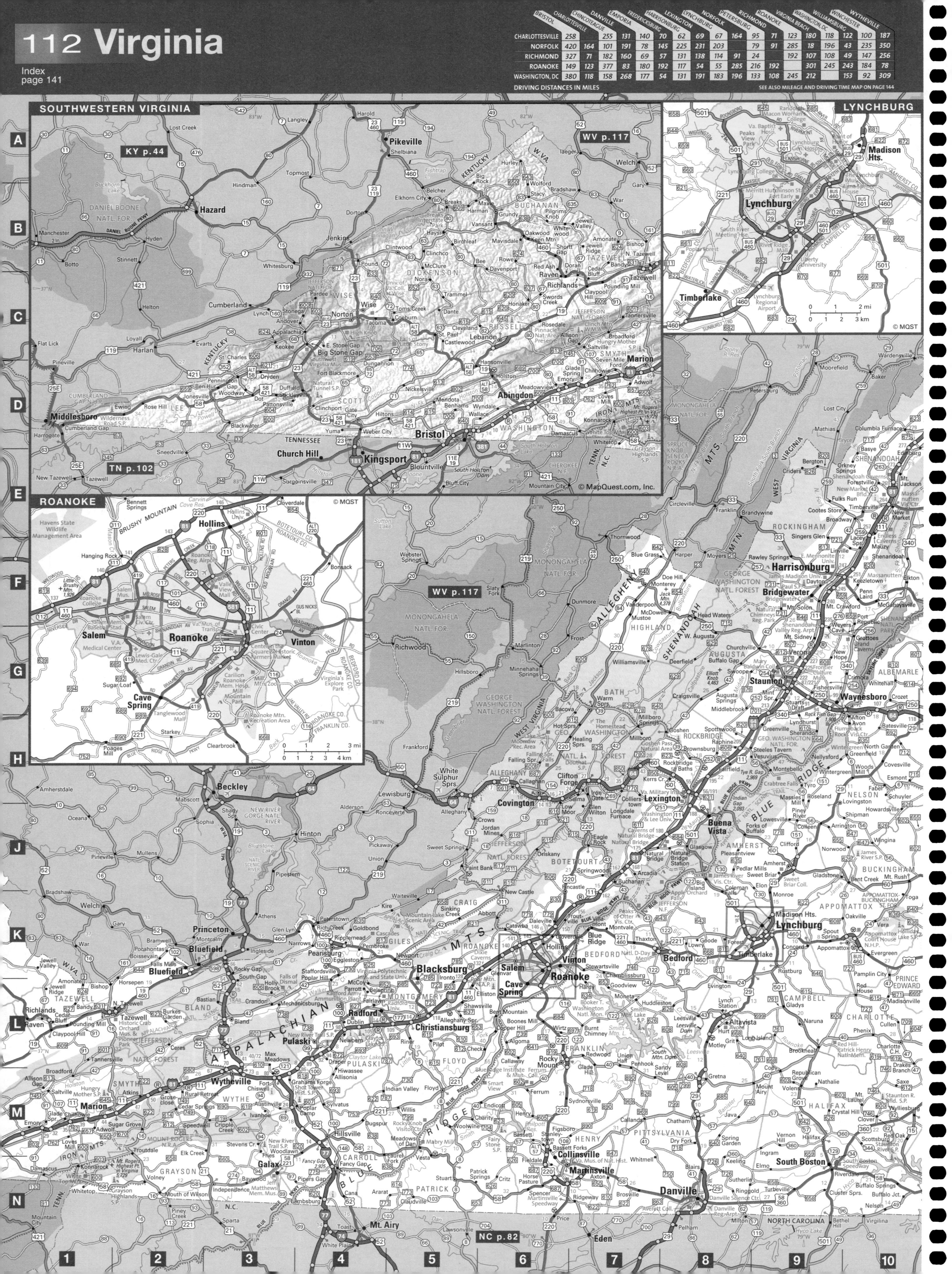

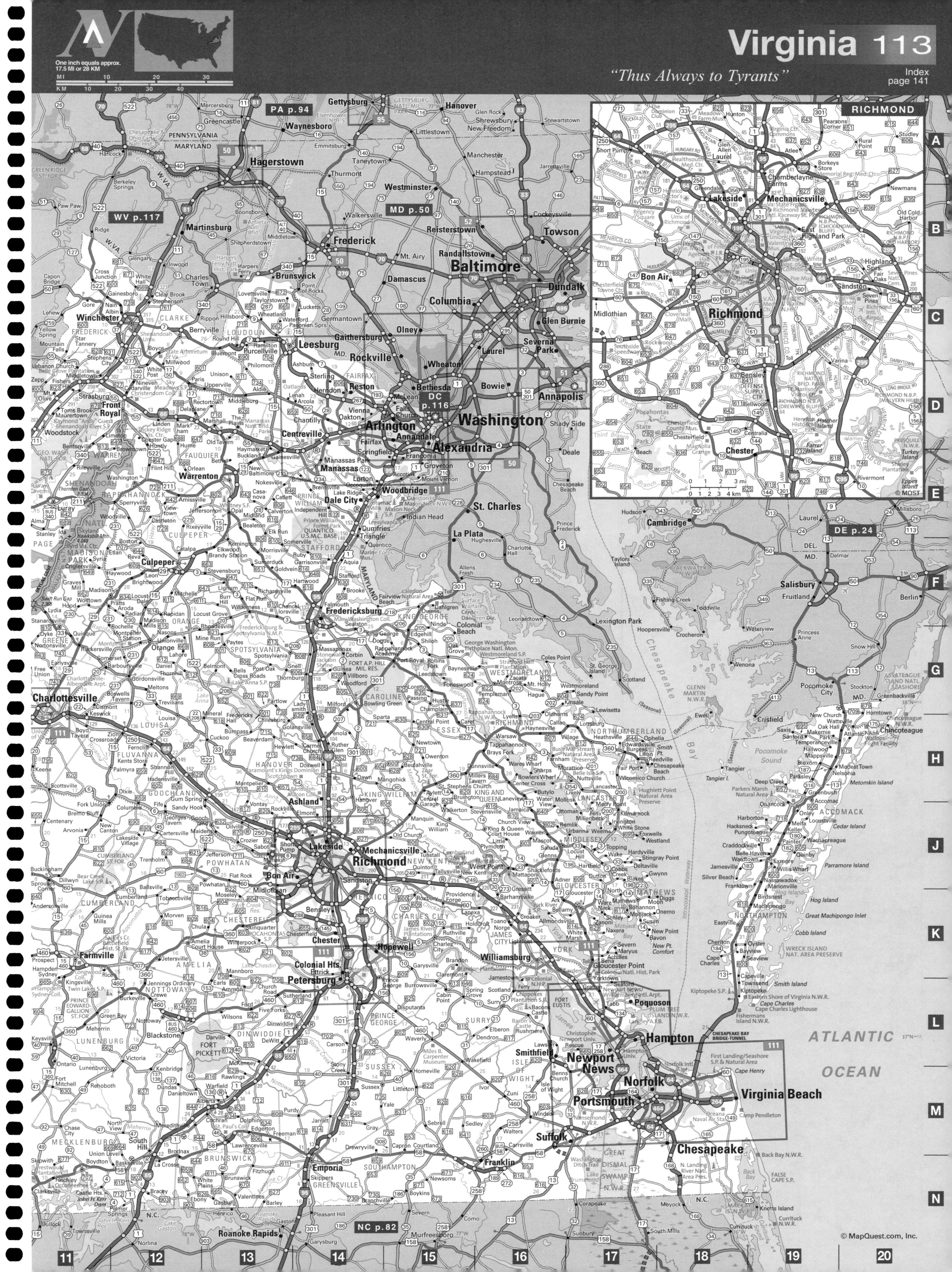
Virginia 113
"Thus Always to Tyrants"
Index page 141
One inch equals approx. 17.5 MI or 28 KM
MI 10 20 30
KM 10 20 30 40
PA p.94
MD p.50
WV p.117
DC p.116
DE p.24
NC p.82
RICHMOND
A
B
C
D
E
F
G
H
J
K
L
M
N
11
12
13
14
15
16
17
18
19
20
PENNSYLVANIA
MARYLAND
Gettysburg
Hanover
Waynesboro
Hagerstown
Martinsburg
Frederick
Westminster
Baltimore
Towson
Dundalk
Columbia
Glen Burnie
Annapolis
Winchester
Leesburg
Rockville
Bethesda
Reston
Arlington
Washington
Alexandria
Centreville
Manassas
Warrenton
Front Royal
Culpeper
Fredericksburg
Charlottesville
Dale City
Woodbridge
St. Charles
La Plata
Cambridge
Salisbury
Ashland
Lakeside
Mechanicsville
Richmond
Bon Air
Chester
Hopewell
Colonial Hts.
Petersburg
Farmville
Williamsburg
Gloucester Point
Poquoson
Hampton
Newport News
Norfolk
Portsmouth
Virginia Beach
Chesapeake
Suffolk
Franklin
Emporia
South Hill
Roanoke Rapids
Chincoteague
ATLANTIC OCEAN
Chesapeake Bay
© MapQuest.com, Inc.
© MOST

Index page 141

	ABERDEEN	BELLINGHAM	EVERETT	KENNEWICK	LEWISTON, ID	LONGVIEW	MOUNT RANIER N.P.	OKANOGAN	OLYMPIA	PORT ANGELES	PORTLAND, OR	PULLMAN	SEATTLE	SPOKANE	TACOMA	WALLA WALLA	WENATCHEE	YAKIMA
BELLINGHAM	196		61	307	420	215	186	195	147	127*	261	390	88	360	122	353	185	221
OLYMPIA	49	147	86	275	387	68	73	282		117	114	358	56	327	27	320	196	188
SEATTLE	105	88	28	226	338	124	96	223	56	83*	170	309		278	31	271	148	140
SPOKANE	376	360	299	139	103	395	290	148	327	362*	351	73	278		303	167	171	203
YAKIMA	237	221	161	86	214	170	87	194	188	223*	187	233	140	203	164	132	115	

DRIVING DISTANCES IN MILES

* DISTANCE INCLUDES FERRY TRAVEL

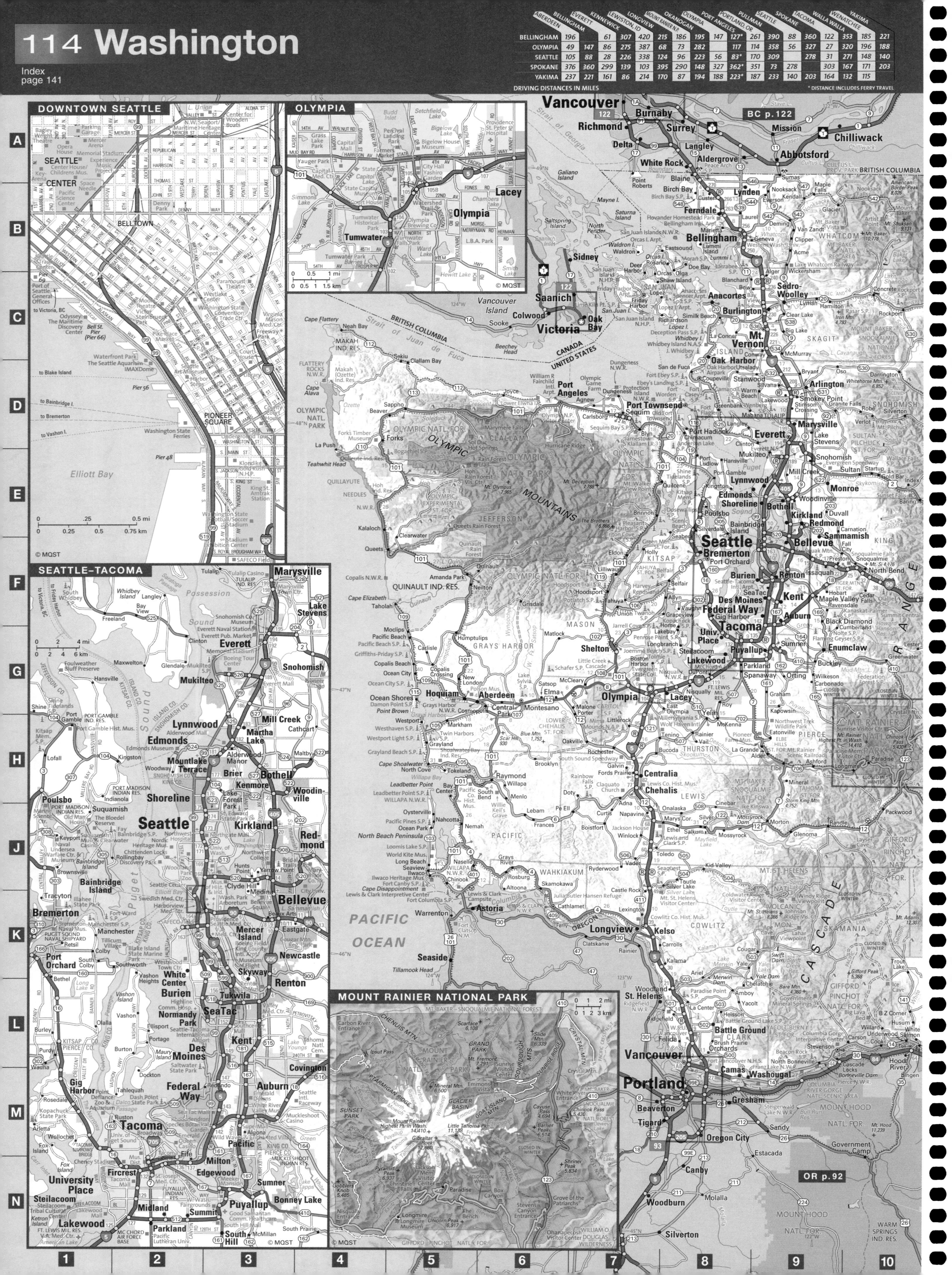

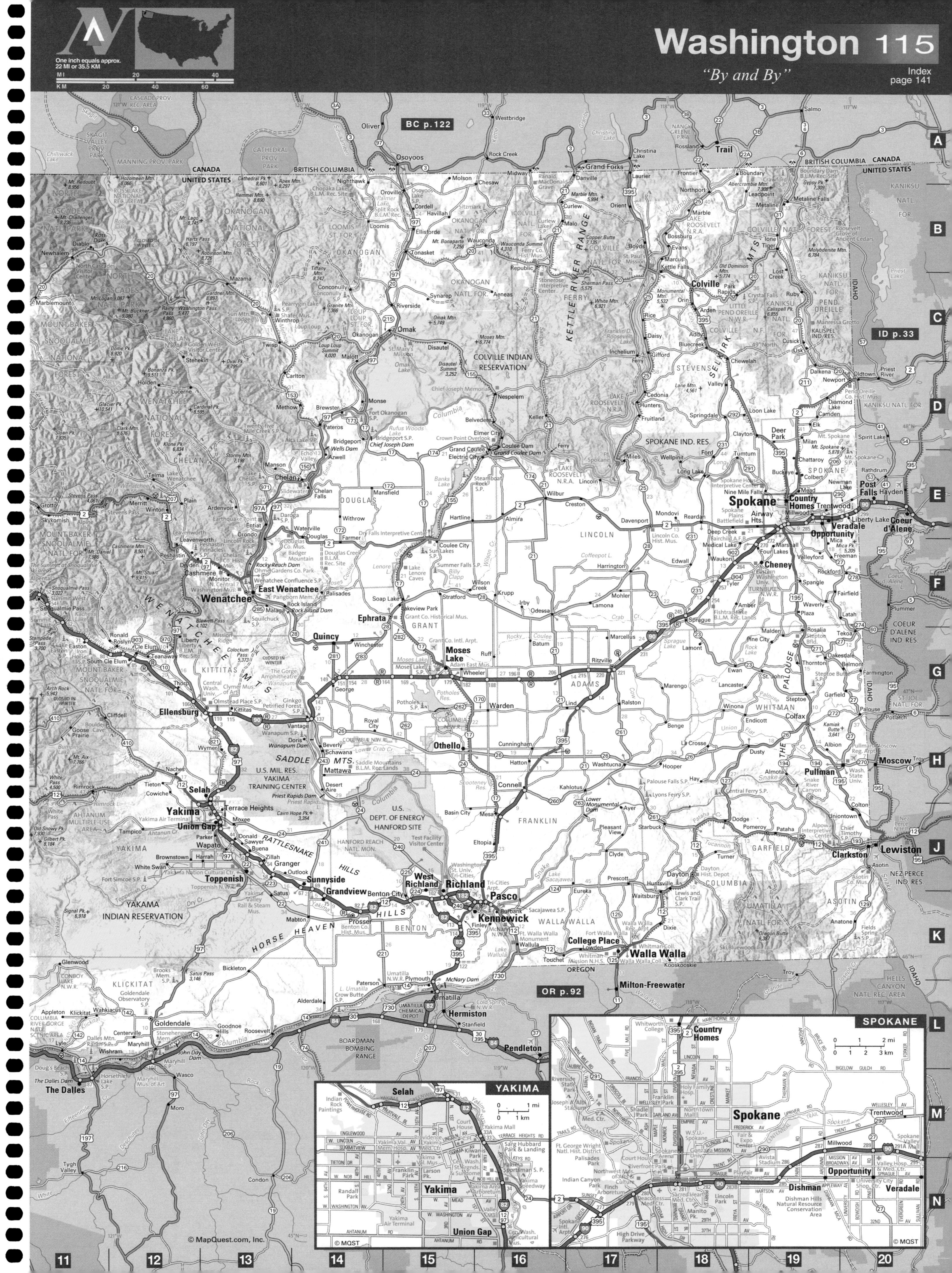
"By and By"
One inch equals approx. 22 MI or 35.5 KM
BC p.122
ID p.33
OR p.92
CANADA
UNITED STATES
BRITISH COLUMBIA
IDAHO
OREGON
Osoyoos
Oliver
Grand Forks
Trail
Rossland
Salmo
Okanogan
Omak
Tonasket
Oroville
Republic
Colville
Kettle Falls
Chewelah
Newport
Spokane
Country Homes
Millwood
Trentwood
Veradale
Opportunity
Cheney
Spokane Valley
Post Falls
Coeur d'Alene
Wenatchee
East Wenatchee
Chelan
Leavenworth
Cashmere
Ellensburg
Cle Elum
Ephrata
Quincy
Moses Lake
Othello
Ritzville
Davenport
Wilbur
Grand Coulee
Coulee Dam
Yakima
Selah
Union Gap
Toppenish
Sunnyside
Grandview
Prosser
Richland
West Richland
Kennewick
Pasco
Walla Walla
College Place
Milton-Freewater
Hermiston
Umatilla
Pendleton
Dayton
Pullman
Colfax
Moscow
Clarkston
Lewiston
Goldendale
The Dalles
Wasco
Moro
Condon
Tygh Valley
Snoqualmie Pass
OKANOGAN NATL. FOR.
COLVILLE NATL. FOR.
COLVILLE INDIAN RESERVATION
SPOKANE IND. RES.
KETTLE RIVER RANGE
YAKAMA INDIAN RESERVATION
U.S. DEPT. OF ENERGY HANFORD SITE
YAKIMA TRAINING CENTER
HORSE HEAVEN HILLS
RATTLESNAKE HILLS
SADDLE MTS.
WENATCHEE MTS.
NORTH CASCADES NATL. PARK
LINCOLN
DOUGLAS
GRANT
ADAMS
WHITMAN
FRANKLIN
BENTON
WALLA WALLA
COLUMBIA
GARFIELD
ASOTIN
KITTITAS
CHELAN
STEVENS
KLICKITAT
YAKIMA
SPOKANE
YAKIMA
Selah
Yakima
Union Gap
0 1 mi
0 1 km
© MQST
SPOKANE
Country Homes
Spokane
Trentwood
Millwood
Opportunity
Dishman
Veradale
0 1 2 mi
0 1 2 3 km
© MQST
© MapQuest.com, Inc.

Index
page 135

One inch equals approx. 2.5 MI or 4 KM

MI 2 4
KM 2 4 6

A B C D E F G H

Randolph Hills
Wheaton
White Oak
Calverton
Beltsville
Potomac
Silver Spring
Takoma Park
Langley Park
College Park
Greenbelt
Bethesda
Chevy Chase
Hyattsville
Riverdale Park
New Carrollton
Glenn Dale
Seabrook
Lanham
Chillum
Mount Rainier
Brentwood
Bladensburg
Cheverly
Landover
Glenarden
Kentland
Palmer Park
Woodmore
Largo
McLean
Tysons Corner
Pimmit Hills
Idylwood
Vienna
Falls Church
Merrifield
Seven Corners
Arlington
Washington
Seat Pleasant
Fairfax
Annandale
Baileys Crossroads
Alexandria
Suitland
District Heights
Hillcrest Heights
Marlow Heights
Temple Hills
Forestville
Camp Springs
Kings Park
North Springfield
West Springfield
Springfield
Franconia
Rose Hill
Groveton
Fort Foote Village
Glassmanor
Oxon Hill
Forest Heights
Huntington
Belle Haven

VA p.112

MD p.50

NATIONAL INSTITUTES OF HEALTH
WALTER REED ARMY MED. CTR.
ROCK CREEK PARK
ARLINGTON NATIONAL CEMETERY
NATIONAL ARBORETUM
ANACOSTIA NAVAL STATION
BOLLING A.F.B.
NAVAL RESEARCH LAB
ANDREWS AIR FORCE BASE
NATIONAL AGRICULTURAL RESEARCH CENTER

THE MALL

GEORGETOWN
FOGGY BOTTOM
LAFAYETTE SQUARE
DOWNTOWN
CHINATOWN
ROSSLYN
CAPITOL HILL
SW/WATERFRONT

Lincoln Memorial
Washington Monument
The White House
Thomas Jefferson Memorial
U.S. Capitol
Tidal Basin
Potomac
Arlington National Cemetery
Theodore Roosevelt Island
Smithsonian Institution Castle
National Air & Space Museum
National Gallery of Art
The Supreme Court
Library of Congress
Union Station

0 0.25 0.5 mi
0 0.25 0.5 0.75 km

WASHINGTON NAVY YARD

1 2 3 4 5 6 7 8 9 10

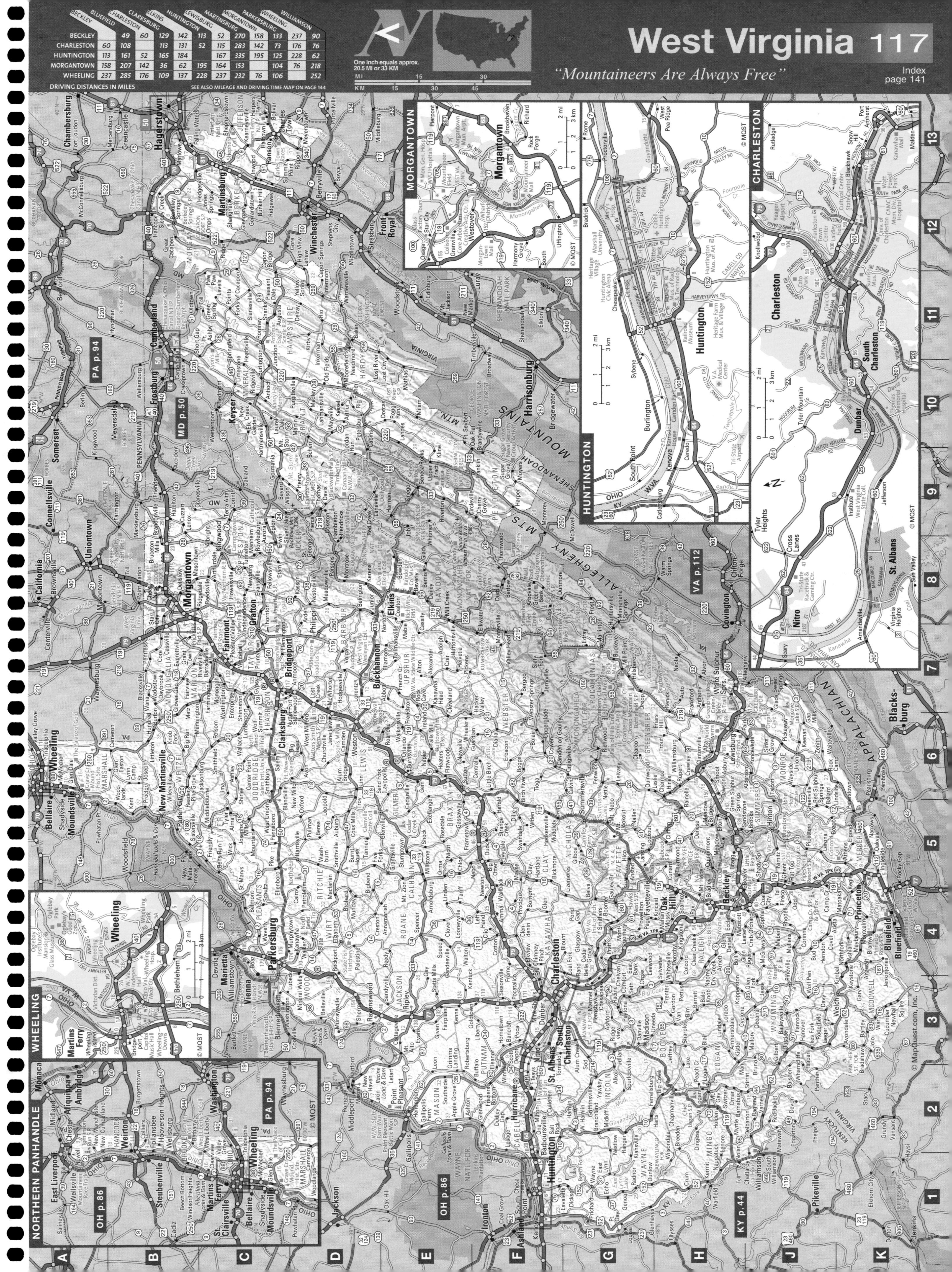

	BECKLEY	BLUEFIELD	CHARLESTON	CLARKSBURG	ELKINS	HUNTINGTON	LEWISBURG	MARTINSBURG	MORGANTOWN	PARKERSBURG	WHEELING	WILLIAMSON
BECKLEY		49	60	129	142	113	52	270	158	133	237	90
CHARLESTON	60	108		113	131	52	115	283	142	73	176	76
HUNTINGTON	113	161	52	165	184		167	335	195	125	228	62
MORGANTOWN	158	207	142	36	62	195	164	153		104	76	218
WHEELING	237	285	176	109	137	228	237	232	76	106		252

Index page 141

	APPLETON	ASHLAND	BELOIT	EAU CLAIRE	GREEN BAY	KENOSHA	LA CROSSE	MADISON	MARINETTE	MILWAUKEE	OSHKOSH	PORTAGE	PRAIRIE DU CHIEN	RHINELANDER	ST. PAUL, MN	SHEBOYGAN	SUPERIOR	WAUSAU
EAU CLAIRE	178	163	225		192	284	81	176	211	246	180	147	151	151	83	227	155	99
GREEN BAY	31	245	189	192		154	205	135	54	115	50	120	234	124	268	61	308	93
MADISON	104	305	56	176	135	116	141		184	78	86	36	102	197	258	132	327	141
MILWAUKEE	105	375	74	246	115	39	211	78	170		87	106	180	239	328	54	397	211
WAUSAU	90	165	190	99	93	249	146	141	112	211	111	105	193	58	174	153	223	

DRIVING DISTANCES IN MILES

SEE ALSO MILEAGE AND DRIVING TIME MAP ON PAGE 144

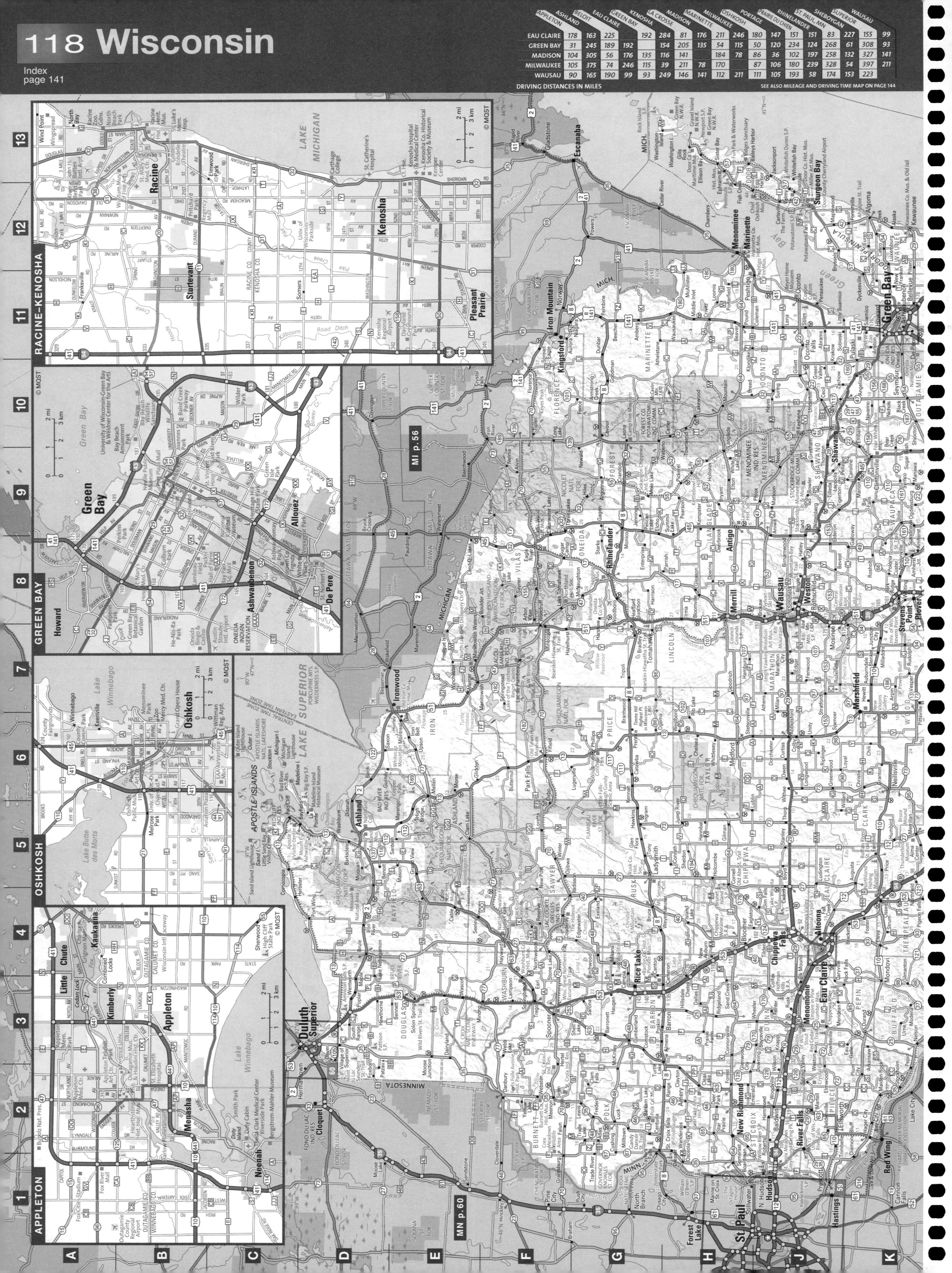

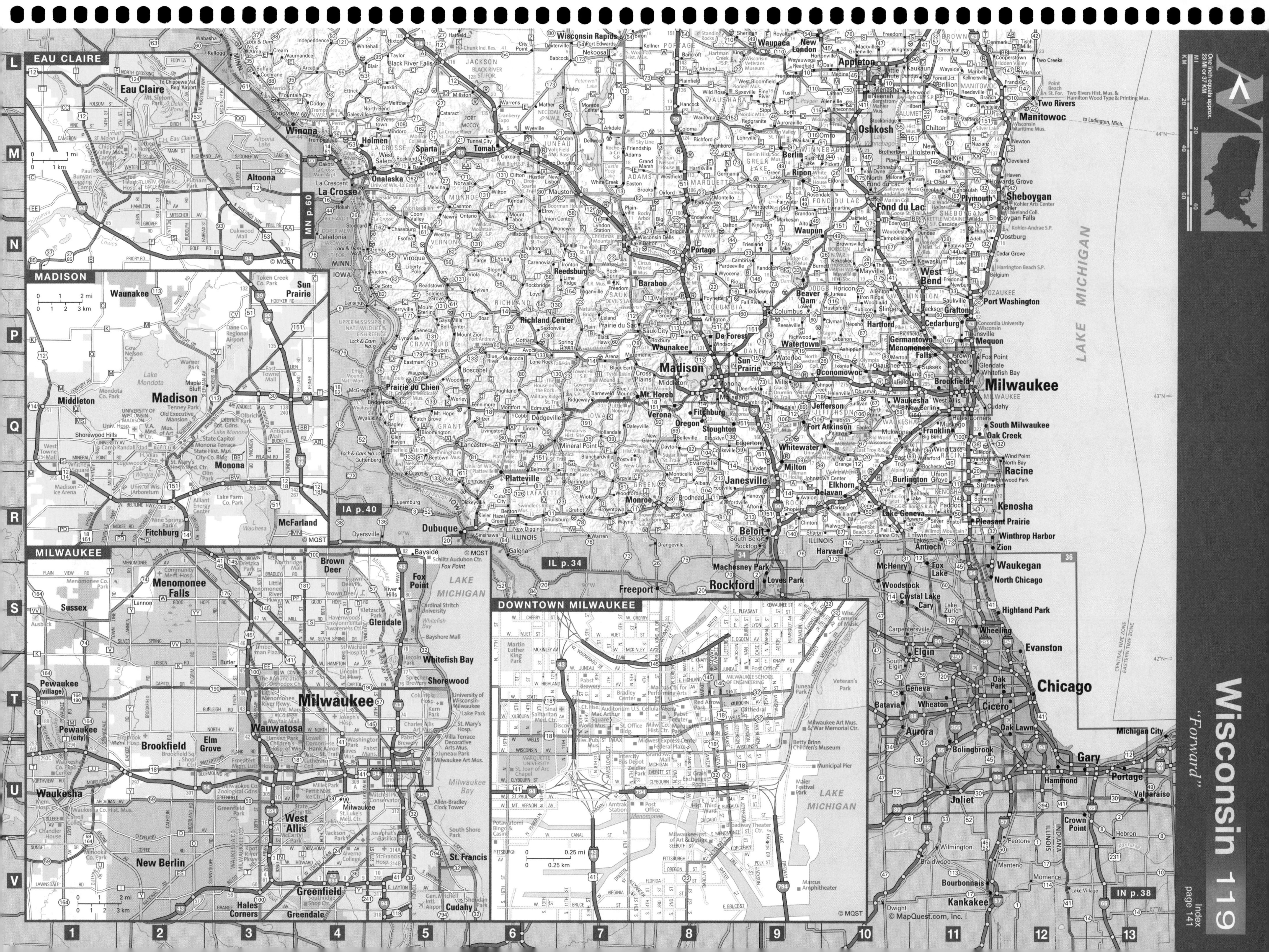
Wisconsin 119
"Forward"
Index
page 141
One inch equals approx.
23 MI or 37 KM
MI 20 40
KM 20 40 60
LAKE MICHIGAN
EASTERN TIME ZONE
CENTRAL TIME ZONE
INDIANA
ILLINOIS
IN p.38
IL p.34
IA p.40
MN p.60
Chicago
Milwaukee
Madison
Appleton
Oshkosh
Fond du Lac
Sheboygan
Manitowoc
Two Rivers
Racine
Kenosha
Waukegan
Rockford
Janesville
Beloit
Freeport
Dubuque
La Crosse
Onalaska
Winona
Tomah
Sparta
Portage
Baraboo
Waupaca
New London
Wisconsin Rapids
Gary
Hammond
Joliet
Kankakee
Aurora
Elgin
Evanston
Platteville
Prairie du Chien
Watertown
Waukesha
West Bend
Beaver Dam
Monroe
Sun Prairie
Stoughton
Lake Geneva
Whitewater
Delavan
Elkhorn
Cedarburg
Port Washington
Plymouth
Ripon
Berlin
Viroqua
Richland Center
Reedsburg
Mt. Horeb
Verona
Middleton
Waunakee
Fitchburg
DOWNTOWN MILWAUKEE
EAU CLAIRE
MADISON
MILWAUKEE
Eau Claire
Altoona
McFarland
Monona
Brookfield
New Berlin
Wauwatosa
West Allis
Greenfield
Glendale
Shorewood
Whitefish Bay
Fox Point
Brown Deer
Menomonee Falls
Cudahy
St. Francis
Greendale
Hales Corners
Elm Grove
Pewaukee
Sussex
© MQST
© MapQuest.com, Inc.
L M N P Q R S T U V
1 2 3 4 5 6 7 8 9 10 11 12 13

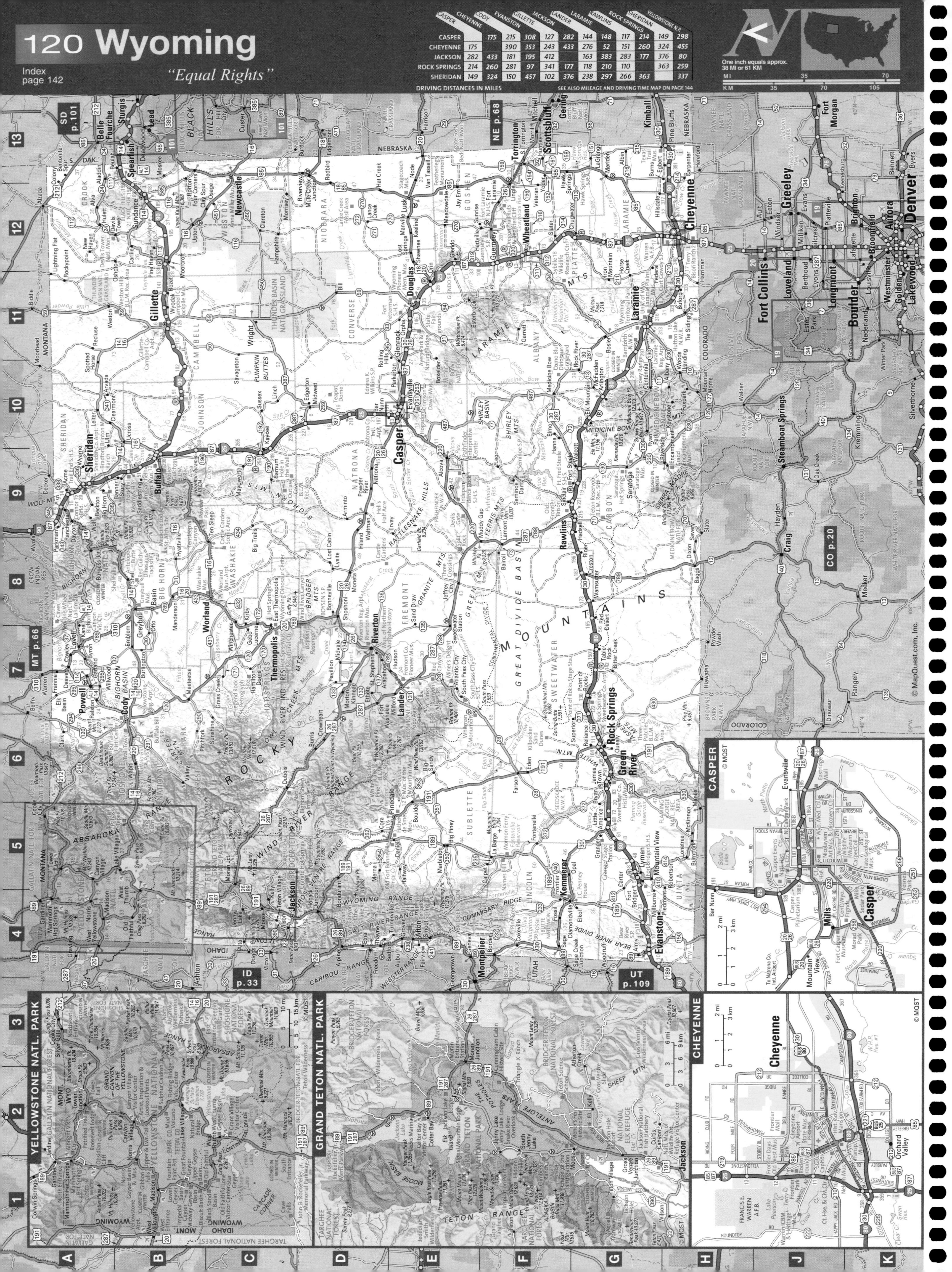

	CASPER	CHEYENNE	CODY	EVANSTON	GILLETTE	JACKSON	LANDER	LARAMIE	RAWLINS	ROCK SPRINGS	SHERIDAN	YELLOWSTONE N.P.
CASPER		175	215	308	127	282	144	148	117	214	149	298
CHEYENNE	175		390	353	243	433	276	52	151	260	324	455
JACKSON	282	433	181	195	412		163	383	283	177	376	80
ROCK SPRINGS	214	260	281	97	341	177	118	210	110		363	259
SHERIDAN	149	324	150	457	102	376	238	297	266	363		337

DRIVING DISTANCES IN MILES

SEE ALSO MILEAGE AND DRIVING TIME MAP ON PAGE 144

Index page 142

One inch equals approx. 259 MI or 417.5 KM

MI 200 400
KM 200 400 600

NOTE: Legislated standard time zone boundaries shown; observed time may differ locally.

DISTANCES BETWEEN CITIES ARE COMPUTED IN KILOMETERS OVER MAIN HIGHWAYS AND INCLUDE FERRY DISTANCES

	BOSTON, MA	BRANDON, MB	CALGARY, AB	CHARLOTTETOWN, PE	CHICAGO, IL	DAWSON CREEK, BC	EDMONTON, AB	FREDERICTON, NB	HALIFAX, NS	KENORA, ON	MINNEAPOLIS, MN	MONTRÉAL, QC	NEW YORK, NY	NORTH BAY, ON	OTTAWA, ON	PRINCE GEORGE, BC	QUÉBEC, QC	REGINA, SK	ST. JOHN'S, NF	SASKATOON, SK	SAULT STE. MARIE, ON	SEATTLE, WA	THUNDER BAY, ON	TORONTO, ON	VANCOUVER, BC	VICTORIA, BC	WHITEHORSE, YT	WINDSOR, ON	WINNIPEG, MB
BANFF, AB	4434	1234	128	4681	2811	1001	412	4432	4802	1648	2156	3652	4104	3137	3500	637	3888	856	6032	729	2725	977	2105	3642	819	874	2219	3280	1429
BOSTON, MA		3220	4318	1049	1614	4950	4353	690	1149	2639	2280	504	346	1036	665	5093	634	3577	2379	3840	1572	4941	2187	917	5156	5235	6268	1181	3006
BRANDON, MB			1117	3468	1598	1749	1152	3217	3589	434	943	2438	2889	1923	2287	1894	2675	377	4817	639	1510	2041	892	2427	2016	2108	3067	2066	216
CALGARY, AB				4566	2696	885	296	4315	4686	1530	2041	3536	3986	3021	3384	755	3772	740	5914	613	2607	1093	1989	3524	900	991	2203	3162	1313
CHARLOTTETOWN, PE					2382	5198	4601	354	322	3035	3048	1030	1381	1574	1204	5341	819	3825	1376	4088	1997	5708	2583	1561	5924	6003	6516	1925	3241
CHICAGO, IL						3328	2731	2134	2504	1577	658	1353	1283	1138	1252	3471	1604	1955	3734	2216	896	3318	1521	821	3534	3613	4646	460	1384
DAWSON CREEK, BC							597	4947	5319	2165	2673	4168	4620	3653	4017	406	4405	1373	6548	1112	3241	1283	2622	4158	1184	1181	1318	3796	1946
EDMONTON, AB								4350	4722	1566	2076	3571	4022	3056	3420	740	3806	776	5950	513	2642	1308	2024	3560	1115	1207	1915	3198	1347
FREDERICTON, NB									452	2784	2797	779	1022	1323	953	5092	568	3574	1688	3837	1746	5457	2333	1310	5673	5752	6265	1674	2990
HALIFAX, NS										3156	3169	1151	1481	1695	1324	5462	940	3946	1402	4208	2118	5829	2704	1682	6045	6123	6637	2045	3362
KENORA, ON											668	2005	2622	1489	1854	2308	2240	792	4384	1052	1077	2456	459	1814	2432	2522	3483	1640	208
MINNEAPOLIS, MN												2020	1949	1802	1918	2816	2271	1299	4398	1561	1173	2662	547	1487	2877	2956	3989	1125	727
MONTRÉAL, QC													616	544	194	4311	250	2795	2379	3058	967	4678	1553	531	4894	4973	5486	895	2211
NEW YORK, NY														999	703	4764	838	3248	2710	3508	1545	4609	2171	816	4825	4905	5938	1001	2675
NORTH BAY, ON															364	3796	795	2280	2924	2541	423	4464	1072	336	3920	4012	4971	679	1696
OTTAWA, ON																4160	444	2644	2552	2906	787	4578	1401	431	4792	4873	5335	793	2060
PRINCE GEORGE, BC																	4548	1516	6691	1255	3384	922	2765	4302	778	821	1580	3940	2089
QUÉBEC, QC																		3032	2168	3293	1218	4929	1790	782	5143	5224	5723	1144	2448
REGINA, SK																			5176	261	1868	1664	1249	2786	1640	1732	2691	2424	573
ST. JOHN'S, NF																				5436	3346	7058	3933	2910	7272	7353	7866	3273	4590
SASKATOON, SK																					2129	1823	1511	3046	1630	1722	2430	2684	834
SAULT STE. MARIE, ON																						4223	649	674	3508	3598	4559	563	1283
SEATTLE, WA																							2913	4147	225	177	2504	3787	2237
THUNDER BAY, ON																								1355	2889	2980	3940	1699	665
TORONTO, ON																									4363	4443	5476	364	2213
VANCOUVER, BC																										93	2311	4001	2213
VICTORIA, BC																											2401	4081	2305
WHITEHORSE, YT																												5114	3264
WINDSOR, ON																													1852

Index page 142

"Splendor Without Diminishment"

	BANFF, AB	CRANBROOK	DAWSON CREEK	JASPER, AB	KAMLOOPS	KELOWNA	NANAIMO	PRINCE GEORGE	PRINCE RUPERT	REVELSTOKE	VANCOUVER	VICTORIA
CRANBROOK	265		985	504	600	513	845*	838	1562	196	765	882*
KAMLOOPS	479	600	931	444		163	359*	525	1249	206	340	396*
KELOWNA	476	513	1094	597	163		383*	688	1409	192	378	420*
PRINCE GEORGE	637	838	406	376	525	688	784*		724	693	778	821*
VANCOUVER	819	765	1184	784	340	378	109*	778	1502	546		93*

DRIVING DISTANCES IN KILOMETERS

* DISTANCE INCLUDES FERRY TRAVEL

One inch equals approx. 46.5 MI or 75 KM

"Strong and Free"

Index page 142

	BANFF	CALGARY	CRANBROOK, BC	DAWSON CREEK, BC	EDMONTON	FORT MC MURRAY	GRANDE PRAIRIE	JASPER	LETHBRIDGE	LLOYDMINSTER	MEDICINE HAT	RED DEER
CALGARY	128		383	885	296	726	750	396	216	534	285	145
EDMONTON	412	296	679	597		439	462	367	512	238	579	150
GRANDE PRAIRIE	665	750	861	124	462	756		397	965	700	1033	603
LETHBRIDGE	344	216	296	1101	512	943	965	612		605	164	360
MEDICINE HAT	413	285	460	1168	579	931	1033	681	164	480		430

DRIVING DISTANCES IN KILOMETERS

SEE ALSO MILEAGE AND DRIVING TIME MAP ON PAGE 144

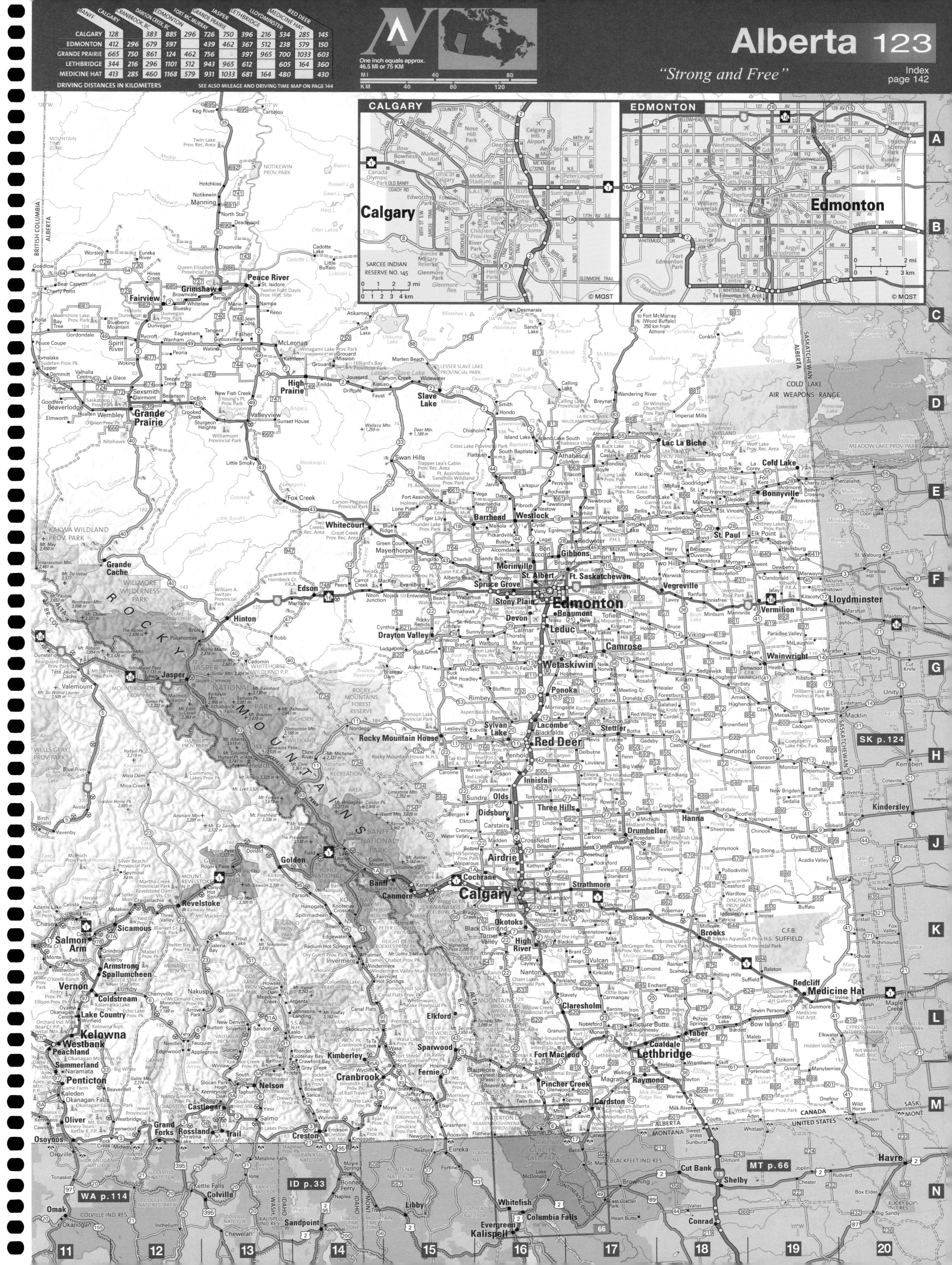

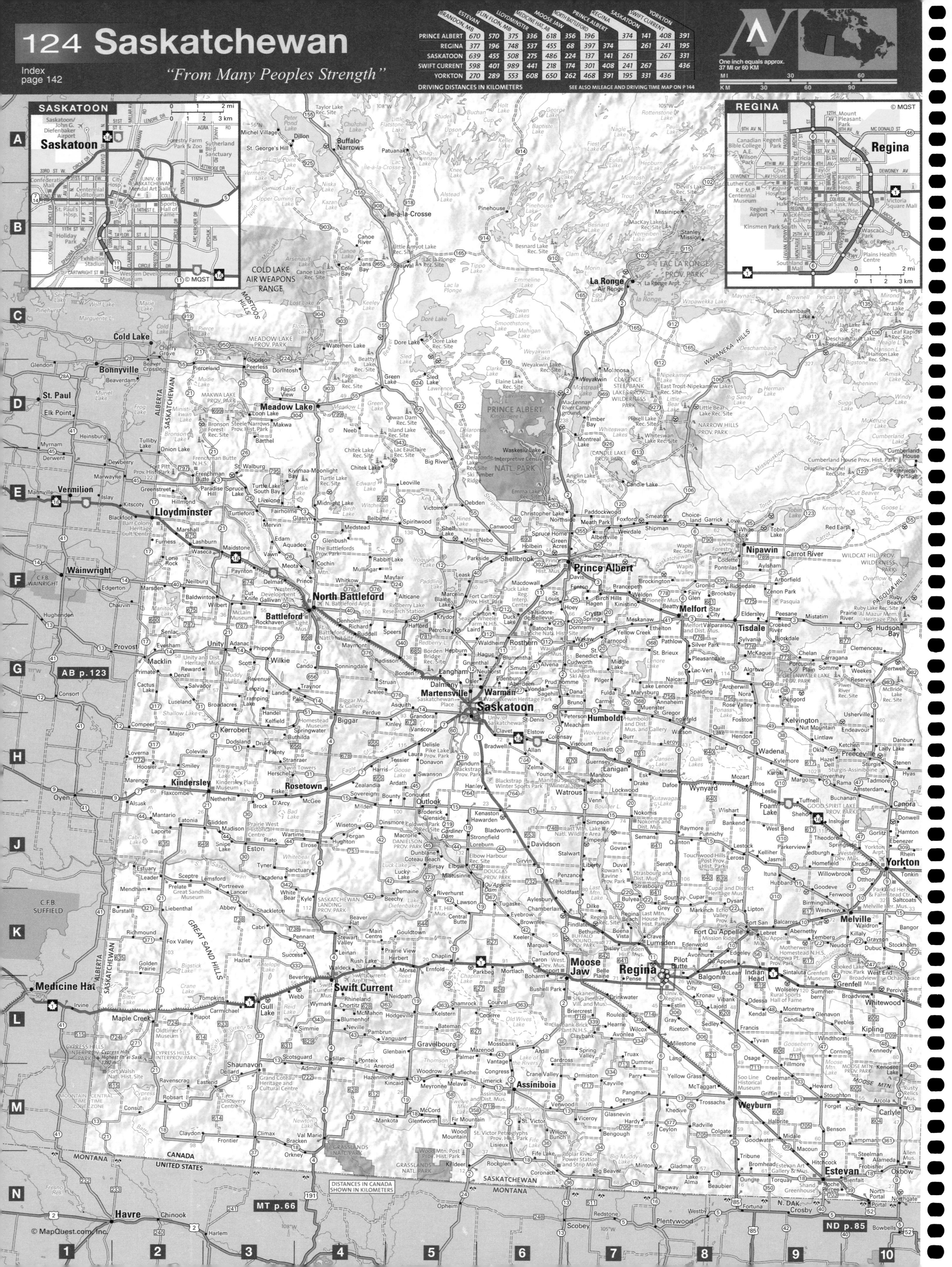

Index page 142

"From Many Peoples Strength"

	BRANDON, MB	ESTEVAN	FLIN FLON, MB	LLOYDMINSTER	MEDICINE HAT, AB	MOOSE JAW	NORTH BATTLEFORD	PRINCE ALBERT	REGINA	SASKATOON	SWIFT CURRENT	YORKTON
PRINCE ALBERT	670	570	375	336	618	356	196		374	141	408	391
REGINA	377	196	748	537	455	68	397	374		261	241	195
SASKATOON	639	455	508	275	486	224	137	141	261		267	331
SWIFT CURRENT	598	401	989	441	218	174	301	408	241	267		436
YORKTON	270	289	553	608	650	262	468	391	195	331	436	

DRIVING DISTANCES IN KILOMETERS

SEE ALSO MILEAGE AND DRIVING TIME MAP ON P 144

Index page 142

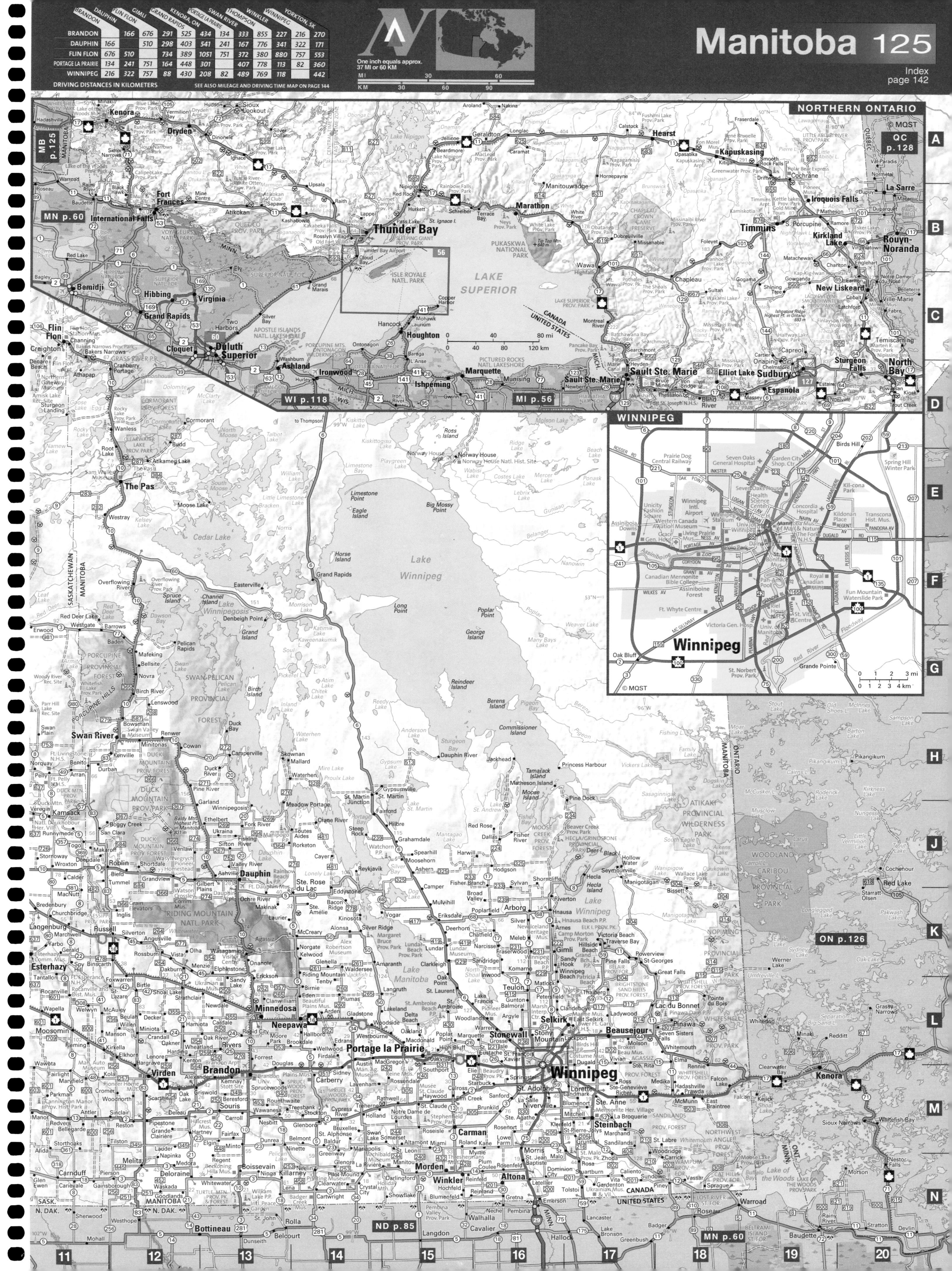

	BRANDON	DAUPHIN	FLIN FLON	GIMLI	GRAND RAPIDS	KENORA, ON	PORTAGE LA PRAIRIE	SWAN RIVER	THOMPSON	WINKLER	WINNIPEG	YORKTON, SK
BRANDON		166	676	291	525	434	134	333	855	227	216	270
DAUPHIN	166		510	298	403	541	241	167	776	341	322	171
FLIN FLON	676	510		734	389	1051	751	372	380	880	757	553
PORTAGE LA PRAIRIE	134	241	751	164	448	301		407	778	113	82	360
WINNIPEG	216	322	757	88	430	208	82	489	769	118		442

DRIVING DISTANCES IN KILOMETERS

SEE ALSO MILEAGE AND DRIVING TIME MAP ON PAGE 144

Index page 142

	Barrie	Hamilton	Kenora	Kingston	Kitchener	London	Niagara Falls	North Bay	Ottawa
LONDON	248	134	1926	434	105		227	499	613
OTTAWA	442	504	1854	179	496	613	574	364	
SUDBURY	319	462	1407	600	453	570	533	124	488
THUNDER BAY	1219	1410	459	1548	1401	1467	1481	1072	1401
TORONTO	105	74	1814	251	104	183	145	336	431

	Owen Sound	Peterborough	Sarnia	Sault Ste. Marie	Sudbury	Thunder Bay	Timmins	Toronto	Windsor
LONDON	208	309	109	818	570	1467	840	183	195
OTTAWA	558	265	714	787	488	1401	705	431	793
SUDBURY	435	404	673	299		948	290	407	751
THUNDER BAY	1335	1371	1621	649	948		735	1355	1699
TORONTO	183	127	285	674	407	1355	677		364

DRIVING DISTANCES IN KILOMETERS

SEE ALSO MILEAGE AND DRIVING TIME MAP ON PAGE 144

"Loyal She Began, Loyal She Remains"

Index page 142

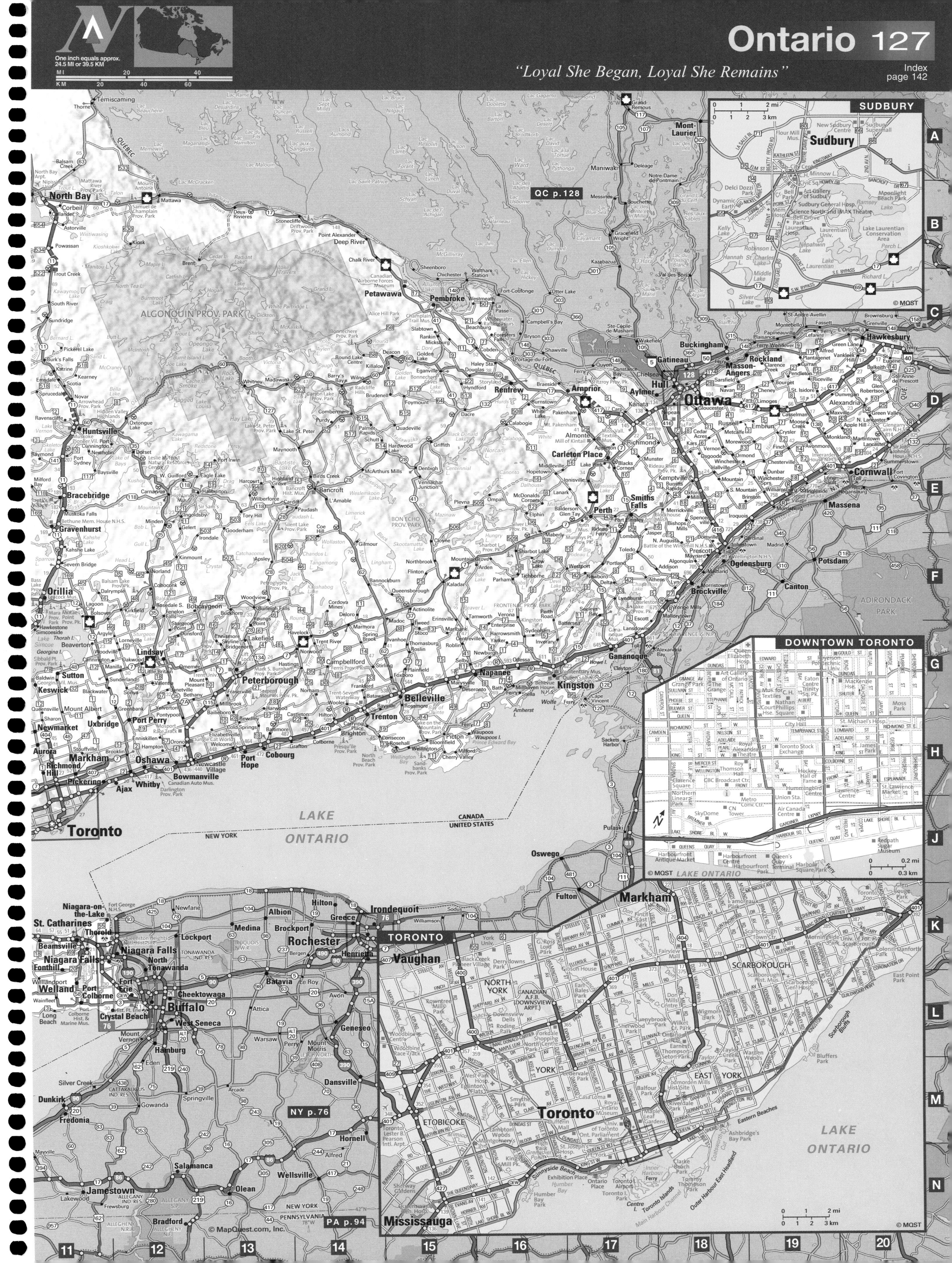

Index page 142

	BAIE-COMEAU	CHICOUTIMI	DRUMMONDVILLE	GASPÉ	MONT-LAURIER	MONTRÉAL	OTTAWA, ON	QUÉBEC	RIMOUSKI	RIVIÈRE-DU-LOUP	ROBERVAL	ROUYN-NORANDA	ST-GEORGES	SEPT-ÎLES	SHERBROOKE	SOREL	TROIS-RIVIÈRES	VICTORIAVILLE
MONTRÉAL	663	461	116	898	230		194	250	535	426	448	616	325	887	143	87	146	164
QUÉBEC	400	211	151	668	439	250	444		305	196	253	879	102	624	233	204	135	114
RIVIÈRE-DU-LOUP	230*	154*	328	472	656	426	620	196	109		249*	1042	272	454*	401	381	333	291
SHERBROOKE	633	444	82	873	373	143	337	233	510	401	417	759	148	857		142	158	97
TROIS-RIVIÈRES	535	346	68	804	376	146	340	135	441	333	296	762	214	759	158	82		65

DRIVING DISTANCES IN KILOMETERS

* DISTANCE INCLUDES FERRY TRAVEL

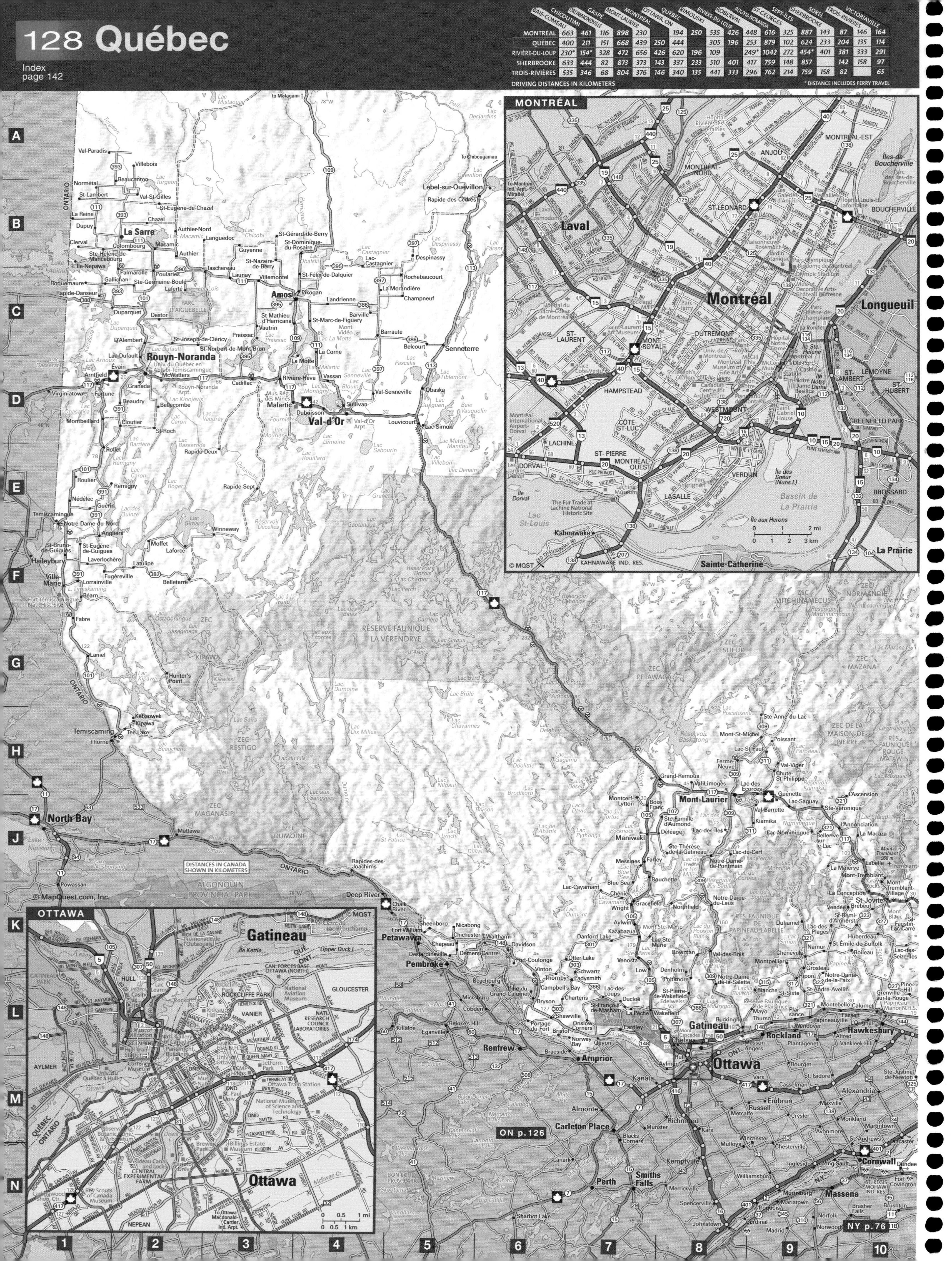

"Je Me Souviens (I Remember)"

Index page 142

One inch equals approx. 24 MI or 39 KM

MI 0 20 40
KM 0 20 40 60

QUÉBEC

© MapQuest.com, Inc.

EASTERN QUÉBEC

SHERBROOKE

QC p.130

ME p.48

NH p.71

VT p.110

NY p.76

A B C D E F G H J K L M N

11 12 13 14 15 16 17 18 19 20

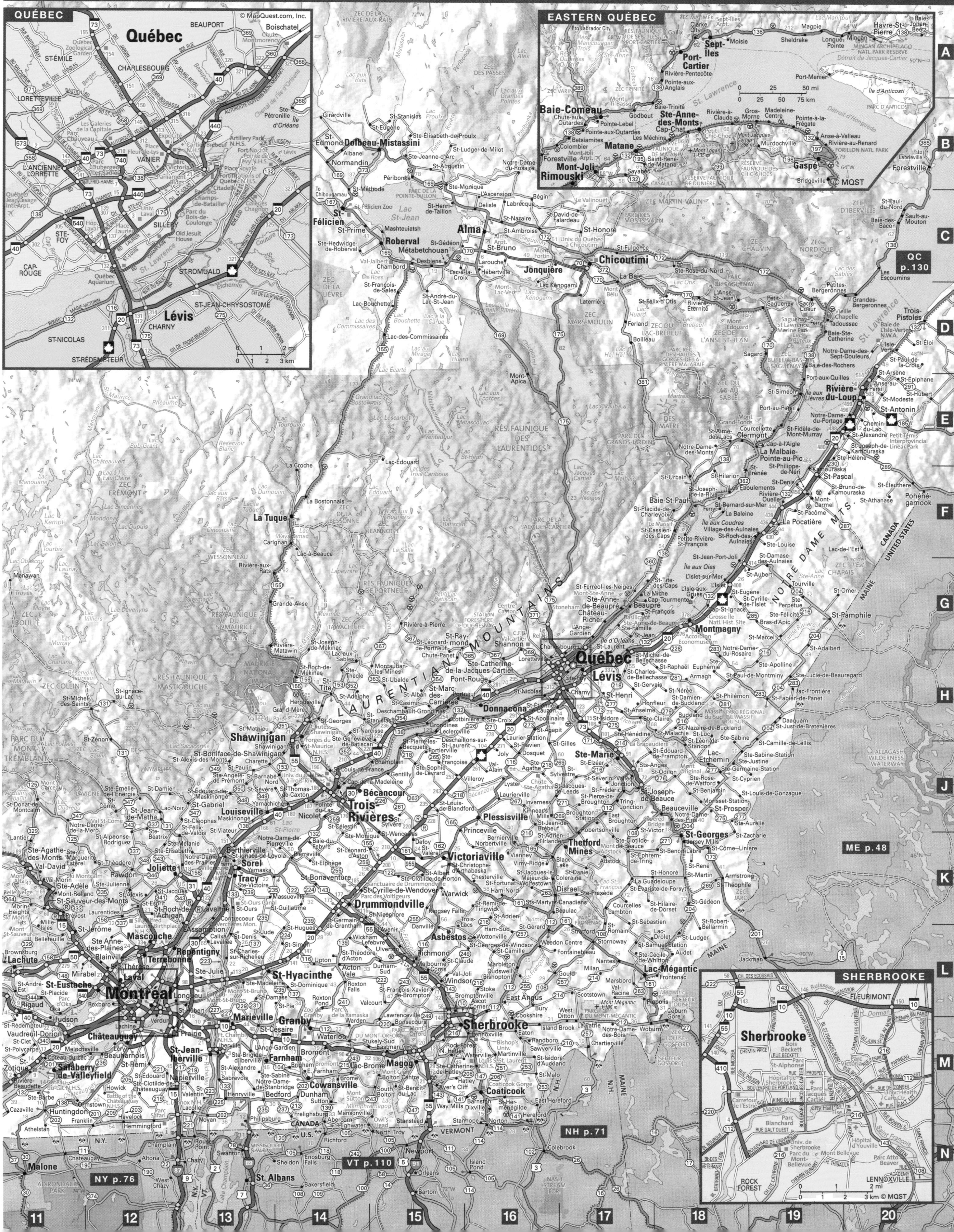

Index page 142

NB: "Hope Restored"

NS: "One Defends and the Other Conquers"

	BATHURST, NB	CAMPBELLTON, NB	CHARLOTTETOWN, PE	DIGBY, NS	EDMUNDSTON, NB	FREDERICTON, NB	GASPÉ, QC	HALIFAX, NS	LUNENBURG, NS	MIRAMICHI, NB	MONCTON, NB	NEW GLASGOW, NS	PORT HAWKESBURY, NS	RIMOUSKI, QC	RIVIÈRE-DU-LOUP, QC	SAINT JOHN, NB	ST. STEPHEN, NB	SYDNEY, NS	TRURO, NS	WOODSTOCK, NB	YARMOUTH, NS
CHARLOTTETOWN, PE	328	434		539	629	354	730	322	419	258	162	110*	224*	620	749	312	417	374*	233	457	616
FREDERICTON, NB	245	351	354	669	275		647	452	549	175	192	425	539	445	395	105	123	689	363	103	746
HALIFAX, NS	452	558	322	217	727	452	854		97	382	260	151	265	744	847	410	515	415	89	555	294
SAINT JOHN, NB	350	456	312	82*	380	105	752	410	258*	280	150	383	497	550	500		105	647	321	208	176*
SYDNEY, NS	689	795	374*	632	964	689	1091	415	512	619	497	264	123	981	1084	647	752		326	792	709

DRIVING DISTANCES IN KILOMETERS

* DISTANCE INCLUDES FERRY TRAVEL

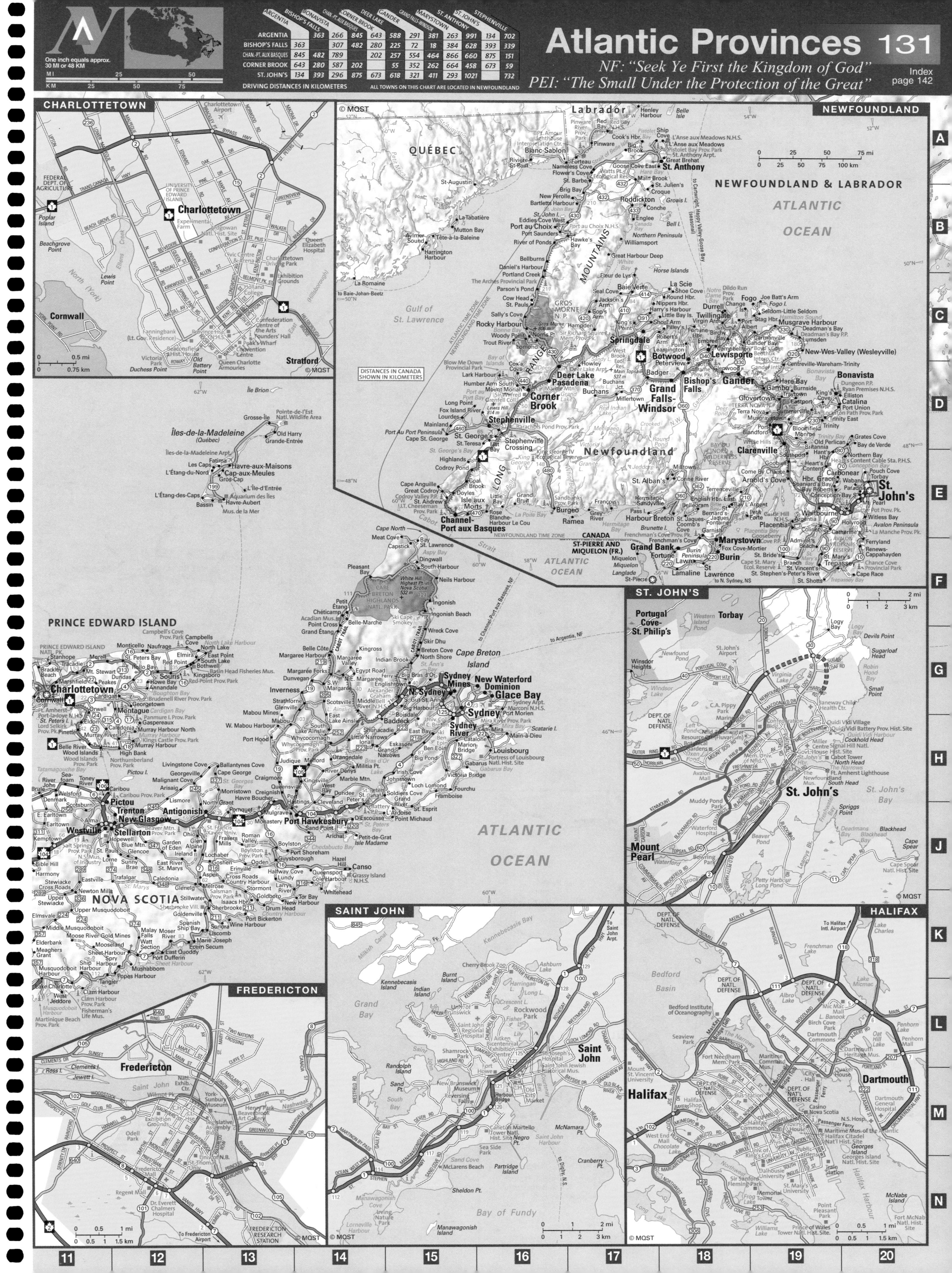

	ARGENTINA	BISHOP'S FALLS	BONAVISTA	CHAN.-PT. AUX BASQUES	CORNER BROOK	DEER LAKE	GANDER	GRAND FALLS-WINDSOR	MARYSTOWN	ST. ANTHONY	ST. JOHN'S	STEPHENVILLE
ARGENTINA		363	266	845	643	588	291	381	263	991	134	702
BISHOP'S FALLS	363		307	482	280	225	72	18	384	628	393	339
CHAN.-PT. AUX BASQUES	845	482	789		202	257	554	464	866	660	875	151
CORNER BROOK	643	280	587	202		55	352	262	664	458	673	59
ST. JOHN'S	134	393	296	875	673	618	321	411	293	1021		732

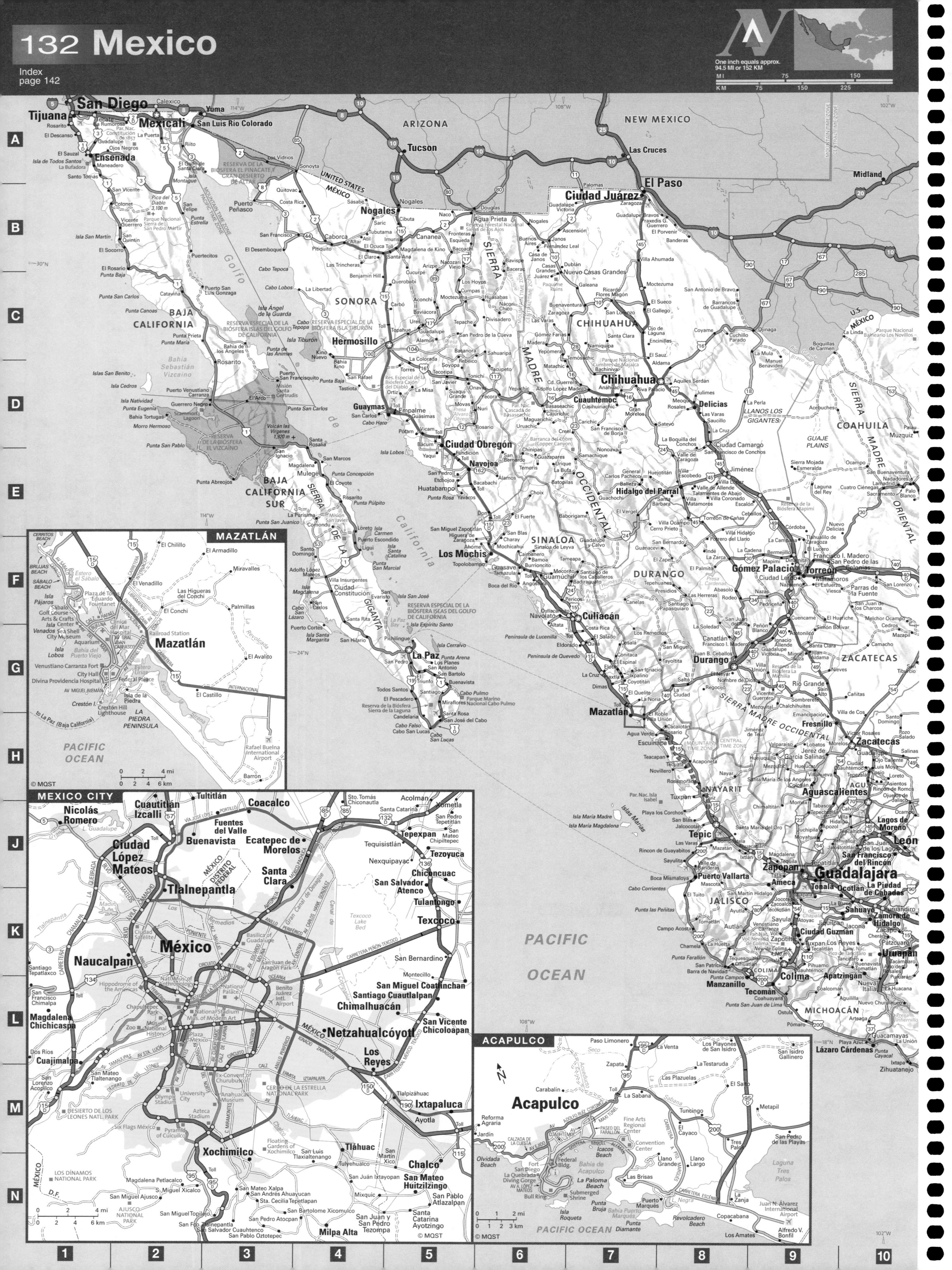

132 Mexico
Index page 142
One inch equals approx. 94.5 MI or 152 KM
MI 75 150
KM 75 150 225
ARIZONA
NEW MEXICO
UNITED STATES
MÉXICO
SONORA
BAJA CALIFORNIA
BAJA CALIFORNIA SUR
CHIHUAHUA
SINALOA
DURANGO
COAHUILA
ZACATECAS
NAYARIT
JALISCO
MICHOACÁN
SIERRA MADRE OCCIDENTAL
SIERRA MADRE ORIENTAL
Golfo de California
PACIFIC OCEAN
Tijuana
San Diego
Mexicali
Yuma
San Luis Río Colorado
Ensenada
Tucson
Las Cruces
El Paso
Ciudad Juárez
Midland
Nogales
Hermosillo
Guaymas
Ciudad Obregón
Navojoa
Los Mochis
Chihuahua
Cuauhtémoc
Delicias
Hidalgo del Parral
Torreón
Gómez Palacio
Culiacán
Mazatlán
Durango
Zacatecas
La Paz
Aguascalientes
Tepic
Puerto Vallarta
Guadalajara
Zapopan
León
Lagos de Moreno
Colima
Manzanillo
Uruapan
Lázaro Cárdenas
MAZATLÁN
PACIFIC OCEAN
© MQST
MEXICO CITY
México
Naucalpan
Tlalnepantla
Ciudad López Mateos
Cuautitlán Izcalli
Coacalco
Ecatepec de Morelos
Netzahualcóyotl
Chimalhuacán
Texcoco
Xochimilco
Chalco
Ixtapaluca
Milpa Alta
Cuajimalpa
© MQST
ACAPULCO
Acapulco
PACIFIC OCEAN
© MQST
A B C D E F G H J K L M N
1 2 3 4 5 6 7 8 9 10

Index page 142

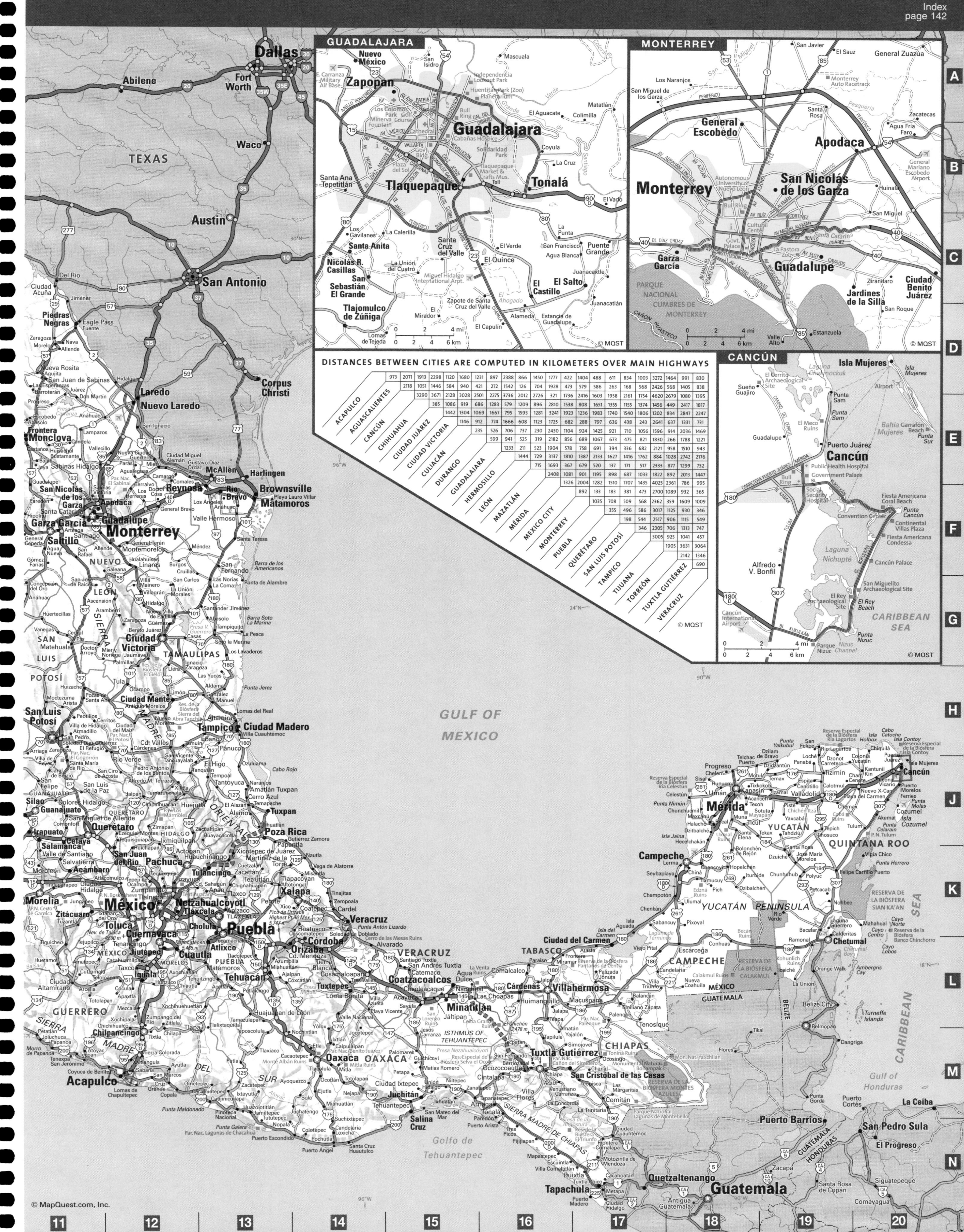

DISTANCES BETWEEN CITIES ARE COMPUTED IN KILOMETERS OVER MAIN HIGHWAYS

	Aguascalientes	Cancún	Chihuahua	Ciudad Juárez	Ciudad Victoria	Culiacán	Durango	Guadalajara	Hermosillo	León	Mazatlán	Mérida	Mexico City	Monterrey	Puebla	Querétaro	San Luis Potosí	Tampico	Tijuana	Torreón	Tuxtla Gutiérrez	Veracruz
ACAPULCO	973	2071	1913	2298	1120	1680	1231	897	2388	866	1450	1777	422	1404	488	611	834	1003	3272	1464	991	830
AGUASCALIENTES		2118	1051	1446	584	940	421	272	1542	126	704	1928	473	579	586	263	168	568	2426	568	1405	838
CANCÚN			3290	3671	2128	3028	2501	2275	3736	2012	2726	321	1736	2416	1603	1958	2161	1754	4620	2679	1080	1395
CHIHUAHUA				385	1086	919	686	1283	579	1209	896	2810	1538	808	1651	1355	1155	1374	1456	449	2417	1817
CIUDAD JUÁREZ					1442	1304	1069	1667	795	1593	1281	3241	1923	1236	1983	1740	1540	1806	1202	834	2847	2247
CIUDAD VICTORIA						1146	912	774	1666	608	1123	1725	682	288	797	636	438	243	2641	637	1331	731
CULIACÁN							235	526	706	737	230	2430	1104	924	1425	921	710	1056	1596	914	2036	1469
DURANGO								599	941	525	319	2182	856	689	1067	673	475	821	1830	266	1788	1221
GUADALAJARA									1233	211	523	1904	578	758	691	394	336	682	2121	958	1510	943
HERMOSILLO										1444	729	3137	1810	1387	2133	1627	1416	1762	884	1028	2742	2176
LEÓN											715	1693	367	679	520	137	171	517	2333	877	1299	732
MAZATLÁN												2408	1081	901	1195	898	687	1033	1822	892	2013	1447
MÉRIDA													1326	2004	1282	1510	1707	1435	4025	2361	786	995
MEXICO CITY														892	133	183	381	473	2700	1089	932	365
MONTERREY															1035	708	509	568	2362	359	1609	1009
PUEBLA																355	496	586	3017	1125	930	346
QUERÉTARO																	198	544	2517	906	1115	549
SAN LUIS POTOSÍ																		346	2305	706	1313	747
TAMPICO																			3005	925	1041	457
TIJUANA																				1905	3631	3064
TORREÓN																					2142	1346
TUXTLA GUTIÉRREZ																						690

© MQST

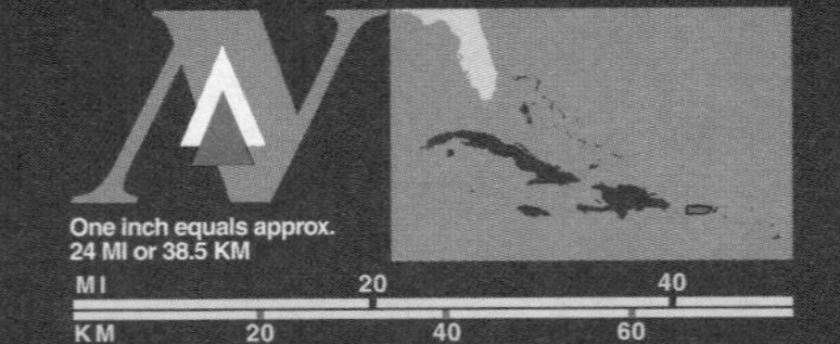

	AGUADILLA	ARECIBO	CAGUAS	CAYEY	FAJARDO	GUAYAMA	HUMACAO	MANATI	MAYAGÜEZ	PONCE	SAN JUAN	UTUADO
ARECIBO	32		59	70	80	87	74	17	48	52	48	20
CAGUAS	90	59		12	36	28	17	41	97	50	17	76
MAYAGÜEZ	16	48	97	85	129	84	114	64		46	96	48
PONCE	62	52	50	39	85	37	67	52	46		67	32
SAN JUAN	80	48	17	28	34	44	33	31	96	67		67

DRIVING DISTANCES IN MILES

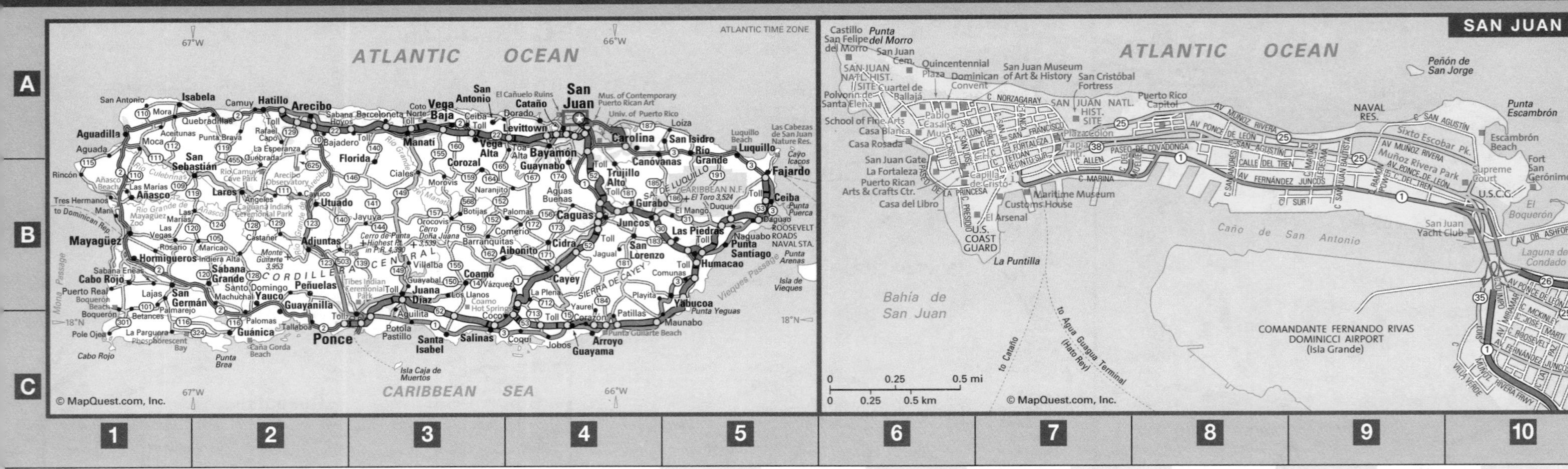

Alabama–California

Note: Population figures are from the latest census or the most recent available estimates.

ALABAMA PG. 4-5

CAPITAL Montgomery

NICKNAME Heart of Dixie

POPULATION 4,447,100, rank 23

AREA 51,705 sq mi, rank 29

STATEHOOD 1819, rank 22

ALASKA PG. 6

CAPITAL Juneau

NICKNAME Great Land

POPULATION 626,932, rank 48

AREA 591,004 sq mi, rank 1

STATEHOOD 1959, rank 49

ARIZONA PG. 7-9

CAPITAL Phoenix

NICKNAME Grand Canyon State

POPULATION 5,130,632, rank 20

AREA 114,000 sq mi, rank 6

STATEHOOD 1912, rank 48

ARKANSAS PG. 10-11

CAPITAL Little Rock

NICKNAME Natural State

POPULATION 2,673,400, rank 33

AREA 53,187 sq mi, rank 27

STATEHOOD 1836, rank 25

BIXBY BRIDGE, BIG SUR, CALIFORNIA

CALIFORNIA PG. 12-19

CAPITAL Sacramento

NICKNAME Golden State

POPULATION 33,871,648, rank 1

AREA 158,706 sq mi, rank 3

STATEHOOD 1850, rank 31

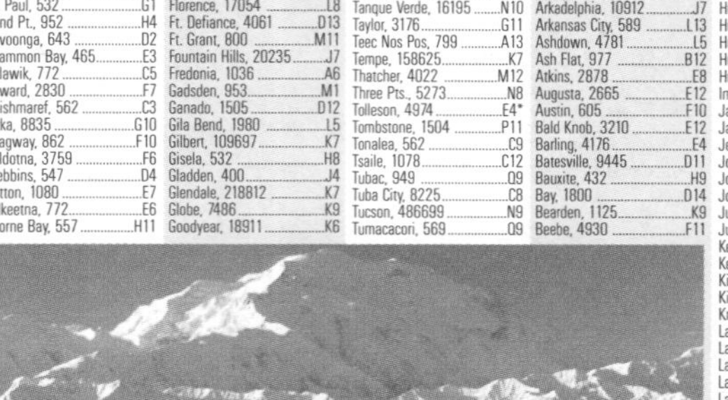

MOUNT MCKINLEY, DENALI NATIONAL PARK AND PRESERVE, ALASKA

COLORADO
PG. 19–21

CAPITAL
Denver

NICKNAME
Centennial State

POPULATION
4,301,261, rank 24

AREA
104,091 sq mi, rank 8

STATEHOOD
1876, rank 38

CONNECTICUT
PG. 22–23

CAPITAL
Hartford

NICKNAME
Constitution State

POPULATION
3,405,565, rank 29

AREA
5,018 sq mi, rank 48

STATEHOOD
1788, rank 5

DISTRICT OF COLUMBIA
PG. 116

POPULATION
572,059

AREA
69 sq mi

BECAME CAPITAL
1800

FLORIDA
PG. 25–28

CAPITAL
Tallahassee

NICKNAME
Sunshine State

POPULATION
15,982,378, rank 4

AREA
58,664 sq mi, rank 22

STATEHOOD
1845, rank 27

SOUTH BEACH, MIAMI BEACH, FLORIDA

DELAWARE
PG. 24

CAPITAL
Dover

NICKNAME
First State

POPULATION
783,600, rank 45

AREA
2,044 sq mi, rank 49

STATEHOOD
1787, rank 1

GEORGIA
PG. 29–31

CAPITAL
Atlanta

NICKNAME
Empire State of the South

POPULATION
8,186,453, rank 10

AREA
58,910 sq mi, rank 21

STATEHOOD
1788, rank 4

HAWAII
PG. 32

CAPITAL
Honolulu

NICKNAME
Aloha State

POPULATION
1,211,537, rank 42

AREA
6,471 sq mi, rank 47

STATEHOOD
1959, rank 50

IDAHO
PG. 33

CAPITAL
Boise

NICKNAME
Gem State

POPULATION
1,293,953, rank 39

AREA
83,564 sq mi, rank 13

STATEHOOD
1890, rank 43

ROCKY COAST NEAR HONOLULU, HAWAII

ILLINOIS
PG. 34–37

CAPITAL
Springfield

NICKNAME
Land of Lincoln

POPULATION
12,419,293, rank 5

AREA
56,345 sq mi, rank 24

STATEHOOD
1818, rank 21

INDIANA
PG. 37–39

CAPITAL
Indianapolis

NICKNAME
Hoosier State

POPULATION
6,080,485, rank 14

AREA
36,185 sq mi, rank 38

STATEHOOD
1816, rank 19

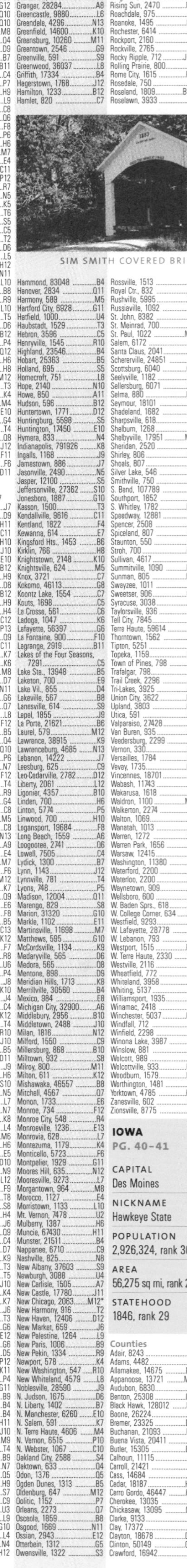

SIM SMITH COVERED BRIDGE, PARKE COUNTY, INDIANA

IOWA
PG. 40–41

CAPITAL
Des Moines

NICKNAME
Hawkeye State

POPULATION
2,926,324, rank 30

AREA
56,275 sq mi, rank 25

STATEHOOD
1846, rank 29

KANSAS
PG. 42–43

CAPITAL
Topeka

NICKNAME
Sunflower State

POPULATION
2,688,418, rank 32

AREA
82,277 sq mi, rank 14

STATEHOOD
1861, rank 34

KENTUCKY
PG. 44–45

CAPITAL
Frankfort

NICKNAME
Bluegrass State

POPULATION
4,041,769, rank 25

AREA
40,409 sq mi, rank 37

STATEHOOD
1792, rank 15

LOUISIANA
PG. 46–47

CAPITAL
Baton Rouge

NICKNAME
Pelican State

POPULATION
4,468,976, rank 22

AREA
47,751 sq mi, rank 31

STATEHOOD
1812, rank 18

KENTUCKY HORSE FARM

Estherwood, 807 K8
Eunice, 11499 J9
Farmerville, 3808 B9
Ferriday, 3723 E11
Florien, 692 F6
Folsom, 525 H15
Fordoche, 933 J11
Franklin, 8354 L11
Franklinton, 3657 H15
French Settlement, 945 J13
Galliano, 7356 M14
Garyville, 2775 K14
Gibsland, 1119 C7
Gilbert, 561 D11
Glenmora, 1558 G8
Golden Meadow, 2193 M15
Goldonna, 457 D7
Gonzales, 8156 K13
Grambling, 4693 C8
Gramercy, 3066 K13
Grand Coteau, 1040 J10
Grand Isle, 1541 N15
Gray, 4958 L13
Grayson, 531 D9
Greensburg, 631 H13
Greenwood, 2458 C5
Gretna, 17423 L15
Grosse Tete, 670 J11
Gueydan, 1598 K8
Hackberry, 1699 K6
Hahnville, 2792 K14
Hammond, 17639 J14
Harahan, 9885 C17
Harrisonburg, 746 E10
Harvey, 22226 C17
Haughton, 2792 C6
Hayes, 750 K7
Haynesville, 2679 A7
Henderson, 1531 J10
Hessmer, 642 G9
Hodge, 492 C8
Homer, 3788 B7
Houma, 32393 M13
Independence, 1724 H14
Inniswold, 4944 G20
Iota, 1376 J8
Iowa, 2663 K7
Jackson, 4130 H12
Jeanerette, 5997 L11
Jean Lafitte, 2137 L15
Jefferson, 11843 B17
Jena, 2971 E9
Jennings, 10986 K8
Jonesboro, 3914 C8
Jonesville, 2469 E10
Junction City, 652 A8
Kaplan, 5177 K9
Kenner, 70517 K15
Kentwood, 2205 G14
Killian, 1053 J14
Killona, 797 B14
Kinder, 2148 J7
Kolin, 600 F9
Krotz Sprs., 1219 J10
Labadieville, 1811 L13
Lacombe, 7518 J15
Lafayette, 110257 K10
Lafitte, 1576 L15
Lake Arthur, 3007 K8
Lake Charles, 71757 K6
Lake Providence, 5104 B12
Laplace, 27684 K14
Larose, 7306 M14
Lawtell, 850 J9
Lecompte, 1366 G9
Leesville, 6753 G6
Leonville, 1007 J10
Livingston, 1342 J13
Livonia, 1339 J11
Lockport, 2624 L14
Logansport, 1630 D5
Lone Star, 1400 C15
Loreauville, 938 K11
Luling, 11512 C15
Lutcher, 3735 K13
Lydia, 1079 L10
Madisonville, 677 J15
Mamou, 3566 H9
Mandeville, 10489 J15
Mangham, 595 C10
Mansfield, 5582 D5
Mansura, 1573 G10
Many, 2889 E6
Maringouin, 1262 J11
Marion, 806 A9
Marksville, 5537 G10
Marrero, 36165 L15
Martin, 625 D7
Mathews, 2003 L14
Maurice, 642 K9
Melville, 1376 H10
Meraux, 10192 L15
Mermentau, 721 K8
Mer Rouge, 721 B10
Merrydale, 10427 E19
Merryville, 1126 H6
Metairie, 146136 K15
Midway, 1505 E9
Mimosa Park, 4500 C15
Minden, 13027 B6
Monroe, 53107 C9
Montegut, 1803 M14
Montgomery, 787 E7
Montz, 1120 B14
Mooringsport, 833 B5
Moreauville, 922 G10
Morgan City, 12703 L12
Morganza, 659 H11
Morse, 759 K8
Moss Bluff, 10535 J7
Napoleonville, 686 L12
Natalbany, 1739 J14
Natchez, 583 E7
Natchitoches, 17865 E7
Newellton, 1482 D12
New Iberia, 32623 K10
New Llano, 2415 G6
New Orleans, 484674 K15
New Roads, 4966 H11
New Sarpy, 1568 B15
Norco, 3579 K14
N. Shore, 1800 K16
Oakdale, 8137 H8
Oak Grove, 2174 B12
Oberlin, 1853 H8
Oil City, 1219 B5
Olla, 1417 E9
Opelousas, 22860 J9
Paincourtville, 884 K12
Paradis, 1252 C14
Parks, 533 K10
Patterson, 5130 L12
Pearl River, 1839 J16
Perry, 1300 L9
Pierre Part, 3239 K12
Pigeon, 600 K12
Pine Prairie, 1087 H9
Pineville, 13829 F8
Plain Dealing, 1071 A5
Plaquemine, 7064 J12
Pleasant Hill, 786 E6
Pointe a la Hache, 475 M16
Ponchatoula, 5180 J14
Port Allen, 5278 J12
Port Barre, 2287 J10
Port Sulphur, 3115 M16
Port Vincent, 463 J13
Poydras, 3886 L16
Prairieville, 950 J13
Provencal, 708 E7
Raceland, 10224 L14
Rayne, 8552 K9
Rayville, 4234 C10
Reserve, 9111 K14
Richmond, 499 C12
Richwood, 2115 C9
Ridgecrest, 801 E11
Ringgold, 1660 C6
River Ridge, 14588 B16
Rosedale, 753 J11
Roseland, 1162 H14
Rosepine, 1390 G6
Ruston, 20546 C8
St. Bernard, 1500 L16
St. Francisville, 1712 H12
St. Gabriel, 5514 K12
St. Joseph, 1340 D12
St. Martinville, 6989 K9
St. Rose, 6540 K14
Sarepta, 925 A6
Schriever, 5880 L13
Scott, 7870 K9
Seymourville, 2200 K12
Shreveport, 200145 C5
Sibley, 1098 C6
Simmesport, 2239 G10
Simpson, 583 F7
Simsboro, 684 C8
Slaughter, 1011 H12
Slidell, 25695 K16
Sorrento, 1227 K13
Springhill, 5439 A6
Starks, 650 J5
Sterlington, 1276 B9
Stonewall, 1668 C5
Sulphur, 20512 K6
Sun, 471 H15
Sunset, 2352 J9
Supreme, 1119 L13
Swartz, 4247 B10
Tallulah, 9189 C12
Tangipahoa, 747 H14
Terrytown, 25430 L15
Thibodaux, 14431 L13
Tickfaw, 617 J14
Tioga, 1500 F9
Triumph, 3358 M17
Urania, 700 E9
Venice, 2220 M17
Vidalia, 4543 F11
Ville Platte, 8145 H9
Vinton, 3338 K5
Violet, 8555 L15
Vivian, 4031 A5
Waggaman, 9435 C16
Walker, 4801 J13
Washington, 1082 H10
Waterproof, 834 E12
Watson, 1400 J13
Welcome, 950 K13
Welsh, 3380 K8
Westlake, 4668 K6
Westminster, 2515 G20
W. Monroe, 13250 C9
Westwego, 10763 L15
White Castle, 1946 K12
Wilson, 668 H12
Winnfield, 5749 D8
Winnsboro, 5344 D11
Wisner, 1140 D11
Woodworth, 1080 G8
Youngsville, 3992 K10
Zachary, 11275 H12
Zwolle, 1783 E5

MAINE
PG. 48-49

CAPITAL
Augusta

NICKNAME
Pine Tree State

POPULATION
1,274,923, rank 40

AREA
33,265 sq mi, rank 39

STATEHOOD
1820, rank 23

Counties
Androscoggin, 103793 O3
Aroostook, 73938 D7
Cumberland, 265612 R3
Franklin, 29467 M3
Hancock, 51791 M9
Kennebec, 117114 P5
Knox, 39618 O6
Lincoln, 33616 O5
Oxford, 54755 N2
Penobscot, 144919 J8
Piscataquis, 17235 G6
Sagadahoc, 35214 R4
Somerset, 50888 K3
Waldo, 36280 N6
Washington, 33941 L11
York, 186742 T2

Cities and Towns
Alfred, 700 T2
Anson, 818 M4
Ashland, 600 D9
Ash Pt., 400 R7
Athens, 325 M5
Auburn, 23203 O3
Augusta, 18560 P5
Bailey Island, 400 S4
Bangor, 31473 M8
Bar Harbor, 2680 P9
Bar Mills, 800 S2
Bass Harbor, 600 O9
Bath, 9266 R5
Beals, 750 P11
Belfast, 6381 P7
Belgrade Lakes, 350 P4
Belmont Corner, 375 P7
Benton, 500 N5
Bernard, 600 O9
Berwick, 1993 U1
Bethel, 475 P2
Biddeford, 20942 T3
Bingham, 856 L4
Blaine, 1428 E10
Blue Hill, 550 P8
Boothbay, 550 R5
Boothbay Harbor, 1237 R5
Bowdoin Ctr., 425 R4
Bowdoinham, 600 R4
Bradley, 650 M8
Brewer, 8987 M8
Bridgton, 2359 R2
Brooks, 550 N7
Brownville Jct., 750 K7
Brunswick, 14816 R4
Buckfield, 325 O3
Bucksport, 2970 N8
Bucksport Ctr., 650 N7
Calais, 3447 L12
Camden, 3934 O7
Cape Cottage, 2300 S3
Cape Elizabeth, 1100 T3
Cape Neddick, 2997 U2
Cape Porpoise, 650 T3
Caribou, 8312 C10
Carmel, 400 M7
Casco, 400 R2
Castine, 900 P8
Cherryfield, 375 N10
Chisholm, 1399 P3
Clarks Mills, 450 T2
Clinton, 1305 N5
Cooks Corner, 425 R4
Cooks Mills, 325 R2
Coopers Mills, 350 O5
Corea, 450 P10
Corinna, 600 M6
Cornish, 400 S2
Cumberland Ctr., 2596 S3
Cumberland Foreside, 500 S3
Damariscotta, 1751 R5
Derby, 900 K7
Dexter, 2201 L6
Dixfield, 1137 N3
Dover-Foxcroft, 2592 L6
Dryden, 1100 N3
Dry Mills, 700 R3
Dyer Cove, 600 S4
Eagle Lake, 600 C8
E. Brownfield, 400 R1
E. Hampden, 800 C12
E. Harpswell, 650 R4
E. Holden, 475 N8
E. Lebanon, 650 T1
E. Limington, 500 S2
E. Millinocket, 1701 J8
E. Northport, 350 P7
Easton, 475 D10
E. Poland, 600 O3
Eastport, 1640 M13
E. Union, 350 O6
E. Wilton, 550 N3
E. Winthrop, 650 P4
Eddington, 700 M8
Eliot, 475 U1
Ellsworth, 6456 N9
Elms, 500 U2
Emery Mills, 350 T1
Fairbanks, 700 N4
Fairfield, 2569 N5
Fairfield Ctr., 500 N5
Falmouth Foreside, 1964 S3
Farmingdale, 1935 O5
Farmington, 4098 N4
Ft. Fairfield, 1600 D10
Ft. Kent, 1978 B8
Ft. Kent Mills, 325 B8
Freeport, 1813 R4
Frenchville, 350 B9
Friendship, 475 R6
Fryeburg, 1549 R1
Gardiner, 6198 O5
Glenburn, 650 M7
Glen Cove, 375 O7
Goodwins Mills, 450 T2
Gorham, 4164 S3
Gray, 800 R3
Greene, 950 O4
Greenville, 1319 J5
Greenville Jct., 850 J5
Guilford, 945 L6
Hallowell, 2467 O5
Hampden, 4126 N7
Harrington, 425 N11
Harrison, 375 O2
Hartland, 872 M6
Hermon, 750 M7
Higgins Beach, 800 T3
Highpine, 325 T2
Hollis Ctr., 450 S2
Houlton, 5270 G10
Howland, 1210 K8
Island Falls, 450 G9
Jackman, 700 J3
Jackman Sta., 750 J3
Jacksonville, 350 N12
Jay, 325 P3
Jonesport, 650 P11
Keegan, 550 B10
Kennebunk, 4804 T2
Kennebunk Beach, 800 T2
Kennebunkport, 1376 T2
Kents Hill, 375 P4
Kezar Falls, 750 S1
Kingfield, 600 M4
Kittery, 4884 V2
Kittery Pt., 1135 V2
Levant, 475 M7
Lewiston, 35690 O3
Limerick, 425 S2
Limestone, 1453 C10
Lincoln, 2933 K8
Lincolnville Ctr., 325 O7
Lisbon, 1800 R4
Lisbon Falls, 4420 R4
Litchfield, 325 O4
Livermore Falls, 1626 P3
Long Cove, 425 R6
Lubec, 650 M13
Machias, 1376 N12
Madawaska, 3326 A9
Madison, 2733 M4
Manchester, 600 P4
Manset, 700 U11
Mapleton, 600 D9
Mars Hill, 1428 E10
Mattawamkeag, 400 J9
Mechanic Falls, 2450 O3
Medway, 650 J8
Mexico, 1946 N2
Milbridge, 475 P10
Milford, 2197 M8
Millinocket, 5190 J8
Milo, 1898 K7
Minot, 400 O3
Monmouth, 500 O4
Moody, 1000 U2
Moody Pt., 800 U2
Moscow, 325 L4
Nequasset, 450 R5
Newcastle, 1751 R5
New Gloucester, 500 R3
Newport, 1754 M6
Nobleboro, 375 O6
Norridgewock, 1557 N5
N. Anson, 400 M4
N. Berwick, 1580 U2
Northeast Harbor, 500 O9
N. Jay, 350 N3
N. Lincoln, 350 K9
N. Monmouth, 600 O4
N. Scarborough, 650 S3
N. Turner, 400 P3
N. Vassalboro, 750 P5
N. Windham, 4568 R3
Norway, 2623 O2
Oakfield, 475 G9
Oakland, 2758 N5
Ocean Park, 3100 T3
Ogunquit, 800 U2
Old Orchard Beach, 8856 T3
Old Town, 8130 M8
Orland, 500 N8
Orono, 8253 M8
Orrington, 325 N8
Orrs Island, 550 S4
Oxford, 1300 O2
Paris, 375 O2
Patten, 850 G9
Pembroke, 475 M12
Phillips, 600 M3
Pine Pt., 600 T3
Pittsfield, 3217 M6
Pittston, 350 O5
Pleasant Pt., 600 M13
Portland, 64249 S3
Presque Isle, 9511 D10
Randolph, 1911 O5
Rangeley, 450 M2
Raymond, 325 R3
Readfield, 475 P4
Richmond, 1864 O5
Riley, 375 P3
Rockland, 7609 O7
Rockport, 900 O7
Round Pond, 325 R6
Rumford, 4795 N2
Sabattus, 1200 O4
Saco, 16822 T3
St. George, 350 R6
Sanford, 10133 T2
Sangerville, 475 L6
Scarborough, 3867 T3
Searsport, 1102 P7
Sebago Lake, 550 S2
Skowhegan, 6696 N5
Songo Lock, 475 R2
S. Berwick, 2300 U1
S. Casco, 650 R2
S. China, 325 P5
S. Eliot, 3445 U1
S. Gray, 400 R3
S. Hancock, 400 P9
S. Harpswell, 550 S4
S. Hiram, 900 S1
S. Lebanon, 350 U1
S. Orrington, 475 N8
S. Paris, 2237 O2
S. Portland, 23324 S3
S. Sanford, 4173 T2
S. Thomaston, 350 R7
Southwest Harbor, 950 O9
S. Windham, 1792 S3
Springvale, 3488 T2
Standish, 600 S2
Stillwater, 1600 M8
Stockton Sprs., 550 P7
Stonington, 850 O8
Stratton, 425 L3
Strong, 550 M3
Tenants Harbor, 500 R6
Thomaston, 2714 O6
Topsham, 6271 R4
Trevett, 325 R5
Turner, 550 O3
Union, 475 O6
Unity, 486 N6
Upper Gloucester, 475 R3
Van Buren, 2369 B10
Vassalboro, 350 P5
Veazie, 1500 M8
Vinalhaven, 750 R8
Waldoboro, 1291 O6
Warren, 900 O6
Washburn, 800 D9
Waterboro, 800 T2
Waterville, 15605 N5
Webster Corner, 1000 R4
Welchville, 600 O3
Wells, 1000 U2
Wells Beach, 500 U2
W. Bowdoin, 325 R4
Westbrook, 16142 S3
W. Buxton, 425 S2
W. Enfield, 350 K8
W. Falmouth, 950 S8
W. Farmington, 3500 N4
W. Gorham, 475 S2
W. Kennebunk, 809 T2
W. Lebanon, 350 T1
W. Paris, 550 P2
W. Peru, 350 P3
W. Poland, 350 R3
W. Rockport, 425 O7
W. Sidney, 400 P5
W. Southport, 325 S5
Wilton, 2290 N3
Winslow, 7743 N5
Winterport, 1307 N7
Winthrop, 2893 P4
Wiscasset, 1203 R5
Woodland (Baileyville), 1044 L12
Woolwich, 325 R5
Yarmouth, 3560 S3
York Beach, 1400 U2
York Harbor, 3321 U2
York Vil., 2000 U2

MARYLAND
PG. 50-52

CAPITAL
Annapolis

NICKNAME
Old Line State

POPULATION
5,296,486, rank 19

AREA
10,460 sq mi, rank 42

STATEHOOD
1788, rank 7

Counties
Allegany, 74930 B5
Anne Arundel, 489656 F13
Baltimore, 754292 C13
Calvert, 74563 H14
Caroline, 29772 G17
Carroll, 150897 B11
Cecil, 85951 C16
Charles, 120546 J12
Dorchester, 30674 J16
Frederick, 195277 C9
Garrett, 29846 C2
Harford, 218590 C15
Howard, 247842 E12
Kent, 19197 E16
Montgomery, 873341 E11
Prince George's, 801515 G13
Queen Anne's, 40563 E17
St. Mary's, 86211 K13
Somerset, 24747 L18
Talbot, 33812 G16
Washington, 131923 B7
Wicomico, 84644 J18
Worcester, 46543 K19

Cities and Towns
* City indexed to pg. 52
\# Independent city population not included in county figures.

Aberdeen, 13842 C15
Abingdon, 950 C15
Accokeek, 7349 H12
Accokeek Acres, 1500 H12
Adamstown, 650 D10
Adelphi, 14998 K4
Annapolis, 35838 F14
Arbutus, 20116 F4*
Arden-on-the-Severn, 1971 K6*
Arnold, 23422 F14
Arundel on the Bay, 1000 F14
Arundel Vil., 8000 G6*
Ashton, 3437 G4
Aspen Hill, 50228 F12
Baldwin, 850 C14
Baltimore, 651154# D13
Baltimore Highlands, 15724 F5*
Barstow, 750 J14
Barton, 478 C3
Bartonsville, 12529 D10
Bay Ridge, 2300 F14
Bel Air, 10080 C15
Belcamp, 1900 C15
Beltsville, 15690 F12
Belvedere Hts., 7900 K8*
Benson, 950 C14
Berlin, 3491 K20
Berwyn Hts., 2942 K5
Bethesda, 55277 F11
Beverly Beach, 1600 G14
Bladensburg, 7661 L5
Bond Mill Park, 3400 H6
Boonsboro, 2803 C9
Bowie, 50269 F13
Bowleys Quarters, 6314 D14
Bowling Green, 2000 C4
Boxhill North, 2900 C15
Braddock Hts., 4627 D9
Brandywine, 1410 H13
Breezy Pt., 800 H14
Brentwood, 2844 L5
Breton Bay, 750 K13
Bridgeport, 2700 B9
Brock Hall, 1200 G13
Brooklandville, 2200 B5*
Brooklyn Park, 10938 F6*
Brunswick, 4894 D9
Bryans Road, 4912 H12
Burtonsville, 7305 E12
Cabin John, 1734 K2
California, 9307 K14
Calvert Beach, 2487 J14
Calvert Manor, 650 H12
Calverton, 12610 F12
Cambridge, 10911 H16
Camp Sprs., 17968 G12
Cape St. Claire, 8022 F14
Capitol Hts., 4138 M5
Cardiff, 650 B15
Carney, 28264 C7*
Cascade, 1141 B10
Catonsville, 39820 E13
Cavetown, 1486 B9
Cearfoss, 800 B8
Cecilton, 474 D17
Cedar Grove, 950 E11
Cedar Lawn, 900 K9
Centreville, 1970 F16
Charlestown, 1019 C16
Charlotte Hall, 1214 J13
Chelsea Beach, 4400 J7*
Cheltenham, 650 H13
Chesapeake Beach, 3180 H14
Chesapeake City, 787 C17
Chesapeake Ranch Estates, 11503 K14
Chester, 3723 F15
Chestertown, 4746 E16
Cheverly, 6433 F12
Chevy Chase, 2726 K3
Chevy Chase View, 863 K3
Chillum, 34252 L4
Church Hill, 530 E16
Churchton, 1800 G14
Churchville, 1200 C15
Clarksburg, 1834 E11
Clarksville, 900 E12
Clinton, 26064 G12
Cloverly, 7835 H4
Cobb Island, 750 K13
Cockeysville, 19388 C13
Colesville, 19810 F12
College Park, 24657 K5
Columbia, 88254 E12
Columbia Beach, 700 G14
Coral Hills, 10720 M5
Cordova, 592 G16
Corriganville, 1000 B4
Cresaptown, 5884 C4
Crisfield, 2723 M17
Crofton, 20091 F13
Crownsville, 1670 F14
Cumberland, 21518 B4
Damascus, 11430 D11
Daniel, 650 D12
Dares Beach, 1400 H14
Darnestown, 6378 E11
Deale, 4796 G14
Deal Island, 578 L16
Delmar, 1859 J18
Denton, 2960 G17
Derwood, 2000 E11
District Hts., 5958 M5
Dorsey, 1000 G7
Doubs, 750 D10
Dowell, 750 K14
Drum Pt., 11503 K14
Dublin, 650 B15
Dundalk, 62306 E14
Dunkirk, 2363 H13
Easton, 11708 G16
Eastview, 650 C12
Eden, 793 K18
Edgemere, 9248 E14
Edgewater, 2900 N7*
Edgewood, 23378 D15
Edmonston, 959 L5
Eldersburg, 27741 D12
Elkridge, 22042 E13
Elkton, 11893 C17
Ellicott City, 56397 E13
Elvaton, 3500 J6*
Emmitsburg, 2290 B10
Emmorton, 4000 C15
Essex, 39078 D14
Fairland, 21738 F12
Fairmount, 537 L17
Fairmount Hts., 1508 M5
Fallston, 8427 C14
Federalsburg, 2620 H17
Ferndale, 16056 G5*
Flohrville, 950 D12
Forest Hts., 2585 N4
Forestville, 12707 N6
Frederick, 52767 D10
Friendly, 10938 G12
Friendsville, 539 B1
Frostburg, 7873 B3
Fruitland, 3774 K18
Fullerton, 10100 C8*
Fulton, 850 E12
Funkstown, 983 L10
Gaithersburg, 52613 E11
Gamber, 1000 C12
Garrett Park, 917 J3
Garrison, 7969 B3*
Germantown, 55419 E11
Gibson, 650 C15
Glenarden, 6318 F12
Glen Burnie, 38922 E13
Glenn Dale, 12609 F13
Glenwood, 650 D12
Glyndon, 1200 C13
Golden Beach, 2665 J13
Goshen, 1300 E11
Grantsville, 619 B2
Grasonville, 2193 F15
Great Mills, 2600 K14
Greenbelt, 21456 F12
Green Haven, 17415 E14
Greensboro, 1632 F17
Green Valley, 12262 D11
Guilford, 12918 G6
Hagerstown, 36687 B9
Halfway, 10065 C8
Hampstead, 5060 C13
Hampton, 5004 B6*
Hancock, 1725 B7
Harewood Park, 3400 D15
Havre de Grace, 11331 C16
Hebbville, 10900 D3*
Hebron, 807 J18
Herald Harbor, 2313 K6*
Hermanville, 1100 K14
Highland, 800 E12
Hillandale, 3054 J4
Hillcrest Hts., 16359 G12
Hillsmere Shores, 2977 N8*
Hollywood, 650 K14
Hughesville, 1537 J13
Huntingtown, 2436 H14
Hurlock, 1874 H17
Hyattsville, 14733 F12
Indian Head, 3422 H11
Jacksonville, 900 C14
Jarrettsville, 2756 C14
Jessup, 7865 E13
Joppatowne, 11391 D15
Keedysville, 482 C9
Kensington, 1873 J3
Kenwood, 9600 D8*
Kettering, 11008 M6
Kingstown, 1644 E16
Kingsville, 4214 A9*
Lake Shore, 13065 E14
Landover, 22900 L5
Landover Hills, 1534 L5
Langley Park, 16214 K4
Lanham, 18190 L6
Lansdowne, 15724 F5*
La Plata, 6551 J12
Largo, 8408 M6
Laurel, 19960 E13
LaVale, 4613 B4
Lawsonia, 1300 M17
Leitersburg, 523 B9
Leonardtown, 1896 K13
Lexington Park, 11021 K14
Linthicum, 7539 G5*
Lochearn, 25269 D13
Loch Lynn Hts., 469 D2
Lonaconing, 1205 C3
Londontown, 7595 F14
Long Beach, 2487 J14
Long Green, 1000 C14
Loveville, 650 K13
Lusby, 1666 J14
Manchester, 3329 B12
Marbury, 1200 H11
Marley, 11200 E14
Marlton, 7798 G13
Martins Additions, 875 K3
Maryland City, 6814 H6
Marywood, 6000 C15
Mattawoman, 3100 H12
Maugansville, 2295 B8
Mayo, 3153 G14
Mays Chapel, 11427 A5*
Mechanicsville, 750 J13
Melrose, 750 B12
Middle River, 23958 D14
Middletown, 2668 D9
Midland, 473 C3
Milford, 26527 D4*
Montgomery Vil., 38051 E11
Montpelier, 11800 J6
Montrose, 4800 J2
Morningside, 1295 N5
Mt. Aetna, 838 C9
Mtn. Lake Park, 2248 D2
Mt. Airy, 6425 D11
Mt. Rainier, 8498 L4
Mt. Savage, 1200 B4
Mt. Vernon, 761 K17
Myersville, 1382 C9
New Carrollton, 12589 F12
New Windsor, 1303 C11
Nikep, 650 C3
Normans, 650 F15
N. Beach, 1880 H14
N. Brentwood, 469 L5
North East, 2733 C16
Oakland, 1930 D1
Oakland, 2100 D12
Ocean City, 7173 K20
Ocean Pines, 10496 J20
Odenton, 20534 F13
Olney, 31438 E12
Orchard Beach, 4400 H7*
Orchard Hills, 3844 J9
Overlea, 12148 D14
Owings, 1325 H14
Owings Mills, 20193 D13
Oxford, 771 H15
Oxon Hill, 35355 G12
Palmer Park, 7000 L6
Paramount, 2722 J10
Park Hall, 800 K14
Parkville, 31118 D14
Parole, 14031 N11
Pasadena, 12093 J6*
Perry Hall, 28705 D14
Perryman, 2461 C15
Perryville, 3672 C16
Pikesville, 29123 D13
Piney Pt., 700 L14
Pittsville, 1182 J19
Pleasant Hills, 2851 C14
Pocomoke City, 4098 L18
Pt. of Rocks, 850 E9
Pomonkey, 750 H12
Poolesville, 5151 E10
Port Deposit, 676 C16
Potomac, 44822 F11
Potomac Hts., 1154 H11
Potomac Park, 1900 C4
Preston, 566 H17
Prince Frederick, 1432 J14
Princess Anne, 2313 K18
Pumphrey, 5317 G5*
Queenstown, 617 F15
Quince Orchard, 23044 E11
Randallstown, 30870 D13
Randle Cliff Beach, 800 H14
Randolph Hills, 14300 J3
Rawlings, 750 C4
Redland, 16998 E11
Reisterstown, 22438 D13
Ridgely, 1352 F17
Rising Sun, 1702 B16
Riva, 3966 N6*
Riverdale Park, 6690 L5
Riviera Beach, 12695 E14
Rockdale, 16100 D13
Rock Hall, 1396 E15
Rock Pt., 750 K13
Rockville, 47388 F11
Romancoke, 800 G15
Rosaryville, 12322 G13
Rosedale, 19199 D14
Rose Haven, 1400 H14
Rossmoor Leisure World, 7569 H3
Rossville, 11515 D8*
Royal Oak, 750 G15
St. Charles, 33379 H12
St. Clement Shores, 800 K13
St. Inigoes, 650 L15
St. James, 1657 C8
St. Leonard, 536 J14
St. Mary's City, 900 L14
St. Michaels, 1193 G15
Salisbury, 23743 K18
Sandy Spr., 3437 G4
Sandyville, 1000 C12
Savage, 12918 E13
Seabrook, 18190 K6
Seat Pleasant, 4885 M5
Secretary, 503 H16
Severn, 35076 E13
Severna Park, 28507 F14
Shady Side, 5559 G14
Sharpsburg, 691 C8
Sharptown, 649 J17
Shoreham Beach, 1300 G14
Silver Hill, 33515 N5
Silver Spr., 76540 F12
Simpsonville, 4400 E12
Smallwood, 950 C12
Smithsburg, 2146 B9
Snow Hill, 2409 L19
Solomons, 1536 K14
Somerset, 1124 K3
S. Gate, 28672 H6*
Sparks, 1800 C13
Spencerville, 2900 H4
Spring Garden Estates, 2400 C10
Stevensville, 5880 F15
Suitland, 33515 G12
Sunderland, 1400 H14
Sunnybrook, 2300 C14
Sykesville, 4197 D12
Takoma Park, 17299 K4
Taneytown, 5128 B11
Tantallon, 7900 H12
Taylorsville, 900 D12
Temple Hills, 7792 N5
Thurmont, 5588 C10
Tilghman, 854 H15
Tonytank, 3500 K18
Towson, 51793 D14
Trappe, 1146 H16
Union Bridge, 989 C11
University Park, 2318 K5
Upper Marlboro, 648 G13
Waldorf, 22312 H12
Walker Mill, 11104 M5
Walkersville, 5192 C10
Washington Grove, 515 G2
Waterloo, 900 E13
Webster, 1200 C15
Westernport, 2104 C3
W. Friendship, 700 D12
Westminster, 16731 C12
Wheaton, 57694 F12
Whiteford, 700 B15
White Marsh, 8485 C9*
White Oak, 20973 J4
White Plains, 3600 H12
Willards, 938 J19
Williamsport, 1868 C8
Willows, 900 H14
Wilson, 1885 B8
Woodfield, 2500 E11
Woodlawn, 1600 B16
Woodlawn, 36079 D4*
Woodmore, 6077 L7
Woodsboro, 846 C10
Yellow Sprs., 1100 C10

MASSACHUSETTS
PG. 53-55

CAPITAL
Boston

NICKNAME
Bay State

POPULATION
6,349,097, rank 13

AREA
8,284 sq mi, rank 45

STATEHOOD
1788, rank 6

Counties
Barnstable, 222230 K17
Berkshire, 134953 D2
Bristol, 534678 H13
Dukes, 14987 M17
Essex, 723419 B14
Franklin, 71535 C5
Hampden, 456228 F7
Hampshire, 152251 E4
Middlesex, 1465396 D13
Nantucket, 9520 N19
Norfolk, 650308 F13
Plymouth, 472822 H15
Suffolk, 689807 E14
Worcester, 750963 D9

Cities and Towns
* City indexed to pg. 53

Abington, 14605 G15
Accord, 2300 F15
Acton, 2700 D12
Acushnet, 3171 K15
Adams, 5784 C3
Agawam, 28144 G6
Amesbury, 12327 A15
Amherst, 17050 E6
Andover, 7900 C14
Arlington, 42389 D14
Ashburnham, 1000 C9
Ashland, 14674 F12
Assinippi, 2700 F15
Assonet, 1200 J14
Athol, 8370 C8
Attleboro, 42068 H13
Auburn, 15901 F10
Ayer, 2960 C11
Baldwinville, 1852 C8
Ballardvale, 3500 C14
Barnstable, 47821 K18
Barre, 1150 D8
Barre Plains, 1200 E8
Bedford, 12595 D13
Belchertown, 2626 E7
Bellingham, 4497 G12
Belmont, 24194 E13
Berkley, 850 J14
Berlin, 650 E11
Bernardston, 1000 C6
Beverly, 39862 C15
Billerica, 38981 C13
Blackstone, 2900 G11
Bliss Corner, 5466 N12
Bondsville, 1876 F7
Boston, 589141 E14
Bourne, 1443 J17
Boxborough, 1400 D12
Boxford, 2340 C14
Braintree, 33698 F14
Brant Rock, 5100 G16
Brewster, 2212 J19
Bridgewater, 6664 G15
Briggsville, 750 B3
Brockton, 94304 G14
Brookfield, 1200 F8
Brookline, 57107 E14
Bryantville, 2600 G15
Burlington, 22876 D13
Buzzards Bay, 3549 J17
Byfield, 850 B15
Cambridge, 101355 E14
Canton, 20775 F14
Carlisle, 800 D13
Carver, 900 H16
Centerville, 9200 K18
Chaffinville, 3100 E10
Charlton, 1100 F9
Charlton City, 1400 F9
Charlton Depot, 1200 F9
Chartley, 1600 H13
Chatham, 1667 K20
Chelmsford, 32400 C13
Chelsea, 35080 D14
Cheshire, 1200 C3
Chester, 800 E4
Chicopee, 54653 F6
Clinton, 7884 D11
Cochituate, 6768 E12
Cohasset, 3300 F16
Concord, 3500 D13
Cordaville, 2515 E12
Cotuit, 2400 K18
Dalton, 4100 D3
Danvers, 25212 C15
Dedham, 23464 F14
Dennis, 2798 J19
Dennis Port, 3612 K19
Dighton, 1200 J14
Douglas, 800 G10
Dover, 2216 F13
Dudley, 1800 G9
Duxbury, 1426 G16
E. Blackstone, 1600 G12
E. Brewster, 850 J20
E. Bridgewater, 4000 G15
E. Brookfield, 1410 F9
E. Dennis, 3299 J19
E. Douglas, 2319 G11
E. Falmouth, 6615 K17
E. Freetown, 1200 J15
Eastham, 1100 J20
Easthampton, 15994 E5
E. Harwich, 4744 J20
E. Longmeadow, 14100 G6
E. Orleans, 1800 J20
E. Pepperell, 2034 C11
E. Sandwich, 3720 J17
E. Templeton, 1200 C9
E. Wareham, 1700 J16
Edgartown, 1100 M17
Essex, 1426 C16
Everett, 38037 D6*
Fairhaven, 16159 K15
Fall River, 91938 K14
Falmouth, 4115 L17
Fiskdale, 2156 G8
Fitchburg, 39102 C10
Five Corners, 2100 G14
Forestdale, 3992 K17
Forge Vil., 2300 C12
Foxboro, 5509 G13
Framingham, 66910 E12
Franklin, 29560 G12
Gardner, 20770 C9
Georgetown, 3000 B14
Gilbertville, 1000 E8
Glen Mills, 750 B15
Gloucester, 30273 C16
Grafton, 2400 F11
Granby, 1344 F6
Great Barrington, 2459 F2
Greenfield, 13716 C6
Green Harbor, 2397 G16
Groton, 1113 C11
Groveland, 2800 B14
Hadley, 1200 E6
Halifax, 1000 G15
Hanover, 2200 G15
Hanson, 2044 G15
Harvard, 800 D11
Harwich, 1832 K19
Harwich Port, 1809 K19
Hatfield, 1298 E6
Haverhill, 58969 B14
Haydenville, 700 E5
Hingham, 5352 F15
Hinsdale, 750 D3
Holbrook, 10785 F14
Holden, 4200 E10
Holland, 1444 G8
Holliston, 3400 F12
Holyoke, 39838 F6
Hopedale, 4158 F12
Hopkinton, 2628 F12
Hortonville, 850 J13
Housatonic, 1335 E1
Hudson, 14388 E11
Hull, 11050 E15
Humarock, 2000 F16
Huntington, 950 F4
Hyannis, 14100 K18
Hyannis Port, 3100 K18
Ipswich, 4161 B15
Jefferson, 1600 E9
Kingston, 5380 G16
Lakeville, 2233 J15
Lancaster, 1700 D11
Lanesboro, 850 D2
Lawrence, 72043 B14
Lee, 2021 E2
Leicester, 2400 F9
Lenox, 1667 E2
Lenox Dale, 1100 E2
Leominster, 41303 D10
Lexington, 30355 D13
Lincoln, 650 D1*
Littleton Common, 2816 C12
Longmeadow, 15633 G6
Long Pond, 1500 H17
Lowell, 105167 C13
Ludlow, 7400 F6
Lunenburg, 1695 C10
Lynn, 89050 D15
Lynnfield, 11542 C14
Malden, 56340 D14
Manchaug, 850 G10
Manchester-by-the-Sea, 3600 C16
Manomet, 2900 H17
Mansfield, 7320 G13
Marblehead, 20377 D15
Marion, 1202 K16
Marlborough, 36255 E12
Marshfield, 4246 G16
Marshfield Hills, 2369 F16
Marstons Mills, 8000 K18
Mashpee, 901 K17
Mattapoisett, 2966 K15
Maynard, 10433 D12
Medfield, 6670 F13
Medford, 55765 D14
Medway, 4000 F12
Melrose, 27134 C6*
Mendon, 1100 G11
Merrimac, 2900 A14
Methuen, 43789 B13
Middleboro, 6913 H15
Middleton, 1200 C14
Milford, 24230 F12
Millbury, 4700 F10
Millers Falls, 1072 C6
Millis, 4607 F13
Milton, 26062 F14
Minot, 1100 F16
Monponsett, 1700 G15
Monson, 2103 G7
Montague, 800 C6
Monument Beach, 2438 J17
Morningdale, 2500 K6
Nahant, 3632 D15
Nameloc Hts., 1500 J17
Nantucket, 3830 N19
Natick, 32170 E13
Needham, 28911 E13
New Bedford, 93768 K15
Newburyport, 17189 A15
Newton, 83829 E13
Norfolk, 1900 G13
N. Acton, 3000 D12
N. Adams, 14681 B3
N. Amherst, 6019 D6
Northampton, 28978 E5
N. Attleboro, 16796 H13
N. Billerica, 5200 C13
Northborough, 6257 E11
Northbridge, 3000 F11
N. Brookfield, 2527 E8
N. Carver, 700 H16
N. Chatham, 750 J20
N. Chelmsford, 4900 C12
N. Cohasset, 1600 E15
N. Dartmouth, 2200 M11
N. Dighton, 1400 H14
N. Eastham, 1915 H20
N. Easton, 3700 G14
N. Falmouth, 3355 K17
Northfield, 1141 B6
N. Grafton, 3600 F11
N. Middleboro, 850 H15
N. Oxford, 1200 F9
N. Pembroke, 2913 G16
N. Plymouth, 3593 H16
N. Reading, 2800 C14
N. Scituate, 5065 F16
N. Swansea, 1100 J13
N. Uxbridge, 4200 G11
Northville, 2400 G15
Norton, 2618 H13
Norwell, 1300 F16
Norwood, 28587 F13
Nutting Lake, 5700 A2*
Oak Bluffs, 1700 L17
Oakdale, 1100 E10
Ocean Bluff, 5100 G16
Ocean Grove, 3012 J13
Onset, 1292 J16
Orange, 3945 C7
Orleans, 1716 J20
Osterville, 2900 K18
Otter River, 850 C9
Oxford, 5899 G10
Palmer, 3900 F7
Paxton, 1000 E9
Peabody, 48129 D15
Pembroke, 2800 G15
Pepperell, 2517 C11
Pigeon Cove, 1700 B16
Pinehurst, 6941 D13
Pittsfield, 45793 D2
Plainville, 3000 G13
Pleasant Lake, 800 J19
Plymouth, 7658 H16
Pocasset, 2671 K17
Provincetown, 3192 G19
Quincy, 88025 F14
Randolph, 30963 F14
Raynham, 1900 H14
Raynham Ctr., 3633 H14
Reading, 23708 D14
Rehoboth, 700 J13
Revere, 47283 D14
Rochdale, 1400 F9
Rock, 850 J15
Rockland, 17670 F15
Rockport, 5606 C16
Rowley, 1434 B15
Rutland, 2205 E9
Sagamore, 3544 J17
Sagamore Beach, 1200 J17
Salem, 40407 D15
Salisbury, 4484 A15
Salisbury Beach, 1300 A15
Sand Hills, 2400 F16
Sandwich, 3058 J17
Saugus, 26078 D14
Scituate, 5069 F16
Scotland, 1900 H14
Sharon, 5941 G14
Sheffield, 750 G2
Shelburne Falls, 1951 C5
Sherborn, 1200 F12
Shirley, 1427 C11
Shrewsbury, 31640 E10
Silver Lake, 3300 C13
Silver Lake, 1000 G16
Sippewisset, 950 L16
Somerset, 18234 J14
Somerville, 77478 E14
S. Acton, 2700 D12
S. Amherst, 5039 E6
S. Ashburnham, 1013 C9
S. Berlin, 800 E11
Southborough, 1700 E12
Southbridge, 12878 G9
S. Bridgewater, 2600 H15
S. Chatham, 800 K20
S. Dartmouth, 1900 K15
S. Deerfield, 1868 D6
S. Dennis, 3679 K19
S. Duxbury, 3062 G16
S. Easton, 3600 G14
S. Hadley, 3900 E6
S. Hadley Falls, 4300 F6
S. Lancaster, 1742 D11
S. Middleboro, 750 J15
S. Orleans, 1100 J20
S. Walpole, 1900 G13
S. Weymouth, 11100 F15
Southwick, 2000 G5
S. Yarmouth, 11603 K19
Spencer, 6032 F9
Springfield, 152082 G6
Sterling, 1300 D10
Stockbridge, 900 E2
Stoneham, 22219 D14
Stoughton, 11200 F14
Sturbridge, 2047 G8
Sudbury, 2300 E12
Sunderland, 850 D6
Sutton, 650 F10
Swampscott, 14412 D15
Swifts Beach, 2700 J16
Taunton, 55976 H14
Teaticket, 1907 L17
Templeton, 800 C8
Tewksbury, 28851 C13
Texas, 1300 F9
Three Rivers, 2939 F7
Topsfield, 2826 C15
Townsend, 1043 C11
Townsend Harbor, 1700 C11
Turners Falls, 4441 C6
Upton, 2326 F11
Uxbridge, 3300 G11
Vallersville, 2000 H17
Vineyard Haven, 2048 L17
Wakeby, 1600 K17
Wakefield, 24804 D14
Wales, 850 G8
Walpole, 5867 F13
Waltham, 59226 E13
Ware, 6174 F8
Wareham, 2874 J16
Warren, 1452 F8
Watertown, 32986 E13
Waterville, 950 B8
Wayland, 1300 E12
Webster, 11600 G9
Wellesley, 26613 E13
Wellfleet, 1000 H20
Wenham, 2300 C15
W. Barnstable, 1500 J18
Westborough, 3983 E11
W. Boxford, 1200 B14
W. Boylston, 1100 E10
W. Bridgewater, 2400 G14
W. Brookfield, 1610 F8
W. Chelmsford, 1400 C12
W. Concord, 5632 D12
W. Dennis, 2570 K19
W. Falmouth, 1867 K16
Westfield, 40072 G5
W. Groton, 750 C11
W. Medway, 3500 F12
Westminster, 1300 C9
W. Pelham, 1300 E6
W. Springfield, 27899 G5
W. Stockbridge, 750 E1
W. Townsend, 1300 B10
W. Upton, 2326 F11
W. Wareham, 1908 J16
W. Warren, 1100 F8
Westwood, 14117 F13
W. Yarmouth, 6460 K19
Weymouth, 53988 F15
White Horse Beach, 2300 H17
White Island Shores, 2133 J16
Whitinsville, 6340 G11
Whitman, 13882 G15
Wilbraham, 3544 F6
Williamstown, 4754 B2
Wilmington, 21363 C13
Winchendon, 4246 B9
Winchester, 20810 D14
Winnecunnet, 750 H14
Winthrop, 18303 E15
Woburn, 37258 D14
Woods Hole, 925 L16
Worcester, 172648 E10
Wrentham, 2600 G13
Yarmouth, 2100 J19
Yarmouth Port, 5395 K18

PEMAQUID POINT LIGHTHOUSE, MAINE

MICHIGAN
PG. 56-58

CAPITAL
Lansing

NICKNAME
Great Lakes State

POPULATION
9,938,444, rank 8

AREA
58,527 sq mi, rank 23

STATEHOOD
1837, rank 26

Counties
Alcona, 11719 K10
Alger, 9862 E3
Allegan, 105665 S5
Alpena, 31314 J10
Antrim, 23110 J7
Arenac, 17269 M10
Baraga, 8746 B12
Barry, 56755 S6
Bay, 110157 N9
Benzie, 15998 K5
Berrien, 162453 U4
Branch, 45787 U7
Calhoun, 137985 T7
Cass, 51104 U5
Charlevoix, 26090 H7
Cheboygan, 26448 G8
Chippewa, 38543 D7
Clare, 31252 M7
Clinton, 64753 R8
Crawford, 14273 K8
Delta, 38520 F3
Dickinson, 27472 E1
Eaton, 103655 S7
Emmet, 31437 G7
Genesee, 436141 Q10
Gladwin, 26023 M8
Gogebic, 17370 C10
Grand Traverse, 77654 K6
Gratiot, 42285 P8
Hillsdale, 46527 U8
Houghton, 36016 C11
Huron, 36079 N11
Ingham, 279320 S9
Ionia, 61518 R7
Iosco, 27339 L10
Iron, 13138 C11
Isabella, 63351 N7
Jackson, 158422 T8
Kalamazoo, 238603 T6
Kalkaska, 16571 K7
Kent, 574335 Q6
Keweenaw, 2301 A12
Lake, 11333 M5
Lapeer, 87904 Q11
Leelanau, 21119 J5
Lenawee, 98890 U9
Livingston, 156951 S10
Luce, 7024 D6
Mackinac, 11943 E7
Macomb, 788149 R12
Manistee, 24527 L5
Marquette, 64634 D1
Mason, 28274 M4
Mecosta, 40553 P6
Menominee, 25326 G1
Midland, 82874 N9
Missaukee, 14478 L7
Monroe, 145945 U11
Montcalm, 61266 P6
Montmorency, 10315 J9
Muskegon, 170200 O5
Newaygo, 47874 P5
Oakland, 1194156 S11
Oceana, 26873 N4
Ogemaw, 21645 L9
Ontonagon, 7818 C10
Osceola, 23197 M6
Oscoda, 9418 J9
Otsego, 23301 H8
Ottawa, 238314 R5
Presque Isle, 14411 H9
Roscommon, 25469 L8
Saginaw, 210039 P9
St. Clair, 164235 R12
St. Joseph, 62422 U6
Sanilac, 44547 P12
Schoolcraft, 8903 E4
Shiawassee, 71687 Q9
Tuscola, 58266 P10
Van Buren, 76263 T4
Washtenaw, 322895 T10
Wayne, 2061162 T11
Wexford, 30484 L6

Cities and Towns
* City indexed to pg. 58

Acme, 650 J6
Addison, 627 U9
Adrian, 21574 U9
Alanson, 785 G7
Albion, 9144 T8
Algonac, 4613 S13
Allegan, 4838 S5
Allendale, 11555 R5
Allen Park, 29376 L6*
Alma, 9275 P8
Almont, 2803 R12
Alpena, 11304 H11
Anchorville, 3200 R13
Ann Arbor, 114024 T10
Argentine, 2285 R10
Armada, 1573 R12
Ashley, 526 Q8
Athens, 1111 U6
Atlanta, 757 J9
Attica, 700 Q11
Auburn, 2011 P9
Auburn Hills, 19837 E7*
Au Gres, 1028 M10
Augusta, 899 T6
Au Sable, 1533 L11
Bad Axe, 3462 N12
Baldwin, 1107 N5
Bancroft, 616 R9
Bangor, 1933 T4
Baraga, 1285 B12
Baroda, 858 U3
Bath, 1200 R8
Battle Creek, 53364 T7
Bay City, 36817 P10
Beaverton, 1106 N8
Beecher, 12793 D2*
Belding, 5877 Q6
Bellaire, 1164 J6
Belleville, 3997 T11
Bellevue, 1365 S7
Benton Harbor, 11182 T4
Benzonia, 519 K4
Berkley, 15531 H7*
Berrien Sprs., 1862 U4
Bertrand, 1700 V4
Bessemer, 2148 C9
Beulah, 363 K4
Beverly Hills, 10437 G6*
Big Rapids, 10849 N6
Bingham Farms, 1030 G6*
Birch Run, 1653 Q10
Birmingham, 19291 S11
Blissfield, 3223 U10
Bloomfield Hills, 3940 F6*
Bloomingdale, 528 T5
Boyne City, 3503 H7
Breckenridge, 1339 P8
Bridgeport, 7849 P10
Bridgman, 2428 U3
Brighton, 6701 S10
Britton, 699 U10
Bronson, 2421 U7
Brooklyn, 1176 T9
Brown City, 1334 Q12
Buchanan, 4681 U4
Buckley, 550 K5
Buena Vista, 7845 P10
Burr Oak, 797 U6
Burt, 1122 Q10
Burton, 30308 Q10
Byron, 595 R10
Byron Ctr., 3777 R5
Cadillac, 10000 L6
Caledonia, 1102 R6
Calumet, 879 A12
Camden, 550 V8
Capac, 1775 Q12
Carleton, 2562 U11
Caro, 4145 P11
Carrollton, 6602 P10
Carson City, 1190 Q7
Carsonville, 502 P13
Caseville, 888 M11
Caspian, 997 D12
Cass City, 2643 N11
Cassopolis, 1740 U5
Cedar Sprs., 3112 Q6
Center Line, 8531 H8*
Central Lake, 990 H6
Centreville, 1579 U6
Charlevoix, 2994 H6
Charlotte, 8389 S7
Chassell, 800 B12
Cheboygan, 5295 G8
Chelsea, 4398 T9
Chesaning, 2548 Q9
Clare, 3173 N8
Clarkston, 962 D5*
Clawson, 12732 G7*
Climax, 791 T6
Clinton, 2293 U10
Clio, 2483 Q10
Coldwater, 12697 U7
Coleman, 1296 N8
Coloma, 1595 T4
Colon, 1227 U6
Columbiaville, 815 Q11
Comstock, 4472 T6
Comstock Park, 10674 Q5
Concord, 1101 T8
Constantine, 2095 U5
Coopersville, 3910 Q5
Corunna, 3381 R9
Covert, 650 T4
Croswell, 2467 P13
Crystal Falls, 1791 D12
Cutlerville, 15114 R5
Davison, 5536 Q11
Dearborn, 97775 T11
Dearborn Hts., 58264 K6*
Decatur, 1838 T5
Deckerville, 944 P12
Deerfield, 1005 U10
Detroit, 951270 T12
Detroit Beach, 2289 U11
De Witt, 4702 R8
Dexter, 2338 T10
Dimondale, 1342 S8
Dollar Bay, 950 A12
Dorr, 2800 R5
Douglas, 1214 S4
Dowagiac, 6147 U4
Dryden, 815 R12
Dundee, 3522 U10
Durand, 3933 R9
Eagle River, 20 A12
E. Grand Rapids, 10764 C3*
E. Jordan, 2507 H7
E. Lansing, 46525 R8
Eastpointe, 34077 H9*
E. Tawas, 2951 L11
Eaton Rapids, 5330 S8
Eau Claire, 656 U4
Ecorse, 11229 L7*
Edmore, 1244 P7
Edwardsburg, 1147 V4
Elk Rapids, 1700 J6
Elkton, 863 N11
Elsie, 1055 Q8
Escanaba, 13140 F2
Essexville, 3766 N10
Evart, 1738 N6
Fairgrove, 627 P10
Fair Haven, 1500 R13
Fair Plain, 7828 U4
Farmington, 10423 H5*
Farmington Hills, 82111 G5*
Farwell, 855 N7
Fennville, 1459 S4
Fenton, 10582 R10
Ferndale, 22105 H7*
Ferrysburg, 3040 Q4
Flat Rock, 8488 T11
Flint, 124943 Q10
Flushing, 8348 Q10
Fowler, 1136 R8
Fowlerville, 2972 S9
Frankenmuth, 4838 P10
Frankfort, 1513 K4
Franklin, 2937 G6*
Fraser, 15297 G9*
Freeland, 5147 P9
Fremont, 4224 P5
Fruitport, 1124 Q4
Galesburg, 1988 T6
Galien, 593 V3
Garden City, 30047 K5*
Gardendale, 800 Q13
Gaylord, 3681 J8
Genesee, 1800 Q10
Gibraltar, 4264 T11
Gladstone, 5032 F2
Gladwin, 3001 M8
Gobles, 815 T5
Goodrich, 1353 R11
Grand Blanc, 8242 R10
Grand Haven, 11168 Q4
Grand Ledge, 7813 R8
Grand Rapids, 197800 R5
Grandville, 16263 R5
Grant, 881 P5
Grass Lake, 1082 T9
Grawn, 1600 K5
Grayling, 1952 K8
Greenville, 7935 Q6
Greilickville, 1415 J5
Grosse Ile, 10894 N7*
Grosse Pointe, 5670 J10*
Grosse Pointe Farms, 9764 J10*
Grosse Pointe Park, 12443 J9*
Grosse Pointe Shores, 2823 J10*
Grosse Pointe Woods, 17080 S12
Gwinn, 1965 E1
Hamilton, 1300 S5
Hamtramck, 22976 J8*
Hancock, 4323 A12
Harbert, 1619 U3
Harbor Beach, 1837 N13
Harbor Sprs., 1567 G7
Harper Woods, 14254 J9*
Harrison, 2108 M7
Harrisville, 514 K11
Hart, 1950 N4
Hartford, 2476 T4
Harvey, 1321 D2
Haslett, 11283 R9
Hastings, 7095 S7
Hazel Park, 18963 H8*
Hemlock, 1585 P9
Hesperia, 954 P5
Highland Park, 16746 J8*
Hillman, 685 H10
Hillsdale, 8233 U8
Holland, 35048 R4
Holly, 6135 R10
Holt, 11315 S8
Homer, 1851 T8
Hopkins, 592 S5
Houghton, 7010 A12
Houghton Lake, 3749 L8
Howard City, 1585 P6
Howell, 9232 S10
Hubbard Lake, 993 J10
Hubbell, 1105 A12
Hudson, 2499 U9
Hudsonville, 7160 R5
Huntington Woods, 6151 H7*
Ida, 1100 U10
Imlay City, 3869 Q12
Indian River, 2008 G8
Inkster, 30115 L5*
Ionia, 10569 R7
Iron Mtn., 8154 D12
Iron River, 3386 D12
Ironwood, 6293 C9
Ishpeming, 6686 D1
Ithaca, 3098 Q8
Jackson, 36316 T8
Jamestown, 750 R5
Jenison, 17211 R5
Jonesville, 2337 U8
Kalamazoo, 77145 T6
Kaleva, 509 L5
Kalkaska, 2226 K7
Kawkawlin, 1600 N10
Keego Harbor, 2769 F5*
Kent City, 1061 Q5
Kentwood, 45255 R6
Kinde, 534 M12
Kingsford, 5549 D12
Kingsley, 1469 K6
Laingsburg, 1223 R9
Lake City, 923 L6
Lake Isabella, 1243 N7
Lake Linden, 1081 A12
Lake Michigan Beach, 1509 T4
Lake Odessa, 2272 R7
Lake Orion, 2715 R11
Lakeport, 700 Q13
Lakeview, 1112 P6
Lakewood Club, 1006 P4
Lambertville, 9299 V10
L'Anse, 2107 B12
Lansing, 119128 R8
Lapeer, 9072 Q11
Lathrup Vil., 4236 H6*
Laurium, 2126 A12
Lawrence, 1059 T5
Lawton, 1859 T5
Leland, 350 J5
Lennon, 517 R10
Leslie, 2044 S8
Lewiston, 990 J9
Lexington, 1104 Q13
Lexington Hts., 1000 Q13
Lincoln Park, 40008 T11
Linden, 2861 R10
Linwood, 1200 N9
Litchfield, 1458 U8
Livonia, 100545 S11
Lowell, 4013 R6
Ludington, 8357 M4
Luna Pier, 1483 U11
Lyons, 726 R7
Mackinac Island, 523 F8
Mackinaw City, 859 F8
Madison Hts., 31101 G8*
Mancelona, 1408 J7
Manchester, 2160 T10
Manistee, 6586 L4
Manistique, 3583 F4
Manitou Beach, 2080 U9
Manton, 1221 L6
Maple Rapids, 643 Q8
Marcellus, 1162 U5
Marine City, 4652 R13
Marion, 836 M7
Marlette, 2104 P12
Marquette, 19661 D1
Marshall, 7459 T7
Marysville, 9684 R13
Mason, 6714 S8
Mattawan, 2536 T5
Maybee, 505 U11
Mayville, 1055 P11
McBain, 584 M6
Melvindale, 10735 L7*
Memphis, 1129 R12
Mendon, 917 U6
Menominee, 9131 H1
Merrill, 782 P9
Metamora, 507 R11
Michigan Ctr., 4641 T9
Middleville, 2721 R6
Midland, 41685 P9
Milan, 4775 U10
Milford, 6272 S10
Millington, 1137 Q11
Mio, 2016 K9
Mohawk, 750 A12
Monroe, 22076 U11
Montague, 2407 P4
Montrose, 1619 Q10
Morenci, 2398 V9
Morrice, 882 R9
Mt. Clemens, 17312 S12
Mt. Morris, 3194 Q10
Mt. Pleasant, 25946 P8
Muir, 634 R7
Mulliken, 557 R7
Munising, 2539 D3
Muskegon, 40105 Q4
Muskegon Hts., 12049 Q4
Napoleon, 1254 T9
Nashville, 1684 S7
Negaunee, 4576 D1
Newaygo, 1670 P5
New Baltimore, 7405 S13
Newberry, 2686 D6
New Buffalo, 2200 U3
New Haven, 3071 R12
New Lothrop, 603 Q9
Niles, 12204 U4
N. Adams, 514 U8
N. Branch, 1027 Q11
N. Muskegon, 4031 Q4
Northport, 648 H6
Northville, 6459 J4*
Norton Shores, 22527 Q4
Norway, 2959 E13
Novi, 47386 S11
Oak Grove, 700 J8
Oak Park, 29793 S11
Okemos, 22805 R8
Olivet, 1758 S7
Onaway, 993 H9
Onekama, 647 L4
Onsted, 813 U9
Ontonagon, 1769 B11
Orchard Lake, 2215 F5*
Ortonville, 1535 R11
Oscoda, 992 L11
Ossineke, 1059 J11
Otisville, 882 Q11
Otsego, 3933 S5
Ovid, 1514 Q9
Owosso, 15713 R9
Oxford, 3540 R11
Parchment, 1936 A6*
Parma, 907 T8
Patterson Gardens, 3900 U11
Paw Paw, 3363 T5
Paw Paw Lake, 3944 T4
Pearl Beach, 3224 S13
Peck, 599 Q12
Pellston, 771 G7
Pentwater, 958 N4
Perry, 2065 R9
Petersburg, 1157 U10
Petoskey, 6080 G7
Pewamo, 560 R7
Pigeon, 1207 N11
Pinckney, 2141 S10
Pinconning, 1386 N9
Plainwell, 3933 S5
Pleasant Lake, 850 T9
Pleasant Ridge, 2594 H7*
Plymouth, 9022 T11
Pontiac, 66337 S11
Portage, 44897 T6
Port Austin, 737 M12
Port Huron, 32338 Q13
Portland, 3789 R7
Port Sanilac, 658 P13
Potterville, 2168 S8
Prudenville, 1737 L8
Pullman, 700 S4
Quincy, 1701 U7
Quinnesec, 1187 E13
Ramsay, 750 C9
Ravenna, 1206 Q5
Reading, 1134 U8
Redford, 51622 J6*
Reed City, 2430 N6
Reese, 1375 P10
Republic, 614 C13
Richland, 593 T6
Richmond, 4897 R12
River Rouge, 9917 L7*
Riverview, 13272 M7*
Rives Jct., 650 T8
Rochester, 10467 E8*

MINNESOTA STATE CAPITOL BUILDING, ST. PAUL, MINNESOTA

Rochester Hills, 68825 R11
Rockford, 4626 Q6
Rockwood, 3442 U11
Rogers City, 3322 G10
Romeo, 3721 R12
Romulus, 22979 T11
Roosevelt Park, 3890 Q4
Roscommon, 1133 K8
Rose City, 721 L9
Roseville, 48129 G9*
Royal Oak, 60062 S11
Saginaw, 61799 P9
St. Charles, 2215 Q9
St. Clair, 5802 R13
St. Clair Shores, 63096 S12
St. Helen, 2993 L8
St. Ignace, 2678 F8
St. Johns, 7485 R8
St. Joseph, 8789 T3
St. Louis, 4494 P8
Saline, 8034 T10
Sandusky, 2745 P12
Sanford, 943 N8
Saranac, 1326 R7
Saugatuck, 1065 S4
Sault Ste. Marie, 16542 D8
Schoolcraft, 1587 T5
Scottville, 1266 M4
Sebewaing, 1974 N11
Shelby, 1914 P4
Shepherd, 1536 P8
Sheridan, 705 Q7
Shields, 6590 P9
Shoreham, 860 U3
Sister Lakes, 1000 U4
Skidway Lake, 3147 M9
Southfield, 78296 S11
Southgate, 30136 M7*
S. Haven, 5021 S4
S. Lyon, 10036 S10
S. Monroe, 6370 U11
S. Range, 727 B12
S. Rockwood, 1284 U11
Sparta, 4159 Q5
Spring Arbor, 2188 T8
Springfield, 5189 T6
Spring Lake, 2514 Q4
Springport, 704 T8
Standish, 1581 M9
Stanton, 1504 Q7
Stephenson, 875 G1
Sterling, 533 M9
Sterling Hts., 124471 S12
Stevensville, 1191 U3
Stockbridge, 1260 S9
Sturgis, 11285 V6
Sunfield, 591 R7
Suttons Bay, 589 J5
Swartz Creek, 5102 R10
Sylvan Lake, 1735 F5*
Tawas City, 2005 L10
Taylor, 65868 T11
Tecumseh, 8574 U10
Tekonsha, 712 U7
Temperance, 7757 U11
Three Oaks, 1829 V3
Three Rivers, 7328 U5
Traverse City, 14532 K6
Trenton, 19584 T11
Trowbridge Park, 2012 D1
Troy, 80959 S12
Twin Lake, 1613 P4
Ubly, 873 N12
Union City, 1804 U7
Union Lake, 2500 F4*
Unionville, 605 N11
Utica, 4577 F8*
Vanderbilt, 587 H8
Vandercook Lake, 4809 T8
Vassar, 2823 P10
Vermontville, 789 S7
Vernon, 847 R9
Vicksburg, 2320 T6
Wakefield, 2085 C9
Waldron, 590 V8
Walker, 21842 R5
Walled Lake, 6713 G4*
Warren, 138247 S12
Waterford, 73150 R11
Watervliet, 1843 T4
Wayland, 3939 S5
Wayne, 19051 L5*
Webberville, 1503 S9
Weidman, 879 N7
W. Branch, 1926 L9
Westland, 86602 T11
Westphalia, 876 R7
White Cloud, 1420 P5
Whitehall, 2884 P4
White Pigeon, 1627 V5
White Pine, 700 B10
Whitmore Lake, 6574 S10
Williamston, 3441 S9
Wixom, 13263 S11
Wolf Lake, 4455 Q4
Wolverine Lake, 4415 G4*
Woodhaven, 12530 T11
Woodland Beach, 2179 U11
Wyandotte, 28006 T11
Wyoming, 69368 R5
Yale, 2063 Q12
Ypsilanti, 22362 T10
Zeeland, 5805 R5
Zilwaukee, 1799 G13

MINNESOTA
PG. 59-61

CAPITAL
St. Paul

NICKNAME
Gopher State

POPULATION
4,919,479, rank 21

AREA
84,402 sq mi, rank 12

STATEHOOD
1858, rank 32

Counties
Aitkin, 15301 L8
Anoka, 298084 Q9
Becker, 30000 J4
Beltrami, 39650 F5
Benton, 34226 P7
Big Stone, 5820 P2
Blue Earth, 55941 U7
Brown, 26911 T5
Carlton, 31671 L10
Carver, 70205 R7
Cass, 27150 J6
Chippewa, 13088 Q4
Chisago, 41101 P9
Clay, 51229 J2
Clearwater, 8423 H4
Cook, 5168 F13
Cottonwood, 12167 U4
Crow Wing, 55099 M7
Dakota, 355904 S9
Dodge, 17731 U9
Douglas, 32821 N4
Faribault, 16181 V7
Fillmore, 21122 U11
Freeborn, 32584 U9
Goodhue, 44127 S10
Grant, 6289 N3
Hennepin, 1116200 Q8
Houston, 19718 V12
Hubbard, 18376 J5
Isanti, 31287 P8
Itasca, 43992 H8
Jackson, 11268 V4
Kanabec, 14996 M9
Kandiyohi, 41203 Q5
Kittson, 5285 D1
Koochiching, 14355 E8
Lac qui Parle, 8067 R2
Lake, 11058 G13
Lake of the Woods, 4522 E5
Le Sueur, 25426 S8
Lincoln, 6429 S2
Lyon, 25425 S3
Mahnomen, 5190 J3
Marshall, 10155 E2
Martin, 21802 U6
McLeod, 34898 R6
Meeker, 22644 Q6
Mille Lacs, 22330 N8
Morrison, 31712 M7
Mower, 38603 V10
Murray, 9165 T3
Nicollet, 29771 S6
Nobles, 20832 U3
Norman, 7442 H2
Olmsted, 124277 T10
Otter Tail, 57159 L3
Pennington, 13584 F3
Pine, 26530 M10
Pipestone, 9895 T2
Polk, 31369 G2
Pope, 11236 P4
Ramsey, 511035 Q9
Red Lake, 4299 G3
Redwood, 16815 S4
Renville, 17154 R5
Rice, 56665 S8
Rock, 9721 U2
Roseau, 16338 D3
St. Louis, 200528 G10
Scott, 89498 S8
Sherburne, 64417 P7
Sibley, 15356 S7
Stearns, 133166 P6
Steele, 33680 T8
Stevens, 10053 P3
Swift, 11956 Q3
Todd, 24426 M5
Traverse, 4134 N2
Wabasha, 21610 T11
Wadena, 13713 L5
Waseca, 19526 U8
Washington, 201130 Q9
Watonwan, 11876 U5
Wilkin, 7138 L2
Winona, 49985 U11
Wright, 89986 Q7
Yellow Medicine, 11080 R3

Cities and Towns
* City indexed to pg. 59

Ada, 1657 H2
Adams, 800 V10
Adrian, 1234 V3
Afton, 2839 G10*
Aitkin, 1984 L8
Albany, 1796 P6
Albert Lea, 18356 V8
Albertville, 3621 Q8
Alden, 652 U8
Alexandria, 8820 N4
Amboy, 575 U7
Andover, 26588 Q8
Annandale, 2684 Q7
Anoka, 18076 Q8
Appleton, 2871 Q3
Apple Valley, 45527 R9
Arden Hills, 9652 C5*
Argyle, 656 E1
Arlington, 2048 S7
Arnold, 3032 K11
Atwater, 1079 Q5
Aurora, 1850 H11
Austin, 23314 V9
Avon, 1242 P6
Babbitt, 1670 G11
Bagley, 1235 H4
Balaton, 637 T3
Barnesville, 2173 K2
Barnum, 525 L10
Battle Lake, 686 M4
Baudette, 1104 D6
Baxter, 5555 M6
Bayport, 3162 Q10
Becker, 2673 P7
Belgrade, 750 P5
Belle Plaine, 3789 S8
Bemidji, 11917 H5
Benson, 3376 Q4
Big Lake, 6063 Q8
Birchwood Vil., 968 D8*
Bird Island, 1195 R5
Biwabik, 954 H10
Blackduck, 696 G6
Blaine, 44942 Q9
Blooming Prairie, 1933 U9
Bloomington, 85172 R9
Blue Earth, 3621 V7
Bovey, 662 J8
Braham, 1276 N9
Brainerd, 13178 M7
Breckenridge, 3559 M2
Breezy Pt., 979 L7
Brooklyn Ctr., 29172 C4*
Brooklyn Park, 67388 B3*
Brooten, 649 P5
Browerville, 735 M5
Brownsdale, 718 U9
Browns Valley, 690 P1
Brownton, 807 R6
Buffalo, 10097 Q7
Buffalo Lake, 768 R6
Buhl, 983 H10
Burnsville, 60220 R9
Butterfield, 564 U5
Byron, 3500 T10
Caledonia, 2965 V12
Cambridge, 5520 P9
Canby, 1903 R2
Cannon Falls, 3795 S9
Carlton, 810 K10
Carver, 1266 R8
Cass Lake, 860 H6
Center City, 582 P9
Centerville, 3202 B7*
Champlin, 22193 B3*
Chanhassen, 20321 R8
Chaska, 17449 R8
Chatfield, 2394 U11
Chisago City, 2622 P9
Chisholm, 4960 H9
Circle Pines, 4663 B6*
Clara City, 1393 R4
Claremont, 620 T9
Clarissa, 609 M5
Clarkfield, 944 R3
Clarks Grove, 734 U8
Clearbrook, 551 G4
Clearwater, 858 P7
Cleveland, 673 T7
Cloquet, 11201 K10
Cohasset, 2481 J8
Cokato, 2727 Q7
Cold Spr., 2975 P6
Coleraine, 1110 J8
Cologne, 1012 R8
Columbia Hts., 18520 D5*
Cook, 622 G10
Coon Rapids, 61607 Q8
Corcoran, 5630 Q8
Cosmos, 582 R6
Cottage Grove, 30582 R9
Cottonwood, 1148 S4
Courtland, 538 T6
Crookston, 8192 G2
Crosby, 2299 L7
Crosslake, 1893 K7
Crystal, 22698 D3*
Danube, 529 R5
Dassel, 1233 Q6
Dawson, 1539 R3
Dayton, 4699 Q8
Deephaven, 3853 F1*
Deer River, 903 H7
Deerwood, 590 L7
Delano, 3837 Q7
Dellwood, 1033 C8*
Detroit Lakes, 7348 K3
Dilworth, 3001 K2
Dodge Ctr., 2226 T9
Duluth, 86918 K11
Dundas, 547 S9
Eagan, 63557 H6*
Eagle Bend, 595 M5
Eagle Lake, 1787 T7
E. Bethel, 10941 P9
E. Grand Forks, 7501 F1
E. Gull Lake, 978 L6
Eden Prairie, 54901 H2*
Eden Valley, 866 Q6
Edgerton, 1033 U2
Edina, 47425 R8
Elbow Lake, 1275 N3
Elgin, 826 T11
Elk River, 16447 Q8
Ellendale, 590 U9
Ellsworth, 540 V3
Elmore, 735 V7
Ely, 3724 G11
Emily, 847 K7
Esko, 1300 K10
Evansville, 566 N4
Eveleth, 3865 H10
Eyota, 1644 U11
Fairfax, 1295 S6
Fairmont, 10889 V6
Falcon Hts., 5572 E5*
Faribault, 20818 T9
Farmington, 12365 S9
Fergus Falls, 13471 M3
Fertile, 893 H2
Foley, 2154 P7
Forest Lake, 6798 Q9
Fosston, 1575 H4
Frazee, 1377 K4
Fridley, 27449 Q9
Fulda, 1283 U4
Gaylord, 2279 S7
Gibbon, 808 S6
Gilbert, 1847 H10
Glencoe, 5453 R7
Glenville, 720 V9
Glenwood, 2594 P4
Glyndon, 1049 K2
Golden Valley, 20281 E2*
Goodhue, 778 S10
Good Thunder, 592 U7
Goodview, 3373 T12
Graceville, 605 P2
Grand Marais, 1353 C11
Grand Meadow, 945 U10
Grand Rapids, 7764 J8
Granite Falls, 3070 R4
Grant, 4026 Q9
Greenbush, 784 D3
Grove City, 608 Q6
Hallock, 1196 D1
Halstad, 622 H1
Hamburg, 538 R7
Ham Lake, 12710 Q9
Hancock, 717 P3
Hanover, 1355 Q8
Harmony, 1080 V11
Harris, 1121 P9
Hastings, 18204 R9
Hawley, 1882 K2
Hayfield, 1325 U10
Hector, 1166 R6
Henderson, 910 S7
Hendricks, 725 S2
Henning, 719 M4
Hermantown, 7448 K11
Heron Lake, 768 U4
Hibbing, 17071 H9
Hills, 565 V2
Hilltop, 766 D4*
Hinckley, 1291 N9
Hoffman, 672 N3
Hokah, 614 U13
Holdingford, 736 N6
Hopkins, 17145 F2*
Houston, 1020 U12
Howard Lake, 1853 Q7
Hoyt Lakes, 2082 H11
Hugo, 6363 Q9
Hutchinson, 13080 R6
Independence, 3236 Q8
International Falls, 6703 E8
Inver Grove Hts., 29751 H7*
Isanti, 2324 P9
Isle, 707 M8
Ivanhoe, 679 S2
Jackson, 3501 V5
Janesville, 2109 T8
Jasper, 597 U2
Jordan, 3833 S8
Kandiyohi, 555 Q5
Karlstad, 794 E2
Kasota, 680 T7
Kasson, 4398 T10
Keewatin, 1164 H9
Kenyon, 1661 T9
Kerkhoven, 759 Q4
Kiester, 540 V8
Kimball, 635 Q6
La Crescent, 4923 U13
Lafayette, 529 S6
Lake Benton, 703 T2
Lake City, 4950 S11
Lake Crystal, 2420 T7
Lake Elmo, 6863 E9*
Lakefield, 1721 U5
Lakeland, 1917 R10
Lake Park, 782 K3
Lake St. Croix Beach, 1140 R10
Lake Shore, 966 L6
Lakeville, 43128 S9
Lamberton, 859 T4
Landfall, 700 F8*
Lanesboro, 788 U11
La Prairie, 605 J8
Lauderdale, 2364 E5*
Le Center, 2240 S8
Le Roy, 925 V10
Lester Prairie, 1377 R7
Le Sueur, 3922 S7
Lewiston, 1484 U12
Lexington, 2214 B5*
Lilydale, 552 F6*
Lindstrom, 3015 P10
Lino Lakes, 16791 A6*
Litchfield, 6562 Q6
Little Canada, 9771 E6*
Little Falls, 7719 N6
Littlefork, 680 E8
Long Lake, 1842 R8
Long Prairie, 3040 N5
Lonsdale, 1491 S8
Loretto, 570 Q8
Luverne, 4617 U2
Lyle, 566 V9
Mabel, 766 V12
Madelia, 2340 T6
Madison, 1768 Q2
Madison Lake, 837 T7
Mahnomen, 1202 H3
Mahtomedi, 7563 C8*
Mankato, 32427 T7
Mantorville, 1054 T10
Maple Grove, 50365 Q8
Maple Lake, 1633 Q7
Maple Plain, 2088 R8
Mapleton, 1678 U7
Maplewood, 34947 E7*
Marble, 695 H8
Marine on St. Croix, 602 Q10
Marshall, 12735 S3
Mayer, 554 R7
Mazeppa, 778 T10
McIntosh, 638 G3
Medford, 984 T9
Medina, 4005 Q8
Melrose, 3091 P5
Menahga, 1220 K5
Mendota Hts., 11434 G6*
Milaca, 2580 N8
Minneapolis, 382618 R9
Minneota, 1449 S3
Minnesota Lake, 681 U7
Minnetonka, 51301 F1*
Montevideo, 5346 R3
Montgomery, 2794 S8
Monticello, 7868 Q7
Montrose, 1143 Q7
Moorhead, 32177 K1
Moose Lake, 2239 L10
Mora, 3193 N9
Morgan, 903 S5
Morris, 5068 P3
Morristown, 981 T8
Motley, 585 M6
Mound, 9435 R8
Mounds View, 12738 C5*
Mtn. Iron, 2999 H10
Mtn. Lake, 2082 U5
Nashwauk, 935 H9
Naytahwaush, 583 J4
New Brighton, 22206 D5*
New Hope, 20873 D2*
New London, 1066 Q5
Newport, 3715 G8*
New Prague, 4559 S8
New Richland, 1197 U8
New Ulm, 13594 T6
New York Mills, 1158 L4
Nicollet, 889 T7
Nisswa, 1953 L7
N. Branch, 8023 P9
Northfield, 17147 S9
N. Mankato, 11798 T7
N. Oaks, 3883 C6*
N. St. Paul, 11929 D8*
Norwood-Young America, 3108 R7
Oakdale, 26653 E8*
Oak Grove, 6903 Q9
Oak Park Hts., 3957 Q10
Olivia, 2570 R5
Onamia, 847 M8
Orono, 7538 R8
Oronoco, 883 T10
Ortonville, 2158 Q2
Osakis, 1567 N5
Osseo, 2434 C2*
Otsego, 6389 Q8
Owatonna, 22434 T9
Parkers Prairie, 991 M4
Park Rapids, 3276 K5
Paynesville, 2267 P6
Pelican Rapids, 2374 L3
Pequot Lakes, 947 L6
Perham, 2559 L4
Pierz, 1277 N7
Pine City, 3043 N9
Pine Island, 2337 T10
Pine River, 928 K6
Pipestone, 4280 T2
Plainview, 3190 T11
Plymouth, 65894 R8
Ponemah, 874 F5
Preston, 1426 U11
Princeton, 3933 P8
Prior Lake, 15917 R8
Proctor, 2852 K11
Ramsey, 18510 Q8
Randall, 535 M6
Raymond, 803 Q4
Redby, 957 G5
Red Lake, 1430 G5
Red Lake Falls, 1590 G3
Red Wing, 16116 S10
Redwood Falls, 5459 S5
Renville, 1323 R5
Rice, 711 N7
Richfield, 34439 G4*
Richmond, 1213 P6
Robbinsdale, 14123 D3*
Rochester, 85806 T10
Rock Creek, 1119 N9
Rockford, 3484 Q8
Rockville, 749 P6
Rogers, 3588 Q8
Rollingstone, 697 T12
Roseau, 2756 D4
Rosemount, 14619 K6*
Roseville, 33690 E5*
Royalton, 816 N6
Rush City, 2102 P9
Rushford, 1696 U12
Rushford Vil., 714 U12
Sacred Heart, 549 R4
St. Anthony, 8012 D5*
St. Augusta, 650 P7
St. Bonifacius, 1873 R8
St. Charles, 3295 U11
St. Clair, 827 T7
St. Cloud, 59107 P7
St. Francis, 4910 P8
St. James, 4695 U6
St. Joseph, 4681 P6
St. Louis Park, 44126 F3*
St. Michael, 9099 Q8
St. Paul, 287151 R9
St. Paul Park, 5070 H8*
St. Peter, 9747 T7
St. Stephen, 860 N6
Sandstone, 1549 M9
Sartell, 9641 P7
Sauk Centre, 3930 N5
Sauk Rapids, 10213 P7
Savage, 21115 R8
Scanlon, 838 K10
Sebeka, 710 L5
Shakopee, 20568 R8
Sherburn, 1082 V5
Shoreview, 25924 C6*
Shorewood, 7400 R8
Silver Bay, 2068 H13
Silver Lake, 761 R7
Slayton, 2072 T3
Sleepy Eye, 3515 T5
S. St. Paul, 20167 G7*
Spicer, 1126 Q5
Springfield, 2215 T5
Spring Grove, 1304 V12
Spring Lake Park, 6772 C4*
Spring Valley, 2518 U10
Stacy, 1278 P9
Staples, 3104 M5
Starbuck, 1314 P4
Stephen, 708 E1
Stewart, 564 R6
Stewartville, 5411 U10
Stillwater, 15143 Q10
Stockton, 682 T12
Taylors Falls, 951 P10
Thief River Falls, 8410 F3
Tracy, 2268 T4
Trimont, 754 U6
Truman, 1259 U6
Twin Valley, 865 J2
Two Harbors, 3613 J12
Tyler, 1218 T3
Ulen, 532 J2
Vadnais Hts., 13069 C7*
Verndale, 575 L5
Victoria, 4025 R8
Vineland, 607 M8
Virginia, 9157 H10
Wabasha, 2599 S11
Wabasso, 643 S4
Waconia, 6814 R7
Wadena, 4294 L5
Waite Park, 6568 P7
Walker, 1069 J6
Walnut Grove, 599 T4
Wanamingo, 1007 T10
Warren, 1678 F2
Warroad, 1722 D4
Warsaw, 550 T8
Waseca, 8493 T8
Watertown, 3029 R7
Waterville, 1833 T8
Watkins, 880 Q6
Waverly, 732 Q7
Wayzata, 4113 E1*
Welcome, 721 V6
Wells, 2494 U8
Westbrook, 755 T4
W. Concord, 836 T9
W. St. Paul, 19405 G7*
Wheaton, 1619 N2
White Bear Lake, 24325 D8*
Willernie, 549 D8*
Willmar, 18351 Q5
Windom, 4490 U5
Winnebago, 1487 U7
Winona, 27069 T12
Winsted, 2094 R7
Winthrop, 1367 S6
Woodbury, 46463 R9
Worthington, 11283 V4
Wyoming, 3048 P9
Zimmerman, 2851 P8
Zumbrota, 2789 T10

MISSISSIPPI
PG. 62

CAPITAL
Jackson

NICKNAME
Magnolia State

POPULATION
2,844,658, rank 31

AREA
47,689 sq mi, rank 32

STATEHOOD
1817, rank 20

Counties
Adams, 34340 K4
Alcorn, 34558 A9
Amite, 13599 K4
Attala, 19661 E7
Benton, 8026 A8
Bolivar, 40633 D4
Calhoun, 15069 C8
Carroll, 10769 D6
Chickasaw, 19440 D8
Choctaw, 9758 E7
Claiborne, 11831 H4
Clarke, 17955 H9
Clay, 21979 D9
Coahoma, 30622 C5
Copiah, 28757 J5
Covington, 19407 J7
DeSoto, 107199 A6
Forrest, 72604 L8
Franklin, 8448 J4
George, 19144 L9
Greene, 13299 K9
Grenada, 23263 D7
Hancock, 42967 M7
Harrison, 189601 M8
Hinds, 250800 H5
Holmes, 21609 E6
Humphreys, 11206 F5
Issaquena, 2274 G4
Itawamba, 22770 C9
Jackson, 131420 M9
Jasper, 18149 H8
Jefferson, 9740 J4
Jefferson Davis, 13962 J6
Jones, 64958 J8
Kemper, 10453 G9
Lafayette, 38744 B7
Lamar, 39070 K7
Lauderdale, 78161 H9
Lawrence, 13258 K6
Leake, 20940 F7
Lee, 75755 B9
Leflore, 37947 E6
Lincoln, 33166 K5
Lowndes, 61586 E9
Madison, 74674 G6
Marion, 25595 K7
Marshall, 34993 B7
Monroe, 38014 D9
Montgomery, 12189 D7
Neshoba, 28684 G8
Newton, 21838 H8
Noxubee, 12548 F9
Oktibbeha, 42902 E8
Panola, 34274 C6
Pearl River, 48621 L7
Perry, 12138 K8
Pike, 38940 K5
Pontotoc, 26726 C8
Prentiss, 25556 B9
Quitman, 10117 C6
Rankin, 115327 H6
Scott, 28423 G7
Sharkey, 6580 F5
Simpson, 27639 J6
Smith, 16182 H7
Stone, 13622 L8
Sunflower, 34369 E5
Tallahatchie, 14903 D6
Tate, 25370 B6
Tippah, 20826 A8
Tishomingo, 19163 B10
Tunica, 9227 B6
Union, 25362 B8
Walthall, 15156 L6
Warren, 49644 G5
Washington, 62977 F4
Wayne, 21216 J9
Webster, 10294 D7
Wilkinson, 10312 K3
Winston, 20160 F8
Yalobusha, 13051 C7
Yazoo, 28149 G6

Cities and Towns
Aberdeen, 6415 D9
Ackerman, 1696 E8
Alcorn, 1200 J4
Algoma, 508 C8
Amory, 6956 C9
Anguilla, 907 F5
Arcola, 563 E4
Arnold Line, 1800 E1
Artesia, 498 E9
Ashland, 577 A8
Baldwyn, 3321 B9
Batesville, 7113 C6
Bay St. Louis, 8209 M8
Bay Sprs., 2097 H8
Beaumont, 977 K8
Belmont, 1961 B10
Belzoni, 2663 E5
Benoit, 611 D4
Bentonia, 500 G6
Beulah, 473 D4
Biloxi, 50644 M9
Blue Mtn., 670 B8
Bogue Chitto, 533 F8
Bolton, 629 G5
Booneville, 8625 B9
Boyle, 720 D5
Brandon, 16436 H6
Brookhaven, 9861 J5
Brooksville, 1182 E9
Bruce, 2097 C8
Bude, 1037 K4
Burnsville, 1034 A10
Byhalia, 706 A7
Byram, 7386 H6
Caledonia, 1015 D10
Calhoun City, 1872 D8
Canton, 12911 G6
Carriere, 600 M7
Carrollton, 408 E6
Carthage, 4637 G7
Cary, 427 F4
Centreville, 1680 K4
Charleston, 2198 C6
Clarksdale, 20645 C5
Cleveland, 13841 D5
Clinton, 23347 G6
Coffeeville, 930 C7
Coldwater, 1674 B6
Collins, 2683 J7
Collinsville, 1823 G9
Columbia, 6603 K7
Columbus, 25944 E9
Como, 1310 B6
Conehatta, 997 G8
Corinth, 14054 A9
Courtland, 460 C6
Crawford, 655 E9
Crenshaw, 916 B6
Crowder, 766 C6
Cruger, 449 E6
Crystal Sprs., 5873 H6
Decatur, 1426 G8
De Kalb, 972 F9
De Lisle, 800 M8
Derma, 1023 D8
Diamondhead, 5912 M8
D'Iberville, 7608 M9
Drew, 2434 D5
Duck Hill, 746 D7
Dumas, 452 B9
Duncan, 578 C5
Durant, 2932 F7
Ecru, 947 C8
Edwards, 1347 G5
Ellisville, 3465 J8
Enterprise, 474 H9
Escatawpa, 3566 M5
Ethel, 452 F7
Eupora, 2326 E8
Farmington, 1810 A9
Fayette, 2242 J4
Flora, 1546 G6
Florence, 2396 H6
Flowood, 4750 C2
Forest, 5987 G7
Friars Pt., 1480 C5
Fulton, 3882 C9
Gautier, 11681 M9
Gloster, 1073 K4
Goodman, 1252 F6
Greenville, 41633 E4
Greenwood, 18425 E6
Grenada, 14879 D7
Gulfport, 71127 M8
Gunnison, 633 D4
Guntown, 1183 B9
Hatley, 476 C9
Hattiesburg, 44779 K8

Hazlehurst, 4400 J5
Heidelberg, 840 J8
Helena, 778 M5
Hernando, 6812 A6
Hickory, 499 H8
Hickory Flat, 565 B8
Hollandale, 3437 E5
Holly Sprs., 7957 B7
Horn Lake, 14099 A6
Houston, 4079 D8
Hurley, 985 M9
Indianola, 12066 E5
Inverness, 1153 E5
Isola, 768 E5
Itta Bena, 2208 E6
Iuka, 3059 A10
Jackson, 184256 H6
Jonestown, 1701 C5
Kilmichael, 830 E7
Kiln, 2040 M7
Kosciusko, 7372 F7
Lambert, 1967 C6
Latimer, 4288 M9
Laurel, 18393 J8
Leakesville, 1026 K9
Leland, 5502 E4
Lexington, 2025 F6
Liberty, 633 K5
Long Beach, 17320 M8
Louisville, 7006 F8
Lucedale, 2458 L9
Lumberton, 2228 L7
Lynchburg, 2959 A6
Maben, 803 D8
Macon, 2461 F9
Madison, 14692 G6
Magee, 4200 J7
Magnolia, 2071 K5
Mantachie, 1107 C9
Marion, 1305 G9
Marks, 1551 C6
Mathiston, 720 E8
Mayersville, 795 F4
McComb, 13337 K5
McLain, 603 K9
Meadville, 519 K4
Mendenhall, 2555 H7
Meridian, 39968 G9
Merigold, 664 D5
Metcalfe, 1109 E4
Mississippi State, 3500 E9
Monticello, 1726 J6
Moorhead, 2573 E5
Morton, 3482 G7
Moss Pt., 15851 M9
Mound Bayou, 2102 D5
Mt. Olive, 893 J7
Natchez, 18464 J3
Nesbit, 700 A6
Nettleton, 1932 C9
New Albany, 7607 B8
New Augusta, 715 K8
New Hebron, 447 J6
New Hope, 1964 E10
New Houlka, 710 C8
Newton, 3699 G8
Nicholson, 1400 M7
N. Carrollton, 499 E6
N. Tunica, 1450 B6
Oak Grove, 1400 K7
Oakland, 586 C6
Ocean Sprs., 17225 M9
Okolona, 3056 C9
Olive Branch, 21054 A7
Osyka, 481 L5
Oxford, 11756 C7
Pascagoula, 26200 M9
Pass Christian, 6579 M8
Paulding, 200 H8
Pearl, 21961 H6
Pearlington, 1684 N7
Pelahatchie, 1461 H7
Perkinston, 700 L8
Petal, 7579 K8
Philadelphia, 7303 F8
Picayune, 10535 M7
Pickens, 1325 F6
Pittsboro, 212 D8
Plantersville, 1144 C9
Pontotoc, 5253 C8
Poplarville, 2601 L7
Port Gibson, 1840 H5
Potts Camp, 494 B8
Prentiss, 1158 J7
Purvis, 2164 K7
Quitman, 2463 H9
Raleigh, 1255 H7
Raymond, 1664 H5
Renova, 623 D5
Richland, 6027 H6
Richton, 1038 K8
Ridgeland, 20173 G6
Ripley, 5478 B8
Rolling Fork, 2486 F4
Rosedale, 2414 D4
Roxie, 569 J4
Ruleville, 3234 D5
Saltillo, 3393 B9
Sanatorium, 900 J7
Sandersville, 789 J8
Sardis, 2038 B6
Saucier, 1303 M8
Scooba, 632 F9
Senatobia, 6682 B6
Shannon, 1657 C9
Shaw, 2312 D5
[illegible]

MISSOURI
PG. 63–65

CAPITAL
Jefferson City

NICKNAME
Show Me State

POPULATION
5,595,211, rank 17

AREA
69,697 sq mi, rank 19

STATEHOOD
1821, rank 24

Counties
[illegible]

Cass, 82092 G3
Cedar, 13733 J4
Chariton, 8438 D6
Christian, 54285 L6
Clark, 7416 B9
Clay, 184006 D3
Clinton, 18979 D3
Cole, 71397 G7
Cooper, 16670 F7
Crawford, 22804 H10
Dade, 7923 J4
Dallas, 15661 J6
Daviess, 8016 B4
DeKalb, 11597 C3
Dent, 14927 J9
Douglas, 13084 L7
Dunklin, 33155 N13
Franklin, 93807 G10
Gasconade, 15342 G9
Gentry, 6861 B3
Greene, 240391 K5
Grundy, 10432 C5
Harrison, 8850 B4
Henry, 21997 G4
Hickory, 8940 H6
Holt, 5351 B2
Howard, 10212 E7
Howell, 37238 L9
Iron, 10697 J11
Jackson, 654880 E3
Jasper, 104686 K3
Jefferson, 198099 G11
Johnson, 48258 F4
Knox, 4361 B8
Laclede, 32513 J6
Lafayette, 32960 E5
Lawrence, 35204 K4
Lewis, 10494 B8
Lincoln, 38944 E10
Linn, 13754 C6
Livingston, 14558 C5
Macon, 15762 C7
Madison, 11800 J12
Maries, 8903 H8
Marion, 28289 C9
McDonald, 21681 L3
Mercer, 3757 A5
Miller, 23564 G7
Mississippi, 13427 L14
Moniteau, 14827 G7
Monroe, 9311 D8
Montgomery, 12136 E9
Morgan, 19309 G6
New Madrid, 19760 M13
Newton, 52636 L3
Nodaway, 21912 A2
Oregon, 10344 L10
Osage, 13062 G9
Ozark, 9542 M7
Pemiscot, 20047 N13
Perry, 18132 J13
Pettis, 39403 F5
Phelps, 39825 H8
Pike, 18351 D10
Platte, 73781 D2
Polk, 26992 J5
Pulaski, 41165 J8
Putnam, 5223 A6
Ralls, 9626 D9
Randolph, 24663 D7
Ray, 23354 D4
Reynolds, 6689 K10
Ripley, 13509 L11
St. Charles, 283883 F11
St. Clair, 9652 H5
Ste. Genevieve, 17842 H12
St. Francois, 55641 J12
St. Louis, 1016315 F11
Saline, 23756 E6
Schuyler, 4170 B7
Scotland, 4983 A8
Scott, 40422 L13
Shannon, 8324 K9
Shelby, 6799 C8
Stoddard, 29705 L13
Stone, 28658 L5
Sullivan, 7219 B6
Taney, 39703 M6
Texas, 23003 K8
Vernon, 20454 H3
Warren, 24525 F10
Washington, 23344 H11
Wayne, 13259 K11
Webster, 31045 K6
Worth, 2382 A3
Wright, 17955 K7

Cities and Towns
* City indexed to pg. 63
# Independent city population not included in county figures.

Adrian, 1780 G3
Advance, 1244 K13
Affton, 20535 F15
Agency, 599 C3
Airport Drive, 622 H9*
Alba, 588 K3
Albany, 1937 B3
Alton, 668 L9
Anderson, 1856 L3
Appleton City, 1314 G4
Arbyrd, 528 N12
Arcadia, 567 J11
Archie, 890 G3
Arnold, 19965 G12
[illegible]

Claycomo, 1267 D5*
Clayton, 12825 F12
Cleveland, 592 F3
Clever, 1010 L5
Clinton, 9311 G4
Cole Camp, 1028 G6
Columbia, 84531 E8
Concord, 16689 F15
Concordia, 2360 E5
Conway, 743 J6
Cool Valley, 1081 D16
Cottleville, 1928 C12
Country Club Hills, 1381 D16
Country Club Vil., 1846 C2
Crane, 1390 L5
Crestwood, 11863 F15
Creve Coeur, 16500 D14
Crocker, 1033 H8
Crystal City, 4247 G12
Cuba, 3230 H9
Dearborn, 529 D3
Dellwood, 5255 C16
Desloge, 4802 H12
De Soto, 6375 H11
Des Peres, 8592 E14
Dexter, 7356 L13
Diamond, 807 L3
Dixon, 1570 H8
Doniphan, 1932 M11
Doolittle, 644 H8
Drexel, 1090 G3
Duenweg, 1034 J10*
Duquesne, 1640 J10*
E. Prairie, 3227 L14
Edgerton, 533 D3
Edina, 1233 B8
Edmundson, 840 C15
Eldon, 4895 G7
El Dorado Sprs., 3775 H4
Ellington, 1045 K10
Elsberry, 2047 E11
Eminence, 548 K10
Eureka, 7676 G11
Excelsior Sprs., 10847 D4
Exeter, 707 L4
Fairfax, 645 B1
Fair Grove, 1107 K6
Farmington, 13924 H12
Fayette, 2793 E7
Fenton, 4360 F14
Ferguson, 22406 C16
Ferrelview, 593 D3
Festus, 9660 G12
Flordell Hills, 931 D16
Florissant, 50497 F12
Fordland, 684 K6
Forsyth, 1686 L6
Four Seasons, 1493 G7
Fredericktown, 3928 J12
Fremont Hills, 597 K6
Frontenac, 3483 E14
Fulton, 12128 F8
Gainesville, 632 M7
Galena, 451 L5
Gallatin, 1789 C4
Garden City, 1500 F4
Gerald, 1171 G10
Gideon, 1113 M13
Gladstone, 26365 E3
Glasgow, 1263 E6
Glasgow Vil., 5234 C17
Glenaire, 553 C6*
Glendale, 5767 E15
Golden City, 884 K4
Goodman, 1183 L3
Gower, 1399 D3
Grain Valley, 5160 E4
Granby, 2121 L3
Grandview, 24881 F3
Grant City, 926 A3
Gray Summit, 2640 G11
Green City, 688 B6
Greendale, 722 D15
Greenfield, 1358 J4
Green Park, 2666 F15
Greenville, 451 K12
Greenwood, 3952 F3
Hallsville, 978 E8
Hamilton, 1813 C4
Hanley Hills, 2124 D15
Hannibal, 17757 C9
Hardin, 614 E4
Harrisonville, 8946 F3
Hartville, 607 K7
Hayti, 3207 N13
Hayti Hts., 771 N13
Hazelwood, 26206 C15
Herculaneum, 2805 G12
Hermann, 2674 F9
Hermitage, 406 H5
Higbee, 623 D7
Higginsville, 4682 E5
Highlandville, 872 L5
High Ridge, 4236 G11
Hillsboro, 1675 G11
Hillsdale, 1477 D16
Holcomb, 696 M13
Holden, 2510 F4
Hollister, 3867 M6
Holts Summit, 2935 F8
Hopkins, 579 A2
Hornersville, 686 N12
Houston, 1992 K8
Humansville, 946 H5
[illegible]

Maryland Hts., 25756 D13
Maryville, 10581 B2
Matthews, 605 L14
Maysville, 1212 C3
Mehlville, 28822 F12
Memphis, 2061 A8
Merriam Woods, 1142 L6
Mexico, 11320 E8
Milan, 1958 B6
Miller, 754 K4
Miner, 1056 L14
Moberly, 11945 D7
Moline Acres, 2662 C16
Monett, 7396 L4
Monroe City, 2588 D9
Montgomery City, 2442 E9
Monticello, 126 B9
Morehouse, 1015 L14
Morley, 792 K14
Moscow Mills, 1742 E11
Mound City, 1193 B2
Mtn. Grove, 4574 K8
Mtn. View, 2430 L9
Mt. Vernon, 4017 K4
Murphy, 9048 G12
Naylor, 610 M11
Neosho, 10505 L3
Nevada, 8607 H3
New Bloomfield, 599 F8
New Florence, 764 E9
New Franklin, 1145 E7
New Haven, 1867 F10
New London, 1001 D9
New Madrid, 3334 M14
Nixa, 12124 K5
Noel, 1480 M3
Norborne, 805 D5
Normandy, 5153 D16
N. Kansas City, 4714 E4*
Northwoods, 4643 D16
Northwye, 550 H9
Norwood, 552 K7
Novinger, 534 B7
Oak Grove, 5535 E4
Oakland, 1540 F15
Oakville, 35309 G12
Odessa, 4818 E4
O'Fallon, 46169 F11
Olivette, 7438 D15
Olympian Vil., 669 H12
Oran, 1264 K13
Oregon, 935 C2
Orrick, 889 E4
Osage Beach, 3662 H7
Osceola, 835 H5
Overland, 16838 D15
Owensville, 2500 G9
Ozark, 9665 L6
Pacific, 5482 G11
Pagedale, 3616 D15
Palmyra, 3467 C9
Paris, 1529 D8
Park Hills, 7861 H12
Parkville, 4059 D3*
Parma, 852 M13
Peculiar, 2604 F3
Perry, 666 D9
Perryville, 7667 J13
Pevely, 3768 G12
Piedmont, 1992 K11
Pierce City, 1385 L4
Pilot Grove, 723 F6
Pilot Knob, 697 J11
Pine Lawn, 4204 D16
Pineville, 768 M3
Platte City, 3866 D2
Plattsburg, 2354 D3
Pleasant Hill, 5582 F3
Pleasant Hope, 548 J6
Pleasant Valley, 3321 E3
Polo, 582 D4
Poplar Bluff, 16651 L12
Portageville, 3295 M13
Potosi, 2662 H11
Princeton, 1047 A5
Purdy, 1103 L4
Puxico, 1145 L12
Queen City, 638 A7
Raymore, 11146 F3
Raytown, 30388 E3
Republic, 8438 K5
Rich Hill, 1461 H3
Richland, 1805 H7
Richmond, 6116 D4
Richmond Hts., 9602 E15
Ridgeway, 530 B4
Riverside, 2979 D4*
Riverview, 3146 C17
Rockaway Beach, 577 L6
Rock Hill, 4765 E15
Rock Port, 1395 A1
Rogersville, 1508 K6
Rolla, 16367 H9
Russellville, 758 G7
St. Ann, 13607 C14
St. Charles, 60321 F12
St. Clair, 4390 G10
Ste. Genevieve, 4476 H12
St. George, 1288 F15
St. James, 3704 H9
St. John, 6871 D15
St. Joseph, 73990 C2
St. Louis, 348189# F12
St. Martins, 1023 F7
St. Paul, 1634 F11
[illegible]

GLACIER NATIONAL PARK, MONTANA

[illegible]

MONTANA
PG. 66–67

CAPITAL
Helena

NICKNAME
Treasure State

POPULATION
902,195, rank 44

AREA
147,046 sq mi, rank 4

STATEHOOD
1889, rank 41

Counties
[illegible]

Cities and Towns
[illegible]

NEBRASKA
PG. 68–69

CAPITAL
Lincoln

NICKNAME
Cornhusker State

POPULATION
1,711,263, rank 38

AREA
77,355 sq mi, rank 15

STATEHOOD
1867, rank 37

Counties
[illegible]

Cities and Towns
[illegible]

NEVADA
PG. 70

CAPITAL
Carson City

NICKNAME
Silver State

POPULATION
1,998,257, rank 35

AREA
110,561 sq mi, rank 7

STATEHOOD
1864, rank 36

Counties
[illegible]

Cities and Towns
[illegible]

NEW HAMPSHIRE
PG. 71

CAPITAL
Concord

NICKNAME
Granite State

POPULATION
1,235,786, rank 41

AREA
9,279 sq mi, rank 44

STATEHOOD
1788, rank 9

Counties
[illegible]

Cities and Towns
[illegible]

Hampton Falls, 600 M10
Hanover, 8162 H5
Harrisville, 400 M5
Haverhill, 500 G5
Henniker, 1627 L6
Hillsborough, 1842 L6
Hillsborough Lower Vil., 400 L6
Hinsdale, 1713 N4
Hollis, 550 N7
Hooksett, 3609 L7
Hopkinton, 700 L7
Hudson, 7814 N8
Jaffrey, 2802 N6
Keene, 22563 M5
Kingston, 1700 M9
Laconia, 16411 J7
Lancaster, 1695 E7
Lebanon, 12568 J5
Lee, 650 L9
Lincoln, 750 G7
Lisbon, 1070 F6
Littleton, 4431 F6
Lockmere, 600 K7
Londonderry, 11417 M8
Madbury, 450 L9
Manchester, 107006 M7
Marlborough, 1089 M5
Mason, 550 N6
Meredith, 1739 J7
Meredith Ctr., 425 J7
Merrimack, 1600 M7
Milford, 8293 M7
Milton, 950 K9
Mont Vernon, 550 M7
Nashua, 86605 N7
New Boston, 550 M7
New Castle, 850 B6
New Durham, 425 K8
Newfields, 900 L9
Newington, 650 L10
New Ipswich, 550 N6
New London, 1000 K6
Newmarket, 5124 L9
Newport, 4008 K5
Newton, 1200 M9
N. Charlestown, 425 K4
N. Chichester, 700 K8
N. Conway, 2069 G9
Northfield, 2200 K7
N. Hampton, 1300 M10
N. Haverhill, 450 G6
N. Pelham, 750 N8
N. Salem, 1600 M8
N. Walpole, 750 L4
Northwood, 500 L9
N. Woodstock, 750 G7
Nottingham, 550 L9
Ossipee, 225 H9
Pelham, 1700 N8
Peterborough, 2944 M6
Pinardville, 5779 M7
Pittsfield, 1669 K8
Plaistow, 2800 M9
Plymouth, 3528 H7
Ponemah, 1000 N7
Portsmouth, 20784 L10
Raymond, 2839 M8
Reeds Ferry, 1400 M7
Rindge, 750 N6
Rochester, 28461 K9
Rollinsford, 1500 L10
Rye, 1100 M10
Rye Beach, 750 M10
Rye N. Beach, 475 C5
Salem, 28112 N8
Sanbornville, 950 J9
Sandown, 600 M8
Seabrook, 2300 M10
Severance, 500 H3
Short Falls, 550 L8
Somersworth, 11477 K9
S. Hooksett, 5282 M8
S. Merrimack, 1900 N7
Spofford, 500 M4
Squantum, 400 N6
Stratham, 1000 M9
Sunapee, 750 K5
Suncook, 5362 L8
Swanzey, 700 M5
Tilton, 3231 K7
Troy, 1300 N5
Union, 425 J9
Wakefield, 475 J9
Wallis Sands, 850 M10
Walpole, 700 L4
Warner, 650 K6
Weare, 400 L7
W. Chesterfield, 500 M4
W. Epping, 1200 L9
W. Hampstead, 700 M8
W. Peterborough, 650 M6
W. Rindge, 475 N6
W. Rye, 1400 M10
W. Swanzey, 1118 M5
Westville, 2100 M9
Whitefield, 1089 E7
Wilton, 1236 M7
Winchester, 1832 N4
Windham, 1600 N8
Winnisquam, 850 J7
Wolfeboro, 2979 J8
Wolfeboro Falls, 1000 J8
Woodsville, 1081 F6

NEW JERSEY
PG. 72–73

CAPITAL
Trenton

NICKNAME
Garden State

POPULATION
8,414,350, rank 9

AREA
7,787 sq mi, rank 46

STATEHOOD
1787, rank 3

Counties
[illegible]

Cities and Towns
[illegible]

COVERED WAGON IN FRONT OF EAGLE ROCK, NEBRASKA

Barnegat Light, 764 P11
Barnegat Pines, 1300 N10
Barnsboro, 2500 P4
Basking Ridge, 3600 F8
Bay Head, 1238 L11
Bayonne, 61842 F10
Bay Side, 1800 P10
Bayville, 4700 N10
Beach Haven, 1278 O10
Beach Haven Gardens, 1200 O10
Beach Haven Terrace, 1100 O10
Beachwood, 10375 M10
Beatyestown, 3223 E6
Beckett, 4726 P3
Beesleys Pt., 1400 S7
Belford, 1340 H11
Belleville, 35928 E10
Bellmawr, 11262 N5
Belmar, 6045 K11
Belvidere, 2771 E5
Bergenfield, 26247 D11
Berkeley Hts., 13407 F8
Berlin, 6149 N6
Bernardsville, 7345 F8
Beverly, 2661 L6
Blackwood, 4692 N5
Blairstown, 950 D5
Blawenburg, 1300 H7
Bloomfield, 47683 E10
Bloomingdale, 7610 D9
Bloomsbury, 886 F5
Blue Anchor, 1500 P6
Bogota, 8249 D6*
Boonton, 8496 D9
Bordentown, 3969 K7
Bound Brook, 10155 G8
Bradley Beach, 4793 K11
Branchville, 845 B7
Brant Beach, 800 O10
Brass Castle, 1507 E5
Bridgeton, 22771 R4
Bridgewater, 3200 G7
Brielle, 4893 L11
Brigantine, 12594 S9
Brooklawn, 2354 F5†
Browns Mills, 11257 M8
Budd Lake, 8100 E7
Buena, 3873 R6
Bunnvale, 950 F6
Burleigh, 1836 U6
Burlington, 9736 L6
Butler, 7420 D9
Caldwell, 7584 E2*
Califon, 1055 F6
Camden, 79904 M4
Cape May, 4034 V6
Cape May C.H., 4704 U6
Cardiff, 2100 R8
Carlls Corner, 1100 R4
Carlstadt, 5917 E6*
Carneys Pt., 6914 P2
Carteret, 20709 G10
Cassville, 900 L9
Cedar Brook, 1100 P6
Cedar Grove, 12300 E10
Cedarville, 793 S4
Centerton, 2000 M6
Chatham, 8460 F9
Cherry Hill, 69300 M5
Chesilhurst, 1520 P6
Chester, 1635 E7
Churchtown, 3300 P2
Cinnaminson, 14600 M5
Clark, 14597 G9
Clarksboro, 2600 N4
Clayton, 7139 P5
Clementon, 4986 N5
Cliffside Park, 23007 E11
Cliffwood Beach, 3538 H10
Clifton, 78672 E10
Clinton, 2632 F6
Closter, 8383 D11
Cokesbury, 850 F6
Cold Spr., 950 V6
Collingswood, 14326 M5
Cologne, 800 R7
Colonia, 17811 G9
Conovertown, 1000 R8
Cranbury, 2008 J8
Cranford, 22578 F9
Cresskill, 7746 C8*
Crestwood Vil., 8392 M9
Cross Keys, 3600 P5
Crosswicks, 900 K7
Dayton, 6235 J8
Deal, 1070 K11
Deepwater, 1700 P2
Delanco, 3300 L5
Del Haven, 1200 U6
Demarest, 4845 B8*
Dover, 18188 D8
Dunellen, 6823 G8
Dutch Neck, 4400 J7
E. Brunswick, 46756 H9
E. Freehold, 4936 J10
E. Hanover, 9900 E9
E. Newark, 2377 G4*
E. Orange, 69824 E10
E. Rutherford, 8716 E5*
Eatontown, 14008 J11
Edgewater, 7677 E7*
Edgewater Park, 8400 L6
Edinburg, 900 J7
[illegible]

Harrison, 14424 F10
Hasbrouck Hts., 11662 D6*
Haworth, 3390 B7*
Hawthorne, 18218 D10
Heathcote, 4755 J8
Helmetta, 1825 J9
High Bridge, 3776 F6
Highland Lakes, 5051 B8
Highland Park, 13999 H9
Highlands, 5097 H11
Hightstown, 5216 J8
Hillsdale, 10087 D11
Hillside, 21747 F10
Hoboken, 38577 F11
Ho-Ho-Kus, 4060 A5*
Holly Park, 2200 N10
Holmdel, 1200 J10
Hopatcong, 15888 D7
Hopewell, 2035 H7
Hurffville, 4300 P5
Interlaken, 900 K11
Irvington, 60695 F10
Iselin, 16698 G9
Island Hts., 1751 M10
Jacobstown, 950 L8
Jamesburg, 6025 J9
Jersey City, 240055 F11
Jerseyville, 1000 K10
Keansburg, 10732 H10
Kearny, 40513 E10
Kendall Park, 9006 H8
Kenilworth, 7675 J2*
Kenvil, 12569 E7
Keyport, 7568 H10
Kingston, 1292 J7
Kinnelon, 9365 D9
Lakehurst, 2522 M9
Lake Mohawk, 1500 C7
Lakewood, 36065 L10
Lambertville, 3868 J6
Lanoka Harbor, 3800 N10
Laureldale, 800 R7
Laurel Sprs., 1970 N5
Laurence Harbor, 6227 H10
Lavallette, 2665 M11
Lawnside, 2692 N5
Lawrenceville, 4081 J7
Lebanon, 1065 F6
Ledgewood, 1100 E7
Leesburg, 850 T5
Leisuretowne, 2535 N7
Leonardo, 2823 H11
Leonia, 8914 D7*
Liberty Corner, 1700 F8
Lincoln Park, 10930 D9
Lincroft, 6255 J10
Linden, 39394 G10
Lindenwold, 17414 N5
Linwood, 7172 S8
Little Falls, 10855 E10
Little Ferry, 10800 E6*
Little Silver, 6170 J11
Livingston, 27391 E9
Lodi, 23971 D6*
Long Branch, 31340 J11
Longport, 1054 S8
Long Valley, 1818 E6
Lumberton, 2500 M6
Lyndhurst, 19383 F5*
Madison, 16530 E9
Mahwah, 5200 C10
Malaga, 1700 O5
Manahawkin, 2004 P10
Manasquan, 6310 L11
Manville, 10343 G8
Maple Shade, 19200 M5
Maplewood, 23868 H2*
Margate City, 8193 S8
Marlboro, 3300 J10
Marlton, 10260 N6
Marmora, 1600 T7
Martinsville, 1800 G8
Masonville, 7300 M6
Matawan, 8910 H10
Mays Landing, 2321 R7
Maywood, 9523 D6*
McAfee, 2600 B8
McKee City, 2800 R7
Medford, 3500 N6
Medford Lakes, 4173 N6
Mendham, 5097 E8
Mercerville, 26419 K7
Metuchen, 12840 G9
Middlesex, 13717 G8
Midland Park, 6947 A4*
Milford, 1195 G5
Millington, 3500 F8
Milltown, 7000 H9
Millville, 26847 S5
Monmouth Beach, 3595 J11
Monmouth Jct., 2721 H8
Montclair, 38977 E10
Montvale, 7034 C11
Montville, 1900 D9
Moonachie, 2754 E6*
Moorestown, 13860 M5
Morganville, 11255 H10
Morris Plains, 5236 E8
Morristown, 18544 E8
Mtn. Lakes, 4256 D8
Mountainside, 6602 F9
Mt. Arlington, 4663 D7
Mt. Bethel, 1000 F8
[illegible]

Plainsboro, 2209 J8
Pleasant Grove, 1100 E6
Pleasant Plains, 2600 M10
Pleasantville, 19012 S8
Pluckemin, 6000 F7
Pt. Pleasant, 19306 L11
Pt. Pleasant Beach, 5314 L11
Pomona, 4019 R8
Pompton Lakes, 10640 D9
Pompton Plains, 6500 D9
Port Monmouth, 3742 H11
Port Norris, 1507 T5
Port Reading, 3829 M2*
Port Republic, 1037 R8
Presidential Lakes Estates, 2332 N8
Princeton, 14203 J7
Princeton Jct., 2382 J7
Prospect Park, 5779 B4*
Rahway, 26500 G9
Ramsey, 14351 C10
Rancocas, 8400 M6
Raritan, 6338 G7
Readington, 1800 G7
Reaville, 1200 H6
Red Bank, 11844 J11
Ridgefield, 10830 E7*
Ridgefield Park, 12873 E7*
Ridgewood, 24936 D10
Ringoes, 1100 H6
Ringwood, 12396 C9
Rio Grande, 2444 V6
Riverdale, 2498 A1*
River Edge, 10946 C6*
Riverside, 8000 L5
Riverton, 2759 M5
Robbinsville, 1900 K7
Robertsville, 9800 J9
Rochelle Park, 5528 C6*
Rockaway, 6473 D8
Rocky Hill, 662 H7
Roebling, 8200 B10†
Roosevelt, 933 K8
Roseland, 5298 E1*
Roselle, 21274 F9
Roselle Park, 13281 F10
Rosenhayn, 1099 R4
Rossmoor, 3129 J8
Rumson, 7137 J11
Runnemede, 8533 N5
Rutherford, 18110 E10
Saddle Brook, 13155 D5*
Saddle River, 3201 C11
Salem, 5857 O2
Sayreville, 40377 H9
Schooleys Mtn., 1100 E6
Scotch Plains, 22732 F9
Sea Bright, 1818 J11
Seabrook, 1719 R4
Sea Girt, 2148 L11
Sea Isle City, 2835 T7
Seaside Hts., 3155 M11
Seaside Park, 2263 M11
Seaville, 1700 T7
Secaucus, 15931 G6*
Sewaren, 2780 M2*
Sewell, 3400 P4
Ship Bottom, 1384 O10
Shore Acres, 4500 M11
Shrewsbury, 3590 J11
Sicklerville, 6000 P5
Silver Ridge, 1211 M10
Silverton, 9200 M10
Smithville, 3100 R8
Somerdale, 5192 N5
Somerset, 23040 H8
Somers Pt., 11614 S8
Somerville, 12423 G8
S. Amboy, 7913 H9
S. Belmar, 1806 K11
S. Bound Brook, 4492 G8
S. Orange, 16964 G2*
S. Plainfield, 21810 G9
S. River, 15322 H9
S. Toms River, 3634 M10
Sparta, 9755 C7
Spotswood, 7880 H9
Springfield, 14429 F9
Spring Lake, 3567 K11
Spring Lake Hts., 5227 K11
Springville, 2400 M6
Stanhope, 3584 D7
Star Cross, 1400 O5
Stockton, 560 H5
Stone Harbor, 1128 U7
Stratford, 7271 N5
Strathmore, 6740 H10
Succasunna, 12569 E7
Summit, 21131 F9
Surf City, 1442 P10
Sussex, 2145 B8
Swedesboro, 2055 P3
Taylortown, 1200 D9
Teaneck, 39260 D11
Tenafly, 13806 D11
Tennent, 1100 J9
Thorofare, 1500 N4
Three Bridges, 850 G6
Tinton Falls, 15053 K11
Titusville, 800 J6
Toms River, 86327 M10
Towaco, 2700 D9
Town Bank, 2700 V5

Trenton, 85403 K7
Tuckerton, 3517 O9
Turnersville, 3867 P5
Twin Rivers, 7422 J8
Union, 54405 F9
Union Beach, 6649 H10
Union City, 67088 E11
Upper Saddle River, 7741 C10
Ventnor City, 12910 S8
Vernon Valley, 1737 B8
Verona, 13533 E10
Victory Gardens, 1546 E8
Vienna, 1264 E6
Villas, 9064 U6
Vineland, 56271 R5
Waldwick, 9622 A5*
Wallington, 11583 E10
Wanamassa, 4551 K11
Wanaque, 10266 C9
Waretown, 1582 N10
Washington, 6712 E5
Washington Crossing, 950 J6
Washington Township, 8938 B6*
Watchung, 5613 F8
Waterford Works, 1000 P6
Wayne, 54069 D10
Weehawken, 12400 E11
Wenonah, 2317 N4
W. Berlin, 4000 N5
W. Caldwell, 11233 E2*
W. Cape May, 1095 V6
W. Creek, 1500 O9
Westfield, 29644 F9
W. Freehold, 12498 K9
W. Long Branch, 8258 J11
W. Milford, 26410 C9
W. New York, 45768 E11
W. Orange, 44943 E10
W. Paterson, 10987 D3*
Westville, 4500 F5†
Westwood, 10999 D11
Wharton, 6298 D8
Whippany, 3800 E9
White Horse, 9373 K7
White House Sta., 1951 G7
Whitesboro, 1836 U6
Whiting, 1800 M9
Wildwood, 5436 V6
Wildwood Crest, 3980 V6
Williamstown, 11812 P5
Willingboro, 36300 M6
Woodbine, 2716 T6
Woodbridge, 18309 G9
Woodbury, 10307 N4
Woodbury Hts., 2988 N4
Woodcliff Lake, 5745 A6*
Woodlynne, 2796 E5†
Woodport, 2000 D7
Wood-Ridge, 7644 E5*
Woodstown, 3136 O3
Wrightstown, 748 M7
Wyckoff, 16508 D10
Yardville, 9208 K7

NEW MEXICO
PG. 74–75

CAPITAL
Santa Fe

NICKNAME
Land of Enchantment

POPULATION
1,819,046, rank 36

AREA
121,593 sq mi, rank 5

STATEHOOD
1912, rank 47

Counties
Bernalillo, 556678 F6
Catron, 3543 J3
Chaves, 61382 J10
Cibola, 25595 F2
Colfax, 14189 B9
Curry, 45044 G12
De Baca, 2240 G10
Dona Ana, 174682 M5
Eddy, 51658 M11
Grant, 31002 L3
Guadalupe, 4680 G9
Harding, 810 D11
Hidalgo, 5932 P2
Lea, 55511 K12
Lincoln, 19411 J8
Los Alamos, 18343 D6
Luna, 25016 M4
McKinley, 74798 E4
Mora, 5180 D9
Otero, 62298 M8
Quay, 10155 F11
Rio Arriba, 41190 C6
Roosevelt, 18018 J12
Sandoval, 89908 D5
San Juan, 113801 B3
San Miguel, 30126 E9
Santa Fe, 129292 D7
Sierra, 13270 L5
Socorro, 18078 H6
Taos, 29979 B7
Torrance, 16911 F7
Union, 4174 C12
Valencia, 66152 G5

Cities and Towns
Acomita, 288 F4
Agua Fria, 2051 E7
Alameda, 4200 F6
Alamo, 1183 G4
Alamogordo, 35582 L7
Albuquerque, 448607 F6
Alcalde, 377 D7
Algodones, 688 E6
Angel Fire, 1048 C8
Anthony, 7904 N6
Armijo, 9500 F6
Arroyo Hondo, 550 C8
Arroyo Seco, 1149 C8
Artesia, 10692 L10
Aztec, 6378 B4
Bayard, 2534 L3
Belen, 6901 G6
Berino, 900 N6
Bernalillo, 6611 E6
Black Rock, 1252 F2
Bloomfield, 6417 B4
Bosque Farms, 3931 F6
Capitan, 1443 J8
Carlsbad, 25625 M11
Carnuel, 872 T13
Carrizozo, 1036 J7
Casa Blanca, 669 F4
Cedar Crest, 1060 F6
Cedar Grove, 599 F7
Chama, 1199 B6
Chamberino, 425 N6
Chamisal, 301 C8
Chaparral, 6117 N6
Chimayo, 2924 D7
Church Rock, 1077 E2
Cimarron, 917 C9
Clayton, 2524 C12
Cloudcroft, 749 L8
Clovis, 32667 G12
Cochiti, 507 E7
Columbus, 1765 P4
Corrales, 7334 E6
Crownpoint, 2630 D3
Crystal, 347 D2
Cuba, 590 D5
Deming, 14116 N4
Dexter, 1235 K10
Doña Ana, 1379 M6
Dulce, 2623 B5
Eagle Nest, 306 B8
Edgewood, 1893 F7
Elephant Butte, 1390 K5
El Prado, 400 C8
El Rito, 425 C7
Espanola, 9688 D7
Estancia, 1584 G7
Eunice, 2562 M13
Fairacres, 1100 M6
Farmington, 37844 B3
Flora Vista, 1383 B3
Ft. Sumner, 1249 G10
Ft. Wingate, 550 E2
Fruitland, 650 B3
Galisteo, 265 E7
Gallup, 20209 E2
Glorieta, 859 E8
Grants, 8806 F4
Hagerman, 1168 K10
Hatch, 1673 M5
Hernandez, 600 D7
High Rolls, 425 L7
Hobbs, 28657 L13
Hurley, 1464 M3
Isleta, 496 F6
Jal, 1996 N13
Jarales, 1434 G6
Jemez Pueblo, 1953 E6
Jemez Sprs., 375 D6
Kirtland, 6190 B3
La Cienega, 3007 E7
Laguna, 423 F5
Lake Arthur, 432 L10
La Luz, 1615 L7
La Mesa, 800 N6
Las Cruces, 74267 M6
Las Vegas, 14565 E9
La Union, 850 N6
Lemitar, 400 H5
Logan, 1094 E12
Lordsburg, 3379 M2
Los Alamos, 11909 D7
Los Chavez, 5033 G6
Los Lunas, 10034 F6
Los Padillas, 1800 F6
Los Ranchos de Albuquerque, 5092 F6
Loving, 1326 M11
Lovington, 9471 L12
Magdalena, 913 H5
Maxwell, 274 B10
Medanales, 450 C7
Melrose, 736 G12
Mescalero, 1233 K8
Mesilla, 2180 N6
Mesita, 776 F5
Mesquite, 948 N6
Midway, 700 K10
Milan, 1891 F4
Mora, 450 D8
Moriarty, 1765 F7
Mosquero, 120 D11
Mountainair, 1116 G7
Nageezi, 296 C4
Nambe, 1200 D7
Naschitti, 360 D2
Navajo, 2097 D2
Newcomb, 387 C2
Paguate, 474 F5
Pajarito, 2700 V10
Paradise Hills, 5500 F6
Pecos, 1441 E8
Pena Blanca, 661 E7
Penasco, 572 C8
Peralta, 3750 F6
Placitas, 3452 E6
Pojoaque, 1261 D7
Ponderosa, 310 D6
Portales, 11131 H12
Questa, 1864 B8
Radium Sprs., 1518 M5
Ramah, 407 F3
Ranchos de Taos, 2390 C8
Raton, 7282 B10
Red River, 484 B8
Rehoboth, 375 E2
Reserve, 387 J2
Rio Rancho, 51765 E6
Rodarte, 350 C8
Roswell, 45293 K10
Roy, 304 D10
Ruidoso, 7698 K8
Ruidoso Downs, 1824 K8
Salem, 795 M5
Sandia Park, 475 F6
San Felipe Pueblo, 2080 E6
San Jon, 306 F12
San Miguel, 1100 N6
Sanostee, 429 C2
Santa Ana Pueblo, 479 E6
Santa Clara, 1944 L3
Santa Cruz, 423 D7
Santa Fe, 62203 D7
Santa Rosa, 2744 F10
Santa Teresa, 2607 P6
Santo Domingo Pueblo, 2550 E6
Shiprock, 8156 B2
Silver City, 10545 L3
Socorro, 8877 H5
Springer, 1285 C10
Sunland Park, 13309 P6
Taos, 4700 C8
Tatum, 683 K12
Tesuque, 909 D7
Texico, 1065 G13
Thoreau, 1863 E3
Tierra Amarilla, 90 B6
Tijeras, 474 F6
Timberon, 309 M8
Tohatchi, 1037 D2
Tome, 2211 G6
Torreon, 297 D5
Truth or Consequences, 7289 K5
Tucumcari, 5989 F11
Tularosa, 2864 L7
Turley, 425 B4
Twin Lakes, 1069 D2
Tyrone, 500 L3
University Park, 2732 N6
Vado, 3003 N6
Valencia, 4500 G6
Vaughn, 539 G9
Wagon Mound, 369 D10
White Rock, 6045 D7
Williamsburg, 527 K5
Yah-Tah-Hey, 580 E2
Zia Pueblo, 646 E6
Zuni Pueblo, 6367 F2

NEW YORK
PG. 76–81

CAPITAL
Albany

NICKNAME
Empire State

POPULATION
18,976,457, rank 3

AREA
49,108 sq mi, rank 30

STATEHOOD
1788, rank 11

Counties
Albany, 294565 N21
Allegany, 49927 P7
Bronx, 1332650 X23
Broome, 200536 R16
Cattaraugus, 83955 P4
Cayuga, 81963 M13
Chautauqua, 139750 R1
Chemung, 91070 O12
Chenango, 51401 N15
Clinton, 79894 B22
Columbia, 63094 P23
Cortland, 48599 N14
Delaware, 48055 O18
Dutchess, 280150 R22
Erie, 950265 N4
Essex, 38851 F22
Franklin, 51134 C21
Fulton, 55073 K20
Genesee, 60370 L6
Greene, 48195 P21
Hamilton, 5379 G19
Herkimer, 64427 H18
Jefferson, 111738 G15
Kings, 2465326 Y22
Lewis, 26944 G16
Livingston, 64328 N7
Madison, 69441 M16
Monroe, 735343 K8
Montgomery, 49708 M20
Nassau, 1334544 X24
New York, 1537195 X22
Niagara, 219846 J5
Oneida, 235469 J15
Onondaga, 458336 L14
Ontario, 100224 M9
Orange, 341367 U20
Orleans, 44171 K6
Oswego, 122377 J14
Otsego, 61676 M17
Putnam, 95745 U23
Queens, 2229379 X23
Rensselaer, 152538 M23
Richmond, 443728 Y22
Rockland, 286753 V22
St. Lawrence, 111931 D18
Saratoga, 200635 K22
Schenectady, 146555 M21
Schoharie, 31582 N20
Schuyler, 19224 P11
Seneca, 33342 N11
Steuben, 98726 P9
Suffolk, 1419369 X25
Sullivan, 73966 S19
Tioga, 51784 Q13
Tompkins, 96501 N13
Ulster, 177749 R20
Warren, 63303 G23
Washington, 61042 J24
Wayne, 93765 K11
Westchester, 923459 V23
Wyoming, 43424 M6
Yates, 24621 M10

Cities and Towns
* City indexed to pg. 80-81

Accord, 622 S21
Adams, 1624 G14
Adams Ctr., 1500 G14
Addison, 1797 Q10
Afton, 836 O16
Airmont, 7799 V22
Akron, 3085 L5
Albany, 95658 N23
Albertson, 5200 G14*
Albion, 7438 K6
Alden, 2666 L5
Alexandria Bay, 1088 D15
Alfred, 3954 O8
Allegany, 1883 O5
Altamont, 1737 M22
Altona, 1056 A23
Amagansett, 1067 W29
Amawalk, 1500 U23
Amenia, 1115 S24
Amherst, 13200 L4
Amityville, 9441 X24
Amsterdam, 18355 L21
Andover, 1073 O8
Angelica, 903 P7
Angola, 2266 N3
Angola on the Lake, 1771 N3
Annandale-on-Hudson, 1700 R22
Annsville, 850 U22
Antwerp, 716 E16
Apalachin, 1126 R14
Aquebogue, 2254 W27
Arcade, 2026 N6
Ardonia, 950 S22
Ardsley, 4269 A10*
Arkport, 832 P8
Arlington, 12481 S22
Armonk, 3461 V23
Asharoken, 625 W25
Athens, 1695 P22
Atlanta, 650 N9
Atlantic Beach, 1986 Y23
Attica, 2597 M6
Auburn, 28574 L12
Aurora, 720 M12
Au Sable Forks, 670 D23
Averill Park, 1517 N23
Avoca, 1008 P9
Avon, 2977 L8
Babylon, 12615 X25
Bainbridge, 1365 P16
Baiting Hollow, 1449 W27
Baldwin, 23455 K14*
Baldwin Harbor, 8147 Y24
Baldwinsville, 7053 K13
Ballston Spa, 5556 L22
Balmville, 3339 T22
Barker, 577 J5
Barnum Island, 2487 L14*
Batavia, 16256 L6
Bath, 5641 P10
Baxter Estates, 1006 E13*
Bay Park, 2300 K13*
Bayport, 8662 X26
Bay Shore, 23852 X25
Bayville, 7135 W24
Beacon, 13808 T22
Bedford, 1724 V23
Bedford Hills, 5500 V23
Belfast, 800 P7
Bellerose, 1173 H12*
Bellerose Terrace, 2157 H12*
Belle Terre, 832 W26
Bellport, 2363 X26
Belmont, 952 O7
Bergen, 1240 K7
Bethlehem Ctr., 2500 T29
Bethpage, 16543 X24
Big Flats, 2482 O11
Billings, 800 S23
Billington Hts., 1691 M5
Binghamton, 47380 O15
Black River, 1285 F15
Blasdell, 2718 M4
Blauvelt, 5207 W22
Bloomfield, 1267 L9
Blooming Grove, 1200 U21
Bloomington, 1100 R22
Blue Pt., 4407 X26
Bolivar, 1173 R6
Bolton Landing, 650 H23
Boonville, 2138 J17
Brasher Falls, 1140 B19
Brentwood, 53917 X25
Brewerton, 3453 K14
Brewster, 2162 U23
Brewster Hill, 2226 U24
Briarcliff Manor, 7696 V23
Bridgehampton, 1381 W28
Bridgeport, 1665 K15
Bridgewater, 579 L17
Brighton, 35584 K9
Brightwaters, 3248 X25
Brinckerhoff, 2734 T22
Broadalbin, 1411 L21
Brockport, 8103 K7
Brocton, 1547 P2
Bronxville, 6543 C10*
Brookhaven, 3570 X26
Brookville, 2126 X24
Brownville, 1022 F14
Buchanan, 2189 V22
Buffalo, 292648 L4
Burlingham, 750 T21
Burnt Hills, 2100 L22
Cadyville, 700 B23
Cairo, 1390 P22
Calcium, 3346 F15
Caledonia, 2327 L8
Calverton, 5704 W27
Cambridge, 1925 L24
Camden, 2330 J15
Camillus, 1249 L13
Campbell Hall, 750 U21
Canajoharie, 2257 L20
Canandaigua, 11264 L10
Canaseraga, 594 P8
Canastota, 4425 L15
Candor, 855 O13
Canisteo, 2336 O9
Canton, 5882 C17
Cape Vincent, 760 E13
Carle Place, 5247 G14*
Carmel, 5650 U23
Carthage, 3721 F16
Cassadaga, 676 P2
Castile, 1051 N7
Castleton-on-Hudson, 1619 N23
Cato, 601 K12
Catskill, 4392 O22
Cattaraugus, 1075 P4
Cayuga Hts., 3273 P13
Cazenovia, 2614 L15
Cedarhurst, 6164 K12*
Celoron, 1295 O2
Center Brunswick, 900 M23
Centereach, 27285 W26
Center Moriches, 6655 X27
Centerport, 5446 W24
Central Bridge, 900 M21
Central Islip, 31950 X25
Central Square, 1646 J14
Central Valley, 1857 U22
Champlain, 1173 A23
Chappaqua, 9468 V23
Charlton, 700 L22
Chateaugay, 798 A21
Chatham, 1758 P23
Chaumont, 592 F14
Cheektowaga, 79988 L4
Chelsea, 2300 T22
Chenango Bridge, 4100 O15
Cherry Valley, 592 M19
Chester, 3445 U21
Chestnut Ridge, 7829 V22
Chittenango, 4855 L15
Churchville, 1887 K8
Circleville, 900 T21
Clarence Ctr., 1747 L5
Clark Mills, 1424 R24
Claverack, 1061 O23
Clayton, 1821 E14
Cleveland, 758 K15
Clifton Park, 4600 L23
Clifton Sprs., 2223 L10
Clinton, 1952 L17
Clintondale, 1424 S22
Clyde, 2269 K11
Cobleskill, 4533 M20
Cohocton, 854 N9
Cohoes, 15521 M23
Colden, 700 N5
Cold Spr., 1983 U22
Colonie, 7916 M22
Columbiaville, 1200 P23
Commack, 36367 X25
Comstock, 1900 H24
Congers, 8303 V22
Conklin, 850 R15
Constantia, 1107 K14
Cooperstown, 2032 M18
Copenhagen, 865 F16
Copiague, 21922 X24
Coram, 34923 W26
Corfu, 795 L6
Corinth, 2474 K22
Corning, 10842 O11
Cornwall-on-Hudson, 3058 U22
Cortland, 18740 N14
Country Knolls, 2155 L22
Coxsackie, 2895 P23
Croghan, 665 F17

MANHATTAN BRIDGE, NEW YORK CITY, NEW YORK

NORTH CAROLINA
PG. 82–84

CAPITAL
Raleigh

NICKNAME
Tar Heel State

POPULATION
8,049,313, rank 11

AREA
52,669 sq mi, rank 28

STATEHOOD
1789, rank 12

Counties

Cities and Towns

NORTH DAKOTA
PG. 85

CAPITAL
Bismarck

NICKNAME
Flickertail State

POPULATION
642,200, rank 47

AREA
70,703 sq mi, rank 17

STATEHOOD
1889, rank 39

Counties

Cities and Towns

OHIO
PG. 86–89

CAPITAL
Columbus

NICKNAME
Buckeye State

POPULATION
11,353,140, rank 7

AREA
41,330 sq mi, rank 35

STATEHOOD
1803, rank 17

Counties

Cities and Towns
* City indexed to pg. 117

OKLAHOMA
PG. 90–91

CAPITAL
Oklahoma City

NICKNAME
Sooner State

POPULATION
3,450,654, rank 27

AREA
69,956 sq mi, rank 18

STATEHOOD
1907, rank 46

Counties

Cities and Towns

CAPE HATTERAS BEACH, OUTER BANKS, NORTH CAROLINA

OREGON
PG. 92–93

CAPITAL
Salem

NICKNAME
Beaver State

POPULATION
3,421,399, rank 28

AREA
97,073 sq mi, rank 10

STATEHOOD
1859, rank 33

Counties

Cities and Towns

PENNSYLVANIA
PG. 94–98

CAPITAL
Harrisburg

NICKNAME
Keystone State

POPULATION
12,281,054, rank 6

AREA
45,308 sq mi, rank 33

STATEHOOD
1787, rank 2

Counties

Cities and Towns
* City indexed to pg. 98

OLD BARN, OREGON

RHODE ISLAND
PG. 99

CAPITAL
Providence

NICKNAME
Ocean State

POPULATION
1,048,319, rank 43

AREA
1,212 sq mi, rank 50

STATEHOOD
1790, rank 13

Counties

Cities and Towns

NEWPORT BRIDGE, NEWPORT, RHODE ISLAND

SOUTH CAROLINA
PG. 100

CAPITAL
Columbia

NICKNAME
Palmetto State

POPULATION
4,012,012, rank 26

AREA
31,113 sq mi, rank 40

STATEHOOD
1788, rank 8

Counties

Cities and Towns

SOUTH DAKOTA
PG. 101

CAPITAL
Pierre

NICKNAME
Mount Rushmore State

POPULATION
754,844, rank 46

AREA
77,116 sq mi, rank 16

STATEHOOD
1889, rank 40

Counties

Cities and Towns

TENNESSEE
PG. 102–103

CAPITAL
Nashville

NICKNAME
Volunteer State

POPULATION
5,689,283, rank 16

AREA
42,144 sq mi, rank 34

STATEHOOD
1796, rank 16

Counties

Cities and Towns

TEXAS
PG. 104–108

CAPITAL
Austin

NICKNAME
Lone Star State

POPULATION
20,851,820, rank 2

AREA
266,807 sq mi, rank 2

STATEHOOD
1845, rank 28

Counties

DELICATE ARCH, ARCHES NATIONAL PARK, UTAH

UTAH
PG. 109

CAPITAL
Salt Lake City

NICKNAME
Beehive State

POPULATION
2,233,169, rank 34

AREA
84,899 sq mi, rank 11

STATEHOOD
1896, rank 45

VERMONT
PG. 110

CAPITAL
Montpelier

NICKNAME
Green Mountain State

POPULATION
608,827, rank 49

AREA
9,614 sq mi, rank 43

STATEHOOD
1791, rank 14

VIRGINIA
PG. 111–113

CAPITAL
Richmond

NICKNAME
Old Dominion

POPULATION
7,078,515, rank 12

AREA
40,767 sq mi, rank 36

STATEHOOD
1788, rank 10

WASHINGTON
PG. 114–115

CAPITAL
Olympia

NICKNAME
Evergreen State

POPULATION
5,894,121, rank 15

AREA
68,138 sq mi, rank 20

STATEHOOD
1889, rank 42

WEST VIRGINIA
PG. 117

CAPITAL
Charleston

NICKNAME
Mountain State

POPULATION
1,808,344, rank 37

AREA
24,231 sq mi, rank 41

STATEHOOD
1863, rank 35

WISCONSIN
PG. 118–119

CAPITAL
Madison

NICKNAME
Badger State

POPULATION
5,363,675, rank 18

AREA
56,153 sq mi, rank 26

STATEHOOD
1848, rank 30

MOUNT RAINIER NATIONAL PARK, WASHINGTON

Black Creek, 1192 K10
Black Earth, 1320 P7
Black River Falls, 3618 L5
Blair, 1273 L4
Blanchardville, 806 O7
Bloomer, 3347 H4
Bloomington, 701 O5
Blue Mounds, 708 O7
Bohners Lake, 1952 R10
Bonduel, 1416 J10
Boscobel, 3047 P5
Boyceville, 1043 J3
Boyd, 680 J5
Brandon, 912 N9
Brillion, 2937 L11
Bristol, 1100 R11
Brodhead, 3180 R8
Brookfield, 38649 O11
Brooklyn, 916 O8
Brown Deer, 12170 P11
Bruce, 787 G4
Buffalo, 1040 L3
Burlington, 9936 R10
Butler, 1881 S3
Cadott, 1345 J5
Cambria, 792 N9
Cambridge, 1101 O9
Cameron, 1546 H3
Campbellsport, 1913 N11
Camp Douglas, 592 M6
Cascade, 666 N11
Cashton, 1005 N5
Cassville, 1085 R5
Cedarburg, 10908 P11
Cedar Grove, 1887 N11
Centuria, 865 G2
Chetek, 2180 H4
Chilton, 3708 M11
Chippewa Falls, 12925 J4
Clear Lake, 1051 H2
Cleveland, 1361 M12
Clinton, 2162 R9
Clintonville, 4736 K9
Colby, 1616 J6
Coleman, 716 J11
Colfax, 1136 J3
Columbus, 4479 P9
Combined Locks, 2422 A4
Como, 1870 R10
Coon Valley, 714 N5
Cornell, 1466 H5
Crandon, 1961 G9
Crivitz, 998 H11
Cross Plains, 3084 P8
Cuba City, 2156 R6
Cudahy, 18429 O11
Cumberland, 2280 G3
Dane, 799 P8
Darien, 1572 R10
Darlington, 2418 R7
Deerfield, 1971 O9
De Forest, 7368 P8
Delafield, 6472 O10
Delavan, 7956 R10
Denmark, 1958 L11
De Pere, 20559 K11
Dickeyville, 1043 R6
Dodgeville, 4220 O7
Dorchester, 827 J6
Dousman, 1584 O10
Dresser, 732 H2
Durand, 1968 K3
Eagle, 1707 O10
Eagle River, 1443 F8
E. Troy, 3564 O10
Eau Claire, 61704 J4
Eden, 687 N10
Edgar, 1386 J7
Edgerton, 4933 O9
Eleva, 635 K4
Elkhart Lake, 1021 M11
Elkhorn, 7305 R10
Elk Mound, 785 J3
Ellsworth, 2909 J2
Elm Grove, 6249 T3
Elmwood, 841 J3
Elroy, 1578 N6
Evansville, 4039 O8
Fall Creek, 1236 J4
Fall River, 1097 P9
Fennimore, 2387 O5
Fitchburg, 20501 O8
Florence, 750 F10
Fond du Lac, 42203 M10
Footville, 788 R9
Ft. Atkinson, 11621 O9
Fountain City, 983 L3
Fox Lake, 1454 N9
Fox Pt., 7012 T4
Francis Creek, 681 L12
Franklin, 29494 O11
Franksville, 1789 O11
Frederic, 1262 G2
Fredonia, 1934 N11
Freedom, 1500 L10
Fremont, 666 L9
Friendship, 698 M7
Galesville, 1427 L4
Gays Mills, 625 P5
Genoa City, 1949 R10
Germantown, 18260 P11
Gillett, 1256 J10
Glendale, 13367 P11
Glenwood City, 1183 H2
Grafton, 10312 P11
Grantsburg, 1369 F1
Green Bay, 102313 K11
Greendale, 14405 V3
Greenfield, 35476 V4
Green Lake, 1100 M9
Greenville, 950 L10
Greenwood, 1079 J6
Gresham, 575 J9
Hales Corners, 7765 O11
Hammond, 1153 J2
Hartford, 10905 P10
Hartland, 7905 P10
Hayward, 2129 F4
Hazel Green, 1183 R6
Hewitt, 670 K7
Highland, 855 O6
Hilbert, 1089 L11
Hillsboro, 1302 N6
Holmen, 6200 M4
Horicon, 3775 N10
Hortonville, 2357 L10
Howard, 13546 K11
Howards Grove, 2792 M11
Hudson, 8775 J1
Hurley, 1818 E7
Hustisford, 1135 P10
Independence, 1244 L4
Iola, 1298 K9
Iron Ridge, 998 P10
Ixonia, 642 P10
Jackson, 4938 P11
Janesville, 59498 R9
Jefferson, 7338 O9
Johnson Creek, 1581 O9
Juneau, 2485 P10
Kaukauna, 12983 L10
Kenosha, 90352 R11
Keshena, 1394 J10
Kewaskum, 3274 N11
Kewaunee, 2806 K12
Kiel, 3450 M11
Kimberly, 6146 A3
King, 2215 L9
Kohler, 1926 N12
Lac du Flambeau, 1646 F7
La Crosse, 51818 M4
Ladysmith, 3932 G5
La Farge, 775 N6
Lake Delton, 1982 N7
Lake Geneva, 7148 R10
Lake Mills, 4843 P9
Lake Nebagamon, 1015 D4
Lancaster, 4070 O5
Lannon, 1009 S2
Laona, 700 G10
Linden, 615 O6
Little Chute, 10476 L10
Livingston, 597 O6
Lodi, 2882 P8
Lomira, 2233 N10
Lone Rock, 929 P6
Loyal, 1308 J6
Luck, 1210 G2
Luxemburg, 1935 K12
Madison, 208054 O8
Manawa, 1330 K9
Manitowoc, 34053 M12
Maple Bluff, 1358 O3
Marathon City, 1640 J7
Marinette, 11749 H12
Marion, 1297 K9
Markesan, 1396 N9
Marshall, 3432 P9
Marshfield, 18800 K7
Mauston, 3740 M7
Mayville, 4902 N10
Mazomanie, 1485 P7
McFarland, 6416 O8
Medford, 4350 H6
Mellen, 845 E6
Menasha, 16331 L10
Menomonee Falls, 32647 P11
Menomonie, 14937 J3
Mequon, 21823 P11
Merrill, 10146 H8
Merrillan, 585 K5
Merton, 1926 P10
Middleton, 15770 P8
Milltown, 888 G2
Milton, 5132 O9
Milwaukee, 596974 O11
Mineral Pt., 2617 O6
Minocqua, 750 F7
Mishicot, 1422 L12
Mondovi, 2634 K3
Monona, 8018 O8
Monroe, 10843 R8
Montello, 1397 M8
Montfort, 663 O6
Monticello, 1146 R8
Montreal, 838 E6
Mosinee, 4063 J7
Mt. Calvary, 956 M10
Mt. Horeb, 5860 O7
Mukwonago, 6162 O10
Muscoda, 1453 P6
Muskego, 21397 O11
Necedah, 888 M7
Neenah, 24507 L10
Neillsville, 2731 K6
Nekoosa, 2590 L7
Neopit, 839 J9
Neosho, 593 P10
New Berlin, 38220 O11
Newburg, 1119 N11
New Glarus, 2111 O8
New Holstein, 3301 M11
New Lisbon, 1436 M7
New London, 7085 L9
New Richmond, 6310 H2
Niagara, 1880 G11
N. Fond du Lac, 4557 M10
N. Freedom, 649 N7
N. Hudson, 3463 J1
N. Prairie, 1571 O10
Norwalk, 653 M6
Oak Creek, 28456 O11
Oakfield, 1012 N10
Oconomowoc, 12382 P10
Oconto, 4708 J11
Oconto Falls, 2843 J11
Okauchee, 2100 P10
Omro, 3177 M9
Onalaska, 14839 M4
Oneida, 1070 K11
Oostburg, 2660 N11
Oregon, 7514 O8
Orfordville, 1272 R8
Osceola, 2421 H1
Oshkosh, 62916 M10
Osseo, 1669 K4
Owen, 936 J6
Paddock Lake, 3012 R11
Palmyra, 1766 O10
Pardeeville, 1982 N8
Park Falls, 2793 F6
Pell Lake, 2988 R10
Pepin, 878 K2
Peshtigo, 3357 J11
Pewaukee (city), 11783 T1
Pewaukee (village), 8170 T1
Phillips, 1675 G6
Pittsville, 866 K7
Plain, 792 P7
Plainfield, 899 L8
Platteville, 9989 R6
Pleasant Prairie, 16136 R11
Plover, 10520 K8
Plymouth, 7781 N11
Portage, 9728 N8
Port Edwards, 1944 L7
Port Washington, 10467 P11
Potosi, 711 R5
Powers Lake, 1500 R10
Poynette, 2266 P8
Prairie du Chien, 6018 O4
Prairie du Sac, 3231 P7
Prentice, 626 G6
Prescott, 3764 J1
Princeton, 1504 M9
Pulaski, 3060 K10
Racine, 81855 O12
Randolph, 1869 N9
Random Lake, 1551 N11
Redgranite, 1040 M9
Reedsburg, 7827 N7
Reedsville, 1187 L11
Reeseville, 703 P9
Rhinelander, 7735 G8
Rib Lake, 878 H6
Rice Lake, 8320 G3
Richland Ctr., 5114 P6
Ridgeway, 689 O7
Rio, 938 N8
Ripon, 6828 M9
River Falls, 12560 J2
River Hills, 1631 S5
Roberts, 969 J2
Rochester, 1149 O11
Rockland, 628 M5
Rosendale, 923 M10
Rothschild, 4970 J8
St. Croix Falls, 2033 G2
St. Francis, 8662 V5
St. Nazianz, 749 M11
Sauk City, 3109 P7
Saukville, 4068 P11
Schofield, 2117 J8
Seymour, 3335 K10
Sharon, 1549 R10
Shawano, 8298 J10
Sheboygan, 50792 M12
Sheboygan Falls, 6772 N11
Shell Lake, 1309 G3
Sherwood, 1550 L10
Shiocton, 954 K10
Shorewood, 13763 T5
Shorewood Hills, 1732 O1
Shullsburg, 1246 R6
Silver Lake, 2341 R11
Siren, 988 F2
Sister Bay, 886 H13
Slinger, 3901 P10
Soldiers Grove, 653 P5
Solon Sprs., 576 E3
Somers, 1100 R11
Somerset, 1556 H1
S. Milwaukee, 21256 O11
Sparta, 8648 M5
Spencer, 1932 J6
Spooner, 2653 F3
Spring Green, 1444 P7
Spring Valley, 1189 J2
Stanley, 1898 J5
Stevens Pt., 24551 K8
Stockbridge, 649 M10
Stoddard, 815 N4
Stoughton, 12354 O9
Stratford, 1523 J7
Strum, 1001 K4
Sturgeon Bay, 9437 J12
Sturtevant, 5287 R11
Suamico, 950 K11
Sullivan, 688 O10
Sun Prairie, 20369 P9
Superior, 27368 D3
Suring, 605 J10
Sussex, 8828 P11
Theresa, 1252 N10
Thiensville, 3254 P11
Thorp, 1536 J5
Tigerton, 764 J9
Tomah, 8419 M6
Tomahawk, 3770 G7
Trempealeau, 1319 M4
Turtle Lake, 1065 H3
Twin Lakes, 5124 R11
Two Rivers, 12639 L12
Union Grove, 4322 R11
Valders, 948 M11
Verona, 7052 O8
Viola, 667 N5
Viroqua, 4335 N5
Wales, 2523 O10
Walworth, 2304 R10
Washburn, 2280 D5
Waterford, 4048 O11
Waterloo, 3259 P9
Watertown, 21598 P10
Waukesha, 64825 O11
Waunakee, 8995 P8
Waupaca, 5676 L9
Waupun, 10718 N9
Wausau, 38426 J8
Wautoma, 1998 M8
Wauwatosa, 47271 T3
Wauzeka, 768 P5
Webster, 653 F2
W. Allis, 61254 O11
W. Bend, 28152 N11
Westby, 2045 N5
Westfield, 1217 M8
Weston, 12079 J8
W. Milwaukee, 4201 U4
W. Salem, 4540 M5
Weyauwega, 1806 L9
Whitefish Bay, 14163 P11
Whitehall, 1651 L4
Whitelaw, 730 L11
Whitewater, 13437 O10
Whiting, 1760 K8
Wild Rose, 765 L8
Williams Bay, 2415 R10
Wind Lake, 5202 O11
Wind Pt., 1853 O12
Windsor, 2533 P8
Winnebago, 1500 A6
Winneconne, 2401 M10
Wisconsin Dells, 2418 N7
Wisconsin Rapids, 18435 L7
Wittenberg, 1177 J9
Wonewoc, 834 N6
Woodruff, 1300 F7
Woodville, 1104 J2
Wrightstown, 1934 L11
Wyocena, 668 N8

WYOMING

PG. 120

CAPITAL
Cheyenne

NICKNAME
Equality State

POPULATION
493,782, rank 50

AREA
97,809 sq mi, rank 9

STATEHOOD
1890, rank 44

Counties
Albany, 32014 F11
Big Horn, 11461 B8
Campbell, 33698 B11
Carbon, 15639 G9
Converse, 12052 D11
Crook, 5887 A12
Fremont, 35804 E8
Goshen, 12538 E12
Hot Sprs., 4882 C7
Johnson, 7075 B10
Laramie, 81607 G12
Lincoln, 14573 F4
Natrona, 66533 D9
Niobrara, 2407 D12
Park, 25786 B6
Platte, 8807 F12
Sheridan, 26560 A10
Sublette, 5920 E5
Sweetwater, 37613 F7
Teton, 18251 C5
Uinta, 19742 H4
Washakie, 8289 C8
Weston, 6644 C12

Cities and Towns
Afton, 1818 E4
Alpine, 550 D4
Alta, 400 C4
Arapahoe, 1766 D7
Auburn, 276 E4
Baggs, 348 H8
Bar Nunn, 936 E10
Basin, 1238 B8
Big Piney, 408 E5
Buffalo, 3900 B9
Burlington, 250 B7
Burns, 285 H13
Byron, 557 A7
Casper, 49644 E10
Cheyenne, 53011 H12
Chugwater, 244 G12
Cody, 8835 B6
Cokeville, 506 F4
Cowley, 560 A7
Dayton, 678 A9
Diamondville, 716 F4
Douglas, 5288 E11
Dubois, 962 C6
E. Thermopolis, 274 C8
Eden, 388 F6
Encampment, 443 H9
Ethete, 1455 D7
Evanston, 11507 G4
Evansville, 2255 E10
Fairview, 277 E4
Farson, 242 F6
Ft. Bridger, 400 G5
Ft. Laramie, 243 F12
Ft. Washakie, 1477 D7
Frannie, 209 A7
Gillette, 19646 B11
Glendo, 229 E12
Glenrock, 2231 E11
Green River, 11808 G6
Greybull, 1815 B8
Guernsey, 1147 F12
Hanna, 873 F10
Hudson, 407 E7
Hulett, 408 A12
Jackson, 8647 C4
James Town, 552 G6
Kaycee, 249 C10
Kemmerer, 2651 F4
La Barge, 431 F5
LaGrange, 332 G13
Lander, 6867 E7
Laramie, 27204 G11
Lingle, 510 F12
Lovell, 2281 A7
Lucerne, 525 C8
Lusk, 1447 E12
Lyman, 1938 G5
Mammoth Hot Sprs., 275 A4
Marbleton, 720 E5
Medicine Bow, 274 F10
Meeteetse, 351 B7
Midwest, 408 D10
Mills, 2591 J4
Moorcroft, 807 B12
Mtn. View, 1153 G5
Newcastle, 3065 C13
Orchard Valley, 550 K2
Osage, 215 C12
Pine Bluffs, 1153 H13
Pinedale, 1412 E5
Pine Haven, 222 B12
Powell, 5373 A7
Ralston, 233 A7
Ranchester, 701 A9
Rawlins, 8538 G9
Reliance, 665 G6
Riverton, 9310 D7
Rock River, 235 G10
Rock Sprs., 18708 G6
Rolling Hills, 449 E11
Saratoga, 1726 G9
Sheridan, 15804 A9
Shoshoni, 635 D8
Sinclair, 423 F9
S. Torrington, 550 F13
Story, 887 B9
Sundance, 1161 B12
Superior, 244 G6
Ten Sleep, 304 C8
Thayne, 341 D4
Thermopolis, 3172 C7
Torrington, 5776 F13
Upton, 872 B12
Wamsutter, 261 G8
Wheatland, 3548 F12
Wilson, 1294 C4
Worland, 5250 C8
Wright, 1347 C11

Canada

ALBERTA

PG. 123

CAPITAL
Edmonton

POPULATION
2,696,826, rank 4

AREA
255,286 sq mi, rank 6

ENTERED CANADA
1905

Cities and Towns
* City indexed to pg. 121

Airdrie, 15946 J16
Alberta Beach, 640 F16
Alix, 765 H17
Athabasca, 2313 E16
Banff, 6098 J15
Barrhead, 4239 E15
Bashaw, 774 G17
Bassano, 1272 K17
Beaumont, 5810 F16
Beaverlodge, 1997 D11
Beiseker, 708 J16
Bellevue, 1046 M16
Bentley, 987 H16
Black Diamond, 1811 K16
Blackfalds, 2001 H16
Blairmore, 2118 L16
Bon Accord, 1493 F16
Bonnyville, 5100 E19
Bowden, 1014 H16
Bow Island, 1688 L19
Boyle, 802 E17
Brooks, 10093 K18
Bruderheim, 1198 F17
Calgary, 768082 K16
Calmar, 1797 G16
Camrose, 13728 G17
Canmore, 8354 K15
Cardston, 3417 M17
Carstairs, 1887 J16
Castor, 970 H18
Chestermere, 1911 K16
Claresholm, 3427 L16
Coaldale, 5731 L17
Cochrane, 7424 J16
Cold Lake, 4089 E19
Consort, 794 H19
Coronation, 1166 H18
Crossfield, 1899 J16
Daysland, 679 G17
Delburne, 641 H17
Devon, 4496 F16
Didsbury, 3553 J16
Drayton Valley, 5883 G15
Drumheller, 6587 J17
Duchess, 693 K18
Eckville, 901 H16
Edmonton, 616306 F16
Edson, 7399 F14
Elk Pt., 1403 E19
Evansburg, 740 F15
Fairview, 3316 C12
Falher, 1149 C13
Forestburg, 930 G18
Ft. Macleod, 3034 L17
Ft. McMurray, 33078 F4*
Ft. Saskatchewan, 12408 F17
Ft. Vermilion, 782 F4*
Fox Cr., 2321 E13
Gibbons, 2748 F16
Grande Cache, 4441 F11
Grande Prairie, 31140 D12
Grimshaw, 2661 C13
Hanna, 3001 J18
Hardisty, 808 G18
High Level, 3093 E3*
High Prairie, 2907 D14
High River, 7359 K16
Hinton, 9961 F13
Hythe, 712 D11
Innisfail, 6116 H16
Irricana, 823 J16
Jasper, 3815 G12
Killam, 1048 G18
Kitscoty, 643 F19
Lac La Biche, 2611 D18
Lacombe, 8018 H16
Lamont, 1581 F17
Leduc, 14305 G16
Legal, 1095 F16
Lethbridge, 63053 L17
Lloydminster, 11317 F19
Magrath, 1867 M17
Manning, 1295 B13
Mannville, 758 F18
Mayerthorpe, 1669 F15
McLennan, 867 C13
Medicine Hat, 46783 L19
Milk River, 929 M18
Millet, 1894 G16
Morinville, 6226 F16
Nanton, 1665 K16
Okotoks, 8510 K16
Olds, 5815 J16
Onoway, 788 F16
Oyen, 1009 J19
Peace River, 6536 C13
Penhold, 1625 H16
Picture Butte, 1669 L17
Pincher Cr., 3659 M16
Ponoka, 6149 G16
Provost, 1904 H19
Rainbow Lake, 1138 E3*
Raymond, 3056 M17
Redcliff, 4104 L19
Red Deer, 60075 H16
Redwater, 2053 F17
Rimbey, 2106 G16
Rocky Mtn. House, 5805 H15
Rycroft, 667 C12
St. Albert, 46888 F16
St. Paul, 4861 E18
Sedgewick, 937 G18
Sexsmith, 1481 D12
Slave Lake, 6553 D15
Smoky Lake, 1087 E17
Spirit River, 1112 C12
Spruce Gr., 14271 F16
Stand Off, 682 M17
Stettler, 5220 H17
Stirling, 874 M17
Stony Plain, 8274 F16
Strathmore, 5282 K17
Sundre, 2028 J15
Swan Hills, 2030 E15
Sylvan Lake, 5178 H16
Taber, 7214 L18
Thorsby, 725 G16
Three Hills, 3022 J17
Tofield, 1726 F17
Trochu, 958 H17
Turner Valley, 1527 K16
Two Hills, 1040 F18
Valleyview, 1906 D13
Vauxhall, 1011 L18
Vegreville, 5337 F18
Vermilion, 3744 F19
Viking, 1081 G18
Vulcan, 1537 K17
Wabamun, 645 F15
Wainwright, 5079 G19
Wembley, 1441 D11
Westlock, 4817 E16
Wetaskiwin, 10959 G16
Whitecourt, 7783 E14

BRITISH COLUMBIA

PG. 122–123

CAPITAL
Victoria

POPULATION
3,724,500, rank 3

AREA
365,946 sq mi, rank 5

ENTERED CANADA
1871

Cities and Towns
* City indexed to pg. 121

Abbotsford, 105403 M8
Armstrong, 3906 K11
Ashcroft, 1858 K9
Barrière, 1653 J10
Black Cr., 1950 L6
Bowen Island, 1791 L7
Burnaby, 179209 M8
Burns Lake, 1793 E6
Cache Cr., 1115 K9
Campbell River, 28851 L6
Canal Flats, 685 L14
Castlegar, 7027 M13
Cawston, 843 M11
Cedar, 3178 M7
Chase, 2460 K11
Chetwynd, 2980 C9
Chilliwack, 60186 M9
Clinton, 729 K9
Cobble Hill, 1527 N7
Coldstream, 8975 L11
Colwood, 13848 M1
Comox, 11069 L6
Coombs, 840 M6
Coquitlam, 101820 M8
Courtenay, 17335 L6
Cranbrook, 18131 M14
Creston, 4816 M14
Cumberland, 2548 L6
Dawson Cr., 11125 C10
Delta, 95411 M7
Denman Island, 866 L6
Duncan, 4583 N7
Elkford, 2729 L15
Esquimalt, 16151 N1
Fernie, 4877 M15
Ft. Nelson, 4401 E3*
Ft. St. James, 2046 E7
Ft. St. John, 15021 C10
Fraser Lake, 1344 E6
Ganges, 1457 N7
Gibsons, 3732 M7
Golden, 3968 J13
Gold River, 2041 L5
Grand Forks, 3994 M12
Greenwood, 784 M12
Hope, 6247 M9
Hornby Island, 894 M6
Houston, 3934 E5
Hudson's Hope, 1122 C9
Invermere, 2687 K14
Kaleden, 1118 M11
Kamloops, 76394 K10
Kaslo, 1063 L13
Kelowna, 89442 L11
Kent, 4844 M9
Keremeos, 1167 M11
Kimberley, 6738 L14
Kitimat, 11136 E3
Ladysmith, 6456 M7
Lake Country, 9007 L11
Lake Cowichan, 2856 N7
Langford, 17484 N7
Langley, 22523 M8
Lazo, 1201 L6
Lillooet, 1988 K9
Lions Bay, 1347 M7
Logan Lake, 2492 K10
Lower Nicola, 780 L10
Lumby, 1689 L12
Mackenzie, 5997 D8
Madeira Park, 669 L7
Maple Ridge, 5673 M8
Masset, 1293 F1*
McBride, 740 G10
Merritt, 7631 L10
Merville, 865 L6
Midway, 686 M12
Mission, 30519 M8
Nakusp, 1736 L13
Nanaimo, 70130 M7
Naramata, 1069 M11
Nelson, 9585 M13
New Westminster, 49350 C5
N. Vancouver, 41475 A2
N. Vancouver (DM), 80418 A4
Oak Bay, 17865 N7
Okanagan Falls, 1874 M11
Oliver, 4285 M11
150 Mile House, 899 H9
100 Mile House, 1850 J9
Osoyoos, 4021 M11
Parksville, 9472 M6
Peachland, 4524 L11
Pemberton, 855 L8
Penticton, 30987 M11
Port Alberni, 18468 M6
Port Alice, 1331 K4
Port Edward, 700 E2
Port Hardy, 5283 K4
Port McNeill, 2925 K4
Port Moody, 20847 A6
Pouce Coupe, 894 C11
Powell River, 13131 L6
Prince George, 75150 F8
Prince Rupert, 16714 E2
Princeton, 2826 M10
Qualicum Beach, 6728 M6
Quesnel, 8468 G8
Revelstoke, 8047 K12
Richmond, 148867 M7
Rossland, 3802 M13
Royston, 1219 L6
Saanich, 101388 N7
Salmo, 1202 M13
Salmon Arm, 14664 K11
Sechelt, 7343 M7
Sicamous, 2827 K12
Sidney, 10701 N7
Smithers, 5624 D4
Sointula, 672 K4
Sooke, 4733 N7
Sorrento, 662 K11
S. Hazelton, 654 D4
Spallumcheen, 5322 L11
Sparwood, 3982 L15
Sproat Lake, 777 M6
Stewart, 858 E2*
Summerland, 10584 M11
Surrey, 304477 M8
Tahsis, 940 L4
Taylor, 1031 C10
Telkwa, 1194 D4
Terrace, 12779 D3
Tofino, 1170 M5
Trail, 7696 M13
Tumbler Ridge, 3775 D10
Ucluelet, 1658 M5
Valemount, 1303 G11
Vancouver, 514008 M7
Vanderhoof, 4401 E7
Vernon, 31817 L11
Victoria, 73504 N7
View Royal, 6441 M1
W. Vancouver, 40882 A3
Whistler, 7172 L8
Williams Lake, 10472 H8
Windermere, 821 K14
Wynndel, 871 M14
Youbou, 797 M6

MANITOBA

PG. 125

CAPITAL
Winnipeg

POPULATION
1,113,898, rank 5

AREA
250,946 sq mi, rank 8

ENTERED CANADA
1870

Cities and Towns
* City indexed to pg. 121

Altona, 3286 N16
Arborg, 1012 K16
Ashern, 692 J15
Beausejour, 2712 L17
Birtle, 720 L12
Boissevain, 1544 N13
Brandon, 39175 M13
Camperville, 579 H13
Carberry, 1493 M14
Carman, 2704 M15
Churchill, 1073 F6*
Cranberry Portage, 800 D12
Dauphin, 8266 J13
Deloraine, 1041 N12
E. Selkirk, 599 L17
Elie, 485 L16
Elkhorn, 514 L12
Emerson, 737 N16
Erickson, 507 L13
Flin Flon, 6572 C11
Gilbert Plains, 748 J12
Gillam, 1158 G6*
Gimli, 1574 K16
Gladstone, 927 L14
Glenboro, 663 M14
Grandview, 856 J12
Gretna, 538 N16
Grunthal, 733 M17
Hamiota, 847 L12
Killarney, 2208 N13
La Broquerie, 472 M17
Lac du Bonnet, 1070 L17
Landmark, 783 M17
La Salle, 600 M16
Lorette, 1474 M17
Lundar, 523 K15
Lynn Lake, 501 F5*
MacGregor, 898 L14
Manitou, 781 N15
McCreary, 537 K14
Melita, 1152 N12
Minitonas, 598 H12
Minnedosa, 2443 L13
Mitchell, 811 M17
Morden, 5689 N15
Morris, 1645 M16
Neepawa, 3301 L14
Niverville, 1615 M16
Notre Dame de Lourdes, 620 M15
Pilot Mound, 716 N14
Pinawa, 1669 L18
Pine Falls, 794 K17
Plum Coulee, 729 N16
Portage la Prairie, 13077 L15
Powerview, 759 K17
Reston, 620 M12
Rivers, 1117 L13
Riverton, 566 K16
Roblin, 1885 J12
Rossburn, 580 K12
Russell, 1605 K12
St. Claude, 609 M15
Ste. Agathe, 477 M16
Ste. Anne, 1511 M17
Ste. Rose du Lac, 1047 K14
St. Jean Baptiste, 515 N16
St. Malo, 846 M17
St-Pierre-Jolys, 925 M16
Sanford, 484 M16
Selkirk, 9881 L17
Shoal Lake, 801 L12
Souris, 1613 M13
Southport, 688 L15
Steinbach, 8478 M17
Stonewall, 3689 L16
Stony Mtn., 1744 L16
Swan River, 3986 H12
Teulon, 1055 L16
The Pas, 5945 E12
Thompson, 14385 G6*
Treherne, 675 M14
Virden, 2956 M12
Warren, 510 L16
Wawanesa, 485 M13
Winkler, 7241 N15
Winnipeg, 618477 M16
Winnipeg Beach, 746 K16
Winnipegosis, 730 J13

NEW BRUNSWICK

PG. 130

CAPITAL
Fredericton

POPULATION
738,133, rank 8

AREA
28,355 sq mi, rank 11

ENTERED CANADA
1867

Cities and Towns
Allardville, 675 E7
Atholville, 1376 C5
Back Bay, 559 K5
Baie-Ste-Anne, 1941 E8
Baker Brook, 629 E2
Balmoral, 1975 D6
Barachois, 783 G9
Bas-Caraquet, 1775 D8
Bath, 629 G4
Bathurst, 13815 D7
Belledune, 2060 D7
Beresford, 4720 D7
Bertrand, 1379 D8
Blacks Hbr., 1148 K5
Blackville, 957 F6
Bouctouche, 2459 G8
Bristol, 707 G4
Burtts Corner, 910 H5
Cambridge-Narrows, 634 H6
Campbellton, 8404 C5
Cap-Pele, 2242 G9
Caraquet, 4653 D8
Centreville, 559 G4
Charlo, 1610 C6
Chipman, 1518 G6
Clair, 905 E2
Dalhousie, 4500 C6
Dieppe, 12497 H8
Doaktown, 986 G6
Dorchester, 1179 H8
Drummond, 983 E4
Edmundston, 11033 E3
Eel River Crossing, 1446 C6
Florenceville, 707 G4
Fredericton, 46507 H5
Fredericton Jct., 736 J5
Gagetown, 660 H6
Geary, 1084 H5
Gondola Pt., 4324 J6
Grand Bay-Westfield, 3713 J6
Grande-Anse, 965 D8
Grand Falls, 6133 E4
Grand Manan, 2577 L5
Hampton, 4081 J6
Hartland, 892 G4
Hillsborough, 1272 H8
Hoyt, 618 J5
Kedgwick, 1221 D4
Keswick Ridge, 581 H5
Kingston, 689 J6
Lamèque, 1671 D8
Lavillette, 541 E7
Lorne, 856 D6
Maisonnette, 675 D8
McAdam, 1570 J4
Memramcook, 4904 H8
Minto, 3056 H6
Miramichi, 19241 E7
Moncton, 59313 H8
Nackawic, 1167 H4
Neguac, 1735 E8
New Maryland, 4284 H5
Nigadoo, 961 D7
Norton, 1390 J7
Notre-Dame, 787 G8
Oromocto, 9194 H5
Paquetville, 731 D8
Perth-Andover, 1861 F4
Petitcodiac, 1425 H7
Petit Rocher, 2078 D7
Pigeon Hill, 674 D8
Plaster Rock, 1220 F4
Pointe-Verte, 1122 D7
Pont-Lafrance, 852 E8
Quispamsis, 8839 J6
Renous, 600 F6
Rexton, 908 F8
Richibucto, 1414 F8
Riverview, 16653 H8
Rivière-du-Portage, 789 E8
Rivière-Verte, 929 E3
Robertville, 1251 D7
Rogersville, 1336 F7
Rothesay, 1695 J6
Sackville, 5393 H9
St. Andrews, 1752 K4
St-Antoine, 1463 G8
St-Arthur, 877 D5
St-Basile, 3321 E3
Ste-Anne-de-Madawaska, 1273 E3
Ste-Marie-de-Kent, 550 G8
St-François-de-Madawaska, 631 E2
St. George, 1414 K5
St-Isidore, 912 D8
St-Jacques, 2767 D3
Saint John, 72494 J6
St. Leonard, 1450 E3
St-Louis de Kent, 1015 F8
St-Quentin, 2424 D4
St. Stephen, 4961 J4
Salisbury, 1878 H8
Shediac, 4664 G8
Shippagan, 2862 D8
Sunny Corner, 705 F6
Sussex, 4293 H7
Sussex Corner, 1337 H7
Tide Head, 1170 C5
Tracadie-Sheila, 4773 D8
Tracy, 605 H5
Wilsons Beach, 925 K5
Woodstock, 5092 G4
Zealand, 602 H5

NEWFOUNDLAND

PG. 131

CAPITAL
St. John's

POPULATION
551,792, rank 9

AREA
156,649 sq mi, rank 10

ENTERED CANADA
1949

Cities and Towns
* City indexed to pg. 121

Arnold's Cove, 1115 E19
Badger, 997 D17
Baie Verte, 1708 C17
Bay de Verde, 594 D20
Bay Roberts, 5472 E19
Belleoram, 564 E18
Birchy Bay, 735 C18
Bishop's Falls, 4048 D18
Bloomfield, 650 D19
Bonavista, 4526 D19
Botwood, 3613 D18
Buchans, 1056 D17
Burgeo, 2098 E16
Burin, 2682 F18
Campbellton, 642 C18
Carbonear, 5168 E20
Carmanville, 913 C19
Cartwright, 628 E12*
Catalina, 1155 D20
Centreville-Wareham-Trinity, 1328 D19
Channel-Port aux Basques, 5243 E15
Churchill Falls, 797 F11*
Clarenville, 5335 D19
Conception Bay S., 19265 E20
Corner Brook, 21893 D16
Cow Head, 665 C16
Cox's Cove, 898 D16
Deer Lake, 5222 D16
Eastport, 557 D19
Embree, 819 C18
Englee, 827 B17
Ferryland, 667 F20
Fogo, 982 C19
Fortune, 1969 F18
Gambo, 2339 D19
Gander, 10364 D18
Garnish, 691 E18
Glenwood, 893 D18
Glovertown, 2292 D19
Grand Bank, 3328 F18
Grand Falls-Windsor, 14160 D18
Hampden, 651 C17
Happy Valley-Goose Bay, 8655 F11*
Harbour Breton, 2290 E18
Harbour Grace, 3740 E19
Hare Bay, 1224 D19
Heart's Content, 538 E19
Hermitage-Sandyville, 687 E18
Holyrood, 2090 E20
Hopedale, 591 E11*
Humber Arm S., 1991 D16
Isle aux Morts, 988 E16
Joe Batt's Arm, 1028 C19
Labrador City, 8455 F11*
Lark Hbr., 681 D16
La Scie, 1254 C18
Lawn, 957 F18
Lewisporte, 3709 C18
Lourdes, 758 D15
Marystown, 6742 F18
Mt. Moriah, 748 D16
Mt. Pearl, 25519 E20
Musgrave Hbr., 1386 C19
Musgravetown, 687 D19
Nain, 996 E11*
New-Wes-Valley, 3061 C19
Norris Pt., 850 B16
Old Perlican, 747 D20
Paradise, 7960 E20
Parson's Pond, 530 C16
Pasadena, 3445 D16
Peterview, 862 D18
Placentia, 5013 E19
Pt. Leamington, 783 C18
Port au Choix, 1146 B16
Port Blandford, 603 D19
Port Saunders, 876 B16
Portugal Cove-St. Philip's, 5773 F17
Port Union, 542 D19
Pouch Cove, 1885 E20
Robert's Arm, 963 C18
Rocky Hbr., 1066 C16
Roddickton, 1103 B17
Rose Blanche-Harbour Le Cou, 814 E16
St. Alban's, 1563 E18
St. Anthony, 2996 A18
St. Bernard's-Jacques Fontaine, 751 E18
St. Bride's, 542 F19
St. George's, 1536 D16
St. John's, 101936 E20
St. Lawrence, 1697 F18
St. Mary's, 617 F19
St. Vincent's-St. Stephen's-Peter's River, 589 F19
Seal Cove, 560 C17
Seldom-Little Seldom, 533 C19
Spaniard's Bay, 2771 E19
Springdale, 3381 C18
Stephenville, 7764 D16
Stephenville Crossing, 2283 D16
Terrenceville, 737 E18
Torbay, 5230 E20
Trepassey, 1084 F19
Trout River, 688 C16
Wabana, 3136 E20
Wabush, 2018 F11*
Whitbourne, 988 E19
Witless Bay, 1118 E20

NORTHWEST TERRITORIES

PG. 121

CAPITAL
Yellowknife

POPULATION
39,672, rank 11

AREA
520,850 sq mi (est.), rank 3

ENTERED CANADA
1870

Cities and Towns
Aklavik, 727 B3
Déline, 616 D3
Ft. Good Hope, 644 C3
Ft. Liard, 512 E3
Ft. McPherson, 878 C3
Ft. Providence, 748 E4
Ft. Resolution, 536 E4
Ft. Simpson, 1257 D3
Ft. Smith, 2441 E4
Hay River, 3611 E4
Inuvik, 3296 B3
Norman Wells, 798 C3
Rae-Edzo, 1662 D4
Tuktoyaktuk, 943 B3
Yellowknife, 17275 E4

NOVA SCOTIA

PG. 130–131

CAPITAL
Halifax

POPULATION
909,282, rank 7

AREA
21,425 sq mi, rank 12

ENTERED CANADA
1867

Cities and Towns
Amherst, 9669 H9
Annapolis Royal, 583 L7
Antigonish, 4860 J13
Arcadia, 770 N6
Arichat, 886 J14
Aylesford, 1121 K8
Baddeck, 1064 H14
Bear River, 881 L7
Bedford, 13638 L10
Berwick, 2195 K8
Blockhouse, 700 L8
Bridgetown, 994 K7
Bridgewater, 7351 L8
Brookfield, 917 J10
Brooklyn, 1253 M8
Brooklyn, 610 K9
Canning, 908 K9
Canso, 1127 J14
Centreville, 1086 K8
Chester Basin, 695 L9
Chéticamp, 979 F14
Clark's Hbr., 980 N7
Conquerall Mills, 549 M8
Dartmouth, 65629 L10
Digby, 2199 L6
Dominion G16
Elmsdale, 1112 K10
Enfield, 2588 K10
Eskasoni, 2076 H15
Glace Bay, 23038 G16
Guysborough, 494 J13
Halifax, 113910 L10
Hebron, 716 M6
Herring Cove, 1923 L10
Ingonish, 607 F15
Inverness, 1785 G14
Joggins, 491 J9
Kentville, 5551 K8
Kingston, 7806 K8
Liverpool, 3048 M8
Lockeport, 692 N7
Louisbourg, 1152 H16
Lower W. Pubnico, 854 N6
Lower Woods Hbr., 494 N6
Lunenburg, 2599 L9
Mahone Bay, 1017 L9
Meteghan, 984 M6
Meteghan River, 553 M6
Middle Musquodoboit, 721 K11
Middleton, 1800 K7
Milton, 1770 M8
Mt. Uniacke, 1359 K9
Mulgrave, 896 J13
Musquodoboit Hbr., 886 L11
New Germany, 892 L8
New Glasgow, 9812 J12
New Waterford, 10713 G16
N. Sydney G15
Oxford, 1352 H9
Parrsboro, 1617 J9
Pictou, 4022 J11
Pomquet, 512 J13
Port Hawkesbury, 3809 J14
Port Hood, 835 H13
Port Maitland, 503 M6
Port Morien, 578 G16
Pugwash, 755 H10
River Hebert, 773 J9
St. Peter's, 731 J14
Sandy Pt., 772 N7
Sheet Hbr., 828 K12
Shelburne, 2132 N7
Shubenacadie, 1192 K10
Springhill, 4193 J9
Stellarton, 4968 J12
Stewiacke, 1405 K10
Sydney, 34871 G15
Sydney Mines, 17294 G15
Sydney River H15
Tatamagouche, 726 H10
Terence Bay, 906 L10
Three Mile Plains, 1295 K9
Trenton, 2952 J12
Truro, 11938 J10
Waverley, 1925 L10
Wedgeport, 739 N6
Western Shore, 1017 L9
Westville, 3976 J11
Whites Lake, 980 L10
Wilmot, 640 K8
Windsor, 3726 K9
Wolfville, 3833 K9
Yarmouth, 7568 N6

NUNAVUT

PG. 121

CAPITAL
Iqaluit

POPULATION
24,730, rank 13

AREA
800,775 sq mi (est.), rank 1

ENTERED CANADA
1999

Cities and Towns
Arctic Bay, 639 B7
Arviat, 1559 E6
Baker Lake, 1385 D6
Cambridge Bay, 1351 C5
Cape Dorset, 1118 D8
Gjoa Haven, 879 C6
Igloolik, 1174 C8
Iqaluit, 4220 D9
Kugluktuk, 1201 C4
Pangnirtung, 1243 C9
Pond Inlet, 1154 B8
Rankin Inlet, 2058 E7
Repulse Bay, 559 D7
Taloyoak, 648 C6

ONTARIO

PG. 125–127

CAPITAL
Toronto

POPULATION
10,753,573, rank 1

AREA
412,579 sq mi, rank 4

ENTERED CANADA
1867

Cities and Towns
* City indexed to pg. 121
† City indexed to pg. 125

Acton, 7632 J9
Ailsa Craig, 1044 K6
Ajax, 64430 H12
Alexandria, 3531 D20
Alfred, 1228 C19
Alliston, 8225 H10
Almonte, 4611 D17
Alton, 955 H9
Alvinston, 1037 L6
Amherstburg, 10245 N3
Angus, 9723 G10
Arnprior, 7113 D17
Arthur, 2139 H8
Athens, 997 F17
Atikokan, 3961 B13†
Atwood, 877 J7
Aurora, 34857 H11
Aylmer, 7018 L8
Ayr, 3151 K9
Bancroft, 2554 E14
Barrie, 79191 G10
Barry's Bay, 1086 D14
Bath, 1389 G16
Bayfield, 833 J6
Beachburg, 902 C16
Beamsville, 7699 K11
Beaverton, 3009 G11
Beeton, 2886 H10
Belle River, 4531 M4
Belleville, 37083 G15
Bewdley, 825 H13
Blenheim, 4873 M5
Blind River, 3152 B4
Blyth, 991 J7
Bobcaygeon, 2753 F12
Bolton, 10569 H10
Bothwell, 990 M6
Bourget, 970 D19
Bowmanville, 27594 H12
Bracebridge, 13223 E11
Bradford, 14869 H10
Brampton, 268251 J10
Brantford, 84764 K9
Bridgenorth, 1671 G13
Brighton, 4584 H14
Brockville, 21752 F18
Brooke, 991 F8
Brooklin, 2063 H12
Brussels, 1131 J7
Burk's Falls, 986 D11
Burlington, 136976 K10
Caledonia, 7038 K10
Caledon Vil., 1365 H9
Cambridge, 101429 K9
Campbellford, 3647 G14
Cannington, 2018 G12
Capreol, 3410 A8
Cardinal, 1777 F18
Carleton Place, 8450 E17
Carlisle, 1886 K9
Casselman, 2877 D19
Cayuga, 1015 L10
Chalk River, 974 B14
Chapleau, 2934 C18†
Chatham, 43409 M5
Chesley, 1904 G7
Chesterville, 1497 E19
Clarksburg, 769 F9
Clifford, 775 H8
Clinton, 3216 J6
Cobalt, 1401 C20†
Cobden, 1020 C16
Cobourg, 16027 H13
Cochrane, 4443 A19†
Colborne, 2054 H14
Colchester, 1960 N4
Coldwater, 1254 F10
Collingwood, 15596 G9
Comber, 1480 N4
Constance Bay, 2325 D17
Cookstown, 1466 G10
Cornwall, 47403 E20
Courtland, 917 L8
Courtright, 1046 L5
Creemore, 1285 G9
Crystal Beach, 6321 L12
Deep River, 4491 B14
Delhi, 4155 L8
Deseronto, 1811 G15
Dowling, 1979 A7
Drayton, 1427 J8
Dresden, 2589 M5
Dryden, 6711 A12†
Dundalk, 1776 G9
Dunnville, 12471 L10
Durham, 2641 G8
Dutton, 1315 L6
Earlton, 911 C20†
Echo Bay, 793 A2
Eganville, 1319 D15
Elliot Lake, 13588 A4
Elmira, 7497 J8
Elmvale, 1860 F10
Elora, 3346 J9
Embro, 838 K8
Embrun, 3946 D19
Englehart, 1703 B20†
Erin, 2633 J9
Espanola, 5454 B6
Essex, 6785 N4
Exeter, 4472 K7
Fenelon Falls, 2040 F12
Fergus, 8884 J9
Forest, 3020 K6
Ft. Erie, 27183 L12
Ft. Frances, 8790 B12†
Foxboro, 1150 G15
Frankford, 2096 G14
Gananoque, 5219 G17
Georgetown, 26193 J10
Geraldton, 2627 A16†
Glencoe, 2178 L6
Gloucester D18
Goderich, 7553 J6
Gore Bay, 907 C5
Grafton, 1134 H14
Grand Bend, 1027 K6
Grand Valley, 1611 H9
Gravenhurst, 10030 E11
Grimsby, 19585 K10
Guelph, 95821 J9
Hagersville, 2364 L9
Haliburton, 1434 E12
Hamilton, 467799 K10
Hampton, 745 H12
Hanover, 6844 H7
Harriston, 2008 H8
Harrow, 2806 N4
Hastings, 1140 G14
Havelock, 1352 G14
Hawkesbury, 10162 C20
Hearst, 6049 A17†
Hensall, 1187 J7
Hillsburgh, 1164 H9
Hornepayne, 1458 A17†
Huntsville, 15918 D11
Huron Park, 969 K7
Ingersoll, 9849 L8
Ingleside, 1894 E19
Iron Bridge, 777 B3
Iroquois, 1278 E19
Iroquois Falls, 5714 B19†
Jarvis, 1710 L9
Kanata, 56247 D17
Kapuskasing, 10036 A18†
Kars, 1575 E18
Kearney, 837 D11
Kemptville, 3272 E18
Kenora, 10063 A11†
Keswick, 17068 G11
Kincardine, 6620 G6
Kingston, 55947 G16
Kingsville, 5991 N4
Kirkland Lake, 9905 B20†
Kitchener, 178420 J8
Komoka, 1060 L7
Lakefield, 2444 G13
Lanark, 865 E17
Lancaster, 825 D20
La Salle, 20566 N3
Leamington, 16188 N4
Limoges, 1236 D19
Lindsay, 17638 G12
Listowel, 5467 J8
Little Current, 1575 C6
Lively, 6890 A7
London, 325646 L7
Longlac, 2074 A16†
Long Sault, 1509 E19
Loretto, 781 H10
L'Orignal, 1999 C20
Lucan, 1958 K7
Lucknow, 1215 H6
Madoc, 1464 F15
Maidstone, 864 N4
Manitouwadge, 3395 B16†
Marathon, 4791 B16†
Markdale, 1354 G8
Markham, 173383 H11
Marmora, 1483 G14
Massey, 1171 B6
Matheson, 984 B19†
Mattawa, 2281 B12
Maxville, 885 D19
Meaford, 4681 F8
Merrickville, 1027 E18
Metcalfe, 1576 D18
Midland, 15035 F10
Mildmay, 1110 H7
Millbrook, 1312 G13
Milton, 32104 J10
Milverton, 1618 J8
Minden, 1111 E12
Mississauga, 544382 J10
Mitchell, 3670 J7
Moose Cr., 894 D19
Moosonee, 1939 H9*
Morrisburg, 2538 E19
Mt. Albert, 2158 H11
Mt. Brydges, 2229 L7
Mt. Forest, 4530 H8
Nanticoke, 23485 L9
Napanee, 5450 G16
Nepean D18
Newburgh, 729 G16
New Dundee, 1082 K8
New Hamburg, 6494 K8
New Liskeard, 5112 C20†
Newmarket, 57125 H11
Niagara Falls, 76917 K11
Niagara-on-the-Lake, 13238 K11
Nobleton, 3177 H10
N. Bay, 54332 B11
Norwich, 2460 L8
Norwood, 1469 G14
Oakville, 128405 J10
Oakwood, 735 G12
Odessa, 1162 G16
Oil Sprs., 773 L5
Omemee, 1271 G12
Onaping, 2402 A7
Orangeville, 21498 H9
Orillia, 27846 F11
Orono, 1653 H12
Osgoode, 2009 E18
Oshawa, 134364 H12
Ottawa, 721136 D18
Otterville, 823 L8
Owen Sound, 21390 F8
Paisley, 1106 G7
Palmerston, 2468 H8
Paris, 8987 K9
Parkhill, 1765 K6
Parry Sound, 6326 D9
Pelham, 14343 K11
Pembroke, 14177 C15
Penetanguishene, 7291 F10
Perth, 5886 E17
Petawawa, 6540 C15
Peterborough, 69535 G13
Petrolia, 4908 L5
Pickering, 78989 H12
Picton, 4673 H15
Plantagenet, 967 D19
Plattsville, 915 K8
Pt. Edward, 2257 L5
Port Burwell, 1023 M8
Port Carling, 838 E10
Port Colborne, 18451 L11
Port Dover, 5398 L9
Port Elgin, 7041 G7
Port Hope, 11698 H13
Port Lambton, 1349 L4
Port McNicoll, 4880 F10
Port Perry, 6019 H12
Port Rowan, 846 M9
Port Stanley, 2499 L7
Pottageville, 1000 H10
Powassan, 1125 B11
Prescott, 4480 F18
Queensville, 1636 H11
Red Rock, 982 B15†
Renfrew, 8125 D16
Richmond, 3177 E18
Richmond Hill, 101725 H11
Ridgetown, 3454 M6
Rockland, 8070 D19
Rockwood, 2506 J9
Rodney, 1165 M6
Russell, 3648 D18
St. Catharines, 130926 K11
St. Clements, 1139 J8
St. George, 1901 K9
St. Isidore, 766 D19
St. Marys, 5952 K7
St. Thomas, 32275 L7
Sarnia, 72738 L5
Sauble Beach, 1009 F7
Sault Ste. Marie, 80054 A1
Schreiber, 1189 B15†
Seaforth, 2302 J7
Sharon, 2237 H11
Shelburne, 3790 H9
Simcoe, 15380 L9
Sioux Lookout, 3469 A13†
Smiths Falls, 9131 E17
Smithville, 2951 K10
Smooth Rock Falls, 1982 A19†
Southampton, 3151 G7
S. River, 1098 C11
Spanish, 842 B5
Stayner, 3598 G9
Stirling, 2173 G14
Stoney Pt., 1104 M4
Straffordville, 907 L8
Stratford, 28987 K8
Strathroy, 11852 L6
Sturgeon Falls, 6162 B10
Sudbury (Gr.-Sudbury), 164049 A8
Sunderland, 1082 G11
Sundridge, 1019 C11
Sutton, 5639 G11
Tamworth, 731 F15
Tara, 903 G7
Tavistock, 2420 K8
Tecumseh, 12828 M4
Teeswater, 1069 H7
Terrace Bay, 906 B16†
Thamesford, 1736 K7
Thamesville, 972 M6
Thedford, 831 K6
Thessalon, 1485 B3
Thornbury, 1763 F9
Thornton, 1001 G10
Thorold, 17883 K11
Thunder Bay, 113662 B14†
Tilbury, 4448 N5
Tillsonburg, 13211 L8
Timmins, 47499 B19†
Tiverton, 824 G6
Toronto, 2385421 J11
Tottenham, 4322 H10
Trenton, 17179 H14
Tweed, 1572 G15
Uxbridge, 5864 H11
Valley East, 20048 A8
Vanastra, 790 J16
Vankleek Hill, 2030 D20
Vaughan, 132549 K15
Verona, 1121 F16
Virginiatown, 782 B20†
Walkerton, 5036 H7
Wallaceburg, 11772 M5
Wasaga Beach, 8698 G9
Waterford, 2995 L9
Waterloo, 77949 J8
Watford, 1660 L6
Wawa, 3690 B17†
Welland, 48411 L11
Wellesley, 1274 J8
Wellington, 1691 H15
Wendover, 836 C19
W. Lorne, 1531 M6
Wheatley, 1657 N5
Whitby, 73794 H12
White River, 941 B17†
Wiarton, 2400 F7
Winchester, 2334 E18
Windsor, 197694 M3
Wingham, 2941 H7
Woodstock, 32086 K8
Woodville, 751 G12
Wyoming, 2131 L5
Zurich, 886 J6

PRINCE EDWARD ISLAND

PG. 130–131

CAPITAL
Charlottetown

POPULATION
134,557, rank 10

AREA
2,185 sq mi, rank 13

ENTERED CANADA
1873

Cities and Towns
Alberton, 1084 F9
Borden-Carleton, 829 G10
Charlottetown, 32531 G11
Cornwall, 4291 G11
Georgetown, 732 G12
Kensington, 1383 G10
Miscouche, 679 G9
Montague, 1995 G12
Murray River, 420 H12
N. Rustico, 650 G10
O'Leary, 877 F9
Souris, 1293 G12
Stratford, 5869 D13
Summerside, 14525 G10
Tignish, 839 F9
Wellington, 427 G9

QUÉBEC

PG. 128–130

CAPITAL
Québec

POPULATION
7,138,795, rank 2

AREA
594,857 sq mi, rank 2

ENTERED CANADA
1867

Cities and Towns
* City indexed to pg. 121
† City indexed to pg. 130

Acton Vale, 4685 L14
Albanel, 1111 B14
Alma, 26127 C16
Amos, 13632 C4
Amqui, 6800 B4†
Anjou, 37308 A9
Armagh, 840 H18
Asbestos, 6271 L15
Ayer's Cliff, 986 M15
Aylmer, 34901 M8
Baie-Comeau, 25554 A3†
Baie-St-Paul, 3569 F18
Barraute, 1159 C4
Beauceville, 3751 J18
Beauharnois, 6435 M12
Beauport, 72920 A13
Beaupré, 2799 G17
Bécancour, 11489 J14
Bedford, 2748 M13
Bernierville, 1871 K16
Berthierville, 3952 K13
Black Lake, 4408 K16
Blainville, 29603 L12
Bonaventure, 1509 C7†
Bromont, 4290 M14
Bromptonville, 3426 L15
Brossard, 65927 E10
Brownsburg, 2583 L11
Bryson, 753 L6
Buckingham, 11678 L8
Cabano, 3086 D2†
Cadillac, 930 D3
Campbell's Bay, 874 L6
Cap-aux-Meules, 1661 E13†
Cap-Chat, 2847 A5†
Cap-de-la-Madeleine, 33438 J14
Cap-Rouge, 14163 C11
Carleton, 2886 C6†
Causapscal, 2080 B4†
Chandler, 3358 C8†
Chapais, 2090 H10*
Charlesbourg, 70942 H17
Charny, 10661 H17
Châteauguay, 41423 M12
Château-Richer, 3579 G17
Chibougamau, 8664 H10*
Chicoutimi, 63061 C17
Chute-aux-Outardes, 2155 A3†
Clermont, 3225 E18
Coaticook, 6653 M16
Contrecoeur, 5331 K13
Cookshire, 1532 M16
Coteau-du-Lac, 1207 M11
Côte-St-Luc, 29705 D7
Cowansville, 12051 M14
Danville, 1796 L15
Dégelis, 3437 D2†
Desbiens, 1202 C15
Disraeli, 2657 K16
Dolbeau-Mistassini, 15214 B15
Donnacona, 5739 H16
Dorval, 17572 E6
Drummondville, 44882 K14
Dunham, 3370 M14
Duparquet, 738 C1
E. Angus, 3642 L16
E. Broughton, 2489 J17
Farnham, 6044 M13
Ferme-Neuve, 2178 H8
Fleurimont, 16262 L20
Forestville, 3894 B20
Fort-Coulonge, 1716 K6
Gaspé, 16517 B9†
Gatineau, 100702 L8
Gentilly, 2325 J15
Girardville, 976 B14
Granada, 910 D2
Granby, 43316 M14
Grande-Rivière, 3888 C9†
Grand-Mère, 14223 H14
Greenfield Park, 17337 D10
Grenville-sur-la-Rouge, 1443 L10
Hampstead, 6986 D7
Havre-St-Pierre, 3020 A20
Hébertville, 1514 C16
Hemmingford, 751 N12
Hudson, 4796 M11
Hull, 62339 M8
Huntingdon, 2746 N11
Iberville, 9635 M13
Joliette, 17541 K12
Jonquière, 56503 C17
Kingsey Falls, 1329 K15
Kuujjuaq, 1726 E10*
La Baie, 21057 D17
Labelle, 1170 J10
Lac-au-Saumon, 1314 B4†
Lac-Bouchette, 1445 D15
Lac-Brome, 5073 M14
Lac-des-Écorces, 989 H9
Lac-Etchemin, 2488 J18
Lachine, 35171 M12
Lachute, 11493 L11
Lac-Mégantic, 5864 L17
Lacolle, 1554 N13
La Guadeloupe, 1772 K17
La Malbaie-Pointe-au-Pic, 4918 E19
L'Ancienne-Lorette, 15895 B11
L'Annonciation, 2085 J9
La Pocatière, 4887 F19
La Prairie, 17128 M12
LaSalle, 72029 E8
La Sarre, 8345 B2
L'Ascension, 1354 C16
L'Assomption, 11366 L13
Laterrière, 4815 D17
La Tuque, 12102 F14
Laurentides, 2703 K12
Laurier-Station, 2399 J16
Laurierville, 915 J16
Laval, 330393 L12
Lavaltrie, 5821 K13
Lebel-sur-Quévillon, 3416 B6
Le Bic, 2999 B2†
Lemoyne, 5052 D10
Lennoxville, 4036 M16
Léry, 2410 M12
Lévis, 40407 H17
L'Islet, 934 G18
L'Isle-Verte, 971 D20
Longueuil, 127977 L12
Loretteville, 14168 H16
Lorrainville, 1061 F1
Louiseville, 7911 J13
Macamic, 1711 B2
Magog, 14050 M15
Malartic, 4154 D3
Maniwaki, 4527 J7
Marieville, 5510 M13
Mascouche, 28097 L12
Maskinongé, 1052 J13
Masson-Angers, 7989 L8
Matane, 12364 A4†
Melocheville, 2486 M12
Métabetchouan, 3474 C15
Mirabel, 22689 L11
Moisie, 897 A18
Montebello, 1066 L9
Mont-Joli, 6267 B3†
Mont-Laurier, 8007 J8
Montmagny, 11885 G18
Montréal, 1016376 L12
Montréal-Est, 3523 A8
Montréal-Nord, 81581 A8
Montréal-Ouest, 5254 E7
Mont-Rolland, 2882 K11
Mont-Royal, 18282 C7
Murdochville, 1595 A7†
Napierville, 3004 M13
New Richmond, 3941 C7†
Nicolet, 4352 J14
Normandin, 3873 B14
Normétal, 1065 B1
N. Hatley, 758 M15
Notre-Dame-du-Lac, 2193 D2†
Ormstown, 1604 M11
Outremont, 22571 C8
Papineauville, 1628 L9
Percé, 3993 B9†
Pierrefonds, 52986 L12
Pierreville, 976 K14
Plessisville, 6810 J16
Pohénégamook, 3259 F20
Pointe-au-Père, 4145 B3†
Pointe-aux-Outardes, 1339 A3†
Pointe-Lebel, 2011 A3†
Pont-Rouge, 4676 H16
Port-Cartier, 7070 B17
Portneuf, 1470 H15
Price, 1916 B3†
Princeville, 3997 K15
Puvirnituq, 1169 E9*
Québec, 167264 H17
Quyon, 789 L7
Rawdon, 3855 K12
Repentigny, 53824 L12
Richmond, 3053 L15
Rigaud, 2448 L11
Rimouski, 31773 B2†
Rimouski-Est, 2119 B3†
Rivière-au-Renard, 2035 A9†
Rivière-du-Loup, 14721 E20
Robertsonville, 1829 K17
Roberval, 11640 C15
Rock Forest, 16604 M15
Rouyn-Noranda, 28819 D2
Roxboro, 5950 L12
Roxton Falls, 1371 L14
Roxton Pond, 991 L14
St-Agapit, 1812 H16
St-Ambroise, 2297 C16
St-André-Avellin, 1710 L9
St-André-Est, 1471 L11
St-Anselme, 1912 H17
St-Apollinaire, 1797 H16
St-Augustin, 741 B15†
St-Boniface-de-Shawinigan, 3998 J14
St-Bruno, 2892 C16
St-Césaire, 2990 M13
St-Charles-de-Bellechasse, 979 H17
St-Côme-Linière, 1001 K18
St-Cyrille-de-Wendover, 1201 K14
St-Damase, 1362 L13
St-Damien-de-Buckland, 1670 H18
St-Denis, 994 L13
St-Dominique, 2236 L14
St-Donat-de-Montcalm, 1396 J11
Ste-Adèle, 5837 K11
Ste-Agathe-des-Monts, 5669 K11†
Ste-Anne-de-Beaupré, 3023 G17
Ste-Anne-des-Monts, 5617 A6
Ste-Anne-des-Plaines, 12908 L12
Ste-Catherine, 13724 F8
Ste-Claire, 2031 H17
Ste-Croix, 1618 H16
Ste-Foy, 72330 H17
Ste-Hedwidge-de-Roberval, 847 C14
Ste-Jeanne-d'Arc, 1158 B15
Ste-Julie, 24030 L13
Ste-Julienne, 1394 K12
Ste-Justine, 1084 J18
St-Elzéar, 952 J17
Ste-Luce-Lucedale, 1421 B3†
Ste-Madeleine, 1993 L13
Ste-Marie, 10966 J17
St-Émile, 9889 A11
St-Éphrem-de-Tring, 1248 K17
Ste-Thècle, 1526 H14
Ste-Thérèse, 23477 L12
St-Étienne-de-Lauzon, 6919 H16
St-Eustache, 39848 L12
Ste-Véronique, 1088 J9
St-Fabien, 1150 B2†
St-Félicien, 9599 C14
St-Félix-de-Valois, 1530 K13
St-Flavien, 796 J16
St-Gabriel, 2862 J13
St-Gédéon, 1770 K18
St-Georges, 20057 K18
St-Georges, 3929 H14
St-Germain-de-Grantham, 1753 K14
St-Guillaume, 741 K14
St-Henri, 1541 H17
St-Honoré, 2023 C17
St-Hubert, 77042 L13
St-Hyacinthe, 38981 L13
St-Isidore, 833 H17
St-Jacques, 2261 K12
St-Jean-Chrysostome, 16161 D13
St-Jean-de-Dieu, 1177 C2†
St-Jean-Iberville, 81125 M13
St-Jean-Port-Joli, 1961 G18
St-Jérôme, 23916 L11
St-Joseph-de-Beauce, 3240 J17
St-Jovite, 4609 K10
St-Lambert, 20971 D9
St-Laurent, 74240 C6
St-Léonard, 71327 B8
St-Léonard-d'Aston, 979 K15
St-Louis-de-France, 7327 J14
St-Marc-des-Carrières, 2955 H15
St-Martin, 1567 K18
St-Michel-des-Sts, 1631 H12
St-Nicolas, 15594 H16
St-Ours, 1619 K13
St-Pacôme, 1177 F19
St-Pamphile, 2990 G19
St-Pascal, 2504 F19
St-Pie, 2249 L14
St-Pierre, 4739 E7
St-Prime, 2685 C14
St-Prosper, 2467 J18
St-Raphael, 1263 H18
St-Raymond, 8733 H15
St-Rédempteur, 6358 D12
St-Rémi, 5707 M12
St-Romuald, 10604 C13
St-Sauveur-des-Monts, 2904 K11
St-Siméon, 1012 E19
St-Tite, 2555 H14
St-Ulric, 754 B4†
St-Victor, 1253 J17
St-Zotique, 3683 M11
Salaberry-de-Valleyfield, 26600 M11
Salluit, 929 E9*
Sawyerville, 832 M16
Sayabec, 1742 B4†
Senneterre, 3488 C5
Sept-Îles, 25224 A18
Shawinigan, 18678 H14
Shawinigan-Sud, 11804 J14
Shawville, 1632 L6
Sherbrooke, 76786 M15
Sillery, 12003 C12
Sorel, 23248 K13
Squatec, 1390 C2†
Stanstead, 3112 N15
Stukely-Sud, 882 M14
Sutton, 1617 M14
Tadoussac, 913 D19
Témiscaming, 3112 H2
Terrebonne, 42214 L12
Thetford Mines, 17635 K17
Thurso, 2498 L9
Tracy, 12773 K13
Tring-Jonction, 1387 J17
Trois-Pistoles, 3807 D20
Trois-Rivières, 48419 J14
Upton, 1070 L14
Valcourt, 2442 L15
Val-David, 3473 K11
Val-d'Or, 24285 D4
Vallée-Jonction, 1144 J17
Vanier, 11174 B12
Vaudreuil-Dorion, 18466 M11
Verdun, 59714 M12
Victoriaville, 38174 K15
Ville-Marie, 2855 F1
Warwick, 2904 K15
Waterloo, 4040 M14
Waterville, 1332 M15
Weedon Ctr., 1213 L16
Westmount, 20420 D8
Windsor, 4904 L15
Yamachiche, 1314 J14

SASKATCHEWAN

PG. 124–125

CAPITAL
Regina

POPULATION
990,237, rank 6

AREA
251,865 sq mi, rank 7

ENTERED CANADA
1905

Cities and Towns
* City indexed to pg. 121

Air Ronge, 957 C7
Allan, 702 H6
Asquith, 533 G5
Assiniboia, 2653 M6
Balcarres, 661 K9
Balgonie, 1132 K8
Battleford, 3936 F4
Beauval, 785 B5
Bienfait, 826 N10
Biggar, 2351 H4
Big River, 826 E5
Birch Hills, 945 F7
Broadview, 751 L10
Bruno, 648 G7
Buffalo Narrows, 1053 A4
Cabri, 529 K3
Canora, 2208 J10
Carlyle, 1252 M10
Carnduff, 1069 N11
Caronport, 1147 K6
Carrot River, 1032 F9
Churchbridge, 815 K11
Coronach, 949 N6
Creighton, 1713 C11
Cudworth, 752 G6
Cumberland House, 836 E10
Cupar, 592 K8
Cut Knife, 585 F3
Dalmeny, 1470 G5
Davidson, 1105 J6
Delisle, 840 H5
Denare Beach, 776 C11
Deschambault Lake, 695 C9
Duck Lake, 667 F6
Eastend, 616 M3
Elrose, 557 J4
Esterhazy, 2602 K11
Estevan, 10752 N9
Eston, 1119 J3
Foam Lake, 1303 J9
Ft. Qu'Appelle, 1997 K8
Gravelbourg, 1211 L5
Green Lake, 536 D4
Grenfell, 1106 L9
Gull Lake, 1078 L3
Hague, 688 G6
Herbert, 855 K5
Hudson Bay, 1883 F10
Humboldt, 5074 H7
Île-à-la-Crosse, 1403 B4
Indian Head, 1833 K9
Ituna, 743 J9
Kamsack, 2264 J11
Kelvington, 1046 H9
Kerrobert, 1109 H3
Kindersley, 4679 H3
Kinistino, 691 F7
Kipling, 1004 L10
La Loche, 1966 F4*
Lampman, 648 M10
Langenburg, 1119 K11
Langham, 1104 G5
Lanigan, 1368 H7
La Ronge, 2964 C7
Lashburn, 674 F2
Leader, 983 J2
Lloydminster, 7636 E2
Lumsden, 1530 K7
Luseland, 622 G2
Macklin, 1281 G2
Maidstone, 962 F3
Maple Cr., 2307 L2
Marshall, 605 E2
Martensville, 3477 G5
Meadow Lake, 4813 D4
Melfort, 5759 F8
Melville, 4646 K10
Milestone, 540 L8
Moose Jaw, 32973 L6
Moosomin, 2420 L11
Naicam, 789 G8
Nipawin, 4318 F8
N. Battleford, 14051 F4
Osler, 618 G6
Outlook, 2116 J5
Oxbow, 1163 N10
Pense, 534 L7
Pilot Butte, 1469 K8
Pinehouse, 922 B6
Ponteix, 544 L4
Porcupine Plain, 866 G9
Preeceville, 1148 H10
Prince Albert, 34777 F7
Qu'Appelle, 632 K8
Radville, 823 M8
Raymore, 667 J8
Redvers, 965 M11
Regina, 180400 K8
Regina Beach, 984 K7
Rocanville, 875 L11
Rosetown, 2496 H4
Rosthern, 1564 G6
St. Walburg, 685 E3
Saltcoats, 531 K10
Saskatoon, 193647 H5
Shaunavon, 1857 M3
Shellbrook, 1234 F6
Southey, 679 K8
Spiritwood, 924 E5
Springside, 542 J10
Stoughton, 726 M9
Strasbourg, 760 J7
Sturgis, 684 H10
Swift Current, 14890 L4
Tisdale, 2966 F8
Unity, 2200 G3
Wadena, 1477 H9
Wakaw, 869 G7
Waldheim, 841 G6
Warman, 2839 G6
Watrous, 1860 H7
Watson, 837 H8
Wawota, 620 L11
Weyburn, 9723 M8
White City, 905 L8
Whitewood, 985 L10
Wilkie, 1364 G3
Wolseley, 821 L9
Wynyard, 1954 H8
Yorkton, 15154 J10

YUKON TERRITORY

PG. 121

CAPITAL
Whitehorse

POPULATION
30,766, rank 12

AREA
186,660 sq mi, rank 9

ENTERED CANADA
1898

Cities and Towns
Carmacks, 466 C2
Dawson, 1287 C2
Faro, 1261 D2
Haines Jct., 574 D1
Mayo, 324 C2
Ross River, 352 D2
Watson Lake, 993 D2
Whitehorse, 19157 D2

Mexico

MEXICO

PG. 132–133

CAPITAL
Mexico City

POPULATION
95,772,462

AREA
756,066 sq mi

Cities and Towns
Acámbaro, 54523 K11
Acapulco, 592528 M12
Acayucan, 49256 L15
Actopan, 24097 K12
Agua Dulce, 39921 L15
Agua Prieta, 54681 B5
Aguascalientes, 537523 H10
Ajalpan, 19212 L13
Álamo, 23281 J13
Altamira, 34523 H13
Alvarado, 23776 L14
Apan, 23625 K13
Apatzingán, 89834 K10
Apizaco, 50593 K13
Apodaca, 212118 F11
Arriaga, 23617 M16
Atlixco, 79556 L13
Atoyac, 19154 M11
Autlán, 36267 K8
Cabo San Lucas, 28483 H5
Caborca, 47032 B4
Campeche, 178160 K18
Cananea, 27614 B5
Cancún, 297183 J20
Cárdenas, 72739 L16
Castaños, 19035 E11
Catemaco, 22965 L15
Celaya, 251724 J11
Cerro Azul, 23573 J13
Chalco, 96978 N5
Champotón, 21894 K18
Chetumal, 115152 L19
Chiapa, 27654 M16
Chihuahua, 613722 D8
Chilpancingo, 123475 M12
Chimalhuacán, 410031 L5
Cholula, 62259 K13
Cintalapa, 32069 M16
Ciudad Acuña, 79221 C11
Ciudad Altamirano, 21936 L11
Ciudad Camargo, 37400 D8
Ciudad Constitución, 35447 F4
Ciudad del Carmen, 114360 L17
Ciudad Guzmán, 81720 K9
Ciudad Hidalgo, 55225 K11
Ciudad Ixtepec, 21127 M15
Ciudad Juárez, 995770 B7
Ciudad Lerdo, 54570 F9
Ciudad Madero, 171091 H13
Ciudad Mante, 81128 H12
Ciudad Mendoza, 34303 L13
Ciudad Obregón, 244028 D5
Ciudad Valles, 102226 H12
Ciudad Victoria, 230304 G12
Coacalco, 202778 J3
Coatepec, 42462 K14
Coatzacoalcos, 222027 L15
Colima, 110977 K9
Comalcalco, 34850 L16
Comitán, 62292 M17
Comonfort, 20088 J11
Córdoba, 132091 L14
Cosamaloapan, 28520 L14
Cosoleacaque, 19674 L15
Costa Rica, 21452 G7
Cozumel, 47841 J20
Cuauhtémoc, 80428 D7
Cuautla, 128781 L12
Cuernavaca, 311095 L12
Culiacán, 505518 F7
Delicias, 94001 D8
Dolores Hidalgo, 45888 J11
Durango, 397687 G8
Ébano, 22777 H13
Ecatepec de Morelos, 1455909 J4
Empalme, 38519 D5
Ensenada, 192550 A1
Escárcega, 25209 L18
Escuinapa, 27679 H8
Francisco I. Madero, 26201 F9
Fresnillo, 89338 H9
Frontera, 60434 E11
Garza García, 120868 F11
General Escobedo, 174486 B18
Gómez Palacio, 192888 F9
Guadalajara, 1633053 J9
Guadalupe, 618610 F11
Guadalupe, 65726 H10
Guamúchil, 56091 F6
Guanajuato, 69970 J11
Guasave, 57581 F6
Guaymas, 90964 D5
Hermosillo, 504009 C5
Hidalgo del Parral, 96267 E8
Huajuapan de León, 38828 L13
Huatabampo, 29313 E5
Huatusco, 24424 K14
Huauchinango, 43613 K13
Huejutla, 30316 J13
Huetamo, 21507 L11
Huimanguillo, 23507 L16
Huixtla, 28356 N17
Hunucmá, 19868 J18
Iguala, 98276 L12
Irapuato, 299604 J11
Ixmiquilpan, 29097 J12
Ixtapaluca, 153138 M5
Ixtlán, 21474 J8
Jacona, 49047 K10
Jalostotitlán, 20201 J10
Jáltipan, 32698 L15
Jerez de García Salinas, 36642 H9
Jiménez, 31517 E8
Jiutepec, 125148 L12
Juchitán, 62065 M15
Kanasín, 31757 J18
La Barca, 30194 K10
La Paz, 154314 G5
La Piedad de Cabadas, 72041 K10
Lagos de Moreno, 75220 J10
Las Choapas, 42132 L15
Lázaro Cárdenas, 63723 L10
León, 941626 J10
Linares, 49921 F12
Loma Bonita, 30826 L14
Morelia, 512169 K11
Moroleón, 40614 K11
Múzquiz, 31071 D10
Naranjos, 19633 J13
Naucalpan, 822358 K2
Navojoa, 94837 E5
Navolato, 24340 F6
Progreso, 40005 J18
Puebla, 1157625 K13
Puerto Peñasco, 26810 B3
Puerto Vallarta, 121844 J8
Puruándiro, 26493 K10
Querétaro, 469542 J11
Reynosa, 320458 E13
San Juan de los Lagos, 39331 J10
San Juan del Río, 84532 K12
San Luis de la Paz, 38287 J11
San Luis Potosí, 586585 H11
Tecomán, 68847 L9
Tehuacán, 172510 L13
Tehuantepec, 36888 M15
Teloloapan, 19355 L12
Tenancingo, 25195 L12
Tenosique, 29134 L17
Teocaltiche, 20648 J10
Tepatitlán, 65930 J10
Tepic, 254551 J8
Tequila, 21611 J9
Tequisquiapan, 24039 J12
Texcoco, 89524 K5
Teziutlán, 50415 K13
Ticul, 26882 J18
Tierra Blanca, 43927 L14
Tijuana, 966097 A1
[illegible], 27855 K12
[illegible]n, 38328 J19
[illegible]c, 214341 M4
[illegible]pantla, 708013 K12
[illegible]pantla, 708013 K2
[illegible], 26409 M13
[illegible]oyan, 29799 K13
[illegible]paque, 434710 J9
[illegible]la, 63335 K13
[illegible], 368384 K12
[illegible], 250058 J9
[illegible], 29557 M16
[illegible]n, 481493 F9
[illegible]alles, 18078 L14
[illegible]ingo, 87458 K13
[illegible], 74692 J13
Tuxpan, 26219 K9
Tuxpan, 22481 H8
Tuxtepec, 77467 L14
Tuxtla Gutiérrez, 378079 M16
Umán, 24989 J18
Uruapan, 215449 K10
Valladolid, 34857 J19
Valle de Santiago, 56517 K11
Valle Hermoso, 39020 F13
Veracruz, 381190 K14
Victor Rosales, 21420 H10
Villa Flores, 28257 M16
Villahermosa, 301238 L16
Xalapa, 324081 K14
Xicotepec de Juárez, [illegible] K13
Xochimilco, 323659 N3
Zacapu, 48307 K10
Zacatecas, 109109 H10
Zacatlán, 26109 K13
Zamora de Hidalgo, 121181 K10
Zapopan, 850315 J9
Zapotiltic, 22002 K9
Zapotlanejo, 25196 [illegible]
Zihuatanejo, 54537 L10
Zitácuaro, 74824 K11
Zumpango, 36123 K12
Zumpango del Río, 18158 L12

Puerto Rico

PUERTO RICO

PG. 134

CAPITAL
San Juan

POPULATION
3,808,610

AREA
3,435 sq mi

Cities and Towns
Adjuntas, 4980 B2
Aguada, 3871 A1
Aguadilla, 16776 A1
Aguas Buenas, 4368 B4
Aguilita, 4922 B3
Aibonito, 9269 B4
Anasco, 5880 B1
Arecibo, 49318 A2
Arroyo, 7244 C4
Bajadero, 3877 A2
Barceloneta, 4253 A3
Bayamón, 203499 A4
Cabo Rojo, 10610 B1
Caguas, 88680 B4
Campo Rico, 3218 B5
Camuy, 4013 A2
Canóvanas, 8069 A4
Carolina, 168164 A4
Cataño, 30071 A4
Cayey, 19940 B4
Ceiba, 6277 B5
Ceiba, 3698 A3
Ciales, 3082 B3
Cidra, 4881 B4
Coamo, 12356 B3
Coco, 5803 C4
Comerio, 4478 B4
Coquí, 3590 C4
Corozal, 11444 B3
Dorado, 12747 A4
Fajardo, 33286 B5
Florida, 5652 B3
Guánica, 9247 C2
Guayama, 21624 C4
Guayanilla, 5110 B2
Guaynabo, 78806 B4
Gurabo, 9046 B4
Hatillo, 5321 A2
Hormigueros, 12444 B1
Humacao, 20682 B5
Isabela, 12818 A1
Jayuya, 3516 B3
Jobos, 3475 C4
Juana Díaz, 9505 B3
Juncos, 8978 B4
Lajas, 5036 B1
Lares, 7042 B2
Las Piedras, 6352 B5
Levittown, 30140 A4
Loíza, 4123 A5
Luquillo, 7947 B5
Manatí, 16173 A3
Mayagüez, 78647 B1
Moca, 4757 A1
Naguabo, 4432 B5
Patillas, 4091 C4
Peñuelas, 6712 B2
Ponce, 155038 C3
Potala Pastillo, 3819 C3
Puerto Real, 6166 B1
Punta Santiago, 5803 B5
Quebradillas, 5319 A2
Rio Grande, 13467 A5
Sabana Grande, 8784 B2
Salinas, 6141 C3
San Antonio, 6456 A3
San Germán, 12033 B1
San Isidro, 8071 A5
San Juan, 421958 A4
San Lorenzo, 8947 B4
San Sebastián, 11598 B2
Santa Isabel, 6993 C3
Santo Domingo, 3633 B2
Toa Alta, 4368 A4
Trujillo Alto, 50841 B4
Utuado, 9887 B2
Vega Alta, 11755 A3
Vega Baja, 28811 A3
Villalba, 4388 B3
Yabucoa, 6636 B5
Yauco, 19609 B2

Distances in chart are in miles. To convert miles to kilometers, multiply the distance in miles by 1.609

Example: New York, NY to Boston, MA = 215 miles or 346 kilometers (215 x 1.609)

	ALBANY, NY	ALBUQUERQUE, NM	AMARILLO, TX	ATLANTA, GA	BALTIMORE, MD	BILLINGS, MT	BIRMINGHAM, AL	BISMARCK, ND	BOISE, ID	BOSTON, MA	BUFFALO, NY	BURLINGTON, VT	CHARLESTON, SC	CHARLESTON, WV	CHARLOTTE, NC	CHEYENNE, WY	CHICAGO, IL	CINCINNATI, OH	CLEVELAND, OH	COLUMBUS, OH	DALLAS, TX	DENVER, CO	DES MOINES, IA	DETROIT, MI	EL PASO, TX	HARTFORD, CT	HOUSTON, TX	INDIANAPOLIS, IN	JACKSON, MS	JACKSONVILLE, FL	KANSAS CITY, MO	LAS VEGAS, NV	LITTLE ROCK, AR	LOS ANGELES, CA	LOUISVILLE, KY	MEMPHIS, TN	MIAMI, FL	MILWAUKEE, WI	MINNEAPOLIS, MN	MOBILE, AL	MONTRÉAL, QC	NASHVILLE, TN	NEW ORLEANS, LA	NEW YORK, NY	NORFOLK, VA	OKLAHOMA CITY, OK	OMAHA, NE	ORLANDO, FL	PHILADELPHIA, PA	PHOENIX, AZ	PITTSBURGH, PA	PORTLAND, ME	PORTLAND, OR	RALEIGH, NC	RAPID CITY, SD	RENO, NV	RICHMOND, VA	ST. LOUIS, MO	SALT LAKE CITY, UT	SAN ANTONIO, TX	SAN DIEGO, CA	SAN FRANCISCO, CA	SEATTLE, WA	TAMPA, FL	TORONTO, ON	VANCOUVER, BC	WASHINGTON,DC	WICHITA, KS
ALBANY, NY		2095	1811	1010	333	2083	1093	1675	2526	172	292	147	913	634	771	1789	832	730	484	621	1680	1833	1155	571	2326	111	1768	795	1331	1094	1282	2586	1354	2859	832	1214	1439	929	1245	1344	230	1003	1440	151	570	1549	1292	1235	223	2561	485	270	2954	639	1750	2747	482	1036	2224	1953	2919	2964	2899	1290	400	3032	369	1471
ALBUQUERQUE, NM	2095		286	1490	1902	991	1274	1333	966	2240	1808	2178	1793	1568	1649	538	1352	1409	1619	1476	754	438	1091	1608	263	2139	994	1298	1157	1837	894	578	900	806	1320	1033	2155	1426	1339	1344	2172	1248	1276	2015	1970	546	973	1934	1954	466	1670	2338	1395	1782	841	1020	1876	1051	624	818	825	1111	1463	1949	1841	1597	1896	707
AMARILLO, TX	1811	286		1206	1618	988	991	1398	1266	1957	1524	1894	1510	1285	1365	534	1069	1126	1335	1192	470	434	808	1324	438	1855	711	1014	874	1517	610	864	617	1092	1036	750	1834	1142	1055	1106	1888	965	993	1731	1686	262	726	1613	1671	753	1386	2054	1695	1499	837	1306	1593	767	964	513	1111	1397	1763	1628	1557	1897	1612	423
ATLANTA, GA	1010	1490	1206		679	1889	150	1559	2218	1100	910	1158	317	503	238	1482	717	476	726	577	792	1403	967	735	1437	998	800	531	386	344	801	2067	528	2237	419	389	661	813	1129	332	1241	242	473	869	558	944	989	440	782	1868	676	1197	2647	396	1511	2440	527	549	1916	1000	2166	2618	2705	455	958	2838	636	989
BALTIMORE, MD	333	1902	1618	679		1959	795	1551	2401	422	370	481	583	352	441	1665	708	521	377	420	1399	1690	1031	532	2045	321	1470	600	1032	763	1087	2445	1072	2705	602	933	1109	805	1121	1013	564	716	1142	192	239	1354	1168	904	104	2366	246	520	2830	309	1626	2623	152	841	2100	1671	2724	2840	2775	960	565	2908	38	1276
BILLINGS, MT	2083	991	988	1889	1959		1839	413	626	2254	1796	2181	2157	1755	2012	455	1246	1552	1597	1608	1433	554	1007	1534	1255	2153	1673	1432	1836	2237	1088	965	1530	1239	1547	1625	2554	1175	839	2019	2093	1648	1955	2049	2141	1227	904	2333	2019	1199	1719	2352	889	2110	379	960	2053	1341	548	1500	1302	1176	816	2348	1762	949	1953	1067
BIRMINGHAM, AL	1093	1274	991	150	795	1839		1509	2170	1215	909	1241	466	578	389	1434	667	475	725	576	647	1356	919	734	1292	1114	678	481	241	494	753	1852	381	2092	369	241	812	763	1079	258	1289	194	351	985	708	729	941	591	897	1723	763	1313	2599	547	1463	2392	678	501	1868	878	2021	2472	2657	606	958	2791	758	838
BISMARCK, ND	1675	1333	1398	1559	1551	413	1509		1039	1846	1388	1773	1749	1347	1604	594	838	1144	1189	1200	1342	693	675	1126	1597	1745	1582	1024	1548	1906	801	1378	1183	1702	1139	1337	2224	767	431	1765	1685	1315	1734	1641	1733	1136	616	2003	1611	1662	1311	1944	1301	1702	320	1372	1645	1053	960	1599	1765	1749	1229	2018	1354	1362	1545	934
BOISE, ID	2526	966	1266	2218	2401	626	2170	1039		2697	2239	2624	2520	2182	2375	737	1708	1969	2040	2036	1711	833	1369	1977	1206	2595	1952	1852	2115	2566	1376	760	1808	1033	1933	1954	2883	1748	1465	2302	2535	1976	2234	2491	2584	1506	1234	2662	2462	993	2161	2795	432	2495	930	430	2496	1628	342	1761	1096	646	500	2677	2204	633	2395	1346
BOSTON, MA	172	2240	1957	1100	422	2254	1215	1846	2697		462	214	1003	741	861	1961	1003	862	654	760	1819	2004	1326	741	2465	102	1890	940	1453	1184	1427	2757	1493	3046	964	1353	1529	1100	1417	1433	313	1136	1563	215	660	1694	1463	1324	321	2706	592	107	3126	729	1921	2919	572	1181	2395	2092	3065	3135	3070	1380	570	3204	458	1616
BUFFALO, NY	292	1808	1524	910	370	1796	909	1388	2239	462		375	899	431	695	1502	545	442	197	333	1393	1546	868	277	2039	401	1513	508	1134	1080	995	2299	1066	2572	545	927	1425	642	958	1165	397	716	1254	400	573	1262	1005	1221	414	2274	217	560	2667	642	1463	2460	485	749	1936	1665	2632	2677	2612	1276	106	2745	384	1184
BURLINGTON, VT	147	2178	1894	1158	481	2181	1241	1773	2624	214	375		1061	782	919	1887	930	817	567	704	1763	1931	1253	652	2409	231	1916	878	1479	1242	1366	2684	1437	2957	915	1297	1587	1027	1343	1492	92	1086	1588	299	718	1632	1390	1383	371	2644	587	233	3052	787	1848	2845	630	1119	2322	2036	3020	3062	2997	1438	419	3130	517	1554
CHARLESTON, SC	913	1793	1510	317	583	2157	466	1749	2520	1003	899	1061		468	204	1783	907	622	724	637	1109	1705	1204	879	1754	901	1110	721	703	238	1102	2371	900	2554	610	760	583	1003	1319	642	1145	543	783	773	437	1248	1290	379	685	2184	642	1101	2948	279	1824	2741	428	850	2218	1310	2483	2934	2973	434	1006	3106	539	1291
CHARLESTON, WV	634	1568	1285	503	352	1755	578	1347	2182	741	431	782	468		265	1445	506	209	255	168	1072	1367	802	410	1718	639	1192	320	816	649	764	2122	745	2374	251	606	994	601	918	837	822	395	926	515	415	1022	952	790	454	2035	217	839	2610	313	1422	2403	322	512	1880	1344	2393	2620	2571	845	537	2705	346	953
CHARLOTTE, NC	771	1649	1365	238	441	2012	389	1604	2375	861	695	919	204	265		1637	761	476	520	433	1031	1559	1057	675	1677	760	1041	575	625	385	956	2225	754	2453	464	614	730	857	1173	572	1003	397	713	631	319	1102	1144	525	543	2107	438	959	2802	158	1678	2595	289	704	2072	1241	2405	2759	2827	581	802	2960	397	1145
CHEYENNE, WY	1789	538	534	1482	1665	455	1434	594	737	1961	1502	1887	1783	1445	1637		972	1233	1304	1300	979	100	633	1241	801	1859	1220	1115	1382	1829	640	843	1076	1116	1197	1217	2147	1012	881	1570	1799	1240	1502	1755	1847	773	497	1926	1725	1004	1425	2059	1166	1758	305	959	1760	892	436	1046	1179	1176	1234	1941	1468	1368	1659	613
CHICAGO, IL	832	1352	1069	717	708	1246	667	838	1708	1003	545	930	907	506	761	972		302	346	359	936	1015	337	283	1543	901	1108	184	750	1065	532	1768	662	2042	299	539	1382	89	409	923	841	474	935	797	890	807	474	1161	768	1819	467	1101	2137	861	913	1930	802	294	1406	1270	2105	2146	2062	1176	510	2196	701	728
CINCINNATI, OH	730	1409	1126	476	521	1552	475	1144	1969	862	442	817	622	209	476	1233	302		253	105	958	1200	599	261	1605	760	1079	116	700	803	597	1955	632	2215	106	493	1141	398	714	731	815	281	820	636	624	863	736	920	576	1876	292	960	2398	522	1219	2191	530	350	1667	1231	2234	2407	2368	935	484	2501	517	785
CLEVELAND, OH	484	1619	1335	726	377	1597	725	1189	2040	654	197	567	724	255	520	1304	346	253		144	1208	1347	669	171	1854	570	1328	319	950	904	806	2100	882	2374	356	742	1250	443	760	981	588	531	1070	466	559	1073	806	1045	437	2085	136	751	2469	568	1264	2262	471	560	1738	1481	2437	2478	2413	1101	303	2547	370	995
COLUMBUS, OH	621	1476	1192	577	420	1608	576	1200	2036	760	333	704	637	168	433	1300	359	105	144		1059	1266	665	192	1706	659	1179	176	801	818	663	2021	733	2281	207	594	1163	454	771	832	725	382	921	535	604	930	802	958	474	1942	190	858	2464	482	1275	2257	517	417	1734	1332	2300	2474	2424	1036	440	2558	416	852
DALLAS, TX	1680	754	470	792	1399	1433	647	1342	1711	1819	1393	1763	1109	1072	1031	979	936	958	1208	1059		887	752	1218	647	1717	241	913	406	1049	554	1331	327	1446	852	466	1367	1010	999	639	1772	681	525	1589	1350	209	669	1146	1501	1077	1246	1917	2140	1189	1077	1933	1309	635	1410	271	1375	1827	2208	1161	1441	2342	1362	367
DENVER, CO	1833	438	434	1403	1690	554	1356	693	833	2004	1546	1931	1705	1367	1559	100	1015	1200	1347	1266	887		676	1284	701	1903	1127	1088	1290	1751	603	756	984	1029	1118	1116	2069	1055	924	1478	1843	1162	1409	1799	1782	681	541	1847	1744	904	1460	2102	1261	1680	404	1054	1688	855	531	946	1092	1271	1329	1862	1512	1463	1686	521
DES MOINES, IA	1155	1091	808	967	1031	1007	919	675	1369	1326	868	1253	1204	802	1057	633	337	599	669	665	752	676		606	1283	1225	992	481	931	1315	194	1429	567	1703	595	720	1632	378	246	1115	1165	725	1117	1121	1213	546	136	1411	1091	1558	791	1424	1798	1157	629	1591	1126	436	1067	1009	1766	1807	1822	1426	834	1956	1025	390
DETROIT, MI	571	1608	1324	735	532	1534	734	1126	1977	741	277	652	879	410	675	1241	283	261	171	192	1218	1284	606		1799	679	1338	318	960	1060	795	2037	891	2310	366	752	1401	380	697	991	564	541	1079	622	714	1062	743	1180	592	2074	292	838	2405	724	1201	2198	627	549	1675	1490	2373	2415	2350	1194	233	2483	526	984
EL PASO, TX	2326	263	438	1437	2045	1255	1292	1597	1206	2465	2039	2409	1754	1718	1677	801	1543	1605	1854	1706	647	701	1283	1799		2364	758	1489	1051	1642	1085	717	974	801	1499	1112	1959	1617	1530	1231	2363	1328	1118	2235	1996	737	1236	1738	2147	432	1893	2563	1767	1834	1105	1315	1955	1242	864	556	730	1181	1944	1753	2032	2087	2008	898
HARTFORD, CT	111	2139	1855	998	321	2153	1114	1745	2595	102	401	231	901	639	760	1859	901	760	570	659	1717	1903	1225	679	2364		1788	839	1351	1082	1326	2655	1391	2944	862	1251	1427	999	1315	1332	338	1034	1461	115	558	1593	1362	1223	219	2605	491	199	3024	627	1820	2817	471	1080	2293	1990	2963	3034	2969	1278	509	3102	357	1515
HOUSTON, TX	1768	994	711	800	1470	1673	678	1582	1952	1890	1513	1916	1110	1192	1041	1220	1108	1079	1328	1179	241	1127	992	1338	758	1788		1033	445	884	795	1474	447	1558	972	586	1201	1193	1240	473	1892	801	360	1660	1360	449	910	980	1572	1188	1366	1988	2381	1198	1318	2072	1330	863	1650	200	1487	1938	2449	995	1561	2583	1433	608
INDIANAPOLIS, IN	795	1298	1014	531	600	1432	481	1024	1852	940	508	878	721	320	575	1115	184	116	319	176	913	1088	481	318	1489	839	1033		675	879	485	1843	587	2104	112	464	1196	279	596	737	872	287	826	715	735	752	618	975	655	1764	370	1038	2280	639	1101	2073	641	239	1549	1186	2122	2290	2249	990	541	2383	596	674
JACKSON, MS	1331	1157	874	386	1032	1836	241	1548	2115	1453	1134	1479	703	816	625	1382	750	700	950	801	406	1290	931	960	1051	1351	445	675		598	747	1735	269	1851	594	211	915	835	1151	187	1514	423	185	1223	944	612	935	694	1135	1482	988	1550	2544	783	1458	2337	914	505	1813	644	1780	2232	2612	709	1183	2746	996	771
JACKSONVILLE, FL	1094	1837	1517	344	763	2237	494	1906	2566	1184	1080	1242	238	649	385	1829	1065	803	904	818	1049	1751	1315	1060	1642	1082	884	879	598		1148	2415	873	2441	766	733	345	1160	1477	410	1325	589	556	953	617	1291	1336	141	866	2072	822	1281	2994	460	1859	2787	609	896	2264	1084	2370	2822	3052	196	1187	3186	720	1337
KANSAS CITY, MO	1282	894	610	801	1087	1088	753	801	1376	1427	995	1366	1102	764	956	640	532	597	806	663	554	603	194	795	1085	1326	795	485	747	1148		1358	382	1632	516	536	1466	573	441	930	1359	559	932	1202	1179	348	188	1245	1141	1360	857	1525	1805	1077	710	1598	1085	252	1074	812	1695	1814	1872	1259	1028	2007	1083	192
LAS VEGAS, NV	2586	578	864	2067	2445	965	1852	1378	760	2757	2299	2684	2371	2122	2225	843	1768	1955	2100	2021	1331	756	1429	2037	717	2655	1474	1843	1735	2415	1358		1478	274	1874	1611	2733	1808	1677	1922	2596	1826	1854	2552	2537	1124	1294	2512	2500	285	2215	2855	1188	2360	1035	442	2444	1610	417	1272	337	575	1256	2526	2265	1390	2441	1276
LITTLE ROCK, AR	1354	900	617	528	1072	1530	381	1183	1808	1493	1066	1437	900	745	754	1076	662	632	882	733	327	984	567	891	974	1391	447	587	269	873	382	1478		1706	526	140	1190	747	814	457	1446	355	455	1262	1076	355	570	969	1175	1367	920	1590	2237	889	1093	2030	983	416	1507	600	1703	2012	2305	984	1115	2439	1036	464
LOS ANGELES, CA	2859	806	1092	2237	2705	1239	2092	1702	1033	3046	2572	2957	2554	2374	2453	1116	2042	2215	2374	2281	1446	1029	1703	2310	801	2944	1558	2104	1851	2441	1632	274	1706		2126	1839	2759	2082	1951	2031	2869	2054	1917	2820	2776	1352	1567	2538	2760	369	2476	3144	971	2588	1309	519	2682	1856	691	1356	124	385	1148	2553	2538	1291	2702	1513
LOUISVILLE, KY	832	1320	1036	419	602	1547	369	1139	1933	964	545	915	610	251	464	1197	299	106	356	207	852	1118	595	366	1499	862	972	112	594	766	516	1874	526	2126		386	1084	394	711	625	920	175	714	739	666	774	704	863	678	1786	394	1062	2362	564	1215	2155	572	264	1631	1125	2144	2372	2364	878	589	2497	596	705
MEMPHIS, TN	1214	1033	750	389	933	1625	241	1337	1954	1353	927	1297	760	606	614	1217	539	493	742	594	466	1116	720	752	1112	1251	586	464	211	733	536	1611	140	1839	386		1051	624	940	395	1306	215	396	1123	937	487	724	830	1035	1500	780	1451	2382	749	1247	2175	843	294	1652	739	1841	2144	2440	845	975	2574	896	597
MIAMI, FL	1439	2155	1834	661	1109	2554	812	2224	2883	1529	1425	1587	583	994	730	2147	1382	1141	1250	1163	1367	2069	1632	1401	1959	1427	1201	1196	915	345	1466	2733	1190	2759	1084	1051		1478	1794	727	1671	907	874	1299	962	1609	1654	232	1211	2390	1167	1627	3312	805	2176	3105	954	1214	2581	1401	2688	3140	3370	274	1532	3504	1065	1655
MILWAUKEE, WI	929	1426	1142	813	805	1175	763	767	1748	1100	642	1027	1003	601	857	1012	89	398	443	454	1010	1055	378	380	1617	999	1193	279	835	1160	573	1808	747	2082	394	624	1478		337	1019	939	569	1020	894	987	880	514	1257	865	1892	564	1198	2063	956	842	1970	899	367	1446	1343	2145	2186	1991	1272	607	2124	799	769
MINNEAPOLIS, MN	1245	1339	1055	1129	1121	839	1079	431	1465	1417	958	1343	1319	918	1173	881	409	714	760	771	999	924	246	697	1530	1315	1240	596	1151	1477	441	1677	814	1951	711	940	1794	337		1335	1255	886	1337	1211	1303	793	383	1573	1181	1805	881	1515	1727	1273	606	1839	1216	621	1315	1257	2014	2055	1654	1588	924	1788	1115	637
MOBILE, AL	1344	1344	1106	332	1013	2019	258	1765	2302	1433	1165	1492	642	837	572	1570	923	731	981	832	639	1478	1115	991	1231	1332	473	737	187	410	930	1922	457	2031	625	395	727	1019	1335		1575	450	146	1203	891	799	1119	506	1115	1662	1019	1531	2731	730	1641	2545	861	688	2000	673	1960	2411	2799	521	1214	2933	970	958
MONTRÉAL, QC	230	2172	1888	1241	564	2093	1289	1685	2535	313	397	92	1145	822	1003	1799	841	815	588	725	1772	1843	1165	564	2363	338	1892	872	1514	1325	1359	2596	1446	2869	920	1306	1671	939	1255	1575		1094	1632	383	801	1625	1300	1466	454	2637	607	282	2963	871	1758	2756	714	1112	2232	2043	2931	2972	2907	1522	330	3041	600	1547
NASHVILLE, TN	1003	1248	965	242	716	1648	194	1315	1976	1136	716	1086	543	395	397	1240	474	281	531	382	681	1162	725	541	1328	1034	801	287	423	589	559	1826	355	2054	175	215	907	569	886	450	1094		539	906	720	703	747	686	818	1715	569	1234	2405	532	1269	2198	626	307	1675	954	2056	2360	2463	701	764	2597	679	748
NEW ORLEANS, LA	1440	1276	993	473	1142	1955	351	1734	2234	1563	1254	1588	783	926	713	1502	935	820	1070	921	525	1409	1117	1079	1118	1461	360	826	185	556	932	1854	455	1917	714	396	874	1020	1337	146	1632	539		1332	1032	731	1121	653	1245	1548	1108	1660	2663	871	1643	2431	1002	690	1932	560	1846	2298	2731	668	1302	2865	1106	890
NEW YORK, NY	151	2015	1731	869	192	2049	985	1641	2491	215	400	299	773	515	631	1755	797	636	466	535	1589	1799	1121	622	2235	115	1660	715	1223	953	1202	2552	1262	2820	739	1123	1299	894	1211	1203	383	906	1332		430	1469	1258	1094	91	2481	367	313	2920	499	1716	2713	342	956	2189	1861	2839	2929	2864	1150	507	2998	228	1391
NORFOLK, VA	570	1970	1686	558	239	2141	708	1733	2584	660	573	718	437	415	319	1847	890	624	559	604	1350	1782	1213	714	1996	558	1360	735	944	617	1179	2537	1076	2776	666	937	962	987	1303	891	801	720	1032	430		1424	1350	758	342	2436	428	757	3012	179	1808	2805	91	927	2282	1560	2725	3022	2957	814	747	3090	196	1368
OKLAHOMA CITY, OK	1549	546	262	944	1354	1227	729	1136	1506	1694	1262	1632	1248	1022	1102	773	807	863	1073	930	209	681	546	1062	737	1593	449	752	612	1291	348	1124	355	1352	774	487	1609	880	793	799	1625	703	731	1469	1424		463	1388	1408	1012	1124	1792	1934	1237	871	1727	1331	505	1204	466	1370	1657	2002	1403	1295	2136	1350	161
OMAHA, NE	1292	973	726	989	1168	904	941	616	1234	1463	1005	1390	1290	952	1144	497	474	736	806	802	669	541	136	743	1236	1362	910	618	935	1336	188	1294	570	1567	704	724	1654	514	383	1119	1300	747	1121	1258	1350	463		1433	1228	1440	928	1561	1662	1265	525	1455	1263	440	932	927	1630	1672	1719	1448	971	1853	1162	307
ORLANDO, FL	1235	1934	1613	440	904	2333	591	2003	2662	1324	1221	1383	379	790	525	1926	1161	920	1045	958	1146	1847	1411	1180	1738	1223	980	975	694	141	1245	2512	969	2538	863	830	232	1257	1573	506	1466	686	653	1094	758	1388	1433		1006	2169	963	1422	3091	601	1955	2884	750	993	2360	1180	2467	2918	3149	82	1327	3283	860	1434
PHILADELPHIA, PA	223	1954	1671	782	104	2019	897	1611	2462	321	414	371	685	454	543	1725	768	576	437	474	1501	1744	1091	592	2147	219	1572	655	1135	866	1141	2500	1175	2760	678	1035	1211	865	1181	1115	454	818	1245	91	342	1408	1228	1006		2420	306	419	2890	411	1686	2683	254	895	2160	1774	2779	2900	2835	1062	522	2968	140	1330
PHOENIX, AZ	2561	466	753	1868	2366	1199	1723	1662	993	2706	2274	2644	2184	2035	2107	1004	1819	1876	2085	1942	1077	904	1558	2074	432	2605	1188	1764	1482	2072	1360	285	1367	369	1786	1500	2390	1892	1805	1662	2637	1715	1548	2481	2436	1012	1440	2169	2420		2136	2804	1335	2249	1308	883	2343	1517	651	987	358	750	1513	2184	2307	1655	2362	1173
PITTSBURGH, PA	485	1670	1386	676	246	1719	763	1311	2161	592	217	587	642	217	438	1425	467	292	136	190	1246	1460	791	292	1893	491	1366	370	988	822	857	2215	920	2476	394	780	1167	564	881	1019	607	569	1108	367	428	1124	928	963	306	2136		690	2590	497	1386	2383	341	611	1859	1519	2494	2599	2534	1019	321	2668	240	1046
PORTLAND, ME	270	2338	2054	1197	520	2352	1313	1944	2795	107	560	233	1101	839	959	2059	1101	960	751	858	1917	2102	1424	838	2563	199	1988	1038	1550	1281	1525	2855	1590	3144	1062	1451	1627	1198	1515	1531	282	1234	1660	313	757	1792	1561	1422	419	2804	690		3223	827	2019	3016	670	1279	2493	2189	3162	3233	3168	1478	668	3301	556	1714
PORTLAND, OR	2954	1395	1695	2647	2830	889	2599	1301	432	3126	2667	3052	2948	2610	2802	1166	2137	2398	2469	2464	2140	1261	1798	2405	1767	3024	2381	2280	2544	2994	1805	1188	2237	971	2362	2382	3312	2063	1727	2731	2963	2405	2663	2920	3012	1934	1662	3091	2890	1335	2590	3223		2923	1268	578	2925	2057	771	2322	1093	638	170	3106	2633	313	2824	1775
RALEIGH, NC	639	1782	1499	396	309	2110	547	1702	2495	729	642	787	279	313	158	1758	861	522	568	482	1189	1680	1157	724	1834	627	1198	639	783	460	1077	2360	889	2588	564	749	805	956	1273	730	871	532	871	499	179	1237	1265	601	411	2249	497	827	2923		1777	2716	157	825	2193	1398	2563	2894	2926	656	820	3060	265	1266
RAPID CITY, SD	1750	841	837	1511	1626	379	1463	320	930	1921	1463	1848	1824	1422	1678	305	913	1219	1264	1275	1077	404	629	1201	1105	1820	1318	1101	1458	1859	710	1035	1093	1309	1215	1247	2176	842	606	1641	1758	1269	1643	1716	1808	871	525	1955	1686	1308	1386	2019	1268	1777		1151	1720	963	628	1335	1372	1368	1195	1970	1429	1328	1620	712
RENO, NV	2747	1020	1306	2440	2623	960	2392	1372	430	2919	2460	2845	2741	2403	2595	959	1930	2191	2262	2257	1933	1054	1591	2198	1315	2817	2072	2073	2337	2787	1598	442	2030	519	2155	2175	3105	1970	1839	2545	2756	2198	2431	2713	2805	1727	1455	2884	2683	883	2383	3016	578	2716	1151		2718	1850	524	1870	642	217	755	2899	2426	898	2617	1568
RICHMOND, VA	482	1876	1593	527	152	2053	678	1645	2496	572	485	630	428	322	289	1760	802	530	471	517	1309	1688	1126	627	1955	471	1330	641	914	609	1085	2444	983	2682	572	843	954	899	1216	861	714	626	1002	342	91	1331	1263	750	254	2343	341	670	2925	157	1720	2718		834	2194	1530	2684	2934	2869	805	660	3003	108	1274
ST. LOUIS, MO	1036	1051	767	549	841	1341	501	1053	1628	1181	749	1119	850	512	704	892	294	350	560	417	635	855	436	549	1242	1080	863	239	505	896	252	1610	416	1856	264	294	1214	367	621	688	1112	307	690	956	927	505	440	993	895	1517	611	1279	2057	825	963	1850	834		1326	968	1875	2066	2125	1008	782	2259	837	441
SALT LAKE CITY, UT	2224	624	964	1916	2100	548	1868	960	342	2395	1936	2322	2218	1880	2072	436	1406	1667	1738	1734	1410	531	1067	1675	864	2293	1650	1549	1813	2264	1074	417	1507	691	1631	1652	2581	1446	1315	2000	2232	1675	1932	2189	2282	1204	932	2360	2160	651	1859	2493	771	2193	628	524	2194	1326		1419	754	740	839	2375	1902	973	2094	1044
SAN ANTONIO, TX	1953	818	513	1000	1671	1500	878	1599	1761	2092	1665	2036	1310	1344	1241	1046	1270	1231	1481	1332	271	946	1009	1490	556	1990	200	1186	644	1084	812	1272	600	1356	1125	739	1401	1343	1257	673	2043	954	560	1861	1560	466	927	1180	1774	987	1519	2189	2322	1398	1335	1870	1530	968	1419		1285	1737	2275	1195	1714	2410	1635	624
SAN DIEGO, CA	2919	825	1111	2166	2724	1302	2021	1765	1096	3065	2632	3020	2483	2393	2405	1179	2105	2234	2437	2300	1375	1092	1766	2373	730	2963	1487	2122	1780	2370	1695	337	1703	124	2144	1841	2688	2145	2014	1960	2931	2056	1846	2839	2725	1370	1630	2467	2779	358	2494	3162	1093	2563	1372	642	2684	1875	754	1285		508	1271	2481	2601	1414	2720	1531
SAN FRANCISCO, CA	2964	1111	1397	2618	2840	1176	2472	1749	646	3135	2677	3062	2934	2620	2759	1176	2146	2407	2478	2474	1827	1271	1807	2415	1181	3034	1938	2290	2232	2822	1814	575	2012	385	2372	2144	3140	2186	2055	2411	2972	2360	2298	2929	3022	1657	1672	2918	2900	750	2599	3233	638	2894	1368	217	2934	2066	740	1737	508		816	2933	2643	958	2834	1784
SEATTLE, WA	2899	1463	1763	2705	2775	816	2657	1229	500	3070	2612	2997	2973	2571	2827	1234	2062	2368	2413	2424	2208	1329	1822	2350	1944	2969	2449	2249	2612	3052	1872	1256	2305	1148	2364	2440	3370	1991	1654	2799	2907	2463	2731	2864	2957	2002	1719	3149	2835	1513	2534	3168	170	2926	1195	755	2869	2125	839	2275	1271	816		3164	2577	140	2769	1843
TAMPA, FL	1290	1949	1628	455	960	2348	606	2018	2677	1380	1276	1438	434	845	581	1941	1176	935	1101	1036	1161	1862	1426	1194	1753	1278	995	990	709	196	1259	2526	984	2553	878	845	274	1272	1588	521	1522	701	668	1150	814	1403	1448	82	1062	2184	1019	1478	3106	656	1970	2899	805	1008	2375	1195	2481	2933	3164		1383	3297	916	1448
TORONTO, ON	400	1841	1557	958	565	1762	958	1354	2204	570	106	419	1006	537	802	1468	510	484	303	440	1441	1512	834	233	2032	509	1561	541	1183	1187	1028	2265	1115	2538	589	975	1532	607	924	1214	330	764	1302	507	747	1295	971	1327	522	2307	321	668	2633	820	1429	2426	660	782	1902	1714	2601	2643	2577	1383		2711	563	1217
VANCOUVER, BC	3032	1597	1897	2838	2908	949	2791	1362	633	3204	2745	3130	3106	2705	2960	1368	2196	2501	2547	2558	2342	1463	1956	2483	2087	3102	2583	2383	2746	3186	2007	1390	2439	1291	2497	2574	3504	2124	1788	2933	3041	2597	2865	2998	3090	2136	1853	3283	2968	1655	2668	3301	313	3060	1328	898	3003	2259	973	2410	1414	958	140	3297	2711		2902	1977
WASHINGTON, DC	369	1896	1612	636	38	1953	758	1545	2395	458	384	517	539	346	397	1659	701	517	370	416	1362	1686	1025	526	2008	357	1433	596	996	720	1083	2441	1036	2702	596	896	1065	799	1115	970	600	679	1106	228	196	1350	1162	860	140	2362	240	556	2824	265	1620	2617	108	837	2094	1635	2720	2834	2769	916	563	2902		1272
WICHITA, KS	1471	707	423	989	1276	1067	838	934	1346	1616	1184	1554	1291	953	1145	613	728	785	995	852	367	521	390	984	898	1515	608	674	771	1337	192	1276	464	1513	705	597	1655	769	637	958	1547	748	890	1391	1368	161	307	1434	1330	1173	1046	1714	1775	1266	712	1568	1274	441	1044	624	1531	1784	1843	1448	1217	1977	1272	

Mileage and Driving Times Map

TEMPERATURE CONVERSIONS

°F	°C	°C	°F
100	37.8	35	95
90	32.2	30	86
80	26.7	25	77
70	21.1	20	68
60	15.6	15	59
50	10.0	10	50
40	4.4	5	41
32	0	0	32
30	-1.1	-5	23
20	-6.7	-10	14
10	-12.2	-15	5
0	-17.8	-20	-4
-10	-23.3	-25	-13
-20	-28.9	-30	-22
-30	-34.4	-35	-31
-40	-40.0	-40	-40
-50	-45.6	-45	-49

VOLUME CONVERSIONS

GALLONS	LITERS	LITERS	GALLONS
1	3.8	1	0.26
2	7.6	2	0.5
3	11.4	3	0.8
4	15.1	4	1.1
5	18.9	5	1.3
10	37.9	10	2.6
15	56.8	20	5.3
20	75.7	30	7.9
25	94.6	40	10.6
30	113.6	50	13.2
40	151.4	75	19.8
50	189.3	100	26.4

DISTANCE CONVERSIONS

MILES	KM	KM	MILES
1	1.6	1	0.6
5	8.0	2	1.2
10	16.1	5	3.1
15	24.1	10	6.2
20	32.2	15	9.3
25	40.2	20	12.4
30	48.3	25	15.5
35	56.3	30	18.6
40	64.4	40	24.9
45	72.4	50	31.1
50	80.5	60	37.3
55	88.5	70	43.5
60	96.6	80	49.7
65	104.6	90	55.9
70	112.7	100	62.1
75	120.7	110	68.4
80	128.7	120	74.6
85	136.8	130	80.8
90	144.8	140	87.0
95	152.9	150	93.2
100	160.9	160	99.4